What They Say About Us

"One organization with a long record of success in helping people find jobs is The Five O'Clock Club."

FORTUNE

"Many managers left to fend for themselves are turning to the camaraderie offered by [The Five O'Clock Club]. Members share tips and advice, and hear experts."

The Wall Street Journal

"If you have been out of work for some time . . . consider The Five O'Clock Club."

The New York Times

"Wendleton has reinvented the historic gentlemen's fraternal oasis and built it into a chain of strategy clubs for job seekers."

The Philadelphia Inquirer

"Organizations such as The Five O'Clock Club are building . . . an extended professional family."

Jessica Lipnack, author, *Professional Teams*

"[The Five O'Clock Club] will ask not what you do, but 'What do you want to do?' . . . [And] don't expect to get any great happy hour drink specials at this joint. The seminars are all business."

The Washington Times

"The Five O'Clock Club's proven philosophy is that job hunting is a learned skill like any other. The Five O'Clock Club becomes the engine that drives [your] search."

Black Enterprise

"Job hunting is a science at The Five O'Clock Club. [Members] find the discipline, direction and much-needed support that keeps a job search on track."

Modern Maturity

"Wendleton tells you how to beat the odds—even in an economy where pink slips are more common than perks. Her savvy and practical guide[s] are chockablock with sample résumés, cover letters, worksheets, negotiating tips, networking suggestions and inspirational quotes from such far-flung achievers as Abraham Lincoln, Malcolm Forbes and Lily Tomlin."

Working Woman

"On behalf of eight million New Yorkers, I commend and thank The Five O'Clock Club. Keep the faith and keep America working!"

David N. Dinkins, former Mayor, The City of New York

What Job Hunters Say

"During the time I was looking for a job I kept Kate's books by my bed. I read a little every night, a little every morning. Her common-sense advice, methodical approach, and hints for keeping the spirits up were extremely useful."

Harold Levine, coordinator, Yale Alumni Career Resource Network

"I've just been going over the books with my daughter who is 23 and finally starting to think she ought to have a career. She won't listen to anything I say, but you she believes."

Newspaper columnist

"Thank you, Kate, for all your help. I ended up with four offers and at least fifteen compliments in two months. Thanks!"

president and CEO, large banking organization

"I have doubled my salary during the past five years by using The Five O'Clock Club techniques. Now I earn what I deserve. I think everyone needs The Five O'Clock Club."

M. S., attorney, entertainment industry

"I dragged myself to my first meeting, totally demoralized. Ten weeks later, I chose from among job offers and started a new life. Bless You!

Senior editor, not-for-profit

I'm an artistic person, and I don't think about business. Kate provided the disciplined business approach so I could practice my art. After adopting her system, I landed a role on Broadway in Hamlet!"

Bruce Faulk, actor

"I've referred at least a dozen people to the Five O'Clock Club since I was there. The Club was a major factor in getting my dream job, which I am now in."

B. R., Research Head

My Five O'Clock Club coach was a God-Send!!! She is truly one of the most dynamic and qualified people I've ever met. Without her understanding and guidance, I wouldn't have made the steps I've made toward my goals.

Operating Room Nurse

The Five O'Clock Club has been a fantastic experience for my job search. I couldn't have done it without you. Keep up the good work.

Former restaurant owner who found his dream job with an organization that advises small businesses.

What Human Resources Executives Say About Five O'Clock Club Outplacement!

*"**This thing works.** I saw a structured, yet nurturing, environment where individuals searching for jobs positioned themselves for success. I saw 'accountability' in a non-intimidating environment. I was struck by the support and willingness to encourage those who had just started the process by the group members who had been there for a while."*

Employee Relations Officer, financial services organization

*"**Wow! I was immediately struck by the electric atmosphere** and people's commitment to following the program. Job hunters reported on where they were in their searches and what they had accomplished the previous week. The overall environment fosters sharing and mutual learning."*

Head of Human Resources, major law firm

*"The Five O'Clock Club program is **far more effective** than conventional outplacement. Excellent materials, effective coaching and nanosecond responsiveness combine to get people focused on the central tasks of the job search. Selecting the Five O'Clock Outpatient Program was one of my best decisions this year."*

Sr. Vice President, Human Resources, manufacturing company

*"**You have made me look like a real genius** in recommending The Five O'Clock Club [to our divisions around the country]!"*

SVP HR, major publishing firm

*"Selecting Five O'Clock outplacement was **one of my best decisions this year.**"*

SVP, HR, consumer products firm

The Five O'Clock Club®
Advising Professionals, Managers, and Executives for Over 25 years

THE FIVE O'CLOCK CLUB
JOB SEARCH WORKBOOK

KATE WENDLETON

THOMSON
DELMAR LEARNING

Australia Brazil Canada Mexico Singapore Spain United Kingdom United States

THOMSON

DELMAR LEARNING

The Five O'Clock Club Job Search Workbook
Kate Wendleton

Vice President, Career Education SBU:
Dawn Gerrain

Director of Learning Solutions:
Sherry Dickinson

Managing Editor:
Robert L. Serenka, Jr.

Acquisitions Editor:
Martine Edwards

Developmental Editor:
Jennifer Anderson

Editorial Assistant:
Falon Ferraro

Director of Production:
Wendy A. Troeger

Production Manager:
J.P. Henkel

Production Editor:
Rebecca Goldthwaite

Director of Marketing:
Wendy E. Mapstone

Channel Manager:
Gerard McAvey

Marketing Specialist:
Erica Conley

Cover Design:
TDB Publishing Services

For information, please contact:

The Five O'Clock Club®
300 East 40th Street – Suite 6L
New York, New York 10016
www.FiveOClockClub.com

Library of Congress Cataloging-in-Publication Data

Wendleton, Kate.

The Five O'Clock Club job-search workbook / Kate Wendleton.
     p. cm.
   Includes index.
   ISBN-13: 978-1-4180-4050-5
   ISBN-10: 1-4180-4050-9
      1. Job hunting. I. Five O'Clock Club (New York, N.Y.).
II. Title.

   HF5382.7.W457 2007
   650.14—dc22

                                                          2005056084

Preface

Dear Member or Prospective Member of The Five O'Clock Club:

We have accumulated over 25 years of research into how successful job hunters land the best jobs at the best pay. Because our series of four job-search books for professionals, managers, and executives has grown in size, our members have asked us to summarize this information in one book they could carry around. This is that book, a companion to the four basic books in our job-search series:

1. *Targeting a Great Career* (this book) tells you *where* to look for a job. It is a relatively painless way to think about the career-planning process. It also contains an extensive overview of the entire Five O'Clock Club approach to job search.

2. *Packaging Yourself: The Targeted Résumé* is quite simply the best résumé book on the market. It uses the résumés of real people and tells you their stories. It refers to over 100 industries and professions.

3. *Shortcut Your Job Search: The Best Way to Get Meetings* tells you *how* to get job leads—part-time or full-time, freelance or consulting. It also contains worksheets, which you may copy for your own use. In addition, it contains the most comprehensive job-search bibliography around.

4. *Mastering the Job Interview and the Money Game* teaches you the consultative approach to job interviews, how to turn those interviews into offers, and how to get the best compensation package—whether for full-time, part-time, freelance or consulting work.

This book, The Five O'Clock Club Job Search Workbook, not only contains an overview of the process, it also provides the most important worksheets, which you can copy for your own use.

The books present the strategies we use at The Five O'Clock Club, our highly successful national job-search strategy program. We use a targeted, strategic approach to career development and job search. The keystone to the Five O'Clock Club process is in teaching our members an understanding of the entire hiring process. A first interview is only a time for exchanging critical information. The real works starts after the interview. We teach our members how to turn job interviews into offers, and how to negotiate the best possible employment package.

We urge you to be thorough in your search: do not by-pass a step. However, this book, like the others, is organized to be used by busy people like you. It allows you to skip to the part you need. Parts One and Two help you decide what to do with your life. If you already know what you want in your next job, go directly to Part Three to learn the most powerful, up-to-date techniques available today for getting interviews. If you have an interview coming up, go to Part Four to find the latest ideas for getting what you want, including how to assess the interview and turn it into an offer.

Running The Five O'Clock Club is one of the most gratifying things I do (in addition to raising children and volunteering in a prison). Those coaches who head up our small job-search groups agree that nothing gives them more satisfaction than coaching someone to land a great job at a great salary.

Even those who have been unemployed a long time find help in our groups. Do not become discouraged if you have been in search a long time. You may be doing something wrong. Some of our best stories are about people who have been unemployed two years or longer, and found the job that was perfect for them at just the right salary. All of the case studies in this and our other books are of actual people.

All of this information is based on the highly successful methods used at The Five O'Clock Club, where the average, regularly attending member finds a job within ten weeks. For information on the Club, take a look at our extensive website, *www.FiveOClockClub.com*, or call 1-800 575-3587 to have a packet of information sent to you.

We are guided by the original Five O'Clock Club, where the leaders of Old Philadelphia met regularly to exchange ideas and have a good time. Today's members are the same—they exchange ideas at the Club or through our website, operate at a high level, brainstorm to help each other, and truly enjoy each other's company. In addition, they work closely with a Five O'Clock Club career coach to find the best strategies for their search.

I thank the members of The Five O'Clock Club, people who care about their careers. Their hard work is reflected in this book series.

I hope these books will assist you as they have so many others. Thank you for supporting The Five O'Clock Club through your purchase of this book. Because of people like you, we can keep the program going and spread to new cities so we'll be there when you need us. Our goal is, and always has been, to provide the best affordable career advice. And—with you as our partners—we will continue to do this.

Cheers, God bless, and good luck!

Kate Wendleton
New York City, 2006
http://www.FiveOClockClub.com

For the women of Bayview

I know you are asking today, "How long will it take?" I come to say to you this afternoon, however difficult the moment, however frustrating the hour, it will not be long, because truth pressed to earth will rise again.

How long? Not long, because no lie can live forever.

How long? Not long, because you still reap what you sow.

How long? Not long, because the arm of the moral universe is long but it bends towards justice.

How long? Not long, 'cause mine eyes have seen the glory of the coming of the Lord, trampling out the vintage where the grapes of wrath of stored. He has loosed the fateful lightning of his terrible swift sword. His truth is marching on.

He has sounded forth the trumpets that shall never call retreat. He is lifting up the hearts of man before His judgment seat. Oh, be swift, my soul, to answer Him. Be jubilant, my feet. Our God is marching on.

> *Rev. Martin Luther King, Jr.,*
> *At the end of his march from Selma*
> *(last lines of his speech)*

Contents

The Five O'Clock Club

PART ONE

The Five O'Clock Club Job-Search Process

(Refer to this section throughout your job search.)

The
Five
O'Clock
Club

An Overview of
The Five O'Clock Club Process

Here's an overview of the entire job-search process—the Five O'Clock Club way. The Five O'Clock Club uses a methodical, organized approach to job search. Each topic in this section, and in this book, is covered in much greater detail in our job-search book series and CDs. The techniques we teach work for those who are looking for consulting work, as well as those who want an on-payroll job. In fact, 15% of the people who attend The Five O'Clock Club are looking for consulting work.

> **These techniques work when you're looking for consulting work, too.**

We have come out of the time when obedience, the acceptance of discipline, intelligent courage, and resolution were most important, into that more difficult time when it is a person's duty to understand the world rather than simply fight for it.

Ernest Hemingway

Most people *think* they're job searching when they get an interview and go on an interview. That's not a job search. That's just getting interviews and going on interviews. They're just hoping they'll get lucky and that somebody will hire them.

Most people follow the latest fads, expecting something magical to save them from having to do a full search. Over the years, job hunters have debated such things as using a certain color of résumé paper to give them an edge. One of the most recent fads was answering ads on the Internet, but studies have shown that only 4 percent of active job hunters get jobs that way. The *Wall Street Journal* once featured a middle-aged professional man who stood on a street corner wearing a sandwich board with the message that he wanted to work. Did he get a job that way? No, but he could then claim that he had tried *everything* and nothing had worked.

So, forget fads and gimmicks and do it *our* way. There is no harm in *trying* something faddish (say, 1 percent of

your time!), but make The Five O'Clock Club approach the basis for your search.

And remember, to get momentum going, someone who is unemployed should spend 35 hours a week on his or her search. There's much more to do than you can imagine. Those who are working full time need to spend 15 hours a week on a part-time search, but most of those hours will be in the evenings and on weekends, doing research, writing letters, and following up after meetings.

The members of your small group are all using our methodical, organized approach to job search. You can land that dream job at *any* point in your search, but don't skip a step in the process. Your search will actually go more quickly if you touch every step. What's more, with the Five O'Clock Club approach, you'll be able to tell if things are working for you or not.

Self-respect is the fruit of discipline; the sense of dignity grows with the ability to say no to oneself.

Abraham J. Heschel, quoted in Ruth M. Goodhill, ed., *The Wisdom of Heschel*

> **Here's one way to look at the process:**
>
> 1. **Figure out the kind of job you want.**
> 2. **Develop a résumé that makes you look appropriate.**
> 3. **Get lots of interviews.**
> 4. **Measure how well you are doing.**
> 5. **Interview like a consultant.**
> 6. **Follow up intelligently.**
> 7. **Have fun!!!**

You've got to get obsessed and stay obsessed.

John Irving, *The Hotel*

First, figure out the kind of job you want by going through the exercises in this book—especially the Seven Stories Exercise and the Forty-Year Vision. You'll come up with job targets—the kinds of places where you want to work in the long run—and be better able to focus on the kind of work you'd like to do in your next job.

Then, you'll develop a *résumé* that makes you look appropriate to these targets—so that you'll be desirable when you go in for an interview.

Next, we'll help you get plenty of *interviews* in your target markets. And, we'll show you how to measure how well you're doing in your search, so you can determine whether or not you're meeting the right people and how well you're doing in those meetings.

We'll teach you how to interview like a consultant, which will keep you calm—and help you ask the right questions during the interview.

Then we'll show you how to follow up intelligently—so you can turn those job interviews into offers and get the salary you deserve.

And, finally, we want you to have FUN in the process. If you're not keeping some fun in your life, you won't interview well, and you'll take longer to get a job.

The world fears a new experience more than it fears anything. Because a new experience displaces so many old experiences. . . . The world doesn't fear a new idea. It can pigeon-hole any idea. But it can't pigeon-hole a real new experience.

D. H. Lawrence

What Is a Target?

Everything starts with your job targets. We say, "If your targets are wrong, everything is wrong." Nothing in your search is going to work out well if your targets are vague or ill-defined for long. Targets are the starting point, the basis for everything else you do in your search.

> **If your targets are wrong, everything is wrong.**

Every man is born into the world to do something unique and something distinctive and if he or she does not do it, it will never be done.

Benjamin E. Mays, "I Knew Carter G. Woodson," *Negro History Bulletin*, January–March 1981

A job target consists of:

- an industry or company size where you think you'd like to work, let's say for example, banking or health care;

- a specific position within those industries, something that you think you'd enjoy doing, such as marketing; and

- a certain geographic area, let's say St. Louis.

Those *three* elements make up a target, and, as you will see, each target may have 5, 10, 20, or more positions. In the beginning of your search, come up with as many targets as you possibly can in case you need more targets later on in your search. You'll conduct a Preliminary Target Investigation (through the Internet and networking) on your first list of targets. This will help you refine your Personal Marketing Plan, which will guide your search. Of course, we'll show you how to do all of this.

> **If you will be working with a private coach in addition to your small group coach: Prior to the first private coaching session, send your coach your current résumé, no matter how good or bad it may be, and the results of the Seven Stories Exercise. You and your coach can discuss your Fifteen- and Forty-Year Vision and brainstorm potential targets. Your coach may assign you other exercises or instruments that are right for you, and will help you with your résumé.**

Prepare Your Résumé

There's a lot of talk about self-esteem these days. It seems pretty basic to me. If you want to feel proud of yourself, you've got to do things you can be proud of. Feelings follow actions.

Oseola McCarty, a washerwoman who gave her life savings of $150,000 to help complete strangers get a college education.

When you have completed the exercises in this book, you will be in a better position to develop a résumé that makes you look appropriate to your targets. Then you will be desirable when you go in for a meeting. Remember, the average résumé is looked at for only 10 seconds. So, it's vital that key ideas or words pop out. Can the reader *easily* figure out your level? If you say, I "install computer systems," you could be making anywhere from $15,000 to $200,000. Is your résumé accomplishment oriented or just a job description? Work with your private coach and your small group to make your résumé stand out. It will *not* stand out if it reads like a job description.

Résumés are a complicated matter, and that's why we have an entire book on the subject.

Duty largely consists of pretending that the trivial is critical.

John Fowles, *The Magus*

ASSESSMENT

Consists of:	**Results in:**
• The Seven Stories Exercise	• As many targets as you can think of
• Interests	• A ranking of your targets
• Values	• A résumé that makes you look
• Satisfiers and Dissatisfiers	appropriate to your first target
• Your Forty-Year Vision	• A plan for conducting your search

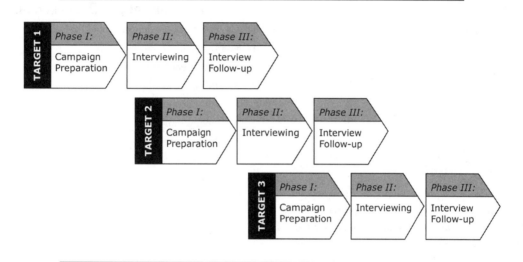

RESULTS

Phase I: **Campaign Preparation.** *Results in:*	**Phase II:** **Interviewing.** *Results in:*	**Phase III:** **Follow-Up.** *Results in:*
❏ Research (list of companies)	❏ Giving them information to keep them interested in you	❏ Aiming to have 6 to 10 things in the works, and
❏ Résumé	❏ Getting information so you can "move it along"	
❏ Cover letter		**Job Offers!**
❏ Plan for getting interviews	❏ Plan for follow-up (You may do several in-depth follow-ups with each person)	
- networking - direct contact - search firms - ads		

Starting Your Personal Marketing Plan

Once you've thought of a few *tentative* job targets, you are ready to work on your Personal Marketing Plan. This Plan will guide you throughout your entire job search.

In my small group, I often ask someone to name something that he or she is targeting and the group helps that person brainstorm how to go after that target. Let's say Joe is targeting *investment advisor*—a job that involves giving investment advice. Jim and his group might start brainstorming where a person could do investment advisory work: perhaps commercial banks, investment banks, hedge funds, insurance companies, or mutual funds.

So far, Joe is targeting a position (investment advisor) and the industries that we just named. Finally, the formula is complete when he names the geographic area. Joe said he was interested in both New York and Chicago.

Develop Your Personal Marketing Plan Based on Targets

The position:

"Investment advisor"—a job where I would give investment advice

The industries:

commercial banks
investment banks
hedge funds
insurance companies
mutual funds

The geographic areas:

New York and Chicago

Segmenting Your Targets

A person may say that she wants to work in the not-for-profit area. This is *not* a target because it's too broad.

Not-for-profit could include associations, hospitals, universities, the government—and each of those subtargets is huge!

Breaking your targets into manageable subtargets is called *segmenting your targets.*

> **"Not-for-profit" is too broad to be useful. It could include:**
>
> - **associations**
> - **hospitals**
> - **universities**
> - **the government**
>
> **—and all of those subtargets are huge!**

What if Susan wants to target health care? Health care is unwieldy as a target! It could include, for example, hospitals, home health care, HMOs, pharmaceutical companies, nursing homes, hospice care, health insurance companies, crisis intervention programs, congregate care facilities, medical billing, health-care consulting firms, medical device manufacturers, and distributors. (Who makes the catheters? And who makes the beds?)

You could go on and on. Health care could also be anything having to do with the aging of America, for example. You could brainstorm lots of other job targets having to do with health care itself.

We'll talk more about Susan's search later, but let's go back to our investment advisor example. I would say to Joe, "How many commercial banks would you say are appro-

priate for you to consider? Name a number, any number." (Of course, job hunters don't really know, but I want them to name *something.*) And Joe would give me a rough guess. "Let's say there are approximately 24 commercial banks," he would say. "Twenty-four investment banks, twenty hedge funds—all within my targeted geographic areas. Let's also say there are six insurance companies, eight mutual funds, and so on."

Break Your Targets Down into Subtargets

Health care, for example, could include:

- hospitals
- home health care
- HMOs
- pharmaceutical companies
- nursing homes
- hospice care
- health insurance companies
- crisis intervention programs
- congregate care facilities
- medical billing
- health-care consulting firms
- medical device manufacturers
- distributors

Rank Your Targets—To Organize Your Work

The only joy in the world is to begin.

Cesare Pavese, Italian writer

So Joe, our investment advisor, has a lot of targets: commercial banks, investment banks, hedge funds. It's just too much. In addition to segmenting his targets, he also has to *rank* his targets. If he doesn't rank them, he will be scattered and ineffective. His list is too big and too unwieldy.

> Health care could also include:
> - Anything having to do with the aging of America
> - Vitamin companies
> - Health-care publishing
> - Lots of other subcategories, depending on your interests

Joe must organize his work. My next question is: "What is your target #1?" Joe says his target #1—the place where he would most like to work—is commercial banking. So I respond, "Let's analyze commercial banks. How many positions would a typical commercial bank have that would be appropriate for you?" Joe doesn't really know the answer. Would there be one position or ten? We're talking about *positions,* not job openings. Positions.

Subtargets for Our Investment Advisor Example

"How many commercial banks are appropriate for you to consider? Name a number, any number."

Approximately:

- 24 commercial banks
- 24 investment banks
- 20 hedge funds—all within your targeted geographic areas
- 6 insurance companies
- 8 mutual funds—and so on

Joe doesn't really know the answer, but I push him to guess. Joe says, "Well, out of 24 commercial banks that I'm targeting, I think each one might have an average of 10 positions that are appropriate for me" (*positions,* not openings). So Joe is targeting 240 positions at just those 24 banks. That is a lot of positions!

In fact, we know from our research that, to be successful in your search in a reasonable time frame, you must target 200 positions. So you can see that Joe is going after 240 positions in just this one target area, increasing the likelihood of a successful search. So you can see that if you are targeting a *smaller* number of positions, you will have a longer search. Chances are, *you* can come up with targets with a total of at least 200 positions. Of course, this takes a lot of research and hard work. You will find a bibliography of job-search resources in the Members Only section of our website (*www.FiveOClockClub.com*) and also in our book *Shortcut Your Job Search.*

Target #1: Commercial Banks

"How many *positions* would a typical commercial bank have that would be appropriate for you?"

So rank your targets. Decide which targets you want to go after first, second, third, fourth. It may be, if you are desperate, you'll focus first on the target where you are most likely to get a job. If you are not desperate and have time to explore—maybe you're employed right now—then maybe your first target is your dream job, the thing you've always wanted to explore. So your first step is to rank your targets.

Then measure your targets. If the total number of positions you're going after is fewer than 200, that's not good.

Remember that we are not totaling job openings, but *positions.* And it does not matter if the positions are filled right now. You are trying to avoid targets that are just too small. Those searches are doomed from the start.

Target #1: 24 Commercial Banks

An average of 10 positions at each bank

Joe is targeting 240 positions at just these 24 banks. That is a lot of positions!

As a separate but very relevant issue, think about the state of the market within each of those targets. Some markets are growing and some markets are retrenching. If your target market is retrenching, you'll need to go after even more positions.

On the other hand, if it's growing and people are getting hired, you may be able to get away with targeting fewer positions.

Calculate the number of *positions,* not job openings. It doesn't matter if the positions are filled right now.

Now, take a look at Joe's targets in more detail. Let's say he's targeting commercial banks as Target #1. And investment banks as Target #2. He's targeting two dozen companies in each of these targets.

Most people start out with targets that are just too small. Their searches are doomed.

If you cannot catch a bird of paradise, better take a wet hen.
Nikita S. Khrushchev, quoted in *Time,* January 6, 1958

Developing Your A-List, B-List, C-List

But Joe needs to divide up his list of commercial banks: The A-list includes companies he would die to work for; the companies that he would consider *okay* to go into are the B-list; and the C-list companies are actually of no interest to him.

Joe should contact his C-list companies first to get his feet wet and use them for practice. Because he does not care that much about them, he will probably be more relaxed and confident and will interview well. He is *practicing.* He will also be testing his market to see if he gets a good response from these C-list companies.

Many are stubborn in pursuit of the path they have chosen, few in pursuit of the goal.

Friedrich Nietzsche

> **To get a job within a reasonable time, target 200 positions—not *openings*— positions.**

If the companies on Joe's C-list are *not* interested in him, that's important for him to know. He needs to talk to the people in his small group to find out what he is doing wrong. However, if he is well received by the companies on his C-list, then Joe can contact the companies on his B-list. He could say something like, "I am already talking to a number of companies in your industry (which is true), but I didn't want to accept a job with any of them (which is also true) until I had a chance to talk with you." This script is just one approach. Be sure to talk to your small group about the right things for you to say to those on your B-list.

> - **Your A-list: You'd love to work there.**
> - **Your B-list: They're okay.**
> - **Your C-list: They don't interest you.**

Your search will have more impact if it is focused by targets and segments of targets. For example, if Susan is going after the health-care market, talking to all of the hospitals on her list within a certain period gives her credibility. She can say, "Oh, I talked to . . ." and name the hospital that she talked to yesterday, "and what is happening there is this. I am really interested in working for a hospital." It makes her sound believable.

> **Contact C-list companies first.**

Remember what we said above about segmenting your targets. The pitch that you use with one of these targets, say, hospitals, will be very different from the pitch you would use with a different target, say, health-care manufacturers.

> **"I am already talking to a number of companies in your industry, but I didn't want to accept a job with any of them until I had a chance to talk with you."**

Your approach cannot be casual—even in the initial stages of your search. You might be tempted to say in an interview, "I don't care whether I work for a hospital or a manufacturer, so long as I have some connection to health care. I can do what I want to do just about anywhere." *You* may not care, but your prospective employers care. They want to know that you understand—and care about—*their* industry.

> **If you are well received by organizations on your C-list, move on to your B-list.**

The
Five
O'Clock
Club

Getting Lots of Meetings

If I try to use human influence strategies and tactics of how to get other people to do what I want, to work better, to be more motivated, to like me and each other—while my character is fundamentally flawed, marked by duplicity and insincerity— then, in the long run, I cannot be successful. My duplicity will breed distrust, and everything I do—even using so-called good human relations techniques—will be perceived as manipulative. . . . Only basic goodness gives life to technique.

Stephen R. Covey, *The Seven Habits of Highly Effective People*

Developing a Detailed Personal Marketing Plan

It's best to focus on one target for a condensed period. For example, Susan can make a list of all of the hospitals within the geographic area she's interested in. This list will become her Personal Marketing Plan. Let's say there are 80 hospitals that are appropriate for her; she would put those on her list. Then she would mount a campaign to get plenty of meetings in that target area, hospitals. A second target could be health-care manufacturers. She would make a second list, this one containing manufacturers she considered appropriate for her in her geographic area.

> **Make a list of organizations within each target. Eighty hospitals in Susan's geographic area are appropriate for her.**

Then, *stagger* your targets so you can focus on each target in turn. Susan will focus on the hospitals first, and when that's under way, she'll start on the health-care manufacturers. To get plenty of meetings, she'll consider all four

basic techniques for getting meetings in her target markets. The techniques are:

- Networking—that is, using someone's name to get a meeting;
- Contacting people directly when you *don't* have a networking contact;
- Answering ads; and
- Talking to search firms.

> *The opposite of love is not hate, it's indifference. The opposite of art is not ugliness, it's indifference. The opposite of faith is not heresy, it's indifference. And the opposite of life is not death, it's indifference.*
>
> Elie Wiesel

If you try all four techniques, you can see which techniques result in meetings for you. Use more of *those* techniques. Use Internet ads, for example, *if* they result in meetings for you. If they don't result in meetings, concentrate on other approaches.

> **Make sure every *manager* in your target market knows that you exist.**

Susan has 80 hospitals in her first target. Remember that the managers in those hospitals don't even know that she *exists*. You want potential employers to hear about you within a reasonable time. Certainly you can contact search firms and answer ads, but only 20 percent of all jobs are filled through search firms and ads. So consider two other techniques—networking and contacting organizations directly. Your goal is to make sure that as many managers as possible know about you within a reasonable time.

Methods for Getting Meetings in Your Target Areas:

- Networking (40 percent of meetings)

- Direct contact (40 percent)

- Search firms (10 percent)

- Ads (print and Internet) (10 percent)

Let's reemphasize an important distinction here. *Networking* means using someone else's name to get a meeting ("Sue suggested I contact you."). *Direct contact* means pursuing people whom you may have known in the past, but especially people you have *never* met: association members, or key people identified on the Internet, through newspaper or magazine articles, or from library research.

Heroes come in all sizes, and you don't have to be a giant hero. You can be a very small hero. It's just as important to understand that accepting self-responsibility for the things you do, having good manners, caring about other people—these are heroic acts. Everybody has the choice of being a hero or not being a hero every day of their lives.

George Lucas, *Star Wars* film director, as quoted in *Time* magazine, April 26, 1999

By the way, when we say that you should "make sure everyone on your target list knows that you exist within a reasonable time," we mean *managers*. We don't mean human resources, *unless* you want a job in human resources.

But you cannot *network* into 80 organizations within a reasonable time. The last thing you want is to find out you're too late! If you rely primarily on networking, you may get around to contacting an organization three months into your search and hear one of them say,

> **"We just filled a position. I wish we had met you before."**

So, if you have a list of 80 companies you want to contact, divide up your list. Perhaps you can network into 5 or 6. If you know someone who can refer you in, use his or her name, contact the hiring manager, and say, "Jim Smith suggested I contact you."

That would leave 75 more organizations out of your list of 80. Select 20 of those that you really want to get in to

see, even though you don't have a connection. It doesn't matter if they don't have any openings—you don't know that anyway. To these 20, you would send a *targeted mailing* and follow up with a phone call.

That would leave 55 organizations on your list. For the remaining 55, you could do a direct-mail campaign. That is, you would send your cover letter and résumé, but you would *not* follow up with a phone call. You're just letting them know that you exist, so *if* they have a need for someone like you, they'll give *you* a call. By combining these various job-search techniques, you will be able to contact all of the organizations on your list within a reasonable time.

Get Lots of Meetings

ABC company
Avrey
Acme
Allister Metal
Goopers
Haskell
Jesking
Alcoa
Fortunoff
Patricin
Costco
Hormel
DiscCity
Oliphant

Divide up your list. If you have a list of 80 companies:

- **Network** into **5 or 6** if you can
- Send a **targeted mailing** to **20** ➝ ☎
- For the remaining **55**, use a **direct-mail campaign** ➝

CASE STUDY

When I was working for a tiny advertising agency in Lancaster, Pennsylvania, a very long time ago, I needed to move to New York because of a family situation. I didn't know anyone in New York, so I could not have networked into any companies there.

I did my research and identified about 60 advertising agencies in New York, as well as the correct people to contact. For the *large* advertising agencies, I identified the names of three managers who seemed appropriate—the president would have been too high up for me to contact. For the small and mid-sized agencies, I wrote directly to the president.

Part of the challenge in your search is picking the right person to contact, say a department head or division head.

> **For my own search,**
> **I identified 60 advertising agencies**
> **and the correct person to contact at each.**
>
> - **For the large advertising agencies, three names of managers who seemed appropriate to me.**
> - **For the small and midsized agencies, I wrote to the president.**

Direct-mail campaigns formed the basis of my search. That is, I wrote to the appropriate people in those companies, but did not make follow-up phone calls. Out of 60 companies, I got about five phone calls saying,

> **"Why don't you come in for a meeting?"**

When I went in for the meetings, I treated them exactly like networking meetings—not job interviews. When I was there, I tried to network into *other* firms in New York. That was my total campaign. Because I was searching from out-of-town, I took off from work every other Friday. Then I could say to a company, "I'll be back in town again in two weeks. Is there anybody else I could meet with in your firm?" This technique is networking: getting in to see someone by using someone else's name.

You can see that I got momentum going by combining direct contact with networking. My search started when I contacted companies directly, met with people, and asked them to help me network into other companies. Or you can start your search by networking into organizations and asking them for a list of other organizations you can contact directly without using that person's name.

> **These meetings are not job interviews, treat them like networking meetings.**
>
> - **Try to network into other firms.**
> - **"I'll be back in town in two weeks. Is there anybody else I could meet in your firm?"**
> - **"Here's a list of companies I'm interested in. What do you think of them?" (Show your Personal Marketing Plan.)**
> - **Combine direct contact with networking.**

So consider *all* four techniques for getting interviews in your target areas: Get momentum going by contacting search firms, answering ads, networking, and also by contacting companies directly.

I have seen the future, and it's a lot like the present, but much longer.

Dan Quisenberry, professional baseball player

This Information Is Based on 25 Years of Research

I know this is a lot for you to digest, but there's even *more* to tell you. And, in the long run, our approach is much more efficient than simply hitting the *send* button on your computer and waiting for a reply. Historically, the average person attending The Five O'Clock Club has found a new job or is in the negotiating stage within 10 weekly sessions.

Most members read the books, listen to the lectures on audio CDs, and attend the small groups at the same time. Our various resources complement each other. Furthermore, your small-group members as well as your career coach will keep you on track and help you with your specific situation. You will master the material over time, and *your future job searches will be easier* because you will use the same methodology the next time you search.

Our methodology is based on more than 25 years of research, and we continually conduct research to develop the best techniques. Let's put this in perspective. During the depths of the 1987 to 1992 recession, when the average American was taking 8.1 months to find a job, the average Five O'Clock Clubber found a new job in just 10 weeks! Even those who had been unemployed 9 to 18 months when we met them found jobs in just 10 weeks. And this was at a time when there were few jobs available.

> **During depths of recession (1987–1992):**
>
> - **Average American took 8.1 months to find a job.**
> - **Five O'Clock Clubbers found a new job in an average of just 10 weekly sessions—even those who had already been unemployed 9 months to 1.5 years when we met them.**
> - **They got paid what they were worth in the market—despite their long-term unemployment.**

Not only did these long-term unemployed people find jobs, they found jobs that paid what they were worth in the market. They did *not* take pay cuts just because they had been unemployed a long time.

So you see, there's hope even for those who are targeted to give up hope. Your situation might not be dire. Or perhaps your situation *is* dire for your market and for the kind of job you're looking for. But the Five O'Clock Club can give you hope. Now you know that there's a methodology you can follow—one that's proven to work. We have specialized in tough searches!

I do not believe they are right who say that the defects of famous men should be ignored. I think it is better we should know them. Then, though we are conscious of having faults as glaring as theirs, we can believe that that is no hindrance to our achieving also something of their virtues.

Somerset Maugham

So, let's see where you are. So far:

1. You've brainstormed your targets. That is, you've thought about the industries and the fields you want to go after. And you've brainstormed as many targets as possible—with the help of your coach or your small group.

2. You've ranked your targets: *Hospitals* is your first target. *Health-care manufacturers* is your second.

3. You're aiming to have a focused, compact search. You've decided to go after all the hospitals at the same time so you can say, "I'm talking to so-and-so at Presbyterian Hospital right now." This gives you credibility.

That's where you are in your search. Now we'll talk about how you can plan and organize your entire job-search campaign. In our books and CDs, we cover each of these areas in great detail: how to do your résumé; how to interview; how to negotiate salary. But here we are presenting an overview of the entire job search.

It is work, work that one delights in, that is the surest guarantor of happiness.

Ashley Montagu, *The American Way of Life*

Job-Search Campaign Management

Every man is born into the world to do something unique and something distinctive and if he or she does not do it, it will never be done.

Benjamin E. Mays, "I Knew Carter G. Woodson," *Negro History Bulletin,* January–March 1981

Campaign Overview

Conduct a Campaign Aimed at Each Target (Industry, Position, Field)

Now we'll give you an overview of how to plan and organize your entire campaign and bring it all together. The goal of your campaign is to get *lots* of meetings. You may get excited when you line up one job interview, but when that interview falls apart, you have to start all over again to get another one. Because of the lack of momentum, this kind of one-at-a-time search can last for many, many months.

We're trying to increase your chance for success, so you'll have three concurrent offers and then you can *pick the job that will position you best for the long term.* So just hang in there. Trust us on this, and follow the rest of the process.

Here's what a campaign aimed at one target might look like. Let's say that target #1 for you is hospitals. There's a planning phase, an interviewing phase, and a follow-up phase.

In the Planning Phase:

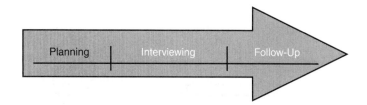

- **Make a list of all the hospitals** that are appropriate for you in your targeted geographic area. We talked about this earlier.

- **Develop what we call your Two-Minute Pitch.** That is, in the hospital market, how do you respond when people say, "Tell me about yourself." For example, your pitch to hospitals might be, "I have 10 years of marketing experience in the health-care industry. In fact, at one company, I increased sales by 50 percent in one product line." Your pitch to hospitals might be very different from your pitch to manufacturing companies in the health-care field. For that target, you may want to emphasize different accomplishments.

- **Be sure your *résumé* makes you look appropriate** to the hospital market. If you've never worked in a hospital before, get rid of jargon that applied to your old industry, and use the jargon of the hospital industry.

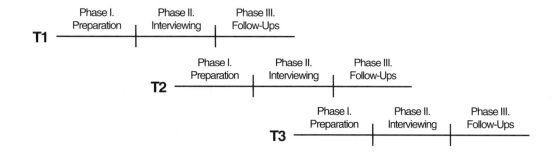

- Next, you'll **develop your plan for getting meetings** in this target market. That is, make a short list of search firms you can contact, scrutinize the ads for information and find those that would require a direct-contact approach, identify the organizations you'll be able to network into, and directly contact the others.

I found that values, for each person, were numerous. Therefore, I proposed to write my value names and to annex to each a short precept—which fully expressed the extent I gave to each meaning. I then arranged them in such a way as to facilitate acquisition of these virtues.

Benjamin Franklin

The Interviewing Phase

After the Planning Phase, you'll be in the Interviewing Phase. With the help of your group, you've figured out how to get meetings in your target market.

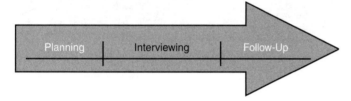

In the **Interviewing Phase:**

- Get information and give information.
- *Don't* try to "close" too soon to get the offer.
- Get another meeting.

Most people think interviews result in job offers. But there are usually a few intervening steps before a final offer is made. **Interviews should result in getting and giving information.**

- Did you learn the issues important to each person with whom you met?
- What did they think were your strongest positives?
- How can you overcome the decision makers' objections?

Most people try to get offers too early. Instead, try to get the next meeting. After all, most organizations need to see you more than once. Keep in the running.

Don't think like a job hunter who is trying to coax people to hire him. Think like a consultant trying to land a $40,000, $90,000, or $150,000 consulting assignment— whatever your salary is. Job hunters are commonly too passive, fielding questions as best they can. They leave interviews thinking, "I did *so* great answering those questions."

Instead, be more proactive in the interview. Have a pad and pen in hand for taking notes. Find out what's *going on* in the company. Ask about their *needs.* How can you satisfy those needs? Who's doing what in this organization? How might you fit in? What are the most important problems the organization faces right now?

The *Two-Minute Pitch*

The way you position yourself is used throughout your search:

- at the top of your résumé;
- in your interviews;
- in your networking meetings; and
- in your cover letters (second paragraph).

It is the response to "So, tell me about yourself." A great pitch helps people see you as appropriate for the kind of job you are going after. At The Five O'Clock Club we say, "If your pitch is wrong, everything is wrong." That is, if the way you are positioning yourself is wrong, you're derailed from the start and everything else about your search will be wrong. It can't work.

The top of your résumé is your written positioning. The Two-Minute Pitch is your oral positioning. And they must correspond. So, the top of Wally's résumé could read:

**Web Press Supervisor
with 20 years' experience and an
emphasis on quality and productivity**

In an interview, when an employer asks, "So tell me about yourself," Wally could start with the verbal version of that same pitch: "I'm a web press supervisor with more than 20 years' experience. I've always emphasized quality and productivity. For example, . . ." And then he could talk about examples of his accomplishments, which would correspond to some of the bulleted accomplishments at the top of his résumé. When your pitch is correct, you will use it throughout your entire search.

A consultant takes notes because a consultant knows he has to *analyze* what happened during the meeting and later make a proposal about how to handle the job. Here is the drill for consultants:

- Research the organization thoroughly.
- Dress and look the part.
- Prepare a 3x5 card including the Two-Minute Pitch, as well as several key points.

Find out:

- What is going on? What are their needs?
- How can I satisfy those needs?

Work to outclass your competition.

- Ask how you stack up against others.
- Make sure you have all the information you need.
- Find out when they hope to decide.
- Find out if they have any objections to you.

Plan your follow-up.

- Get and give information.
- Don't try to get an offer right now.
- Get the next meeting.
- Consultants write proposals. So will you!

Think about your competition. You do have competition, you know. And if you *think* you're the only one being interviewed, you could come away dumb and happy—confident that you did a great job. But you won't know how you stack up *against others* unless you ask! Say to the hiring manager:

- Where are you in the hiring process? Am I first? Second? Last?

- How many other people are you talking to?

- And how do you see me compared with the other people you're talking to?

Ask yourself: Have I gathered all the information I need to write a good proposal about what I would do for this organization? Find out if they're ready to decide now, or if it will take a few months.

Do all you can to keep in the running.

> Everything you need to know about interviewing, following up after the interview, and salary negotiation is covered extensively in our book *Mastering the Job Interview and Winning the Money Game.*

Just a few other points before we go on to the Follow-Up Phase:

Handling Difficult Interview Questions

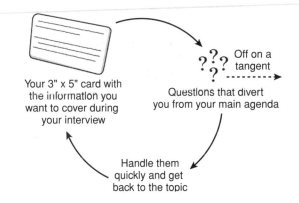

Your 3" x 5" card with the information you want to cover during your interview

??? Off on a tangent

Questions that divert you from your main agenda

Handle them quickly and get back to the topic

> Do not allow the interview to get off track. When the interviewer brings up something that takes you in a direction in which you don't want to go, briefly give a response that satisfies the interviewer, and then get back on track.

> Give your answer, and then say, for example, "But I really wanted to tell you about a special project I worked on." It is your responsibility to get the conversation back on track.

Conduct a campaign aimed at a company. If Miss Gold is the hiring manager, don't try to see her just yet. Surround the hiring manager. Meet with others, so when you finally get in to see her, you will have several advocates and know a lot about the organization.

Dig for the information you need. Say to the person who set up the meeting: "I'd like to go in prepared. With whom will I meet?" Ask:

- names and job titles

- issues important to each of them

- what they are like

- tenure with organization

Uncover their objections, just as a consultant would:

- Where are you in the hiring process?

- How many others are you considering?

"Relax, Mr. Gray, this is just a simple job interview for a sales position. So, please stop pleading the 5th everytime I ask you a question."

- How do I stack up against them?
- Is there any reason why you might be reluctant to bring someone like me on board?

Get each interviewer to see you as the ideal. If you speak to several people, you want each one to advocate having you on board. If anyone objects to you, handle it now.

Always have 6 to 10 possibilities going:

- Always try to get the offer—even at companies you don't want to work for. Otherwise, you'll never get 6 to 10 possibilities. *That's* what momentum is all about.
- Even when an offer seems certain, do not drop other search activities.

Chaos often breeds life, while order breeds habit.
Henry Adams, American historian

In the interviewing phase, you're also *planning* your follow-up. You're not sitting there thinking, "I hope they make me an offer." Instead you're thinking, "I wonder what I should do to follow up after this interview."

Great is the art of beginning, but greater the art of ending.
Henry Wadsworth Longfellow

The Follow-Up Phase

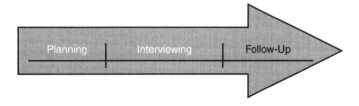

After the Planning and Interviewing phases, now you're in the Follow-Up Phase. This is the brainiest part of the process. In our book *Mastering the Job Interview and Winning the Salary Game*, you'll read lots of case studies to help you understand this part. But here's a brief story right now.

By the time Jeffrey came to The Five O'Clock Club, he had been interviewing with a telemarketing company for *four* months for the job of marketing head. Yet he wasn't getting an offer. So his small group said to him, "Jeffrey, what do you think might be their *objection* to bringing someone like you on board?" He said, "They're afraid that I don't understand their industry."

Jeffrey's situation was easy for his small group: He needed to let his prospective employer know that he understood their industry. The group suggested he do some research, and find out about the company's competitors. So after doing that, Jeffrey wrote the hiring team a letter that essentially said, "If I came in as head of marketing, here's

what I would do." He identified their competitors, how he saw them stacking up against their competitors, and what he would do as head of marketing. They offered Jeffrey a job immediately—*once* he had overcome their objections.

Actually, you'll be doing this intensive follow-up with 6 to 10 different prospective employers at the same time. It's a lot of hard work *and* brainpower. In fact, you should put as much time and energy into the follow-up phase as you did into the planning and interviewing phases.

Five O'Clock Clubbers know that they must put more effort into this part of the process—more than any of their competitors do. They want to make sure their follow-up is better than anyone else's. Then they have a better chance of turning their job interviews into job offers.

Change does not roll in on the wheels of inevitability, but comes through continuous struggle. And so we must straighten our backs and work for our freedom. A man can't ride you unless your back is bent.
Martin Luther King, Jr., "The Death of Evil upon the Seashore," sermon given at the Cathedral of St. John the Divine, New York City, May 17, 1956

---

1. **The brainiest part of the process:**
   - **Takes as much time as getting interviews and interviewing.**
   - **Keeps things alive with 6 to 10 organizations.**
   - **Requires brainpower—be sure to get help from your group.**
2. **Do not write silly *thank-you* notes after *job* interviews. Instead, write thoughtful letters and proposals to *influence* the decision makers.**

Using all of these techniques will help you to turn job interviews into OFFERS!

The more I want to get something done, the less I call it work.
Richard Bach, *Illusions*

It's takes brainpower because the kind of follow-up you do depends on:

- the kind of organization you're interviewing with;
- your personality;
- the number of times you've met with the prospective employer (Have you met with five people for one hour each, or have you met with just one person for half an hour?);

- the information you've gathered in those meetings; and
- who your competitors are.

Tell your small group what's going on and get their help to decide what you should do next.

Give every phase of your job search the attention it requires, and do as well as you can in each area of your campaign: Planning, Interviewing, Follow-Up. Don't skip any step in the process.

Passion costs me too much to bestow it on every trifle.
Thomas Adams

Overlap Your Campaigns

All changes, even the most longed for, have their melancholy; for what we leave behind is part of ourselves; we must die to one life before we can enter into another.

Anatole France, French writer

When you're in the *interviewing* phase of Target # 1, say, hospitals, then your main focus will be hospitals, which means you will customize your Two-Minute Pitch, your résumé, and your cover letter. But once those letters are in the mail and you have had a few meetings with hospitals, you can start working on Target #2, say, health-care equipment manufacturers. When you're in the *interviewing* phase of Target #2, you can start working on Target #3, say, HMOs. This staggered, focused search will result in more meetings and also keep your momentum going.

> **For each target:**
>
> - **Conduct research to develop a list of all the organizations. Find the names of people you should contact in the appropriate departments in each of those companies.**
> - **Develop your cover letter. (Paragraph 1 is the opening; Paragraph 2 is a summary about yourself appropriate for this target; Paragraph 3 contains your bulleted accomplishments ("You may be interested in some of the things I've done"); Paragraph 4 is the close. (Lots of sample letters are in our book *Shortcut Your Search*.)**
> - **Develop your plan for getting lots of meetings in this target.**

These organized, overlapping campaigns give you a structured search, as opposed to a *scattered* search. If you talk to hospitals, health-care manufacturers, HMOs, and anybody else *whenever you feel like it*:

- your pitches will become blurred;
- you will sound less committed to the target;
- you'll have less powerful cover letters;
- you'll get confused;
- your search will take longer; and
- you'll get fewer offers.

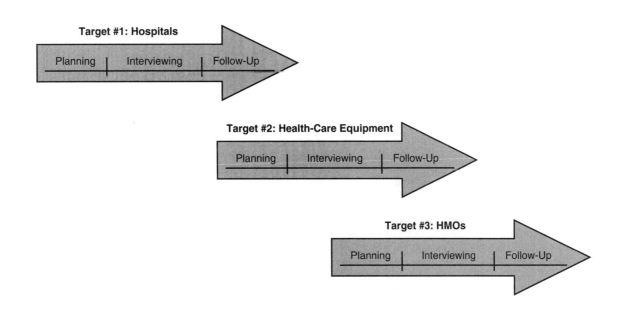

Instead, have structured campaigns. So, the most effective approach is to contact every organization in your first target. Give your first target a good try, and within a week or two, you can start on your second target.

Even if you're going after very small targets, where there are only two or three very small companies in each industry, you should still focus on one target at a time.

For example, Marilyn wanted a job in high-end marketing. One of her targets was watch companies, and there were only two watch companies that were of interest to her. Marilyn was also interested in tabletop companies, that is, companies that made fine china. There were only three tabletop companies that were of interest to her in her geographic area.

These are very small targets. Still, Marilyn contacted the two watch companies at the same time, then the three tabletop companies at the same time. Altogether, she had *18* very small targets, and she focused on one at a time. Even if *your* targets are very small, focus on one target at a time—even a few hours apart—and you'll do better. Your research will be better, as will your cover letters and your pitch.

> • **Conduct a structured search: Contact every organization in your first target.**
> • **Even if your targets are small, focus on one target at a time.**

. . . [W]e have to create a new organizational architecture flexible enough to adapt to change. We want an organization that can evolve, that can modify itself as technology, skills, competitors, and the entire business change.

Paul Allaire, CEO, XEROX Corporation

At the Five O'Clock Club, we:

- advocate a structured search;
- conduct targeted campaigns;
- prepare for *each* campaign;
- interview *well* in each campaign; and
- follow up with every *person* in every *organization* in each campaign.

As a splendid palace deserted by its inmates looks like a ruin, so does a man without character, all his material belongings notwithstanding.

Mohandas Gandhi

The
Five
O'Clock
Club

The Stages of Your Search

*The last thing one discovers in composing
a work is what to put first.*

Blaise Pascal

Measure How Well You Are Doing in Your Search

So, how can you tell whether you're doing well in your search? It's *not* good enough to say, "I'll know my search was effective when I get a job." That's too late.

The first guidepost in evaluating your search is the Preliminary Target Investigation, which will help you check out your various targets and prevent you from wasting months going after targets that are inappropriate for you.

Then, we'll tell you how to measure the effectiveness of your search in terms of Stages 1, 2, and 3. It took us *four years of research* to develop this method for measuring the effectiveness of your search.

You'll find that the search process is a *research* process. As you go along in your search, try to be objective about yourself: Which targets are working for you? Which techniques are resulting in interviews for you? It's ongoing research.

---

*Dying is no big deal. The least of us will
manage that. Living is the trick.*

Walter ("Red") Smith, funeral eulogy for
golf impresario Fred Corcoran

Stage 1: Your Preliminary Target Investigation

During Stage 1, network and make *contacts* in your target markets. As you gather information, analyze it: which markets seem worth pursuing and which do not? Don't waste months on targets that are unlikely to work out.

So it may be that at the beginning of your search, you've brainstormed plenty of targets—maybe you've come

---

Measuring the Effectiveness of Your Search

During a five-month search, you sent 100 résumés and talked to 75 people. But was this *effective*? Measure where you are.

Stage 1 means *keeping in touch with* 6 to 10 people in your target area. Get information on the targets and feedback.

Stage 2 is the core of your search. *Keep in touch* with 6 to 10 of the right *people* at the right *level* in the right *organizations.* When they say, "I wish I had an opening right now—I'd love to have someone like you on board," you have a GREAT search. Now, aim for 10 to 20 ongoing Stage 2 contacts.

But if you're *not* getting this kind of positive feedback, your target is wrong or your positioning is wrong.

Stage 3 will happen naturally: 6 to 10 job possibilities. Aim for three concurrent offers.

Don't select the job that simply pays $2,000 or $20,000 more. Select the job that positions you best for the long term, because it probably will not be your last job. You *will* have to search again.

---

up with 3 to 10 targets. Maybe you thought, "Gee, I think I'd like to work for a hospital." But in your Preliminary Target Investigation, you talked to managers at 4 hospitals—briefly—just to see what hospitals are like. And then you said to yourself, "Now that I have a feel for hospitals, I don't think hospitals are a good match for me." Because you've gathered some information, you can eliminate that target.

If you did not talk to hospitals in a concentrated way, it would be more difficult to assess whether or not you'd want to work for a hospital. You would be like all the other job hunters out there who are just going on interviews in a random manner and hoping they get an offer. Instead, assess the hospital market:

- Is this a good industry for me or not?
- Are my skills easily transferable or not?
- How can I make myself more appealing to hospitals?

Preliminary Target Investigation

- Networking or contacting people directly to gather information.
- Building contacts in your target market.
- Analyzing your target markets: Which targets are working for you and which are not?

All of the above will continue throughout your search.

A Solid Stage 1

- Maintaining 6 to 10 good contacts *on an ongoing basis.*
- You must stay in touch with them.

With a *structured* search, you can say, "This hospital target does not work for me. I need to get rid of it!" Otherwise, you're just wasting your time—going on interviews—and not even realizing that this target is not working for you.

So, eliminate inappropriate targets and decide which targets are worth a full campaign. Rank them: Target 1, Target 2, Target 3, and so on, depending on which ones you want to go after first, second, and third.

All of this happens during your Preliminary Target Investigation: brainstorm as many targets as you can, select the ones worth checking out, investigate them, eliminate some, rank the remaining ones, and mount your campaigns with overlapping targets.

You *must* stay in touch with a certain number of the people you've met during this investigative period. Those are your Stage 1 Contacts. For a good Stage 1, you need to have 6 to 10 people with whom you want to *stay in touch.* If you have *no* intention of staying in touch with some people you've contacted, they don't go on your Stage 1 List.

Stage 2 is the meat of your search, and this is where you should put most of your effort. You're in a good, solid Stage 2 when you're talking to 6 to 10 of the right people at the right level at the right organizations. The *quality* of your contacts has changed and you're being well received. That is, they're saying to you, "I'm so sorry we don't have an opening right now. We'd love to have someone like you on board."

Stage 2—The Stage That Matters Most

Get in to see the right people

- at the right level,
- at the right organizations, and
- make sure you are being well received.

"I wish we had an opening right now. I'd love to have someone like you on board."

That's a solid Stage 2 search, and it means that you've got a great search going.

You're talking to the *right* people, and they *like* you; they really like you. They'd love to have someone like you on board. It just so happens they don't have an opening right now. But that's okay because the positive feedback means you're working the right targets with the right pitch.

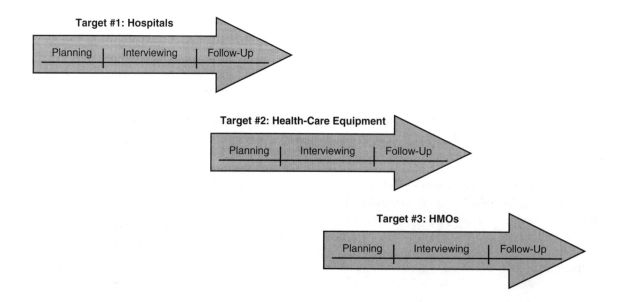

What should you do next? Work hard to get more quality meetings: Talk to *more* of the right people at the right level in the right organizations.

What *else* should you do? Stay in touch with all of them—because someday they're going to need someone like you—they already said they *want* you!

This is the description of a terrific search! You shouldn't expect that a company would have an opening just because you happened to talk to them at this moment. Stay in touch with them—with at least 6 to 10 people *on an ongoing basis.* But if you *don't* intend to talk to them again, *they don't count* as Stage 2 contacts.

This Is a Terrific Search!

- **Although they don't have an opening for you right now . . .**
- **Talk with people and stay in touch with . . .**
- **At least 6 to 10 on an *ongoing basis.***
- **Someday, they'll need you.**

Simon: We can walk right outta here if you want.
Eric: And where we gonna go?
Simon: Anywhere man. It's a big world.

Bruce Faulk, *You Still Got to Come Home to That*

Develop *more* quality contacts. That's right: 6 to 10 are not enough, 6 to 10 was a minimum range to help you test your presentation to this marketplace. It worked. Now, increase that number, and *aim for 12 to 20 or even 40,* and keep in touch with all of them. We're not suggesting the impossible! These recommended numbers are the result of solid research, which we are now passing on to you. Stage 2 is crucial: We know that Five O'Clock Clubbers who follow this methodology and generate these numbers end up with multiple offers to choose from.

Instead of 6 to 10, aim for 12 to 20, or even 40.

Refining Your Search

Look at your Stage 2 contacts by target, and notice which targets are best for you. Become a researcher on your own behalf. You might notice, "Hospitals are being responsive to me. I think I need to contact more people in the hospital market." If you notice which targets are working and which are not, you'll have a better, faster search, and you'll feel calmer in your search because you'll have more control.

Notice which targets are being most responsive to you.

If you can't get a healthy Stage 2 going—if you are not being well received—ask your small group and your coach to help you figure out what's wrong. But you have to bring them good information. For example, if you're in a meeting—not a job interview, but a meeting where there *is* no job opening—ask the manager, "If you had an opening right now, would you consider having someone like me on board?" If the manager is candid and gives you reasons *why not,* tell this information to your group.

This is what I love about The Five O'Clock Club process: It's a research-based approach. There can be only two possible problems here: either your *target* is wrong (you're going after the wrong industries, positions, or geographic areas), or your *positioning* is wrong (your pitch is wrong, you don't look the part, your résumé positions you incorrectly). Ask your coach and your small group for feedback.

- **If Stage 2 is working, do more of the same.**
- **If Stage 2 is *not* happening:**
  —Your targets are wrong, or
  —Your positioning is wrong.
  —Ask your small group and your coach what is wrong.

If you've done Stage 2 well, Stage 3 will take care of itself. Being in Stage 3 means you're talking to 6 to 10 organizations *on an ongoing basis* about a *real* job, or the *possibility* of creating a job for you. Don't worry about Stage 3. Worry about Stage 2.

In Stage 3, we want you to aim to have 6 to 10 *job* possibilities. Don't stop at 2 or 3! That's not enough. Out of 6 to 10, *5 will fall away through no fault of your own.* So you see that two or three possibilities are not enough. Chances are they will disappear for reasons beyond your control, or as we say at the Club, "fall away through no fault of your own."

Out of 6 to 10 job possibilities, 5 will fall away through no fault of your own.

To get more job possibilities, don't worry about Stage 3. Instead, develop more Stage 1 and Stage 2 contacts. Some Stage 1 contacts will bubble up and become Stage 2 contacts. Build up the number of Stage 2 contacts. Instead of 6 to 10, aim to have 20, 30, or even 40. A certain number of those will bubble up to become Stage 3 contacts—that is, where people are considering you for a real job or the possibility of creating a job for you.

Keep that momentum going. Your small group is so helpful here. Just when you think, "There's no *way* I can get more interviews," your small group will tell you how to keep the momentum going in your campaign.

> *We're a society that's not about perfection, but about rectifying mistakes. We're about second chances.*
>
> Harry Edwards, in "Hardline," *Detroit Free Press*

> **To get more job possibilities going:**
>
> - **Develop more Stage 1 and Stage 2 contacts.**
> - **Some Stage 1 contacts will bubble up to Stage 2.**
> - **Instead of 6 to 10, develop more.**
> - **A certain number of Stage 2 contacts will bubble up to Stage 3.**
> - **Keep your momentum going.**

Remember, talk about your search in terms of stages. If your small group asks how your search is going, don't say, "I don't have a job yet" or "I think I might get a job." Instead, analyze your search. Say, "My search is going great. I have 6 things in Stage 2; 12 in Stage 1; and one Stage 2 contact may become a Stage 3." If you use this mind-set and this shorthand, you will become better at analyzing how well you really are doing, and your small-group members will also be able to tell—and we can help you more.

> **How is your search going? Talk in terms of stages.**

Also tell your small group how you're *keeping in touch* with your contacts. It's okay if prospective employers don't have an opening right now. In another month or two, some of the organizations you're keeping in touch with *may* have an opening. So you must keep in touch with them *so they will think of you when something comes up.* Your coach and your small group can help you with this part as well.

Three Concurrent Job Offers

Yes, we want you to have three concurrent job offers. It sounds like a lot, but often the first offer you get is not the best. If you have three offers, you are in a better position to compare the jobs as well as the salaries, *and* you increase your chance of getting *more* offers.

Then you should pick the job that *positions you best for the long term.* Memorize that phrase! When you have choices—and we want you to have choices—don't pick the job that pays you $500 more or $5,000 more or $50,000 more! Think long term. The average American has been in his or her job only four years. Chances are, you will have to search again. So pick the job that positions you best for the long term.

> **Aim for three concurrent job offers, and then pick the job that positions you best for the long term. Don't pick the one that pays the most. Remember your Forty-Year Vision!**

Have Fun!

Finally, we want you to have three hours of fun a week—whether you like it or not. It's a little joke of ours, but the fact is, if you don't get three hours of fun a week, you won't interview well. You'll be too stressed and come across like a drone, rather than seeming like a person who everyone wants to work with.

> **Attend The Five O'Clock Club consistently. It's fun, and our research shows that those who attend on a regular basis get better jobs faster and at higher rates of pay than those who attend sporadically.**

We advocate a structured, disciplined search. If you think you can stop attending the club for a few weeks, and go out and search on your own for a while, you may be buying trouble. If you come back only when you *think* you have a problem, chances are your group could have helped you *avoid* the problem.

Attend consistently and the group will become familiar with your search and notice when you are going off track. You may even be targeting the wrong kind of job, and the group will notice that in your expression, or in your report of what happens when you go to meetings. We don't want you to just get a job—any job. We want you to get the job that's right for you. If you skip meetings and search on your own—without the benefit of weekly peer review—it's easy to get off track. Then when you finally come back to the group, everything's a *mess.*

Instead, attend The Five O'Clock Club week after week after week.

That also means you should job search in the summer and during the holidays. In fact, those are very opportune times to search. Your competition drops out of the job market because they think nothing is going on. Yet there's plenty of hiring going on during the summer and holidays.

Keep going with your job search. Don't use any excuse to drop out. In fact, Five O'Clock Clubbers put their foot to the pedal and move ahead whatever time of year it is!

- **Get three hours of fun a week— whether you like it or not!**
- **Attend The Five O'Clock Club consistently.**
- **Job search in the summer and during the holidays, too.**
- *They* **never call when they say they will.**

And always remember how vital it is to take the initiative and follow up. When they say, "I'll call you on Tuesday," they really mean it. But they will *never* call you when they say they will. *The ball is always in your court.* It is always up to you to figure out what to do next—and your small group can help you do that.

Let the past drift away with the water.

Japanese saying

Study our books as if you were in graduate school. Work with your coach and your small group. You'll *love* your small group. Everyone does. You'll be in a small group of your peers. So if you're making $60,000 a year, for example, you'll be in a group of people earning, say, $50,000 to $80,000. If you're earning more than $100,000 a year, you'll be in a group in which everyone earns more than $100,000 a year. And those earning more than $200,000 a year are in a group of *their* peers.

It's important to be in a group of your peers because everyone's brainstorming with you about what you need to do next in your search.

"Going up?"

Now you have an <u>overview</u> of The Five O'Clock Club approach. You have a lot more ahead of you—in our other books and CDs and at the meetings.

Take good care of yourself and your career. Good luck to you. And the next time you need us, we'll be here.

The price one pays for pursuing any profession or calling is an intimate knowledge of its ugly side.

James Baldwin, *Nobody Knows My Name*

The
Five
O'Clock
Club

PART TWO

Finding Good Jobs:
THE CHANGING JOB-HUNTING PROCESS
(Start here if you are just beginning your job search.)

The Five O'Clock Club

11 Hints for Job-Hunting in a Tight Market

If you haven't the strength to impose your own terms upon life, then you must accept the terms it offers you.

T. S. Eliot, *The Confidential Clerk*

1. Expand Your Job-Hunting Targets

If you are searching only in Los Angeles or only in Detroit, for example, think of other geographic areas. If you are looking only in large public corporations, consider small or private companies. If you are looking for a certain kind of position, investigate what other kinds of work you could also do.

2. Expect to Be "In Search" for the Long Haul

The average professional or managerial worker takes six months to get a job. So though you may find something right away, it is sensible to develop financial backup plans. What kind of side work could you do to earn money in the short run? How could you reduce your expenses? Join a job-hunting group to get support, ideas, and contacts.

When you meet someone who doesn't "have" anything for you right now, that's okay. Plan to get in touch with that person again. In fact, you may meet dozens of people who don't have anything right now. Get to know them and their needs better, and tell them about yourself. Build relationships so you can contact them later.

3. Keep Your Spirits Up

An alarming number of job hunters in the United States are becoming discouraged and dropping out of the job market. Don't you be one of them. Read the next section, "When You've Lost the Spirit to Job Hunt."

Be aware that what you are going through is not easy, and that many of the things you are experiencing are being experienced by just about everybody else. Hang in there, get a fresh start, and eventually you will find something.

4. Think about Developing New Skills

If you suspect your old skills are out-of-date, develop new ones. If you can't get a job because you don't have the experience, *get* the experience. The several months that you will probably be searching is long enough for you to develop new skills. Take a course. Do volunteer work to gain expertise that you can then market. Join an association related to your new skill area.

If you need to earn money immediately, try to do something that will enhance your job search. For example, if you decide to do temporary work, and you want a job in the airline industry, consider doing your temporary work with an airline.

Consider doing something for little or no money simply because it would improve your résumé. A Five O'Clock Clubber got a 12-week assignment with a Sears consignee during the Christmas rush. The pay was terrible but the job title was Regional Manager. He needed something to do, and the job looked great on his résumé.

5. Become a Skilled Job Hunter

Being good at your job does not make you good at *getting* jobs. Good job hunters know what they want, what the market wants, and how to present themselves. Stay competitive. Learn how to job hunt like an expert. Your future depends on it.

6. Look for Opportunities

In this economy, opportunities probably will not come knocking on your door. You have to look for them—both inside and outside your present company. Chances are, your present company and even the industry you are in are going to change. So rather than just doing the same old job, think of how you can take on new assignments so you are at the forefront of the changes. Put out feelers to find out whether you are marketable outside your company. Continually test the waters.

When you are on an interview, try to negotiate a job that suits both you and the hiring manager. For example, if the job is for an administrator, and you would like to do some writing, see if they will allow you to do that too.

Don't passively expect to be told where you could fit in. Actively think about your place in their organization. Create a job for yourself.

7. Target What You Want

As Lily Tomlin said, "I always wanted to be somebody, but I should have been more specific." Be sure you select specific geographic areas, specific industries, and specific positions within those industries.

For example, you may want to be a writer in publishing or advertising in Manhattan or Chicago. Find the names of the people to contact in those cities and industries—or people who know people in those targets. If you target, you have a better chance of finding the job you want.

8. Learn How to Get Interviews

There are a lot of techniques for generating interviews. The basic ones are: answering ads, using search firms, contacting companies directly, and networking. Only 10 percent of all jobs are filled through ads and search firms, so it is wise to learn how to contact companies directly and how to network properly.

Identify all of the companies you need to contact, and then contact them as quickly as possible. Make sure you consider *every* technique for getting interviews in your target area. Don't focus on getting a job: Focus on getting interviews.

9. See People Two Levels Higher than You Are

When you are in the initial stages of exploring a target area, you will want to do some library research and con-tact people at your level to find out about that area and see how well your skills match up.

But after you have decided to conduct a full campaign in a target area, contact people who are at a higher level than you are. They are the ones who are in a position to hire you or recommend that you be hired.

Make sure you talk to lots of people. It will give you practice and actually relax you. You will find out how much in demand you are, and how much you can charge.

10. Work at Your Job Hunt the Same Way You Would Work at a Job

Plan your job-hunting campaign. Work at it 35 hours a week if you are unemployed, and 15 hours a week if you are employed. It's only when you are devoting a certain number of hours a week to your search that you can get some momentum built up. Of course, you also need to be concerned about the *quality* of your campaign. You can have an organized and methodical search by carefully following the process in this book.

11. Follow-Up, Follow-Up, Follow-Up

After you meet with someone who has no job for you, keep in touch with that person by letting him or her know how your search is going or by sending a magazine article that would be of interest, for example. After a job interview, consider what they liked about you and what they didn't, and how you could influence their hiring decision. Follow-up is the main opportunity you have to turn a job interview into a job offer.

You think you understand the situation, but what you don't understand is that the situation just changed.

Putnam Investments advertisement

The
Five
O'Clock
Club

When You've Lost the Spirit to Job Hunt

*"I can't explain myself, I'm afraid, Sir," said
Alice, "because I'm not myself, you see."
"I don't see," said the Caterpillar.*

Lewis Carroll, *Alice in Wonderland*

They're all doing terrific! You're not. You're barely hanging on. You used to be a winner, but now you're not so sure. How can you pull yourself out of this?

I've felt like that. Everyone in New York had a job except me. I would never work again. I was ruining interviews although I knew better—I had run The Five O'Clock Club for years in Philadelphia. Yet I was unable to job hunt properly. I was relatively new to New York and divorced. Even going to my country house depressed me. A woman wanted me to sell it, join her cult, and have a 71-year-old as my roommate. It seemed to be my fate.

Then I got a call from my father—a hurricane was about to hit New York. When I told him my situation, he directed me to get rid of the cult lady and take the next train out. I got out just as the hurricane blew in, and he and I spent three beautiful days alone at my parents' ocean place. He encouraged me, even playing 10 motivational tapes on "being a winner"! One tape taught me:

The winners in life think constantly in terms of I can, I will and I am. Losers, on the other hand, concentrate their waking thoughts on what they should have or would have done, or what they can't do.

Dr. Dennis Waitley, *The Psychology of Winning*

My father wined and dined and took care of me. We watched a six-hour tape of my family history—the births, and birthdays, Christmases past, marriages, and parties. We talked about life and the big picture. I had no strength. He nurtured me and gave me strength.

What can *you* do if you can't get this kind of nurturing? Perhaps I've learned a few lessons that may help you.

> **There seem to be phases and cycles in a job hunt—there is the initial rush, the long haul, the drought, followed by the first poor job offer and the later better offers.**

1. Put Things in Perspective

A depressing and difficult passage has prefaced every new page I have turned in life.

Charlotte Brontë

You've worked 10 or 20 years, and you'll probably work 10 or 20 more. In the grand scheme of things, this moment will be a blip: an aberration in the past.

Focusing on the present will make you depressed and will also make you a poor interviewee. You will find it difficult to brag about your past or see the future. You will provide too much information about what put you in this situation.

Interviewers don't care. They want to hear what you can do for *them*. When they ask why you are looking, give a brief, light, logical explanation, and then drop it.

Focus on what you have done in the past, and what you can do in the future. You *do* have a future, you know, although you may feel locked into your present situation. Even some young people say it is too late for them. But a lot can happen in 10 years—and *most* of what happens is up to you.

---

*My life seems like one long obstacle course,
with me as the chief obstacle.*

Jack Paar

Woe to him that is alone when he falleth,
for he hath not another to help him up.

The Wisdom of Solomon

2. Get Support

The old support systems—extended families and even nuclear families—are disappearing. And we no longer look to our community for support.

Today, we are more alone; we are supposed to be tougher and take care of ourselves. But relying solely on yourself is not the answer. How can you fill yourself up when you are emotionally and spiritually empty?

Job hunters often need some kind of emotional and spiritual support because this is a trying time. Our egos are at stake. We feel vulnerable and uncared for. We need realistic support from people who know what we are going through.

There is no such thing as a self-made man. I've had
much help and have found that if you are willing to
work, many people are willing to help you.

O. Wayne Rollins

- Join a job-hunting support group to be with others who know what you're going through. Many places of worship have job-hunting groups open to anyone. During a later job hunt when I was employed, I reported my progress weekly to The Five O'Clock Club I formed in New York. It kept me going.

  Statistics show that job hunters with regular career-coaching support get jobs faster and at higher rates of pay. A job-hunting group gives emotional support, concrete advice, and feedback. Often, however, these are not enough for those who are at their lowest.

The more lasting a man's ultimate work, the
more sure he is to pass through a time, and,
perhaps a very long one, in which there seems
to be very little hope for him.

Samuel Butler

- If possible, rely on your friends and family. I could count on a call from my former husband most mornings after I returned from breakfast—just so we could both make sure I was really job hunting. I scheduled lunches with friends and gave them an honest report or practiced my job-hunting lines with them.

- Don't abuse your relationships by relying on one or two people. Find lots of sources of support. Consider joining a church, synagogue, or mosque (they're *supposed* to be nice to you).

3. Remember That This Is Part of a Bigger Picture

We, ignorant of ourselves, Beg often our own harms,
Which the Wise Power Denies us for our own good;
so we find profit by losing of our prayers.

Shakespeare, *Antony and Cleopatra*

. . . so are My ways higher than your ways and My thoughts
than your thoughts.

Isaiah 55:9

You are a child of the universe no less than the trees and the
stars; you have a right to be here. And whether or not it is clear
to you, no doubt the universe is unfolding as it should.

Max Ehrmann

Why me? Why now? Shakespeare thought there might be someone bigger than ourselves watching over everything—a Wise Power. My mother (and probably yours, too) always said "everything happens for the best."

We know that in all things God works for the good of those who
love Him.

Romans 8:28

If you believe things happen for a purpose, *think about the good in your own situation.* What was the *purpose* of my own unemployment? Because of it:

- I experienced a closeness with my father that still affects me;
- I became a better counselor; and
- I stopped working 12-hour days.

Though shattered when they lose their jobs, many say in retrospect it was the best thing that could have happened to them. Some say this time of transition was the most rewarding experience of their lives.

Every adversity has the seed of an
equivalent or greater benefit.

W. Clement Stone

Perhaps you, too, can learn from this experience and also make some sense of it. This is a time when people often:

- decide what they *really* should be doing with their careers—I had resisted full-time career coaching because I liked the prestige of the jobs I had held;
- better their situations, taking off on another upward drive in their careers;

- develop their personalities; learn skills that will last their entire lives, and
- reexamine their values and decide what is now important to them.

For what shall it profit a man, if he shall gain the whole world, and lose his own soul?

Mark 8:36

The trouble with the rat race is that if you win, you're still a rat.

Lily Tomlin

4. Continue to Do Your Job

When you were in your old job, there were days you didn't feel like doing it, but you did it anyway because it was your responsibility. *Job hunting is your job right now.* Some days you don't feel like doing it, but you must. Make a phone call. Write a proposal. Research a company. Do your best every day. No matter how you feel. Somehow it will get done, as any job gets done. Some practical suggestions:

- Make your job hunting professional. Organize it. Get a special calendar to use exclusively to record what you are doing. Use The Five O'Clock Club's Interview Record in this book to track more professionally your efforts and results.
- Set goals. Don't think of whether or not you want to make calls and write letters. Of course you don't. Just do them anyway. Spend most of your time interviewing— that's how you get a job.

   Depression ➡ Inactivity ➡ Depression.

- If you're at the three-month mark or beyond, you may be at a low point. It's hard to push on. Get a fresh start. Pretend you're starting all over again.
- Finding a job is your responsibility. Don't depend on anyone else (search firms, friends) to find it for you.
- Watch your drinking, eating, smoking. They can get out of hand. Take care of yourself physically. Get dressed. Look good. Get some exercise. Eat healthful foods. You may need a few days off to recharge.

- Don't postpone having fun until you get a job. If you are unemployed, schedule at least three hours of fun a week. Do something you normally are unable to do when you are working. I went out to breakfast every morning, indulged in reading the *Times,* and then went back to my apartment to job hunt. I also went to the auction houses, and bought a beautiful desk at Sotheby's when I sold my country house.
- Assess your financial situation. What is your backup plan if your unemployment goes on for a certain number of months? If need be, I planned to get a roommate, sell furniture, and take out a loan. It turned out not to be necessary, but by planning ahead, I knew I would not wind up on the street.
- Remember: You are distracted. Job hunters get mugged, walk into walls, lose things. This is not an ordinary situation, and extraordinary things happen. Be on your guard.
- Observe the results of what you do in your job hunt. Results are indicators of the correctness of your actions and can help refine your techniques.

All's well that ends well.

Shakespeare

- Become a good job hunter so you can compete in this market. It takes practice, but the better you are, the less anxious you will be.

In nature there are neither rewards nor punishments—there are consequences.

Robert Green Ingersoll

In the depths of winter I discovered that there was in me an invincible summer.

Albert Camus

Finally, two sayings especially helped me when I was unemployed:

You don't get what you want. You get what you need.
and
When God closes a door, He opens a window.

Good luck.—Kate

The
Five
O'Clock
Club

Job Hunting versus Career Planning

Most people say their main fault is a lack of discipline. On deeper thought, I believe that is not the case. The basic problem is that their priorities have not become deeply planted in their hearts and minds.

Stephen R. Covey,
The Seven Habits of Highly Effective People

*Afoot and light-hearted
I take to the open road,
Healthy, free, the world before me,
The long brown path before me,
leading wherever I choose.*

Walt Whitman,
Complete Poetry and Collected Prose

You are probably reading this because you want a job. But you will most likely have to find another job after that one, and maybe after that. After all, the average American has been in his or her job only four years. To make smoother transitions, learn to plan ahead.

If you have a vision and keep it in mind, you can continually *position* yourself for your long-range goal by taking jobs and assignments that lead you there. Then your next job will be more than just a job. It will be a stepping stone on the way to something bigger and better.

When faced with a choice, **select the job that fits best with your Forty-Year Vision—the job that positions you best for the long term.**

It takes less than an hour to make up a rudimentary Forty-Year Vision. But it is perhaps the single most important criterion for selecting jobs. Do the exercise quickly. Later, you can refine it and test it against reality. Do the Forty-Year Vision using the worksheet in this book. This is exactly what helped the people in the following case studies. **All of the people described are real people and what happened to them is true.**

CASE STUDY *Bill*
Bypassing the *Ideal* Offer

For most of his working life, Bill had been a controller in a bank. He was proud of the progress he had made, given his modest education. Now he was almost 50 years old. It was the logical time to become a chief financial officer (CFO), the next step up, ideally in a company near home, since his family life was very important to him. At just this point, he lost his job.

Following The Five O'Clock Club method, Bill got three job offers:

1. as CFO for a bank only 10 minutes from home—the job of his dreams.
2. as controller for a quickly growing bank in a neighboring area—still a long commute.
3. as controller for the health-care division of an insurance company 200 miles from home.

Bill wisely selected the job that would put him in the strongest position for the long term, and would look best in his next job search. He selected job #3 because it would allow him to include two new industries on his résumé. Health care was growing, and insurance would broaden his financial-services experience.

Bill wanted to hedge his bets, and not uproot his family. So he got an apartment close to the new company, and went home on weekends. After a year and a half, the company was taken over, an unpredictable event. The new management brought in their own people. He was out.

But this time, Bill was not worried. Since he now had valuable new experience on his résumé, he was sought after. He was offered and took a key post in a consulting firm that served the health-care and financial industries.

CASE STUDY *Charlotte*
Positioning over Money

Charlotte, a marketing manager, received three offers:

1. with a credit-card company in a staff marketing position dealing with international issues.
2. with a major music company as head of marketing for the classical-music division.
3. with a nonprofit research organization as head of marketing.

The first two positions paid about the same, let's say $90,000. The position with the not-for-profit offered $75,000, and there was no room for moving the salary higher.

How did Charlotte decide which position to take? The music company was not a good fit for her: She was not compatible with the people, and she would probably have failed in that job. The credit-card job would have been easy but boring, and she would not have learned anything new.

Charlotte selected the not-for-profit position, the lowest-paid job. In her Forty-Year Vision, she saw herself as the head of a not-for-profit someday. Since she was only 35, she did not now need a position with a not-for-profit. But she felt good when she interviewed there. So she took the job that best fit with her long-term vision.

Charlotte loved the people, and her position put her in contact with some of the most powerful business people in America. Top management listened to her ideas, and she had an impact on the organization.

After one-and-a-half years, there was a reorganization. Charlotte was made manager of a larger department. She received a pay increase to match her new responsibilities, which brought her salary higher than the salaries of the other two job offers. But, best of all, Charlotte's job was a good fit for her, and made sense in light of her Forty-Year Vision.

CASE STUDY *Harry*
Stuck in a Lower-Level Job

Harry was a window-washer for the casinos, earning an excellent hourly salary. The pay was high because the building was slanted, making the job more dangerous.

Harry did a great job, and was responsible and well liked. He was offered a supervisory position that could lead to other casino jobs. But the base pay was less than his current pay including overtime, and allowed for no overtime pay. Harry decided he could not afford to make the move and stayed as a window-washer paid by the hour. Today, several years later, he still cleans windows.

There's nothing wrong with washing windows, or any other occupation. But if you make this kind of choice based on short-term gain, be aware that you may be closing off certain options for your future. **<u>Sometimes we have to make short-term sacrifices to get ahead—if indeed we *want* to get ahead.</u>**

A man may not achieve everything he has dreamed, but he will never achieve anything great without having dreamed it first.

William James

Selecting the Right Offer

Doing the exercises will give you some perspective when choosing among job offers. I hope that you will attempt to get 6 to 10 job possibilities in the works (knowing that five will fall away through no fault of your own). Then most likely you will wind up with three offers at approximately the same time.

If you have three offers, the one to choose is the one that positions you best for the long run.

People Who Have Goals Do Better

Money is not the only measure of success. When you have a clear, long-term goal, it can affect everything: your hobbies and interests, what you read, the people to whom you are attracted. Those who have a vision do better at reaching their goals, no matter what those goals are. A vision gives you hope and direction. It lets you see that you have plenty of time—no matter how young or how old you are.

CASE STUDY *Bill Clinton*
A Clear Vision

Bill Clinton is a good example of the power of having a vision. A small-town boy, Bill decided in his teens that he wanted to become president. He developed his vision, and worked his entire life to make that dream come true.

CASE STUDY *Bruce*
Plenty of Time

Bruce—young, gifted, and black—was doing little to advance his career. Like many aspiring actors, he worked at odd jobs to survive and auditioned for parts when he could.

But, in fact, Bruce spent little time auditioning or improving his craft because he was too busy trying to make ends meet. What's more, he had recently been devastated by a girlfriend.

Optimism Emerges as Best Predictor to Success in Life

"Hope has proven a powerful predictor of outcome in every study we've done so far," said Dr. Charles R. Snyder, a psychologist at the University of Kansas. . . . "Having hope means believing you have both the will and the way to accomplish your goals, whatever they may be. . . . It's not enough to just have the wish for something. You need the means, too. On the other hand, all the skills to solve a problem won't help if you don't have the willpower to do it."

Dr. Snyder found that people with high levels of hope share several attributes:

- Unlike people who are low in hope, they turn to friends for advice on how to achieve their goals.

- They tell themselves they can succeed at what they need to do.

- Even in a tight spot, they tell themselves things will get better as time goes on.

- They are flexible enough to find different ways to get to their goals.

- If hope for one goal fades, they aim for another. Those low on hope tend to become fixated on one goal, and persist even when they find themselves blocked. They just stay at it and get frustrated.

- They show an ability to break a formidable task into specific, achievable chunks. People low in hope see only the large goal, and not the small steps to it along the way.

People who get a high score on the hope scale have had as many hard times as those with low scores, but have learned to think about it in a hopeful way, seeing a setback as a challenge, not a failure.

Daniel Goleman,
The New York Times,
December 24, 1991

Using The Five O'Clock Club assessment, Bruce realized he was going nowhere. His first reaction was to attempt to do everything at once: quit his part-time jobs, become a film and stage director, and patch things up with his girlfriend. With the help of the Forty-Year Vision, Bruce discovered that his current girlfriend was not right for him in the long run, and that he had plenty of time left in his life to act, direct, and raise a family.

Because of his vision, Bruce knew what to do next to get ahead. He was prompted to look for a good agent (just like a job hunt), and take other steps for his career. Six months later, Bruce landed a role in *Hamlet* on Broadway. He is on tour with another play now.

The psychic task which a person can and must set for himself is not to feel secure, but to be able to tolerate insecurity, without panic and undue fear.

Erich Fromm, *The Sane Society*

CASE STUDY *Sophie*
Making *Life* Changes First

Sophie, age 22, had a low-level office job, wanted a better one, and did the assessment.

She did her Forty-Year Vision, but was depressed by it. Like many who feel stuck, Sophie imagined the same uninspiring situation from year to year. It seemed her life would never change.

With encouragement and help, she did the exercise again, and let her dreams come out, no matter how implausible they seemed. She saw herself eventually in a different kind of life. Although she initially did the exercise because she wanted to change jobs, she saw she needed to change other things first.

She moved away from a bad situation at home, got her own apartment, broke up with the destructive boyfriend she had been seeing for eight years, and enrolled in night school. It took her two years to take these first steps.

She is now working toward her long-term goal of becoming a teacher and educational filmmaker. She says that she is off the treadmill and effortlessly making progress.

CASE STUDY *Dave*
A New Life at *Sixty-Two*

After Dave had worked for his organization for more than 25 years, it eliminated his job. He still had a lot of energy and a lot to offer, and he wanted to work. But he was depressed by his prospects until he did his Forty-Year Vision.

His dream for his new life included: working two days a week developing new business for a small organization, volunteering on the board of a not-for-profit, heading a state commission, and consulting for an international not-for-profit. Instead of slowing down, Dave became busier and happier than he had been in his old job. He was able to quickly implement most of his vision.

I don't think in terms of failure. I think of things as not the right time or something that's outside of my capabilities. I don't feel like anyone outside of me should be setting limitations. People should be encouraged to shoot for the moon.

Whoopi Goldberg, as quoted by Isabel Wilkerson,
The New York Times, Nov. 29, 1992

CASE STUDY *Bob*
Sticking with His Vision

Bob was feeling restless about his career. This prompted him to do a Forty-Year Vision. He wanted to end up at age 80 having done something significant for the community, and having earned a good living doing it. At age 43, he was offered a substantial promotion at his current job—but it was at odds with his community-service goal. After much soul-searching, Bob turned down the promotion, and took steps to implement his plan. He ended up starting his own not-for-profit that eventually would impact communities across America.

CASE STUDY *Karen*
Our Values Change over Time

Karen had been a high-powered executive, earning more than $300,000 a year. When she took time off to have her first baby, she was surprised by how much she loved taking care of her daughter. After Karen had stayed at home for two years, her husband lost his job. She had to look for work.

At first, her vision was to *have it all.* She assumed she needed another $300,000-a-year job to keep up their lifestyle, yet she also wanted time with her child. The assessment helped her see that she had never really enjoyed the grueling hours she had to work before, and she now imagined a better balance between work and family.

Karen received three offers: one for $300,000; one for $200,000, which required a lot of travel; and one for $125,000, which she knew fit into her Forty-Year Vision. Although she was at first embarrassed by having taken a lower-level position, she grew to love it and her new lifestyle.

Over time, our values change. As her daughter grows older, Karen may decide again that a higher-powered job is fine for her.

Men experience value changes, too—easing up a little when they want to spend time with the kids, for example, and focusing more on their careers at other times.

CASE STUDY *Hank*
Thinking Too Small

Hank, a senior executive who lost his job, chose a new field just because it was lucrative. But the assessment showed it would not position him well for the job *after* that one.

Instead, Hank became a senior executive with a major organization in his old field. The quick route to financial success no longer appealed to him. He took a more sure road that would position him well for the future. In fact, the job he took paid well enough to make his family very comfortable.

Thinking Big; Thinking Small

A Forty-Year Vision gives you perspective. Without one, you may think too small or too big. Writing it down makes you more reasonable, more thoughtful, and more serious. **Having a vision also makes you less concerned about the progress of others because you know where *you are going.***

CASE STUDY *Jim*
Objective versus Subjective

Jim had to choose between two job offers, one paying $350,000 and another at $500,000. The thought process is the same regardless of salary. To prove it, let's pretend the positions were paying $35,000 and $50,000. Which should he take?

Jim's wife wanted him to take the $50,000 job. It paid more and had a better title.

Jim liked the people at the $35,000 job, and they appreciated him and listened to his suggestions. But they could pay no more than $35,000. He delayed the start date while we talked, and listed the pros and cons of each position. He *still* could not decide. After all, $15,000 is a big difference.

Finally, I said to Jim: "I'm going to make it easy for you. The $35,000-a-year job no longer exists. Let's not talk about it. You will take the $50,000 a year job, have a very nice commute, make your wife happy, have a title you can be proud of, and make $50,000."

Jim sat in silence. Then he said: "The thought of going there depresses me. I think the job is not doable. They may be offering me an impossible job."

Sometimes objective thinking alone is not enough. The exercise helped Jim find out what his gut was telling him. During the interview process, things had turned him off about the $50,000 organization—but not enough to turn down the extra $15,000. It wasn't logical.

When Jim finally made up his mind to take the "$35,000" job, he was so happy, he bought presents for everyone. Even his wife was pleased. He had made the right choice.

Consider Objective and Subjective Information

If you tend to pay too much attention to subjective information, balance it by asking: "What is the logical thing for me to do regardless of how I feel?"

If you tend to be too objective, ask: "I know the logical thing to do, but how do I really feel about it?"

For most of us, it is easier to think about how to get what we want than to know what exactly we should want.

Robert N. Bellah et al., *Habits of the Heart*

CASE STUDY *Dean*
Expect to Be Paid Fairly

Dean had been making $60,000. He lost his job and uncovered two choices: one at $75,000 and one at $100,000. He asked to meet with me.

Dean was not worth $100,000 at this stage in his career, and I told him so. In addition, that organization was not a good fit for him.

The $75,000 job seemed just right for Dean. He had an engineering degree, and the work dealt with high-tech products.

Yet he took the $100,000 position. Within four months, he was fired.

Dean met with me again to discuss two more possibilities: another position for $100,000 and one at a much lower salary. Since he had most recently been making $100,000, interviewers thought perhaps he was worth it. Again, he opted for the $100,000 position—he liked making that kind of money. Again he could not live up to that salary, and again he was fired.

Life Skills, Not Just Job-Hunting Skills

A vision helps people see ahead, and realize that they can not only advance in their careers but also change their life circumstances—such as who their friends are and where they live.

Your career is not separate from your life. If you dream of living in a better place, you have to earn more money. If you would like to be with better types of people, you need to **become a better type of person yourself.**

The Forty-Year Vision cannot be done in a vacuum. Research is the key to *achieving* your vision. Without research, it is difficult to imagine what might be out there, or to imagine dream situations. Be sure to read the two chapters on research in this book.

> **Whatever your level, to get ahead you need:**
>
> - **exposure** to other possibilities and other dreams;
> - **hard facts** about those possibilities and dreams (through networking and research);
> - the **skills** required in today's job market; and
> - **job-search training** to help you get the work for which you are qualified.

Targeting the Jobs of the Future

The time is not far off when you will be answering your television set and watching your telephone.

Raymond Smith, chairman and chief executive of the Bell Atlantic Corporation, *The New York Times*, February 21, 1993

The Times Are Changing

Ten years from now, half the working population will be in jobs that do not exist today. Positions and industries will disappear almost completely—edged out by technological advances or new industries. When was the last time you saw a typewriter repairman? Or even a typewriter? There are few TV or radio repair jobs. They have been replaced by new jobs.

Some industries retrench—or downsize—slowly and trick us into thinking they are solid and dependable. At the turn of the last century, there were literally thousands of piano manufacturers. A few still remain, but that industry was affected by new industries: movies, TV, radio, and other forms of home entertainment—most recently, the Internet, CD-ROMs, and video game systems.

In 1900, most people probably thought: "But we'll *always* need pianos." People today think the same way about the industries they are in.

All our lives we are engaged in the process of accommodating ourselves to our surroundings; living is nothing else than this process of accommodation. When we fail a little, we are stupid. When we flagrantly fail, we are mad. A life will be successful or not, according as the power of accommodation is equal to or unequal to the strain of fusing and adjusting internal and external chances.

Samuel Butler, *The Way of All Flesh*

Temporary Setbacks

Some industries and occupations ebb and flow with supply and demand. When there is a shortage in a well-paid field, such as nursing, engineering, or law, school enrollments increase, creating an excess. Then people stop entering these fields, creating a shortage. So, sometimes it's easy to get jobs and sometimes it isn't.

The overall economy may also temporarily affect a field or industry. Real estate, for example, may suffer in a down economy and pick up in a strong one.

Ahead of the Market

When the Berlin Wall came down in 1989, there was a rush of companies wanting to capitalize on the potential market in Eastern Europe. Given all they were reading in the papers, job hunters thought it would be a good market for them to explore as well. They were ahead of the market. It took a few years before the market caught up with the concept. Now many people are employed in Eastern Europe or in servicing that market.

The same may be true for the area that you are in or are trying to get into: The market may not be there because it has not yet developed.

Another growth area is *new media.* This is such a rapidly changing area that it is still hard to define. As of this writing, it can include cable stations, a number of which are devoted to home shopping; *imaging* of medical records and credit card receipts; supermarket scanners and other devices that promote items or record what you buy; multimedia use of the computer (sound, motion, and color instead of just text, which you now take for granted); virtual reality; interactive TV; telephone companies (with cable already going into every home); cell phones; CD-ROMs (compact discs containing *read-only memory*), which put materials such as games and encyclopedias on CDs; the increasingly important Internet; and gadgets such as personal data assistants, and DVD and MP3 players.

And let's not forget biotech, health care, and related areas (gyms, nutritionists, physical fitness instructors). Americans now take it as their right that they should have anything that makes them healthier. Such industries make up a significant part of the GNP, and are projected to grow strongly. Often, large corporations have divisions or areas in a division that are in these new media areas. You can find out your company's involvement by looking at its website, talking to HR managers, looking through the company directory, and finding appropriate people knowledgeable about the company's operations. This could be an excellent opportunity to use your skills in a growing area, as well as learn new skills and make an exciting career move.

What about *Your* Industry or Profession?

Is your dream industry or field growing, permanently retrenching, or in a temporary decline because of supply and demand or other economic conditions? If you are lucky, your employer is ahead of the market, and the industry will pick up later. Often, you can find out just by reading your organization's annual report and other information it gives out to the public.

Most people in permanently retrenching industries, including the leaders, incorrectly think the decline is temporary. You have to decide for yourself. You could perhaps gain insight and objectivity by researching what those outside your industry have to say.

It has been predicted that if things continue as they are going, there will soon be a great divide in America, with technologically and internationally aware workers making fine salaries, while the unaware and unskilled earn dramatically lower wages. (Even high-level executives can be unaware and unskilled, and thus face reductions in their salaries as they become less useful.) If this does come to pass, the best a career coach can do is to encourage people to try to be on the winning side of that divide.

Today's workers need to forget jobs completely and look instead for work that needs doing—and then set themselves up as the best way to get that work done.

William Bridges, *JobShift: How to Prosper in a Workplace Without Jobs*

CASE STUDY *Debbie*
Hedging Her Bets for the Future

Debbie had been an account manager in advertising for 15 exciting years. She loved learning everything she could about her shampoo or detergent account, or whatever she was assigned. Debbie was reluctant to change industries despite some negatives: She had a long commute. (Those

who want to stay in a retrenching industry often must commute long distances or relocate.) And her job was not as much fun as it used to be. (Companies that survive in retrenching industries tend to experience greater pressure on their bottom line; thus employees have to work longer hours with smaller rewards.) She decided to stay on, but took proactive steps to better ensure her future in two ways:

1. She asked to be assigned to a high-tech account. She knew that if she learned that business, she could someday get a job in the marketing or advertising department of a high-tech organization in an industry that is growing.

2. In addition to proposing traditional advertising solutions for her clients' problems, she also began to investigate and propose that they take advantage of the new media, such as home shopping and the Internet. This would help her clients, but would also give Debbie experience in the way companies market their goods in the early 2000s and give her an edge over those who knew only traditional advertising.

Debbie continues to hold her own as her colleagues get squeezed out of advertising. Some are forced to commute longer distances or relocate just so they can stay in the industry. Although many have lost their jobs, or work for half what they used to, there are still enough people making good money to create the illusion that things are the same as they were.

Traditional advertising may revive and prove the doomsayers wrong, but at least Debbie has hedged her bets: She can either stay in the industry or be valuable outside.

You can be like Debbie: you can position yourself for the future by gaining new experience on the job you are now in, or by doing volunteer work or taking a course to learn the new skills you need to remain competitive.

Retrenching Markets Are All Alike

When an industry retrenches, the results are predictable. A retrenching market, by definition, has more job hunters than jobs. The more that market retrenches, the worse it gets.

Those who want to stay in the field have increasingly longer searches as more people chase fewer jobs. They will also tend to stay in their new jobs for less time as companies in the retrenching industry continue to downsize or go out of business.

Profit margins get squeezed as companies compete for a slice of a shrinking pie. Those companies become less enjoyable to work for because there is less investment in training and development, research, internal communications, and the like. Of course, salaries are cut.

Many young people are enticed into glamour fields, regardless of the practicality, or into fields their parents or friends are in, regardless of the fit for them personally, despite the projections for those fields. Yes, you should pursue your dreams, but check them out a little first.

Most people target only their current industries, fields, or professions at the start of their search. They consider other targets only after they have difficulty getting another job in their present field. They would probably have found something faster if they had looked in other fields from the beginning. **Those in retrenching industries who also target new industries have a shorter search time.**

> **The new fields are new to everyone. An outsider has a chance of becoming an insider.**

The Attributes of a High-Growth Industry

By definition, growth industries must hire from outside: They don't have enough people inside the industry. The new industry attracts new competitors—many of whom will fail—and there is a shake-out. But if the industry is still growing, those who got in early are the most knowledgeable and valuable, and can command larger salaries. If the industry does *not* continue to grow, new entrants create a surplus of labor and salaries decrease.

As long as the industry continues to grow, there is an open window: Those outside the industry can get in. As the industry stabilizes, there will be plenty of experienced people, companies will want only those with direct experience, and the window will close.

> **HMOs, cellular technology, for-profit schools— and the Internet—were essentially nonexistent industries just 20 years ago.**

Expanding Your Search Geographically; Targeting Small Companies

Studies show that more jobs are created in the suburbs than in major metropolitan areas, and there is greater job creation in the *new* suburbs than in the *old* suburbs. Oops! It's good to know the facts, because you can conduct your search accordingly. If you have been ignoring the suburbs, think about them.

Job growth has been in smaller companies. Large companies do most of the downsizing. **In New York City, for example, there are 193,000 companies. Only 270 of them employ 1,000 people or more.** James Brown, an economist for the New York State Department of Labor specializing in the New York City labor market, advised members of the mid-Manhattan Five O'Clock Club to look to the other 192,730 companies—those that employ fewer than 1,000 employees.

Think about your geographic area, and think about the companies you are targeting. Most job hunters naturally think about the big companies that are in the news, but perhaps you should think about the new *hidden job market*: the suburbs, and companies with fewer than 1,000 employees.

The Bad News Is Good News— If You Are *FLEXIBLE*

Virtually every industry and field has been and will continue to be affected by technological changes. Whether you are in education, work for the Post Office, or sell books, your field will be affected. As Alice said about Wonderland: It takes all the running you can do to stay in the same place.

The good news is that many fields are much easier to enter today than they were in times when careers were more stable. There is room for you if you target properly and stay flexible. If you continue to learn in the field you are now in, and get to know the areas you are pursuing, you will be able to make changes as the world changes.

If your current industry or profession is retrenching (and you expect to be working more than 5 or 10 more years), it makes sense to investigate some of the growing fields.

Even if you end up back in your old retrenching industry, the time you have spent exploring a new industry is not wasted, because you will probably have to search again.

For workers, there are dark spots, but the overall picture is still far brighter than commonly believed. Real wages are starting to turn up, after years of decline. The old factory jobs are disappearing, but new jobs in other industries are being generated at an unprecedented rate. Rather than becoming a nation of hamburger flippers, we are becoming a nation of schoolteachers, computer programmers, and health-care managers. About 11 million new jobs have been created since 1989, and of those, approximately two-thirds are managerial and professional positions. There is a tremendous surge in creativity and new opportunities, ranging from new forms of entertainment to cheap global communications.

Michael Mandel, *The High-Risk Society*

Bull Market for Labor Likely to Continue into the Foreseeable Future

Richard Bayer, Ph.D., an economist and the chief operating officer for The Five O'Clock Club, is optimistic. He notes that both the Bureau of Labor Statistics and the Conference Board project labor shortages over the next 10 years.

Predictions are of course uncertain, and there could easily be a recession or two in this time frame, but the overall employment trend line remains strongly positive.

He notes:

- The demand for labor will continue to grow. The supply of labor will barely be adequate to meet the demand.

- There will almost surely be pockets of "skills mismatch" in which some positions are very difficult to fill.

- Overall, the educational level required to function in this new economy will rise.

- Although workers will continue to be needed at all levels, it is important to note that the larger increases in employment are coming in the various managerial, professional, and skilled technical ranks. This goes against the myth that the new economy is producing mainly low-skill and low-wage jobs.

- The occupations with the greatest declines tend to be lower skilled and lower paid: garment workers, customer-service (those who answer 800 telephone calls), farmworkers, textile machine operators.

So, what might the implications of all this be for Five O'Clock Clubbers and others?

This is a great time to be alive and have a career! The efforts you put into your education, into career development, into salary negotiation, into networking, into targeting a meaningful job, have never had such a strong chance of bearing good fruit!

There is guidance for each of us, and by lowly listening, we shall hear the right word.

Ralph Waldo Emerson

Getting More Sophisticated

Whether you are relatively new to the labor force or have been working a while, think past the obvious and think more deeply about the changes that are occurring.

Listed below are a few of the industries business experts project will grow in the near future. Try to discover other areas that may be affected by these or how your own job may be affected by growth in these areas. Each is huge and changing, and can be better defined by your investigation through networking, as well as Internet and library research.

Here is the list of some of the industries expected to grow:

- Health care and biotech, or anything having to do with them. Health care is considered a sure bet because of the aging population and the advances being made in medical technology.

- Anything high-tech, or the high-tech aspect of whatever field or industry you are in.

- The international aspect of the field/industry you are considering.

- The environmental area; waste management.

- Safety and security (especially since the September 11th attack on the United States).

- Telecommunications, the news media, and global communications (movie studios, TV networks, cable companies, computer companies, consumer-electronics companies, and publishers).

- Education in the broadest sense (as opposed to the traditional classroom), including computer-assisted instruction. (Researchers have found that people who are illiterate learn to read better with computer-assisted instruction than they do in a classroom.)

Because all of us will have to keep up-to-date in more areas in order to do our jobs well, technology will play an important part in our continuing education. Further, with America lagging so far behind other countries educationally, both the for-profit and not-for-profit sectors are working hard to revamp our educational system.

- Alternative means of distributing goods. Instead of retail stores, think not only about direct mail but also about purchasing by TV—or the Internet.

- Anything serving the aging population, both products and services.

In studying the preceding list, think of how you can combine different industries to come up with areas to pursue. For example: Combine the aging population with education, or the aging population with telecommunications, or health care with education, and so on. The more you research, the more sophisticated your thoughts will get.

If you combine education with the new media, you will be thinking like many experts. Students in schools are learning from interactive multimedia presentations on computers—presentations that will be as exciting as computer games and MTV combined, and almost as up-to-date as the morning news (most textbooks are years out of date). Teachers will do what computers cannot do: facilitate the groups, encourage, reinforce learning.

A computer-based approach can be used to train and update the knowledge of the U.S.'s workers: Employees can learn when they have the time and at their own pace, rather than having large numbers of workers leave their jobs to learn in a classroom situation.

When you read predictions that there will be a huge growth in a certain industry, say, home health-care workers, personal and home care aides, and medical assistants, medical secretaries, radiology technologists and technicians, and psychologists, you may think: "I don't want to be any of those." Think more creatively. Companies will have to spring up to supply and train those workers. (Some of the training could be done on multimedia.) People will be needed to manage the companies, regulate the care given, coach patients on how to select and manage such workers, and so on. If you read about the tremendous growth in the temporary help business, you *may* become a temporary worker yourself, or you could go to work running one of the temporary help companies.

Think about the field you are interested in, and how it is being affected by technology. Virtually every job and industry—whether it is publishing, entertainment, manufacturing, or financial services—is being impacted by technology, and by the global marketplace. If you are not aware, you will be blindsided.

Your Age: How Much Longer Do You Want to Work?

If you want to work only two more years, it may not be worth investing the time to learn a new area. (This is assuming you can get a job in your old area if it is retrenching.)

If you want to work another 10 years, learn new things—if only to keep up with what is happening in your present field.

The trouble with the future is that it usually arrives before we're ready for it.

Arnold H. Glasow

Some Areas Are Safer Bets

The rate of change is so fast that technologies you read about may never reach the mainstream or may be replaced with new developments. However, some areas are safer bets than others. *Hard skills* are more marketable than *soft skills.* For example, a person who wants to get a job as a general writer will have more difficulty than someone who can bring more to the party—such as some specialization or computer skills.

When there is no vision, the people perish.

Old Testament, Proverbs 29:18

Figure It Out

It's your job to figure out how your dream industry or field is being impacted by technology, global competition, and the market in general. Think where you fit into the future. Do research.

We are now on the ground floor of many industries, and at an exciting time for those who choose to take advantage of the revolutionary changes that are taking place.

So, once again, remember the definition of job hunting that The Five O'Clock Club developed:

> **Job hunting in a changing economy means continuously becoming aware of market conditions inside, as well as outside your present organization, and learning more about what you have to offer.**

A New Way of Thinking

Any assignment (or job) you get is a temporary one. You're doing work, but you don't have a permanent job. It's like an actor who lands a part. He or she does not really know how long it may last. Furthermore, actors tend to worry about whether or not a role will typecast them and potentially cause them to lose future roles. Or they may intentionally decide to be typecast, hoping it will increase their chances going forward. Actors understand that they will most likely have to land another role after this one, and they constantly think about how a certain role will position them going forward. And so must you. Your next job is only a temporary assignment.

Work today is not just doing; it is, more than ever, thinking. Today's corporation needs thinking, flexible, proactive workers. It wants creative problem solvers, workers smart and skilled enough to move with new technologies and with the ever-changing competitive environment. It needs workers accustomed to collaborating with co-workers, to participating in quality circles, to dealing with people high and low. Communication skills and people skills have become parts of the necessary repertoire of the modern worker.

Hedrick Smith, *Rethinking America*

The
Five
O'Clock
Club

Case Studies: Targeting the Future

While your basic emotional temperament may not change much during your lifetime, you can make significant day-to-day adjustments in the way you perceive events and respond to them. When you face an emotionally trying situation, guard against exaggerating or over-generalizing, and focus instead on your specific options for taking direct action. Avoid putting yourself down by doing something that will exercise your good traits. And seek the company of others, whether it's to gather more rational views on the situation or simply to change your mood.

Jack Maguire, *Care and Feeding of the Brain*

What about Your Field, Industry, or Geographic Area?

A job target is a clearly selected geographic area, an industry or organization size, and a function or position within that industry. An accountant, for example, may target a certain industry (such as telecommunications or hospitals), or may see himself in the accounting function and may not care which industry he is in but prefer instead to focus on *organization size.* This means he wants to target a small, medium, or large organization, regardless of industry.

Examine your targets to see how each is doing. Perhaps, for example, your industry is okay, but large organizations are not doing well, while smaller organizations are hiring. In this case, target smaller organizations.

What changes are taking place in your industry or function? If you think your industry or function will continue to retrench, find a *new horse to ride*: an industry or function that is on a growth curve, or one that will give you transferable skills.

The person who fears to try is thus enslaved.

Leonard E. Read

CASE STUDY *Ed*
The Benefit of Targeting

Ed and Steve were both administrative managers in the retail industry. Both had lost their jobs. Both had spent 20 years—their entire working lives—in retail. Both wanted to work in health care.

Steve actually had hands-on health-care experience. A few years earlier, his organization had lent him to a major hospital to serve as the interim administrative head for a full year. He loved that assignment, did very well at it, and swore he would get a job like that again someday.

But Steve decided to be *practical*: "All my contacts are in retail, and I need a job *now*. It's true I would like to move into a growth area, but I don't have time to learn a new industry. I have no choice but to focus on the retail industry."

Ed, on the other hand, targeted health care, and had retail as a separate target. Ed joined health-care associations that dealt with administration, read all the health-care administration trade magazines, and became knowledgeable about the industry. He met with lots of people, largely through the associations. He was even willing to take a temp job doing data entry in the administrative area of hospitals so he could see what was happening from the inside. His ego did not get in the way.

A job came up: exactly the same hospital job Steve had worked in for a full year. Both Ed and Steve heard about the job, and interviewed extensively.

Who got the job? Ed did—because he sounded more believable, more committed to the industry. Even though he had never held a job in that industry, Ed had *proven* by all his activities that he was sincerely interested in health care.

Steve sounded like all the other job hunters: He wanted this job just because there happened to be an opening.

He had nothing to talk about except the fact that he had held that job before and that they had liked him. Of course, he tried to maximize that experience. But what was noticed was that he had given no recent indication that he was committed to hospital work—he had not interviewed at other hospitals, etc.

This story is a vivid example of the benefits of thoroughly targeting an industry. It is also encouraging proof that people can enter new industries with no prior experience.

Progress might have been all right once,
But it has gone on too long.

Ogden Nash

"People in That Industry Won't Let Me In."

Job hunters always say it's hard to change from one industry to another. "Hiring managers don't believe I want to get into that field." I don't believe those job hunters either because they never read anything about the field, and don't know anyone in the field who would serve as a reality check for them. How do you prove to the hiring managers that you are truly interested? As we say in the chapter *How to Change Careers*:

- Read the industry's trade journals.
- Get to know people in that industry or field.
- Join its organizations; attend its meetings.
- Be persistent.
- Write proposals.
- Be persistent.
- Take relevant courses, part-time jobs, or do volunteer work related to the new industry or skill area.
- Be persistent.

If you want to get into an industry or field, learn about it.

It's Time to Take Control of Your Own Career

If you succeed in judging yourself rightly,
then you are indeed a man of true wisdom.

Antoine de Saint-Exupéry, *The Little Prince*

Get in the habit of reading the papers and noticing what news may affect the industry or field you are in. Learn about some of the industries of the future.

Even if all you want is a job right now, instead of a career, do the exercises in the next section. Be sure to include at least the Seven Stories Exercise, Interests, Values, and Forty-Year Vision. They won't take a long time to do, and they will shorten the length of your search.

Illness strikes men when they are
exposed to change.

Herodotus, Greek historian

CASE STUDY *Scott*

What Should I Be When I Grow Up?

Scott is 38, a lawyer with a varied background. He had worked for the DA's office and a stock exchange, and wrote for a magazine. With his diverse past, he didn't know what to do next.

I know only one way to figure out what a person should be, and it's to use the methodology in this book. So that's what I did with Scott—a shortened version of the exercises.

Seven Stories Exercise

First, we did the Seven Stories Exercise. I said: "Tell me something you've done that you really enjoyed doing, know you did well, and felt a sense of accomplishment about. It doesn't matter what other people thought, how old you were, whether or not you earned money doing it. You may want to start with: 'There was the time when I . . .'"

Scott said: "There was the time when I argued my first case before a jury."

I asked him to tell me the details and what he enjoyed about it.

"I liked being independent, I was calling the shots. I had to plan the whole thing myself . . ."

I asked for another story.

Scott said: "I wrote an exposé for a magazine."

I asked Scott to tell me more. He said he enjoyed the same things: being independent, calling the shots, etc. Seemingly, the only time Scott enjoyed a bureaucratic environment was when he broke away from it.

Scott thought that he had a scattered background, and that everything was different. To my mind, those two stories were alike, so I had enough to go on. (If the stories had been in conflict, I would have asked him for as many as seven stories.)

Values Exercise

"Scott, tell me the things that are important to you." He replied, "Money is important, and independence."

Interests Exercise

"Scott, what are your interests?" Languages were very important to him; he had command of a few. The international area was central to his interests.

Scott's exercise results will serve as a template. He can make sure that his next job will allow him to be independent, to earn the money he wants, to enjoy the international area, and so on.

Forty-Year Vision

Then I guided him through an abbreviated version of the Forty-Year Vision. I don't know how to help people unless I know where they are heading. If all I know is their past, their future will be more of the same. We spent only five minutes on this exercise.

I start with the present to get people grounded in the present. If I simply ask: "What do you want to be?" it doesn't work. They have nothing to base it on.

"Tell me what your life is like right now. What is your relationship with your family, however you define family? Where do you live? What is it physically like? What are your hobbies and interests? How is your health? What do you do for exercise? How would you describe the job you have right now? And tell me anything else you want to about your life today."

Next, I asked Scott to tell me about his life at age 43. Then I asked about his life at age 53. In part, he said:

"I am living in the suburbs. I have a wife and four kids. The oldest is sixteen; the youngest is nine. (It is helpful to put down how old your kids are at each stage so you feel yourself getting older.) I have a small consulting firm, with perhaps four employees who do research and support me in what I am doing. I do a lot of business in Europe. Whatever I am doing is 'at the center of the world'—I feel I'm on top of the important things that are happening."

From my point of view, there were no conflicts in the results of his exercises. They all showed him in an independent situation.

Scott seemed to me to be the stereotypical entrepreneur. I do think he should have his own business, but not right now. Having people work for him sounded right because he seemed disorganized. As he himself suggested, one person could keep him in line and clean up after him. His business might have to do with international business, and also with high-tech. He wants to be at the center of what's happening.

Scott needs to *focus* on something that is a growth area and also satisfies his other needs. There are lots of areas that could fulfill him. The danger is that he may spend 20 years never selecting something to focus on. If a person like Scott is always exploring, it may be best to just arbitrarily pick something, because there is no one correct answer. Other people who are in a rut may need to spend more time exploring.

Scott happens to have contacts in the telecommunications industry. If he can get into the telecommunications field, he should try to learn what he can, and develop a business plan while he is there.

Scott now has a vision. He can follow the vision, or not. If he continues to try out every field he comes across,

he will be in constant turmoil. He will simply go from job to job, wind up in his sixties with a lot of experiences but no career, and never reach his dream.

It's the same for you. Figure out the things you enjoy doing and also do well. Do your Forty-Year Vision. These exercises will serve as your anchor as well as your guide. You won't get as irritated in your next job, because you'll know what you're getting out of it. You will keep up your research and your knowledge of the field. You will gain the skills you need to go forward.

When I examined myself and my methods of thought,
I came to the conclusion that the gift of fantasy
has meant more to me than my talent for
absorbing positive knowledge.

Albert Einstein

Retraining Is for Everybody—Even Executives

When people talk about retraining in the United States, they are usually talking about lower-level workers who don't have computer skills. Retraining is necessary at all levels. Do research to learn the terminology of the industry you want to enter so you can be an insider, not an outsider.

By definition, new industries must hire people from outside the industry. If a job hunter studies the field, and develops a sincere interest in it, he or she has a good chance of being hired.

Careful research is a critical component, and will become a central part of every sophisticated person's job search.

If you just think off the top of your head about the areas you should be targeting, your ideas will probably be superficial—and outdated.

Change is happening at an increasingly faster rate. Industries disappear, and new ones spring up quickly. Instead of simply hunting for the next job, think about your long-range career.

You can pick the *right horse to ride* into your future rather than hanging on for dear life in a declining market. If you pick the right horse, you'll have a much easier ride.

Achieving Stability in a Changing World

How can you keep yourself stable in a constantly changing economy? If the world is being battered, and organizations are being battered, and many CEOs cannot keep their jobs, what are you going to do?

The benefit of doing the following exercises is that they give you confidence and a sense of stability in a changing world. You will learn to know yourself and become sure of exactly what you can take with you wherever you go.

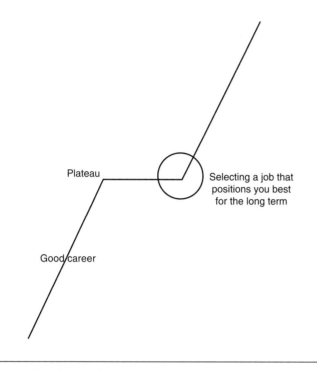

Plateau

Good career

Selecting a job that positions you best for the long term

One doesn't discover new lands without consenting to lose sight of the shore for a very long time.

André Gide

The Result of Assessment Is Job Targets

If you go through an assessment with a career coach or vocational testing center, and do not wind up with tentative job targets, the assessment has not helped you very much. You must go one more step, and decide what to *do* with this information.

The Result of Assessment Is Power

The more you know about yourself, the more power you have to envision a job that will suit you. The exercises give you power.

People find it hard to believe that I went through a period of about 30 years when I was painfully shy. In graduate school, I was afraid when they took roll because I obsessed about whether I should answer "here" or "present." When I had to give a presentation, the best I could do was read the key words from my index cards. (Today, my throat is actually hoarse from all the public speaking I do.) I will be forever grateful for the kindness of strangers who told me I did well when I knew I was awful.

The only thing that ultimately saved me was doing the Seven Stories Exercise. When I was little, I led groups of kids in the neighborhood, and I did it well. It gave me strength to know that I was inherently a group leader regardless of how I was behaving now. (I was in my thirties at the time.)

The Seven Stories Exercise grounds you, and the Forty-Year Vision guides you. When people said: "Would you like to lead groups?" I said to myself, "Well, I led groups when I was 10. Maybe I can do it again." The transition was painful, and took many years, but my Seven Stories Exercise kept me going. And my Forty-Year Vision let me know there was plenty of time in which to do it.

Enjoy yourself. If you can't enjoy yourself, enjoy somebody else.

Jack Schaefer

I was going to buy a copy of The Power of Positive Thinking, *and then I thought: What the hell good would that do?*

Ronnie Shakes

The
Five
O'Clock
Club

PART THREE
Deciding What You Want:
START BY UNDERSTANDING YOURSELF
(If you are already in a field you love and know why,
and know where you're going, go to Part Four.)

The Five O'Clock Club

Deciding What You Want: Selecting Your Job Targets

It may sound surprising when I say, on the basis of my own clinical experience as well as that of my psychological and psychiatric colleagues, "that the chief problem of people in the middle decade of the twentieth century is emptiness." By that I mean not only that many people do not know what they want; they often do not have any clear idea of what they feel.

Rollo May, *Man's Search for Himself*

Studies have shown that up to 85 percent of all American workers are unhappy in their jobs. They feel that they would be happier elsewhere, but they don't know where. After going through an evaluation process (assessment), many decide that their present situation is not so bad after all, and that no change is required. Some may find that a small change is all that is needed. On the other hand, some may want to make a major career change.

The exercises in this book will help you assess your work life so that you can better understand the situations in which you perform your best and are happiest. And, since we will *all* have to change jobs—and probably even careers—more often in the future, we should get to know ourselves better.

Assessment is helpful even if you do not want to change jobs. You will learn more about the way you operate and how to improve the situation where you are currently working.

In the Nazi death camps where Victor Frankl learned the principle of proactivity, he also learned the importance of purpose, of meaning in life. The essence of "logotherapy," the philosophy he later developed and taught, is that many so-called mental and emotional illnesses are really symptoms of an underlying sense of meaninglessness or emptiness. Logotherapy eliminates the emptiness by helping the individual to detect his unique meaning, his mission in life. Once you have that sense of mission, you have the essence of your own proactivity. You have the vision and the values which direct your life. You have the basic direction from which you set long- and short-term goals.

Stephen R. Covey,
The Seven Habits of Highly Effective People

Getting Started

The following exercises help you identify the aspects of your jobs that have been satisfying and dissatisfying. You will know which parts need to be changed and which parts need to stay the same.

You may do certain exercises and skip others. But don't skip the Seven Stories Exercise, and try to do the Forty-Year Vision. If you have had problems with bosses, you need to discover what those problems were and analyze them. Or perhaps examining your values may be an issue at this time. Your insights about yourself from the Seven Stories Exercise will be the primary source for your accomplishment statements, help you interview better, and serve as a template for selecting the right job.

After you do the exercises, brainstorm a number of possible job targets. Then research each target to find out what the job possibilities are for someone like you.

This workbook will guide you through the entire process.

To have a great purpose to work for, a purpose larger than ourselves, is one of the secrets of making life significant; for then the meaning and worth of the individual overflow his personal borders, and survive his death.

Will Durant

Consider Your History

If you have enjoyed certain jobs, attempt to understand exactly what about them you enjoyed. This will increase your chances of replicating the enjoyable aspects.

For example, an accounting manager will probably not be happy in just any accounting-management job. If what he really enjoyed was helping the business manager make the business profitable, and if this thread of helping reappears in his enjoyable experiences (Seven Stories Exercise), then he would be unhappy in a job where he was *not* helping.

If, however, his enjoyment repeatedly came from resolving messy situations, then he needs a job that has messes to be resolved and the promise of more messes to come.

Furthermore, if he wants to do again those things he enjoyed, he can state them in the summary on his résumé. For instance:

Accounting Manager
Serve as right hand to Business Manager, consistently improving organization's profitability.

or

Accounting Manager
A troubleshooter and turnaround manager.

The Results of Assessment: Job Targets— *Then* a Résumé

A job target contains three elements:

- industry or organization size (small, medium, or large organization);
- position or function; and
- geographic location.

If a change is required, a change in any one of these may be enough.

Geographic Location

Let's take Joseph, for example. Joseph had been in trusts and estates for 25 years, and had taken early retirement. He didn't know what he wanted to do next, but he knew that it had to be *completely different.*

Joseph did all of the exercises in this section. I also gave him a personality test, and did *confidential phone calls* on his behalf—a process by which I called people who knew him well and asked them about him. I assured them that I would compile the results and not tell him who said what.

Based on all of this information, we developed a number of targets for him to investigate. We also developed a résumé that positioned him for these new targets.

Joseph conducted a campaign to get interviews in each of his three target areas. However, once he clearly looked at these new fields, his old field began to look more appealing. (This happened to me years ago when I desperately wanted museum work—until I actually looked into it and found it wasn't for me.)

Joseph decided to stay in his old field—but on the West Coast rather than the East—because he is bothered by the climate in the East and because many of his old friends had moved West. This change in location would get him out of the old rut and give him a new lease on life. But it was a relatively minor change compared with what he originally had in mind.

"Johnson, if you're going to have negative thoughts, I suggest you get rid of that thought balloon!"

Industry or Organization Size

Many unhappy people may be in essentially the right position but in the wrong industry. A minor adjustment may be all that is needed.

A person could be a lawyer, but it makes a great deal of difference whether that person is a lawyer in a corporation, in a stuffy law firm, or in a not-for-profit organization. A change in industry may end the dissatisfaction.

By the same token, moving from a large organization to a small one—or vice versa—could increase your satisfaction.

Position or Function

On the other hand, a new field may be what is called for. My own career is a case in point. I had a successful career in computers, advertising, and the financial end of business, with a respectable amount of prestige and money. However, when I did the Seven Stories Exercise (to identify those things I enjoyed doing and also did well), I discovered that only one of my *stories* related to my work life. The message was clear: My true enjoyment was coming from those things I was doing on the outside, such as running The Five O'Clock Club and other entrepreneurial ventures. I had a choice to make:

- I could stay in the lucrative field I was in, and continue to do on the side those things that gave me the most satisfaction; or
- I could move my career in the direction of those things I found most satisfying.

Being risk averse, I was reluctant to give up the 20-plus years I had invested in a business career for a profession that might prove to be financially or otherwise unsatisfying. I decided to hedge my bets. I took a job as the chief financial officer of a major outplacement firm, and *also* headed up one of their career coaching offices. That way, I could slide into the new career, or go back into the old one if I was unhappy.

Many major career changes are made this way. A person *somehow* gets some experience in the new field while holding on to the old one. In general, it is relatively easy to get experience in the new field if you really want it.

. . . and then I decided that to turn your life around you had to start from the inside.

Ethan Canin, *Emperor of the Air*

Looking Ahead—A Career Instead of a Job

Assessment will help you decide what you want to do in your next job as well as in the long run. You will become clearer about the kind of boss you work best with and about all the other things that are important to you in a job.

Through your Forty-Year Vision, you will have the opportunity to look ahead to see whether there is some hidden dream that may dramatically influence what you will want to do in both the short and long run. I did my own Forty-Year Vision about 15 years ago, and the idea I had about my future still drives me today, even though that vision was actually rather vague at the time. Knowing where you would like to wind up in 10, 20, 30, or 40 years can broaden your ideas about the kinds of jobs you would be interested in today.

The Forty-Year Vision is a powerful exercise. It will help you think long term and put things into perspective.

The Seven Stories Exercise is equally powerful. Without it, many job hunters develop stilted descriptions of what they have accomplished. But the exercise frees you up to brag a little, and express things very differently. The results will add life to your résumé and your interviews, and also dramatically increase your self-confidence.

No Easy Way

It would be nice if you could simply take a test that would tell you what you should be. Unfortunately, there is no such sure-fire test. But fortunately, in today's rapidly changing world, we are allowed to be many things: we can be a doctor, a lawyer, *and* an Indian chief. We have an abundance of choices.

A man is what he thinks about all day long.

Ralph Waldo Emerson

A Clear Direction

People are happy when they are working toward their goals. When they get diverted from their goals, they are unhappy. Businesses are the same. When they get diverted from their goals (for instance, because of major litigation or a threatened hostile takeover), they too are unhappy. Life has a way of sneaking up and distracting both individuals and businesses. Many people are unhappy in their jobs because they don't know where they are going.

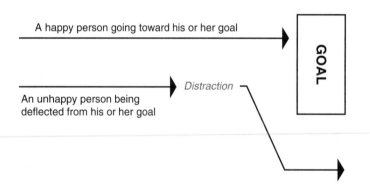

People without goals are more irked by petty problems on their jobs. Those with goals are less bothered because they have bigger plans. To control your life, you have to know where you are going, and be ready for your next move—in case the ax falls on you.

Even after you take that next job, continue to manage your career. Organizations rarely build career paths for their employees any more. Make your own way.

I've never been poor, only broke.
Being poor is a frame of mind.
Being broke is only a temporary situation.

Mike Todd

The Seven Stories Exercise® Worksheet

This exercise is an opportunity to examine the most satisfying experiences of your life and to discover those skills you will want to use as you go forward. You will be looking at the times when you feel you did something particularly well that you also enjoyed doing. It doesn't matter what other people thought, whether or not you were paid, or when in your life the experiences took place. **All that matters is that you felt happy about doing whatever it was, thought you did it well, and experienced a sense of accomplishment.** You can even go back to childhood. When I did my own Seven Stories Exercise, I remembered the time when I was 10 years old and led a group of kids in the neighborhood, enjoyed it, and did it well.

This exercise usually takes a few days to complete. Many people review different life phases in order to capture the full scope of these experiences. Most carry around a piece of paper to jot down ideas as they think of them.

Section I

Briefly outline below *all* the work/personal/life experiences that meet the above definition. Come up with at least 20. We ask for 20 stories so you won't be too selective. Just write down anything that occurs to you, no matter how trivial it may seem. Try to **think of concrete examples, situations, and tasks, not generalized skills or abilities**. It may be helpful if you say to yourself, **"There was the time when I . . ."**

RIGHT	WRONG
• Got extensive media coverage for new product launch.	• Writing press releases.
• Delivered speech to get German business.	• Delivering speeches.
• Coordinated blood drive for division.	• Coordinating.
• Came in third in Nassau Bike Race.	• Cycling.
• Made basket in second grade.	• Working on projects alone.

1. _____
2. _____
3. _____
4. _____
5. _____
6. _____
7. _____
8. _____
9. _____
10. _____
11. _____
12. _____
13. _____
14. _____
15. _____
16. _____
17. _____
18. _____
19. _____
20. _____

Section II

<u>Choose the seven experiences from the above</u> that you enjoyed the most and felt the most sense of accomplishment about. (Be sure to include non-job-related experiences also.) Then **<u>rank them.</u>** Then, for each accomplishment, describe what *you* did. Be specific, listing each step in detail. Notice the role you played and your relationship with others, the subject matter, the skills you used, and so on. Use a separate sheet of paper for each.

If your highest-ranking accomplishments also happen to be work related, you may want them to appear prominently on your résumé. After all, those were things that you enjoyed and did well. And those are probably experiences you will want to repeat again in your new job.

Here's how you might begin:

Experience #1: Planned product launch that resulted in 450 letters of intent from 1,500 participants.

a. Worked with president and product managers to discuss product potential and details.

b. Developed promotional plan.

c. Conducted five-week direct-mail campaign prior to conference to create aura of excitement about product.

d. Trained all product demonstrators to make sure they each presented product in same way.

e. Had great product booth built; rented best suite to entertain prospects; conducted campaign at conference by having teasers put under everyone's door every day of conference. Most people wanted to come to our booth.

—and so on—

Analyzing Your Seven Stories

Now it is time to analyze your stories. You are trying to look for the threads that run through them so that you will know the things you do well that also give you satisfaction. Some of the questions below sound similar. That's okay. They are a catalyst to make you think more deeply about the experience. The questions don't have any hidden psychological significance.

If your accomplishments happen to be mostly work related, this exercise will form the basis for your *positioning* or summary statement in your résumé, and also for your Two-Minute Pitch.

If these accomplishments are mostly not work related, they will still give you some idea of how you may want to slant your résumé, and they may give you an idea of how you will want your career to go in the long run.

For now, simply go through each story without trying to force it to come out any particular way. Just think hard about yourself. And be as honest as you can. When you have completed this analysis, the words in the next exercise may help you think of additional things. **Do this page first.**

Story #1. _____

What was the *main accomplishment* for you?_____
_____

What about it did you *enjoy most?*_____
_____

What did you *do best?*_____
_____

What was your *key motivator?*_____
_____

What *led up to your getting involved?* (e.g., assigned to do it, thought it up myself, etc.) _____
_____

What was your *relationship with others?* (e.g., leader, worked alone, inspired others, team member, etc.)
_____

Describe the *environment* in which you performed. _____
_____

What was the *subject matter?* (e.g., music, mechanics, trees, budgets, etc.) _____
_____

Story #2. _____
Main accomplishment? _____
Enjoyed most? _____
Did best? _____
Key motivator? _____
What led up to it? _____
Your role? _____
Environment? _____
Subject matter? _____

Story #3. _____
Main accomplishment? _____
Enjoyed most? _____
Did best? _____
Key motivator? _____
What led up to it? _____
Your role? _____
Environment? _____
Subject matter? _____

Story #4. _____
Main accomplishment? _____
Enjoyed most? _____
Did best? _____
Key motivator? _____
What led up to it? _____
Your role? _____
Environment? _____
Subject matter? _____

Story #5. _____
Main accomplishment? _____
Enjoyed most? _____
Did best? _____
Key motivator? _____
What led up to it? _____
Your role? _____
Environment? _____
Subject matter? _____

Story #6. _____
Main accomplishment? _____
Enjoyed most? _____
Did best? _____
Key motivator? _____
What led up to it? _____
Your role? _____
Environment? _____
Subject matter? _____

Story #7. _____
Main accomplishment? _____
Enjoyed most? _____
Did best? _____
Key motivator? _____
What led up to it? _____
Your role? _____
Environment? _____
Subject matter? _____

We are here to be excited from youth to old age, to have an insatiable curiosity about the world. . . . We are also here to help others by practicing a friendly attitude. And every person is born for a purpose. Everyone has a God-given potential, in essence, built into them. And if we are to live life to its fullest, we must realize that potential.

Norman Vincent Peale

Your Current Work-Related Values

What is important to you? Your values change as you grow and change, so they need to be reassessed continually. At various stages in your career, you may value money, or leisure time, or independence on the job, or working for something you believe in. See what is important to you *now*. This will help you not be upset if, for instance, a job provides you with the freedom you wanted, but not the kind of money your friends are making.

Sometimes we are not aware of our own values. It may be that, at this stage of your life, time with your family is most important to you. For some people, money or power is most important, but they may be reluctant to admit it—even to themselves.

Values are the driving force behind what we do. It is important to truthfully understand what we value in order to increase our chances of getting what we want.

Look at the list of values below. Think of each in terms of your overall career objectives. Rate the degree of importance you would assign to each for yourself, using this scale:

1—Not at all important in my choice of job   3—Reasonably important
2—Not very but somewhat important   4—Very important

Add other values that don't appear on the list or substitute wording you are more comfortable with.

____ chance to advance
____ work on frontiers of knowledge
____ have authority (responsibility)
____ help society
____ help others
____ meet challenges
____ work for something I believe in
____ public contact
____ enjoyable colleagues
____ competition
____ ease (freedom from worry)
____ influence people
____ enjoyable work tasks
____ work alone
____ be an expert
____ personal growth and development
____ independence

____ artistic or other creativity
____ learning
____ location of workplace
____ tranquility
____ money earned
____ change and variety
____ have time for personal life
____ fast pace
____ power
____ adventure/risk taking
____ prestige
____ moral fulfillment
____ recognition from superiors, society, peers
____ security (stability)
____ physical work environment
____ chance to make impact
____ clear expectations and procedures

Of those you marked "4," circle the five **most** important to you today:

• If forced to compromise on any of these, which one would you give up? _____

• Which one would you be most reluctant to give up? _____

Describe in 10 or 20 words what you want most in your life and/or career.

_____

Your health is bound to be affected if, day after day, you say the opposite of what you feel, if you grovel before what you dislike and rejoice at what brings you nothing but misfortune.

Boris Pasternak, *Dr. Zhivago*

Other Exercises: Interests, Satisfiers, and Bosses

CASE STUDY *Laura*

Using Her Special Interests

For many people, interests should stay as interests—things they do on the side. For others, their interests may be a clue to the kinds of jobs they should do next or in the long run. Laura had food as her special interest. She had spent her life as a marketing manager in cosmetics, but she assured me that food was *very* important to her.

We redid her résumé to downplay the cosmetics background. Next, Laura visited a well-known specialty food store. She spoke to the store manager, a junior person, asked about the way the company was organized, and found that there were three partners, one of whom was the president. Laura said to the store manager, "Please give my résumé to the president, and I will call him in a few days." We prepared for her meeting with the president, in which she would find out the company's long-term plans, and so on. At the meeting, he said he wanted to increase revenues from $4 million to $40 million. Laura and I met again to decide how she could help the business grow through her marketing efforts, and to decide what kind of compensation she would want, including equity in the company. She met with the president again, and got the job!

It was the Interests exercise that prompted her to get into that field. Remember, all you need to do is make a list of your interests. Laura simply wrote *food*. Other people list 20 things. Here is the exercise:

Interests Exercise

List all the things you really like to do. List anything that makes you feel good and gives you satisfaction. List those areas where you have developed a relatively in-depth knowledge or expertise. For ideas, think back over your day, your week, the seasons of the year, places, people, work, courses, roles, leisure time, family, etc. These areas need not be work related. Think of how you spend your discretionary time.

If you cannot think of what your interests may be, think about the books you read, the magazines you subscribe to, the section of the newspaper you turn to first. Think about the knowledge you've built up simply because you're interested in a particular subject. Think about the volunteer work you do—what are the recurring assignments you tend to get and enjoy? Think about your hobbies—are there one or two you have become so involved in that you have built up a lot of expertise/information in those areas? What are the things you find yourself doing—and enjoying—all the time, things you don't *have* to do?

Your interests may be a clue to what you would like in a job. Rob was a partner in a law firm, but loved everything about wine. He left the law firm to become general counsel in a wine company. Most people's interests should stay as interests, but you never know until you think about it.

Satisfiers and Dissatisfiers Exercise

Simply list every job you have ever had. List what was satisfying and dissatisfying about each job. Some people are surprised to find that they were sometimes most satisfied by the vacation, pay, title, and other perks, but were not satisfied with the job itself.

Bosses Exercise

Simply examine those bosses you have had a good relationship with and those you have not, and determine what you need in your future relationship with bosses. If you have had a lot of problems with bosses, discuss this with your counselor.

My illness helped me to see that what was missing in a society is what was missing in me: a little heart, a lot of brotherhood.
The 80s were about acquiring wealth, power, prestige. I acquired more . . . than most. But you can acquire all you want and still feel empty. . . . I don't know who will lead us through the 90s, but they must be made to speak to this spiritual vacuum at the heart of American society, this tumor of the soul.

Lee Atwater, formerly of the Republican National Committee, shortly before he died,
Life magazine, February 1991

Your Special Interests

For many people, interests should stay as interests—things they do on the side. For others, their interests may be a clue to the kinds of jobs they should do next or in the long run. Only you can decide whether your interests should become part of your work life.

List all the things you really like to do—anything that makes you feel good and gives you satisfaction. List those areas in which you have developed a relatively in-depth knowledge or expertise. For ideas, think of your day, your week, the seasons of the year, places, people, work, courses, roles, leisure time, friends, family, etc. Think of how you spend your discretionary time.

- Think about the books you read, the magazines you subscribe to, the section of the newspaper you turn to first.
- Think about knowledge you've built up simply because you're interested in it.
- Think about the volunteer work you do—what are the recurring assignments you tend to get and enjoy?
- Think about your hobbies—are there one or two you have become so involved in that you have built up a lot of expertise/information in those areas?
- What are the things you find yourself doing all the time and enjoying, even though you don't have to do them?

Satisfiers and Dissatisfiers in Past Jobs

*Wherever I went, I couldn't help noticing, the place fell apart. Not that I was ever a big enough wheel
in the machine to precipitate its destruction on my own. But that they let me—and other drifters
like me—in the door at all was an early warning signal. Alarm bells should have rung.*

Michael Lewis, *Liar's Poker*

For each job you have held in the past, describe as fully as possible the factors that made the job especially exciting or rewarding (satisfiers) and those that made the job especially boring or frustrating (dissatisfiers). **Be as specific as possible.** (See the example below, which shows that sometimes the satisfiers can be the perks, while the dissatisfiers can be the job itself.)

JOB	SATISFIERS	DISSATISFIERS
VP of Mfg., ABC Co.	1. Status—large office, staff of 23, exec. dining room 2. Fringes—four weeks' vacation, travel allowance, time for outside activities	1. Manager—cold and aloof, too little structure and feedback, no organizational credibility 2. Limited promotional opportunities—none laterally, only straight line
JOB	**SATISFIERS**	**DISSATISFIERS**

Your Relationship with Bosses

1. Make a list of all the *bosses* you have ever had in work situations. Use a very broad definition. They don't have to have been *bosses* in the strictest sense of the word. Include bosses from part-time jobs, summer jobs, and even professors with whom you worked closely in your student days.

_____   _____
_____   _____
_____   _____
_____   _____

2. Divide the names from above into three lists: those people with whom you had no problems, those with whom you had some problems, and those with whom you had severe problems.

NO PROBLEMS	SOME PROBLEMS	SEVERE PROBLEMS

3. Look for factors that might help explain why you had some problems or severe problems with some bosses and not with others (or why you have never had problems). For example, consider:
   - the type of people involved: age, sex, personality, etc.
   - the structure of your relationship with the people: how much and what type of power they had over you.
   - the broader contexts: the kind of work involved, the type of organizations involved, etc.

Think about it. Do you see any patterns . . .

. . . regarding the type of people?

_____
_____
_____

. . . regarding the structure of the relationship?

_____
_____
_____

. . . regarding the contexts?

_____
_____
_____

This exercise is based on lectures given by John P. Kotter in his classes in power dynamics at the Harvard Business School.

Natural talent, intelligence, a wonderful education—none of these guarantees success. Something else is needed: the sensitivity to understand what other people want and the willingness to give it to them. Worldly success depends on pleasing others. No one is going to win fame, recognition, or advancement just because he or she thinks it's deserved. Someone else has to think so too.

John Luther

The
Five
O'Clock
Club

Your Fifteen-Year Vision® and Your Forty-Year Vision®

In my practice as a psychiatrist, I have found that helping people to develop personal goals has proved to be the most effective way to help them cope with problems.

Ari Kiev, M.D., *A Strategy for Daily Living*

If you could imagine your ideal life five years from now, what would it be like? How would it be different from the way it is now? If you made new friends during the next five years, what would they be like? Where would you be living? What would your hobbies and interests be? How about 10 years from now? Twenty? Thirty? Forty? Think about it!

Some people feel locked in by their present circumstances. Many say it is too late for them. But a lot can happen in five, 10, 20, 30, or 40 years. Reverend King had a dream. His dream helped all of us, but his dream helped him too. He was living according to a vision (which he thought was God's plan for him). *It gave him a purpose in life.* Most successful people have a vision.

A lot can happen to you over the next few decades—and most of what happens is up to you. If you see the rest of your life as boring, I'm sure you will be right. Some people pick the "sensible" route or the one that fits in with how others see them, rather than the one that is best for them.

On the other hand, you can come up with a few scenarios of how your life could unfold. In that case, you will have to do a lot of thinking and a lot of research to figure out which path makes most sense for you and will make you happiest.

When a person finds a vision that is right, the most common reaction is fear. It is often safer to *wish* a better life than to actually go after it.

I know what that's like. It took me two years of thinking and research to figure out the right path for myself—one that included my motivated abilities (Seven Stories Exercise) as well as the sketchy vision I had for myself. Then it took *10 more years* to finally take the plunge and commit to that path—running The Five O'Clock Club. I was 40 years old when I finally took a baby step in the right direction, and I was terrified.

You may be lucky and find it easy to write out your vision of your future. Or you may be more like me: It may take a while and a lot of hard work. You can speed up the process by reviewing your assessment results with a Five O'Clock Club career counselor. He or she will guide you along. Remember, when I was struggling, the country didn't *have* Five O'Clock Club counselors or even these exercises to guide us.

Test your vision and see if that path seems right for you. Plunge in by researching it and meeting with people in the field. If it is what you want, chances are you will find some way to make it happen. If it is not exactly right, you can modify it later—after you have gathered more information and perhaps gotten more experience.

Start with the Present

Write down, in the present tense, the way your life is right now, and the way you see yourself at each of the time frames listed. **This exercise should take no more than one hour**. Allow your unconscious to tell you what you will be doing in the future. Just quickly comment on each of the questions listed on the following page, and then move on to the next. If you kill yourself off too early (say, at age 60), push it 10 more years to see what would have happened if you had lived. Then push it another 10, just for fun.

When you have finished the exercise, ask yourself how you feel about your entire life as you laid it out in your vision. Some people feel depressed when they see on paper how their lives are going, and they cannot think of a way out. But they feel better when a good friend or a Five O'Clock Club counselor helps them think of a better future to work toward. If you don't like your vision, you are allowed to change it—it's your life. Do what you want with it. Pick the kind of life you want.

Start the exercise with the way things are now so you will be realistic about your future. Now, relax and have a good time going through the years. Don't think too hard. Let's see where you wind up. You have plenty of time to get things done.

> The 15-year mark proves to be the most important for most people. It's far enough away from the present to allow you to dream.

There are more things in heaven and earth, Horatio, than are dreamt of in your philosophy.

William Shakespeare, *Hamlet*

Your Fifteen-Year Vision® and Your Forty-Year Vision® Worksheet

1. The year is **xxxx** (current year).
   You are _____ years old right now.

- Tell me what your life is like right now. (Say anything you want about your life as it is now.)
- Who are your friends? What do they do for a living?
- What is your relationship with your family, however you define "family"?
- Are you married? Single? Children? (List ages.)
- Where are you living? What does it look like?
- What are your hobbies and interests?
- What do you do for exercise?
- How is your health?
- How do you take care of your spiritual needs?
- What kind of work are you doing?
- What else would you like to note about your life right now?

Year: _____ Your Age _____

Don't worry if you don't like everything about your life right now. Most people do this exercise because they want to improve themselves. They want to *change* something. What do *you* want to change? **Please continue.**

2. The year is **xxxx** (current year + **5**).
   You are _____ years old.
   (Add 5 to present age.)
   Things are going well for you.

- What is your life like now at this age?
  (Say anything you want about your life as it is now.)
- Who are your friends? What do they do for a living?
- What is your relationship with your "family"?
- Married? Single? Children? (List their ages now.)
- Where are you living? What does it look like?
- What are your hobbies and interests?
- What do you do for exercise?
- How is your health?
- How do you take care of your spiritual needs?
- What kind of work are you doing?
- What else would you like to note about your life right now?

Year: _____ Your Age _____

3. The year is **xxxx** (current year + **15**).
   You are _____ years old.
   (Current age plus 15.)

- What is your life like now at this age? (Say anything you want about your life as it is now.)
- Who are your friends? What do they do for a living?
- What is your relationship with your "family"?
- Married? Single? Children? (List their ages now.)
- Where are you living? What does it look like?
- What are your hobbies and interests?
- What do you do for exercise?
- How is your health?
- How do you take care of your spiritual needs?
- What kind of work are you doing?
- What else would you like to note about your life right now?

Year: _____   Your Age _____

The 15-year mark is an especially important one. This age is far enough away from the present that people often loosen up a bit. It's so far away that it's not threatening. Imagine _your_ ideal life. What is it like? Why were you put here on this earth? What were you meant to do here? What kind of life were you meant to live? Give it a try and see what you come up with. If you can't think of anything now, try it again in a week or so. On the other hand, if you got to the 15-year mark, why not keep going?

4. The year is **xxxx** (current year + **25**).
   You are _____ years old!
   (Current age plus 25.)

Year: _____   Your Age _____
Using a blank piece of paper, answer all of the questions for this stage of your life.

5. The year is **xxxx** (current year + **35**).
   You are _____ years old!
   (Current age plus 35.)

Repeat.

6. The year is **xxxx** (current year + **45**).
   You are _____ years old!
   (Current age plus 45.)

Repeat.

7. The year is **xxxx** (current year + **55**).
   You are _____ years old!
   (Current age plus 55.)

Keep going. How do you feel about your life? You are allowed to change the parts you don't like.

(Keep going—don't die until you are past 80!)

You have plenty of time to get done everything you want to do. Imagine wonderful things for yourself. You have plenty of time. Get rid of any "negative programming." For example, if you imagine yourself having poor health because your parents suffered from poor health, see what you can do about that. If you imagine yourself dying early because that runs in your family, see what would have happened had you lived longer. It's your life—your only one. As they say, "This is the real thing. It's not a dress rehearsal."

The
Five
O'Clock
Club

The Ideal Scene

*Every great personal victory was preceded by
a personal goal or dream.*

Dennis R. Webb

This is another exercise to help you imagine your future. Relax for a while. Arrange a time when you will not be distracted. Set aside about an hour. Sit by yourself, have a cup of tea, take out a pad of paper, and imagine yourself 5, 10, 15, or 20 years from now—at a phase in your life when all is going well. Just pick one of these time frames.

Imagine in very general terms the kind of life you were meant to have. Start writing—it's important to write it down, rather than just thinking about it.

What is your ideal life like? Describe a typical day. What do you do when you get up in the morning? Where are you living? Who are your friends?

If you are working, what is it like there? What kind of people do you work with? How do they dress? What kind of work are they doing? What is the atmosphere (relaxed? frantic?)? What is your role in all of this? Describe it in greater and greater detail.

In addition to describing your work situation, think about the other parts of your life. Remember: we each have 24 hours a day. How do you want to spend your 24 hours? Where are you living? What do you do for exercise? How is your health? What is your social life like? Your family life? What are your hobbies and interests? What do you do for spiritual nourishment? What are you contributing to the world? Describe all of these in as much detail as possible. But don't worry if you are not able to identify seemingly important things, such as the city in which you are living, and the field in which you are working.

Keep on writing—include as many details as you can—and develop a good feel for that life. Work on your Ideal Scene for a while, take a break, and then go back and write some more. Change the parts you don't like, and include all the things you really enjoy doing or see yourself doing at this imaginary time in the future.

For whatever we do, even whatever we do not do prevents us from doing the opposite. Acts demolish their alternatives, that is the paradox. So that life is a matter of choices, each one final and of little consequence, like dropping stones into the sea. We had children, he thought; we can never be childless. We were moderate, we will never know what it is to spill out our lives . . .

James Salter, *Light Years*

CASE STUDY *Max*
Identifying His Future Career

Max, age 40, is a lawyer. A temporary placement firm sends him on assignments to various organizations. He imagined working in a suburban office of six casually dressed people who were on the phone all day talking excitedly to people all over the world. He had a partner in this business. His own role was one of making contacts with prospective customers. He also saw himself writing about the topic they were engaged in, and becoming relatively well-known within their small segment of the industry.

Max's Ideal Scene may seem general, but it contains a lot of information. It appears that he would like to be in his own small but hectic business, operating on an international level. It would be a niche business where he could develop an expertise and become known to his small marketplace.

The international element was strong in this exercise. It was also evident in his Seven Stories Exercise and his Forty-Year Vision. It was clear that an international focus had to be central in his future.

You Can Develop Multiple Scenarios for Your Future

If you simply do the exercise up to this point, you will have done more than most people. You will have developed one scenario for your future. Some people develop multiple scenarios and think about the various possible futures they could have. Then they decide which they would like best, and which they think is doable.

It all starts with describing an Ideal Scene, but it takes a lot more than that. Writing down the scene makes it more serious, and is the start of a more concrete vision. The written vision and the plan are a lot of work, so you can see why most people do not develop visions—and therefore may tend to drift. But those who write down their visions usually find that they have a lot of fun doing it, and those who keep going realize that their future is, in large part, up to them.

Some people become less self-conscious and braver when they think not of what *they* would like to do, but what they think God has in mind for them. They try to discern God's plan for them, and it is this that motivates and inspires them. Whatever technique or inspiration you use to develop your vision, you will be better off for having done it.

Difficulty need not foreshadow despair or defeat. Rather achievement can be all the more satisfying because of obstacles surmounted.

William Hastie, *Grace under Pressure*

The Next Step: Define It Better and Research It

Some people are more ambitious, and want to go on to the next step: They want to flesh out their vision and then test it against reality. In Max's case, he had to figure out what kind of international business he could go into that would rely on his skills and support his values. He came up with a few ideas that excited him. Now he needs to investigate the potential for the various ideas, come up with a plan, develop new skills in the areas where he may be lacking, and take other steps toward fulfilling that vision.

You too will need to flesh out your bare-bones idea and then check it against reality. But be aware that other people will almost always tell you that it's not doable. Conduct enough research so that you can decide for yourself.

Then, if you are serious about achieving the kind of life that you have envisioned, think of what you need to do to succeed. Take a few little steps immediately to help you advance toward your goal.

. . . [I]n my foolishness and crude want of learning, everything I didn't know seemed like a promise.

Ethan Canin, *Emperor of the Air*

Encountering Roadblocks

Remember that this is not a sprint; it is a long-distance run. Do not become discouraged the first time you venture out. You will come up against lots of roadblocks along the way. That's life. Say to yourself, "Isn't this interesting? Another roadblock. I'll take a short breather (and perhaps even allow myself to feel a tingle of discouragement for a little while) and then I'll think of how I can get around this barrier."

Ask yourself what you have learned from the experience, because these experiences are here to teach us something. "What is the lesson for me in this setback?" And then get moving again.

What we do is nothing but a drop in the ocean; but if we didn't do it, the ocean would be one drop less.

Mother Teresa

My Forty-Year Vision

My own Ideal Scene evolved from the Forty-Year Vision I did 20 years ago. I imagined myself at age 80 in a beautiful living space with a housekeeper. I had a strong visual image of someone from the community coming to the door to ask my advice. What this *vision* meant to me was that I had lived my life in such a way that I had

---

**From *The Art of the Long View*
by Peter Schwartz**

In order to make effective decisions, you must articulate them to begin with. Consider, for example, the choice of a career in biotechnology. A scenario-planner would tackle the decision differently. It depends, he or she might argue, on another set of questions: What is the future of the biotechnology industry? (That in turn depends on:) What is the path of development in the biotech industry? (Moreover:) What skills will have enduring value? (And:) Where will be a good place to begin? The hardest questions will be the most important. What is it that interests you about biotechnology in the first place? What sorts of things about yourself might lead you to make a decision with poor results? What could lead you to change your mind?

Scenarios are not predictions. It is simply not possible to predict the future with certainty.

For individuals and small businesses, scenarios are a way to help develop their own gut feeling and assure that they have been comprehensive, both realistic and imaginative, in covering all important bases.

If you look at yourself on the level of historical time, as a tiny but influential part of a century-long process, then at least you can begin to know your own address. You can begin to sense the greater pattern, and feel where you are within it, and your acts take on meaning.

Michael Ventura, quoted by P. Schwartz

had a great impact on the community—people were asking my advice even when I was old. However, I wasn't poverty stricken because of my devotion to the community.

In my Forty-Year Vision I hadn't yet thought of The Five O'Clock Club or even considered a life in career counseling. But the image that came to me, and which I later developed, served as a template for my ideas and my research. My Seven Stories Exercise told me I had better be working with groups, and perhaps writing and lecturing. My Forty-Year Vision eliminated other interests of mine that would not have helped the community as much as career counseling.

It took many years to develop the concept and the focus of The Five O'Clock Club. For years, I continually used the Seven Stories Exercise and the Forty-Year Vision as my template. If an idea fit in with my vision and abilities, I consid-ered it. If an idea didn't fit, I rejected it. I spent many long hours doing library and other research to select the field I wanted to be in. All of this finally evolved into the concept of The Five O'Clock Club.

As you can see, the Forty-Year Vision is simply a vision of your future. By studying it, along with the Ideal Scene, you can get at unconscious desires you may have. Making your desires conscious increases your chances of being able to do something about them.

First, write out your Ideal Scene. Then in the next section, follow Howard step by step as he uncovers his dream.

He was, after all, a good father—that is to say, an ineffective man. Real goodness was different, it was irresistible, murderous, it had victims like any other aggression; in short, it conquered.

James Salter, *Light Years*

The Ideal Scene Worksheet

Imagine yourself 5, 10, 15, or 20 years from now—at a phase in your life when all is going well. Just pick one of these time frames. Imagine in very general terms the kind of life you were meant to have. Start writing—it's important to write it down, rather than just think about it.

What is your ideal life like? Describe a typical day. _____
_____
_____
_____
_____
_____

What do you do when you get up in the morning? Where are you living? _____
_____
_____
_____

Who are your friends? _____
_____
_____
_____

If you are working, what is it like there? _____
_____
_____

What kind of people do you work with? How do they dress? _____
_____

What kind of work are they doing? _____
_____

What is the atmosphere (relaxed or frantic)? _____
_____

What is your role in all of this? _____
_____

Use another sheet of paper to describe it in greater and greater detail.

In addition to describing your work situation, think about the other parts of your life. How do you want to spend your 24 hours?

Where are you living? _____
_____

What do you do for exercise? _____

_____

How is your health? _____

_____

What is your social life like? _____

_____

Your family life? _____

_____

What are your hobbies and interests? _____

_____

What do you do for spiritual nourishment? _____

_____

What are you contributing to the world? _____

_____

Describe all of these in as much detail as possible. But don't worry if you are not able to identify seemingly important things, such as the city in which you are living, and the field in which you are working.

Keep on writing—include as many details as you can—and develop a good feel for that life. Work on your Ideal Scene for a while, take a break, and then go back and write some more. Change the parts you don't like, and include all the things you really enjoy doing or see yourself doing at this imaginary time in the future. _____

_____

_____

_____

_____

_____

_____

Describing Your Ideal Job Worksheet

Thinking back over what you just visualized, answer the following questions as specifically as possible in order to describe your ideal work outcomes. Your answers will help you determine how you will know when you have achieved your goals.

What has happened in your career? _____

_____

What are the signs that you are successful? _____

_____

Looking around you, what do you see? _____

_____

What are you saying? _____

_____

How do you feel? _____

_____

How do you talk about yourself? _____

_____

What was the first step you took? _____

_____

Who did you use as resources in achieving this goal? _____

_____

When did you contact them? _____

_____

What was the hardest lesson you learned in achieving your outcome? _____

_____

What was the best lesson you learned? _____

Even if you did not work with your Career Buddy on this, the two of you may want to discuss these results. Spend some time describing your ideal job and how you got there.

If you are not satisfied right now with your description of your ideal job, that's okay. Some people feel locked in by their present circumstances. Others simply have a hard time using visualization. Try it again in a few days, and see what you come up with. Or ask your Career Buddy to help you. If that still doesn't work, you may have to meet with a career coach.

Visualization can be a highly effective technique for creating a picture of what you want in your career. Once you have begun to see it in your mind's eye, a goal becomes much easier to realize. Knowing what you want sets the stage for achieving it.

Life can only be understood backwards; but it must be lived forwards.

Kierkegaard

The
Five
O'Clock
Club

Case Study: Howard— Developing a Vision

In the thick of active life, there is more need to stimulate fancy than to control it.

George Santayana, *The Life of Reason*

Howard attended a Five O'Clock Club group that specializes in helping people who are not yet in professional-level jobs. He had done the Seven Stories and other exercises, and had tried to do the Forty-Year Vision. Like most people, he had left out important parts, such as what he would be doing for a living. That's okay. I asked him if he would mind doing it in the small discussion group.

At the time, Howard was 35 years old and worked in a lower-level job in the advertising industry. He wanted to advance in his career by getting another job in advertising. Based on our research into the jobs of the future, which showed that his current industry was a shaky choice, we asked him to postpone selecting an industry while we helped him complete his Forty-Year Vision.

HAPPY: All I can do now is wait for the merchandise manager to die. And suppose I get to be merchandise manager? He's a good friend of mine, and he just built a terrific estate on Long Island. And he lived there about two months and sold it, and now he's building another one. He can't enjoy it once it's finished. And I know that's just what I would do. I don't know what the hell I'm workin' for.

Arthur Miller, *Death of a Salesman*

Howard was just getting started on his career even though he was 35. You're just getting started too. Regardless of your age, take pen to paper and force yourself to write something. You can always change it later.

Filling in His Forty-Year Vision

Kate: "Howard, you're 35 years old right now. Tell me: Who are your friends and what do they do for a living?"

Howard: "John is a messenger; Keith minds the kids while his wife works; and Greg delivers food."

Kate: "What do you do for a living?"

Howard: "I work in the media department of an advertising agency."

Kate: "Okay. Now, let's go out a few years. You're 40 years old, and you've made a number of new friends in the past five years. Who are these people? What are they doing for a living?"

Howard: "One friend is a medical doctor; another works in finance or for the stock exchange; and a third is in a management position in the advertising industry."

Kate: "That's fine. Now, let's go out further. You're 50 years old, and you have made a lot of new friends. What are they doing for a living?"

Howard: "One is an executive managing 100 to 200 people in a corporation and is very well respected; a second one is in education—he's the principal or the administrator of an experimental high school and gets written up in the newspapers all the time; a third is a vice president in finance or banking."

Kate: "Those are important-sounding friends you have, Howard. But who are you and what are you doing that these people are associating with you?"

Howard: "I'm not sure."

Kate: "Well, how much money are you making at age 50 in today's dollars?"

Howard: "I'm making $150,000 a year."

Kate: "I'm impressed. What are you doing to earn that kind of money, Howard? What kind of place are you working in? Remember, you don't *have* to be specific about the industry or field you're in. For example, how do you dress for work?"

Howard: "I wear a suit and tie every day. I have a staff of 60 people working for me: six departments, with 10 people in each department."

Kate: "And what are those people doing all day?"

Howard: "They're doing paperwork, or computer work."

Kate: "That's great, Howard. We now have a pretty good idea of what you'll be doing in the future. We just need to fill in some details."

I said to the group: "Perhaps Howard won't be making $150,000, but he'll certainly be making a lot by his own standards. And maybe it won't be 60 people, but it will certainly be a good-sized staff. What Howard is talking about here is a concept. The details may be wrong, but the concept is correct."

*If I see what I want real good in my mind,
I don't notice any pain in getting it.*

George Foreman, former heavyweight boxing
champion of the world

Howard: "But I'm not sure if that's what I really want to do."
Kate: "It may not be exactly what you want to do, Howard, but it's in the right direction and contains the elements you really want. What you just said fits in with your Seven Stories exercise (one story was about your work with computers; another was about an administrative accomplishment). Think about it for next week, but I'll tell you this: You won't decide you want to be a dress designer, like Roxanne here. Nor will you say you want to sell insurance, like Barry. What you will do will be very close to what you just described.

"If you come back next week and say that you've decided to sell ice cream, for example, I'll tell you that you simply became afraid. Fear often keeps people from pursuing their dreams. Over the week, read about the jobs of the future, and let me know the industries you may want to investigate for your future career. It's usually better to pick growth industries rather than declining ones. You stand a better chance of rising with the tide."

The Next Week

When it was Howard's turn in the group the next week, he announced that he had selected health care as the industry he wanted to investigate. That sounded good because it is a growth field and because there will be plenty of need for someone to manage a group of people working on computers.

We brainstormed the areas within health care that Howard could research. He could work in a hospital, an HMO, a health-care association, and so on. He could learn about the field by reading the trade magazines having to do with health care administration, and he could start networking by meeting with someone else in the group who had already worked in a hospital.

Week #3

Howard met with the other person in the group and got a feel for what it was like to work in a hospital. He also got a few names of people he could talk to—people at his level who could give him basic information. He had spent some time in a library reading trade magazines having to do with health-care administration.

Howard needed to do a lot more research before he would be ready to meet with higher-level people—those in a position to hire him.

Week #4

Howard announced to the group that he had done more research, which helped him figure out that he should start in the purchasing area of a hospital, as opposed to the financial area, for example. In previous jobs, he had worked both as a buyer and as a salesman, so he knew both sides of the picture. He would spend some time researching the purchasing aspect of health care. That could be his entry point, and he could make other moves after he got into the field.

A human being certainly would not grow to be seventy or eighty years old if his longevity had no meaning for the species.

C. G. Jung

Week #5

Today Howard is ready to meet with higher-level people in the health-care field. As he networks around, he will learn even more about the field, and select the job and the organization that will position him best for the long run—the situation that fits in best with his Forty-Year Vision.

After Howard gets his next job, he will occasionally come to the group to ask the others to help him think about his career and make moves within the organization. He will be successful in living his vision if he continues to do what needs to be done, never taking his eye off the ball.

If Howard sticks with his vision, he will make good money, and live in the kind of place in which he wants to live. Like many people who develop written plans, Howard has the opportunity to have his dream come true.

You can either say the universe is totally random and it's just molecules colliding all the time and it's totally chaos and our job is to make sense of that chaos, or you can say sometimes things happen for a reason and your job is to discover the reason. But either way, I do see it meaning an opportunity and that has made all the difference.

Christopher Reeve, former star of *Superman*, in an
interview with Barbara Walters—Reeve became a
quadriplegic after a horseback-riding accident

You Can Do It Too

As I mentioned earlier, the group that Howard attended is a special Five O'Clock Club program that works mostly with adults who are not yet in the professional or managerial ranks, and helps them get into professional-track jobs. For example:

Emlyn, a 35-year-old former babysitter, embarked on and completed a program to become a nurse's aide. This is her first step toward becoming an R.N., her ultimate career goal.

Calvin, who suffers from severe rheumatoid arthritis, hadn't worked in 10 years. Within five weeks of starting with us, he got a job as a consumer advocate with a center for the disabled, and has a full caseload. We are continuing to work with him.

These ambitious, hard-working people did it, and so can you. It's not easy, but what else are you doing with your 24 hours a day? The people who did it followed this motto: "Have a dream. Make a plan. Take a step. Keep on climbing."

You can complain that you haven't gotten lucky breaks, but Howard, Emlyn, and Calvin didn't either.

They made their own breaks, attended a branch of The Five O'Clock Club, and kept plugging ahead despite difficulties. If they can do it, you can do it too.

Self-Assessment Summary

Summarize the results of all of the exercises. This information will help define the kind of environment that suits you best, and will also help you brainstorm some possible job targets. Finally, it can be used as a checklist against job possibilities. When you are about to receive a job offer, use this list to help you analyze it objectively.

1. **What I need in my relationship with bosses:** _____

2. **Job satisfiers/dissatisfiers:**

   Satisfiers: _____

   Dissatisfiers: _____

3. **Most important work-related values:** _____

4. **Special interests:** _____

5. **Threads running through the Seven Stories analysis:**
   Main accomplishments: _____
   Key motivators: _____
   Enjoyed most; did best: _____
   My role: _____
   Environment: _____
   Subject matter: _____

6. **Top six or seven Specialized Skills:**

   _____
   _____
   _____
   _____
   _____
   _____
   _____

7. **From Fifteen- or Forty-Year Vision:**

   Where I see myself in the long run: _____
   _____
   _____

   What I need to get there: _____
   _____
   _____

8. **My basic personality and the kinds of work cultures into which it will fit:**

   _____
   _____

The
Five
O'Clock
Club

Brainstorming Possible Jobs

Use the Brainstorming Possible Jobs worksheet on page 53, to help you brainstorm possible jobs that you can then explore.

1. **Across the top of the page**, list the following elements as they apply to you. Use as many columns as you need for each category.

- Your basic personality
- Interests
- Values
- Specialized skills
- From the Seven Stories Exercise:
  - the role you played
  - the environment in which you worked
  - the various subject matters in your stories
- Long-range goals
- Education
- Work experience
- Areas of expertise

Here is one person's list of column headings across the top:

- Personality: **outgoing**
- Interests: **environment, computers, world travel** (three different interests—takes three columns)
- Values: **a decent wage** so I can support a family
- Specialized Skills: **use of PC**
- From the Seven Stories Exercise:
  - being **part of a research group**
  - enjoy **Third World countries** (takes two columns)
- Goals from the Forty-Year Vision: **head up not-for-profit organization**
- Education: **masters in public policy**
- Work Experience: **seven years' marketing experience.**

This takes a total of 11 columns across the top.

2. **Down the side of the page, list possible jobs, fields, or functions** that rely on one or more of these elements. For example, combine marketing with environment, or computers with research and Third World countries.

At this point, do not eliminate anything. Write down whatever ideas occur to you. Ask your friends and family. Do library research and talk to lots of people. Open your eyes and your mind when you read or walk down the street. Be observant and generate lots of ideas. Write down whatever anyone suggests. A particular suggestion may not be exactly right for you, but may help you think of other things that *are* right.

3. **Analyze each job possibility.** Check off across the page the elements that apply to the first job. For example, if the job fits your basic personality, put a checkmark in that column. If it uses your education or relies on your work experience, put checkmarks in those columns. If it fits in with your long-range goals, put a checkmark there.

Do the same for every job listed in the left column.

It is never too late to be what you might have been.

George Eliot

4. **Add up the checkmarks for each job, and write the total in the right-hand column.** Any job that relies on only one or two elements is probably not appropriate for you. Pay attention to the ones with the most checkmarks. Certain elements are more important to you than others, so you must weight those more heavily. In fact, some elements probably *must* be present so you will be satisfied, such as a job that meshes with your values.

Those jobs that seem to satisfy your most important elements are the ones you will list as some of the targets to explore on the Preliminary Target Investigation worksheet (see page 81). Also list positions that would be logical next steps for you in light of your background.

You must have long-range goals to keep you from being frustrated by short-range failures.

Charles C. Noble, major general

CASE STUDY *Agnes*
Broadening Her Targets

Agnes has been a marketing/merchandising/promotion executive in the fashion, retail, and banking industries. Her only love was retail, and her dream job was working for one specific, famous fashion house. Perhaps she could actually get a job with that fashion house, but what kind of job could she go for after that? The retail and fashion industries were both retrenching at the time of her search, although she could probably get a job in one of them. She needed more targets, and preferably some targets in growing industries so she would have a more reasonable career path.

In addition to the retail and fashion industries, what other industries could Agnes consider? In the banking industry, where she had been for only three years, some of the products she promoted had been computerized. In combining *computers* with *retail,* we came up with *computerized shopping,* a new field that was threatening the retail industry. Computerized shopping and related areas were good fields for Agnes to investigate. What about something having to do with debit cards and credit cards or Prodigy—all computer-based systems aimed at retail? Or what about selling herself to banks that were handling the bankrupt retail companies that she was so familiar with? We came up with 20 areas to explore. Agnes's next step is to conduct a Preliminary Target Investigation (which you will read about soon) to determine which fields may be worth pursuing in that they hold some interest for her and there is some possibility of finding a job in them. At this point she has an exciting search lined up—one with lots of fields to explore and one that offers her a future instead of just a job.

I've got peace like a river ina my soul.

African-American spiritual

Brainstorming Possible Jobs Worksheet

Assessment Results →

Possible Jobs

Total Check-marks Across

The
Five
O'Clock
Club

Having a Balanced Life

*Let our advance worrying become
advance thinking and planning.*

Winston Churchill

It is very easy to have a life that is out of balance. Some people intentionally have an *out-of-balance* life so they may achieve in a specific area. Or a person's life may become out of balance in one area for a certain length of time so that he or she may *catch up* in that area. However you decide to live your life, it is still good to know what you are missing.

> ### Pay attention to all areas.
> ### For a balanced life, grow in all areas:
>
> - **Spiritual**
> - **Financial**
> - **Career**
> - **Health and fitness**
> - **Recreation**
> - **Family**
> - **Social**

People need to pay attention to their careers to meet their basic obligations. But be sure you have a *career* and not just *work*. **Career** has a concept of personal development. **Work** has a concept of "I need money to do something else with."

To grow in every area:

1. Have goals in every category.
2. Set priorities.
3. Develop a plan.
4. Live.
5. Review. (Go back to step 1.)

Man dreams dreams, but God directs his steps.

Proverbs 16:9

It's a good idea to review annually what you did last year and what you plan for next year. Keep your plans in a folder and review them over the years. Look for growth in each area. Or do it twice a year. You can pick a theme for the year—something that needs extra focus. Some people do a 5-year or 10-year plan.

Set goals for yourself. The goals you set must be measurable: you must be able to tell when you've accomplished a particular goal.

Set goals that make you stretch. All successful people have failed. It's how you deal with it that's key. If you've never failed, you've never reached.

Life planning is a lot like business planning. A common approach is this one:

1. Get a dream/vision. Formulate a purpose.
2. Write it down.
3. Create long-term, measurable goals.
4. Create a series of strategies and action steps to get there.
5. Evaluate these goals and strategies: Make sure they represent a *stretch*, yet are reasonable.
6. Share these goals with someone.
7. Get some good counsel and advice. (Be prayerful about it.)
8. Act on it.

The more time we spend planning a project, the less total time is required for it. Don't let today's busywork crowd planning time out of your schedule.

Edwin C. Bliss, *Getting Things Done*

Criteria for SUCCESS

Someone found this on a plane and passed it on to me:

S— Sense of purpose—written goals.

E— Excellence—commitment to be the best at whatever you do.

C— Contribution.

R—Responsibility for your actions—you don't work for a company; you work for yourself.

E— Effort.

T— Time management.

S— Stay with it.

Write down your goals for each area, and your steps for reaching your goals in each area. Some people review their lives once or twice a year. Some families develop a plan together every year. Pay attention to all areas. Feel free to add extra areas that have specific importance to you. For a balanced life, *grow* in all areas:

Area to Plan/Grow	Goals for Each Area	Steps for Getting There
• Spiritual		
• Financial		
• Career		
• Health and fitness		
• Recreation		
• Family		
• Social		
• Other		

BIFF: And suddenly I stopped, you hear me?
And in the middle of that office building, do you
hear this? I stopped in the middle of that building
and I saw—the sky. I saw the things that I love in this world.
The work and the food and time to sit
and smoke. And I looked at the pen and said to myself, what the
hell am I grabbing this for? Why am I trying to become what I
don't want to be? What am I doing in an office, making a
contemptuous, begging fool of myself, when all I want is out
there, waiting
for me the minute I say I know who I am!

Arthur Miller, *Death of a Salesman*

The most difficult thing—but an
essential one—is to love Life,
to love it even while one suffers,
because Life is all. Life is God,
and to love Life means to love God.

Leo Tolstoy, *War and Peace*

It is often said that accomplishment makes
[dying] easier, that those who have achieved what they set out to
do in life die more contentedly
than those who have not.

Judith Viorst, *Necessary Losses*

Preliminary Target Investigation: Jobs/Industries Worth Exploring

The Five O'Clock Club

Until you know that life is interesting—and find it so—you haven't found your soul.

Geoffrey Fisher, Archbishop of Canterbury

Although it takes up only a few paragraphs in this book, Preliminary Target Investigation is essential.

Your Preliminary Target Investigation could take only a few weeks if you are high in energy and can devote full time to it. You have to test your ideas for targets in the marketplace to see which ones are worth pursuing. As you research at the library, on the web, and by meeting with people in your fields of choice, you will refine those targets and perhaps develop others. Then you will know where to focus your job search, and the search will be completed much more quickly than if you had skipped this important step.

People who conduct a Preliminary Target Investigation while employed sometimes take a year to explore various fields while they continue in their old jobs. If you are not at all familiar with some of the job targets you have selected, do some Preliminary Target Investigation *now* through the web, library research (be sure to read this section), and networking. You will find that some targets are not right for you. Eliminate them and conduct a full campaign in those areas that seem right for you and that offer some reasonable hope of success.

Whether you are employed or between jobs, Preliminary Target Investigation is well worth your time and a lot of fun. It is the difference between blindly continuing in your old career path because it is the only thing you know, and finding out what is really happening in the world so you can latch on to a field that may carry you forward for many, many years. This is a wonderful time to explore—to find out what the world offers. Most job hunters narrow their targets down too quickly, and wind up later with not much to go after. It is better for you emotionally as well as practically to develop more targets than you need *now* so you will have them when you are actively campaigning. If, on the other hand, you do not have the inclination or time to explore, you can move on. *Just remember, you can come back to this point if your search dries up and you need more targets.*

Most job hunters target only one job type or industry, take a very long time to find out that this target is not working, get depressed, try to think of other things they can do with their lives, pick themselves up, and start on one more target.

Life is God's novel. Let him write it.

Isaac Bashevis Singer

Instead, **brainstorm as many targets as possible before you begin your real job search**. *Then you can overlap your campaigns, going after a number of targets at once. If some targets do not seem to be working as well for you as others, you can drop the targets in which you are no longer interested. And when things don't seem to be going well, you will have other targets to fall back on.*

1. **List below all of the jobs/industries that interest you at this point.**

2. If you are not at all familiar with some of the targets you have selected, do some Preliminary Target Investigation *now* through library research or networking. Eliminate the targets that are not right for you, and conduct a full campaign in those areas that *do* seem right for you and seem to offer you some reasonable hope of success.

   As you find out what is happening in the world, new fields will open up for you. Things are changing so fast that if you conduct a serious search without some exploration, you are probably missing the most exciting developments in an area.

   Spend some time exploring. Don't narrow your targets down too quickly; you will wind up later with not much to go after. It is better for you emotionally, as well as practically, to develop more targets than you need *now* so you will have them when you are actively campaigning. If, on the other hand, you do not have the time or inclination to explore, you can move on to the next step. **Just remember: you can come back to this point if your search dries up and you need more targets.**

JOBS/INDUSTRIES THAT INTEREST ME AT THIS POINT:
(Conduct a Preliminary Target Investigation to determine what is really going on in each of them.)

Counterbalance sources of stress in your life with sources of harmony. Develop closer ties to the people you love. Set up dependable routines in your schedule to which you can look forward during times of stress: a few moments each evening in a hot bath, regular nights to eat out, one day per month in bed, seasonal vacations. Create environments around you that are physically and emotionally restorative: a peaceful workspace, a blossom-filled window box you can see from where you eat, a permanent exercise nook. Regularly perform simple tasks that you can be certain will give you a sense of accomplishment.

Jack Maguire, _Care and Feeding of the Brain_

The Five O'Clock Club

Targeting: The Start of an Organized Search

Dream. Dream big dreams! Others may deprive you of your material wealth and cheat you in a thousand ways, but no man can deprive you of the control and use of your imagination. Men may deal with you unfairly, as men often do; they may deprive you of your liberty; but they cannot take from you the privilege of using your imagination. In your imagination, you always win!

Jesse Jackson

To organize your targeting:
1. Brainstorm as many job targets as possible. You will not conduct a campaign aimed at all of them, but will have backup targets in case certain ones do not work out.
2. Identify a number of targets worthy of preliminary research. (If they are large targets and represent a lot of job possibilities for you, you will need fewer targets.)
3. Research each one enough—through the Internet, the library, and a few networking meetings—to determine whether it is worth a full job-search campaign. This is your Preliminary Target Investigation.
4. If your research shows that a target now seems inappropriate, cross it off your list, and concentrate on the remaining targets. **As you continue to network and research, keep open to other possibilities that may be targets for you. Add those to your list of targets to research.**

    As you add new targets, reprioritize your list so you are concentrating first on the targets that should be explored first. Do *not* haphazardly go after everything that comes your way.
5. If you decide the target is worth pursuing, conduct a full campaign to get interviews in that area:
    * Develop your pitch.
    * Develop your résumé.
    * Develop a list of all the companies in the target area and the name of the person you want to contact in each company.
6. Then contact each organization through networking, direct contact, ads, or search firms.

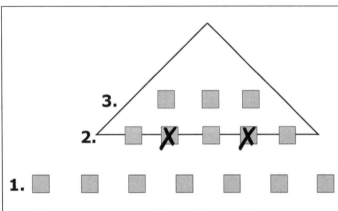

The boxes above represent different job targets. The triangle represents your job search. As you investigate targets, you will eliminate certain ones and spend more time on the remaining targets. You may research your targets by reading or by talking to people. The more you find out, the clearer your direction will become.

During Targeting Phase 1 *you brainstormed lots of possible job targets, not caring whether or not they made sense.*

During Targeting Phase 2 *you conducted preliminary research to determine whether or not you should mount a full campaign aimed at these targets.*

During Targeting Phase 3 *you will focus on the targets that warrant a full campaign. This means you will do full research on each target, and consider using all of the techniques for getting interviews: networking, direct contact, search firms, and ads.*

Serendipitous Leads

Make a methodical approach the basis of your search, but also keep yourself open to those serendipitous *lucky leads* outside of your target areas that may come your way. In general, it is a waste of your energy to go after single serendipitous leads. It is better to ask yourself if this lead warrants a new target. If it does, then decide where it should be ranked in your list of targets, and research it as you would any serious target.

Target Selection

After you have done some preliminary research, select the targets that you think deserve a full campaign. List first the one you will focus on in your first campaign. If you are currently employed and have time to explore, you may want to select as your first target the most unlikely one, but the one that is the job of your dreams. Then you can concentrate on it and find out for sure whether you are still interested and what your prospects are.

On the other hand, if you must find a job quickly, you will first want to concentrate on the area where you stand the best chance of getting a job—probably the area where you are now working. After you get that job, you can explore your other targets. (To expand your targets quickly, consider broadening your search geographically.)

If you are targeting a geographic area different from where you are now, be sure to conduct a serious, complete campaign aimed at that target. For example, you will want to contact search firms in that area, do Internet or library research, perhaps conduct a direct-mail campaign, and network.

Target 1: Industry or organization size: _____

Position/function: _____

Geographic area: _____

Target 2: Industry or organization size: _____

Position/function: _____

Geographic area: _____

Target 3: Industry or organization size: _____

Position/function: _____

Geographic area: _____

Target 4: Industry or organization size: _____

Position/function: _____

Geographic area: _____

Target 5: Industry or organization size: _____

Position/function: _____

Geographic area: _____

Measuring Your Targets

You've selected one to five (or more) targets on which to focus. Will this be enough to get you an appropriate job?

Let's say, for example, that your first target aims at a small industry (10 organizations) having only a few positions that would be appropriate for you.

Chances are, those jobs are filled right now. In fact, chances are there may be no opening for a year or two. The numbers are working against you. Now, if you have targeted 20 small industries, each of which has 10 organizations with a few positions appropriate for you, the numbers are more in your favor.

On the other hand, if one of your targets is large and has a lot of positions that may be right for you, the numbers are again on your side.

Let's analyze your search and see whether the numbers are working for you or against you.

Fill out the following on your own target markets. You will probably have to make an educated guess about the number. A ballpark figure is all you need to get a feel for where you stand.

Target 1: Industry or organization size: _____

       Position/function: _____

       Geographic area: _____

How big is the market for my *product* in this target?

A. Number of organizations in this target market: _____

B. Number of probable positions suitable for me in the average organization in this target: _____

A x B = Total number of probable positions appropriate for me in this target market: _____

For Target 2: Industry or organization size: _____

       Position/function: _____

       Geographic area: _____

How big is the market for my *product* in this target?

A. Number of organizations in this target market: _____

B. Number of probable positions suitable for me in the average organization in this target: _____

A x B = Total number of probable positions appropriate for me in this target market: _____

For Target 3: Industry or organization size: _____

       Position/function: _____

       Geographic area: _____

How big is the market for my *product* in this target?

A. Number of organizations in this target market: _____

B. Number of probable positions suitable for me in the average organization in this target: _____

A x B − Total number of probable positions appropriate for me in this target market: _____

Rule of thumb:

A target list of 200 positions in a healthy market results in seven interviews, which result in one job offer. Therefore, if there are fewer than 200 potential positions in your targets, develop additional targets or expand the ones you already have. Remember: When aiming at a target of less than 200 potential positions, a more concentrated effort is required.

The
Five
O'Clock
Club

Elizabeth: What a Difference a Story Makes

Every résumé has a pitch—although it may not be what the job hunter wants it to be. In scanning Elizabeth's "before" résumé, we can easily see that she has had communications and advertising positions in a number of computer companies. That's the total extent of her pitch. When she went on interviews, managers commented: "You sure have worked for a lot of computer companies." Her résumé read like a job description: She wrote press releases, product brochures, employee newsletters, and so on.

Thousands of people can write press releases, so citing those skills will not separate Elizabeth from her competition. But we can get to know her better if she tells us about specific accomplishments.

Elizabeth agreed to do the Seven Stories Exercise. She didn't feel like writing down "the things she enjoyed doing and also did well" because she felt as though she kept doing the same things again and again in every company for which she worked, and she enjoyed them all. Still, I urged her to be specific—details can make a résumé more interesting. And working on the Seven Stories Exercise is a sure way to develop a strong overall message.

She started with an experience on a job early in her career. She had thought of a terrific idea: Her company's product could be sold through the same computer systems that were used to sell airline tickets and car and hotel reservations. She convinced the company to let her go ahead with the idea, and she promoted it to travel agents across the country and also to the salespeople in her own company. It was so successful, it became the standard way to sell foreign currencies when people were going on a trip.

Most job hunters tend to ignore accomplishments that took place when they were young. But if you had accomplishments early in your career, they may be worth relating because they let the reader know that you have always been a winner.

I said, "That sounds great. Where is it on your résumé?" Elizabeth said, "Well, it's not said exactly that way. . . ." Many times job hunters are constricted when they write their résumés, but the Seven Stories Exercise can free them up to express things differently. So we restated that accomplishment.

Elizabeth then worked on another story. She had participated in a conference that had "generated 450 letters of intent."

I said, "It's nice the conference generated 450 letters of intent. But from what you said, I can't tell that you had anything to do with those results, and I don't know if 450 is good or not. Tell me more about it."

Elizabeth said, "There were only 1,500 participants in the conference, and 450 letters of intent is a lot because our product is very expensive. I had a lot to do with those results because I developed an aura of excitement about the product by putting teasers under everyone's hotel door every morning.

"And before the conference, I had sent five weekly teasers to everyone who planned to attend. For example, one week, I sent each person a bottle of champagne. This direct-mail campaign had everyone talking about us before the convention started. People were asking one another whether or not they had gotten our mailers. When they got to the convention and found teasers under their doors, they were eager to come to our booth.

"I also trained the teams of employees who were demonstrating the product at the convention. I made sure that each demonstrator delivered the same message."

Now I understood how Elizabeth had played a major part in generating those letters of intent.

Next we needed to think of the message behind this accomplishment. Was her message that she could stick mailers under doors? Or send out bottles of champagne? No, her message was that she knew how to launch a product, and that's what we put on her résumé as the main point for that accomplishment.

In her "before" résumé, Elizabeth said that she wrote press releases and did direct-mail campaigns. Her "after" résumé provides some examples of what she accomplished with those efforts and gives us a feel for her ingenuity and hard work.

The successful person has the habit of doing things failures don't like to do. They don't like doing them either necessarily. But their disliking is subordinated to the strength of their purpose.

E. M. Gray, *The Common Denominator of Success*

The Summary

After we reviewed all of her accomplishments, we tackled the summary. What was the most important point Elizabeth wanted to get across? It wasn't just that she could write press releases and speeches or do direct-mail campaigns.

She had to think hard about this. The most important thing was that Elizabeth was a key member of the management team. She sat in on meetings when the company was discussing bringing out a new product or planning how to handle a possible crisis. Elizabeth would not be happy—or effective—in a job where she simply wrote press releases. She needed to be part of the strategy sessions.

What you put on your résumé can both include you and exclude you. A company that does not want the communications person included in those meetings would not be interested in Elizabeth—but then, she wouldn't be interested in them either.

In her summary, instead of highlighting the companies she had worked for, Elizabeth highlighted the industries represented by those companies. She listed Information Services and High-Tech first, because they represented areas of greater growth than Financial Services did.

Elizabeth was—and wanted to be again—a corporate strategist, a crisis manager, and a spokesperson for the corporation. That's how we positioned her.

In every summary in this book, the reader can tell something about the writer's personality. It is not enough that someone knows what you have done; they also need to know your style in doing it. For example, a person who had run a department and doubled productivity could have done it in a nasty, threatening way or could have motivated people to do more, instituted training programs, and encouraged workers to come up with suggestions for improving productivity. Your style matters.

Look at this case study, and then do the Seven Stories Exercise. Come up with accomplishments that will interest your reader. Let him or her know what to expect from you if you are hired.

In Elizabeth's case, we hope the hiring manager will look at her résumé and say: "That's exactly what I need: a corporate strategist who knows how to handle crises and can also serve as a spokesperson for us."

This is the response you want the reader to have: "That's exactly the person I need!" Look at your résumé. What words pop out? Is this how you want to be seen? If not, let's get going.

Great minds have purposes, others have wishes. Little minds are tamed and subdued by misfortune; but great minds rise above it.

Washington Irving,
Elbert Hubbard's Scrap Book

ELIZABETH GHAFFARI

207 Dobbs Ferry   Home: (609) 555-6666
Phoenix, AZ 44444

EXPERIENCE

CITRUS COMPUTER SYSTEMS   1999–Present
<u>Director Corporate Communications</u>

Plan and supervise all corporate communications staff and activities for diversified financial information services company on a global basis.

- Develop, direct, and implement global media, public relations, and internal-communications programs in support of corporate and sales objectives, working closely with executive management team.

- Direct all media-relations activities related to new product introductions and product enhancements; initiate media contacts; respond to press inquiries; coordinate and conduct interviews; and develop all press materials.

- Develop and direct advertising and promotional literature activities, overseeing all corporate publications, including corporate and product brochures, sales materials, and customer and employee newsletters.

ELECTRONIC DATABASE SYSTEMS   1997–1999
<u>Manager, Advertising and Promotion</u>

Developed and implemented marketing and promotion strategies for the company and its North American subsidiaries.

- Worked with market and product managers to identify opportunities for product and sales promotions and new product development for multiple market segments. Conducted market research, developed marketing strategies, and implemented tactical plans (e.g., direct response marketing and sales incentive programs).

- Responsible for planning biannual securities analyst meetings and communication product information to investors and industry analysts.

- Orchestrated six product introductions during three-month period, including public-relations activities, promotional literature and training materials.

- Responsible for forecasting and maintaining $4 million budget.

- Managed corporate and product advertising programs, hiring and working with various agencies.

CREDIT LYONNAIS   1995–1997
<u>Corporate Investment Officer and Product Manager</u>

Planned and directed the sales and promotion efforts for the bank's corporate and correspondent sales staff for a variety of products including foreign exchange and precious metals.

- Developed active and profitable business relationships with correspondent banks for sale of precious metals and foreign exchange products.

- Established and developed new account relationships. Brought in eleven new corporate accounts which produced significant business in precious metals and foreign exchange trading areas.

- Managed market study to identify size, segments, and opportunities of various markets. Prepared analysis and recommendations for new product development and trading vehicles.

ELIZABETH GHAFFARI   Page 2

WASSERELLA & BECKTON   1990–1995
Director of Marketing

Managed all activities of the Marketing Department, including product development, sales promotion, advertising, and public relations activities for diversified financial services company.

- Conceptualized and developed national marketing strategy for foreign exchange services offered to travel industry professionals via automated airline reservation systems.

- Developed and implemented business plans for a variety of products, including responsibility for product positioning, pricing, contracts, advertising, and promotional materials.

- Promoted from Foreign Exchange Trader to Marketing Representative to Director of Marketing in three years.

EDUCATION

B.A., Psychology, University of Phoenix   1990

ELIZABETH GHAFFARI

207 Dobbs Ferry
Phoenix, AZ 44444

e.ghaffari@hotmail.com

Residence: (609) 555-6666
Work: (493) 345-7777

CORPORATE COMMUNICATIONS EXECUTIVE
with 14 years' experience in

- **High-Tech** • **Information Services** • **Financial Services**

Experience includes:

- **Global Media and Investor Relations**
- **Customer Videos and Newsletters**
- **Advertising/Promotional Literature**
- **Employee Newsletters**
- **Employee Roundtables/Awards Programs**
- **Speech Writing/Papers/Public Speaking**

- **A corporate strategist and key member of the management team** with extensive knowledge of financial markets.

- **A crisis manager:** bringing common sense, organizational skills, and a logical decision-making process to solving sensitive, time-critical problems.

- **A spokesperson for the corporation:** developing and communicating key corporate messages accurately and convincingly, under deadline pressure, to multiple audiences including employees, the media, customers, and investors.

Proven team leader and troubleshooter with highly developed analytical, organizational, and strategic planning skills.

CITRUS COMPUTER SYSTEMS   1999–Present

Director, Corporate Communications

- Gained extensive positive media coverage in conjunction with launch of company's first product for new market segment.
  - Planned and conducted **media events in 8 countries**.
  - Resulted in **positive stories in 30 major publications** and trade press: *The Wall Street Journal, The New York Times, Barron's, The Financial Times, Forbes,* and various foreign publications.
  - A first for the company, **positive TV coverage in the United States**: CNN, CNBC, **and Europe**: Sky Financial Television, Business Daily, The City Programme.
- Successfully **avoided communications crisis,** gained positive press coverage and customer support when company sold a major division. Within a 60-day period:
  - Planned and managed all aspects of a **13-city, interactive teleconference**.
  - Developed all written materials including various employee and customer communications, background materials, and press releases.
  - Wrote speeches for six executives including both company presidents (present and acquiring companies).
  - Wrote and produced an extensive question-and-answer document covering **union, compensation, and benefits issues and business rationale**.
  - Selected and trained staff representatives for each of 13 cities.
- Developed and implemented **company's first employee awards program** for service excellence.
  - Honored employees who participated in planning sessions.
  - **Led to changes in key areas** including improvements in software manufacturing efficiencies, shortening of the product development cycle, and improved employee morale.
- **Introduced desktop publishing** program for in-house production of all promotional materials and various customer and employee newsletters.
  - **Reduced outside services expense by 75%.**
  - Created new **corporate standards manual** and reorganized promotional literature system to replace inconsistent product literature.
- Conducted group and individual **employee meetings** to gain and disseminate critical information in identifying and resolving employee-relations problems.

ELIZABETH GHAFFARI - Page 2

CITRUS COMPUTER SYSTEMS, contd.

Director, Corporate Communications, contd.
- Prepared quarterly management reports and written/oral presentations to top management and employees to describe corporate accomplishments compared to goals.
- Managed all customer/media/employee communications for sale of three business units.

ELECTRONIC DATABASE SYSTEMS   1997–1999

Manager, Advertising and Promotion
- Prepared written and oral **presentations to boards of directors** and senior managers on various services, concepts and results.
- Planned **product launch** and company participation in global foreign exchange conference. Successful product launch resulted in **generating 450 letters of intent from 1,500 participants.** Assured successful product introduction:
  - Developed 5-week **direct-mail campaign** to stimulate interest and create an aura of excitement around product prior to conference. Campaign continued at conference with daily newsletter and door stuffer.
  - Maximized impact of **product demonstrations** through use of compelling visual presentation and environment.
  - **Trained teams** of product demonstrators to assure that information regarding benefits and features would be delivered in a consistent way.
- Strengthened company relationships with **industry analysts and investors** by arranging product demonstrations in conjunction with biannual industry analyst meetings. Demonstrations stimulated interest and **gained support for strategic direction from investor community** by communicating important strategic and product information.
  - Selected products to be demonstrated, developed promotional materials, organized display area, selected and trained product demonstrators to assure delivery of consistent corporate message.

CREDIT LYONNAIS   1995–1997

Product Manager
- Established and developed new account relationships.

  Brought in **11 new corporate accounts during 10-month period,** producing significant business in precious metals and foreign exchange trading areas.

WASSERELLA & BECKTON   1990–1995

Director of Marketing

Developed breakthrough idea to sell foreign exchange services (currency and travelers' checks) through travel agents the same way hotel space and airline tickets are sold

via automated airline reservation systems.

- Sold concept to senior management and **negotiated contracts with three major airlines.**
- Developed sales and operational procedures. **Hired and trained 10-person sales and operations staff.**
- **Promoted concept to travel agents** across the country through industry trade shows and sales program.

EDUCATION

B.A., Psychology, University of Phoenix, 1990

The
Five
O'Clock
Club

Writing the Summary at the Top of Your Résumé

Greatness is not measured by what a man or woman accomplishes, but by the opposition he or she has overcome. . . .

Dr. Dorothy Height, President,
National Council of Negro Women

Feel stuck in your present position? Peel off your old label, slap on a new one, and position yourself for something different.

Whether you're an accountant who wants to go into sales or an operations person who dreams of being a trainer, the challenge you face is the same: You have to convince people that, even though you don't have experience, you can handle the new position.

It's a little like show biz: You play the same role for years and then you get typecast. It can be difficult for people to believe that you can play a different role. To move on to new challenges, you have to negotiate into the new job by offering seemingly unrelated skills as an added benefit to the employer. The key to these negotiations is *positioning* yourself.

Positioning

Simply put, positioning yourself means stating your skills and qualities in a way that makes it easy for the prospective employer to see you in the position that is open or in other positions down the road.

You may want to stay in your present organization. In that case, you are positioning yourself to the person in charge of hiring for the particular department you want to enter. Or you may want to go to a new organization or even a new industry. In this case, you are positioning yourself to a new employer. Either way, the steps are the same.

1. Determine what skills and qualities your prospective employer wants.

2. Search your background to see where you have demonstrated skills and qualities that would apply.

3. Write a summary at the top of your résumé to position yourself.

4. Use the same summary to sell yourself in an interview.

Your summary says it all. It should sell your ability, experience, and personality. It brings together all your accomplishments.

The rest of your résumé should support your summary. For example, if the summary says that you're a top-notch marketer, the résumé had better support that. It's completely within your control to tell whatever story you want to tell. You can emphasize certain parts of your background and de-emphasize others.

> **You can get typecast. To move on, you have to negotiate into the new job by *positioning* yourself.**

Thinking through your summary is not easy, but it focuses your entire job hunt. It forces you to clarify the sales pitch you will use in interviews.

However, many people *don't* put a summary that positions them on their résumés. They say they want "a challenging job in a progressive and growth-oriented company that uses all my strengths and abilities." That doesn't say anything at all, and it doesn't do you any good.

Résumé: Your Written Pitch

Make sure the first words on your résumé position you for the kind of job you want next, such as "Accounting Manager." Line *two* of your résumé, also centered, should separate you from all those other accounting managers. For example, it could say, "Specializing in the publishing industry." These headlines in your summary could then be followed by bulleted accomplishments that would be of interest to your target market.

Most people write boring résumés. To avoid this, keep in mind to *whom you are pitching.* Tell readers the most important things you want them to know about you. List your most important accomplishments right there in your summary.

It all starts with the Seven Stories Exercise. After you have done this exercise, you will talk about your accomplishments very differently than if you just sit down and try to write a résumé. The Seven Stories Exercise is the foundation for the résumé. Write out your work-related stories in a way that is *expressive* of you as an individual. *Brag* about yourself the way you would brag to the people in your family or to your friends. Put *those* words at the top of your résumé. It will make for a much more compelling piece of paper.

Let's consider a few examples of summaries that *will* work for you.

Pursuing the Dream Job

Jane, a client-relationship manager at a major bank, has handled high-net-worth clients for more than 20 years. She is taking early retirement and thinking about a second career. Two directions are of interest to her: a job similar to what she has done but in a smaller bank, and the job of her dreams—working as one of the top administrative people for a high-net-worth family (such as the Rockefellers), handling their business office, and perhaps doing some of the things that involve her hobbies over the years: staffing and decorating.

If Jane were to continue on her current career path and go for a position as a relationship manager at a smaller bank, she would highlight the years she has worked at the bank. Her summary, if used in her résumé, would look like this:

Over 20 years handling all aspects of fiduciary relationships for PremierBank's private banking clients. Successfully increased revenue through new business efforts, client cultivation, and account assessment. Consistently achieved fee increases. Received regular bonus awards.

However, to pursue her dream job, Jane's regular résumé won't do. She has to reposition herself to show that her experience fits what her prospective employer needs. Her summary would read like this:

Administrative manager
with broad experience in running operations

- In-depth work with accountants, lawyers, agents, and others
- Over 20 years' experience handling all aspects of fiduciary relationships for bank's private banking clients (overall net worth of $800 million)
- Expert in all financial arrangements (trust and estate accounts, asset management, nonprofit, and tenant shareholder negotiations)

Her résumé would also focus on her work *outside* PremierBank because these activities would interest her prospective employer: first, her work on the board of the high-class apartment building of which she was president for 14 years, and then the post she held for 10 years as treasurer of a nonprofit organization. Finally, Jane would highlight accomplishments at PremierBank that would be of interest to her prospective employer, such as saving a client $300,000 in taxes.

Ready to Take Charge

Robert had worked in every area of benefits administration. Now he would like to head up the entire benefits administration area—a move to management. His summary:

14 years in the design and administration
of all areas of employee benefit plans

- Five years with Borgash Benefits Consultants
- Advised some of the largest, most prestigious companies in the country
- Excellent training and communications skills
- MBA in Finance

From Supporting to Selling

Jack wants to move into sales after being in marketing support. His prior résumé lacked a summary. Therefore, people saw him as a marketing support person rather than as a salesperson—because his most recent job was in marketing support. He has been an executive in the sales promotion area, so his summary stresses his internal sales and marketing as well as his management experience:

Sales and Marketing Professional
with strong managerial experience

- Devise superior marketing strategies through qualitative analysis and product repositioning
- Skillful at completing the difficult internal sale, coupled with the ability to attract business and retain clients
- Built strong relationships with the top consulting firms
- A team player with an enthusiastic approach to top-level challenges.

Notice how he packages his experience running a marketing department as *sales*. His pitch will be: "It's even more difficult to sell inside because, in order to keep my job, I have to get other people in my company to use my marketing services. I have to do a good job, or they won't use me again."

If you do not have a summary, then, by default, you are positioned by the last job you held. In Jack's case, the employer would receive the new résumé with the new summary and say, "Ah-ha! Just what we need—a salesperson!"

Sophisticated Positioning

Here are how some people repositioned their backgrounds in a sophisticated way. Jeff had been in loan-processing operations in a bank. Outside financial services, not many organizations do loan processing. To position himself to work in a hospital, Jeff changed his positioning to *transaction* processing because hospitals process a large number of *transactions,* but not loans. Otherwise, they would look at his résumé and say, "We don't need to have loans processed."

In fact, a lot of people work in banking, but many see themselves as working for information services companies.

Money is sent via computer networks and wire transfers. They are passing information, not currency.

Nydia had worked both at banks and at pharmaceutical companies. Because of her target, she positioned herself as having worked in *regulated industries.*

David saw himself as an international human resources generalist but was having difficulty with his search. There were no international jobs in his field, so he should not position himself as "international."

Now, think about *your* target market and how you should position your background for that target.

 The
Five
O'Clock
Club

Elliott: Getting Back into a Field He Loved

Think like a duchess, act like a duchess, talk like a duchess, and one day you will be a duchess!

Henry Higgins to Eliza Doolittle in
George Bernard Shaw's *Pygmalion*

E lliott had been in sports marketing years ago and had enjoyed it tremendously. However, he had spent the past four years in the mortgage industry and was having a hard time getting back into sports marketing.

The sports people saw him as a career changer—and they saw him as a mortgage man. Even when he explained that marketing mortgages is the same as marketing sports, people did not believe him. He was being positioned by his most recent experience, which was derailing his search.

A job hunter who wants to change industries—or go back to an old industry—cannot let the most recent position act as a handicap. For example, if a person has always been in pharmaceuticals marketing and now wants to do marketing in another industry, the résumé should be rewritten to make it generic marketing, and most references to pharmaceuticals should be removed.

In Elliott's case, the summary in the new résumé helps a great deal to bring his old work experience right to the top of the résumé. In addition, Elliott has removed the word *mortgage* from the description of his most recent job, his title at the mortgage company now stands out more than the company name, and he has gotten rid of company and industry jargon, such as the job title of "segment director," because it is not something easily understood outside his company.

Notice in his new résumé that the description of what Elliott did for the mortgage business is now written generically—it can apply to the marketing of *any* product. With his new résumé, Elliott had no trouble speaking to people in the sports industry. They no longer saw his most recent experience as a handicap, and he soon had a terrific job as head of marketing for a prestigious sporting-goods company.

If you want to move into a new industry or profession, state what you did generically so people will not see you as tied to the old.

> **For a thorough discussion of how to change careers, see our book *Targeting a Great Career* to figure out what you want to do and our book *Shortcut Your Job Search* to tell you how to do it.**

Bring Something to the Party

When it comes down to negotiating yourself into a new position, seemingly unrelated skills from former positions may actually help you get the job.

For example, some of my background had been in accounting and computers when I decided to go into coaching. My CFO (chief financial officer) experience helped me ease into that career. I applied at a 90-person career counseling company and agreed to be their CFO for a while—provided I was also assigned clients to coach. They wanted a cost-accounting system, so my ability to do that for them was what I *brought to the party*. I was willing to give the company something they wanted (my business experience) in exchange for doing something I really wanted to do (coaching executives).

Combining the new with the old, rather than jumping feet first into something completely new, is often the best way to move your career in a different direction. You gain the experience you need in the new field without having to come in at the entry level. Equally important, it is less stressful because you are using some of your old strengths while you build new ones.

Coming from a background different from the field you are targeting can also give you a bargaining chip. If you are looking at an area where you have no experience, you will almost certainly be competing with people who do have experience. You can separate yourself from the competition by saying, "I'm different. I have the skills to do this job, and I can also do other things that these people can't do." It works!

This book contains dozens of additional positioning (summary) statements. In addition, you will see how the positioning statements are used to set the tone for the rest of the résumé.

"Before" Résumé

Elliott Jones

421 Morton Street

Chase Fortune, KY 23097

Sears Mortgage Company
Vice President, Segment Director, Shelter Business

2002–present

- Director of $4.6 billion residential mortgage business for the largest mortgage lender
- Organized and established regional marketing division for the largest mortgage lender, a business which included first and second mortgages and mortgage life insurance

SportsLife Magazine

1999–2002

Publisher and Editor

- Published and edited largest health/fitness magazine. Increased circulation 175%.
  And so on. . .

"After" Résumé

Elliott Jones

421 Morton Street   Chase Fortune, KY 23097   ejones@yahoo.com

**Fifteen years: domestic and international marketing management
in the <u>leisure/sporting goods industry</u>**

- Multibrand expertise specializing in marketing, new business development, strategic planning, and market research.
- Identify customer segments, develop differentiable product platforms, communication strategies, sales management, share growth, and profit generation.

Sears Mortgage Company   2003–present
<u>VICE PRESIDENT, BUSINESS DIRECTOR</u>
Residential Real Estate Business

- Business director of a $4.6 billion business. Managed strategic planning, marketing, product development, and compliance.
- Consolidated four regional business entities into one; doubled product offerings. Grew market share 150 basis points and solidified #1 market position.
- Developed and executed nationally recognized consumer and trade advertising, public relations, and direct-response programs.
- Structured a product development process that integrated product introductions into the operations and sales segments of the business.
- Organized and established regional marketing division.

SPORTSLIFE MAGAZINE   2000–2003
<u>Publisher and Editor</u>

- Published and edited largest health/fitness magazine. Increased circulation 175%, and so on . . .

The
Five
O'Clock
Club

Researching Your Job Targets

Why Is Research Important?

Research can help you decide which fields and industries you want to work in. In our book *Shortcut Your Job Search* we'll tell you how to research those targets, eliminate some, add others, and develop a detailed list of organizations to contact and how to contact them. But for right now, you simply want a list of *tentative* targets. You need to explore what kinds of positions *may* be appropriate for you. Which industries? Which geographic areas?

During the course of your research, look for the following about each industry in your tentative target list:

1. trends and future prospects in a particular industry;

2. areas of growth and decline in that industry;

3. the kinds of challenges the industry faces that could use your skills;

4. the culture of the industry; and

5. the major-league organizations in the industry, of course, but also the second- and third-tier firms as well.

In the bibliography at the back of our *Shortcut Your Job Search* book, you will find many sources for exploring these issues and concerns. Having a *lot* of information will help you determine whether or not you are in sync with a particular industry and whether or not there is a place for you. It generally requires only a small amount of information to decide that an industry should go on your tentative target list. You will continue to research throughout your search because, as you will see, the entire job-search process is a *research* process. You will continue to refine your targets and your list of organizations as you go forward.

Library Research

Find a university or big-city library that's conveniently located and has an extensive business collection. The great thing about libraries is that you will not be on your own: Librarians

are usually experts at helping job hunters, so plan to spend some time with the business reference librarian. Be specific. Tell the librarian what you want to accomplish. I have always said, "The librarian is your friend." I personally love libraries (although I now do most of my research on the Internet). I was a librarian in both high school and college. Get comfortable with the environment. Spend time using the reference books. Photocopy articles you can read at home.

If electronic information at the library is a new frontier for you, do not be intimidated. Ask for assistance. Computer-aided research will make your work immeasurably faster, easier, and more accurate. Let it work for you. If you are of a certain age or inclination and *don't like computers,* the best advice I can give you is *get over it.* In about any field I can think of, information sharing is now done by computer— you *will* need to adapt.

There are going to be no survivors.
Only big winners and the dead.
No one is going to just squeak by.
Ronald Compton, CEO, Aetna Insurance Company

Basic Research

For most job hunts, you should **set aside at least two full days strictly for library or Internet research**. If you are not sure of the industry you want to pursue, you can spend two days just researching industries (or professions). One of my favorite tools is the *Encyclopedia of Business Information Sources.* It lists topics, such as *oil* or *clubs* or *finance* or *real estate.* Under each topic, it lists the most important sources of information on that topic: periodicals, books, and associations. Using this resource, you can quickly research any field in depth. You also may want to read the U.S. Department of Labor's reports on various industries or professions (*www.bls.gov/emp* and *www.bls.gov*).

Two important Internet resources on careers are *www.vault.com* **and** *www.wetfeet.com.*

Vault.com provides information on more than 1,200 organizations. If you click on *fashion,* for example, it will bring up links to articles about the fashion industry and its leading players. You can click on health care and investment banking and many other major industries. Vault.com doesn't offer information on minor industries, but its goal is to provide you with the *inside scoop* on key industries *from a job hunter's point of view.* There are plenty of sites out there where you can find out about an industry from the financial investor's point of view, but Vault.com offers the *employee* perspective.

Vault.com covers the following industries: accounting, advertising and PR, consulting, entertainment, fashion, government, health/biotech/pharmaceutical, investment banking, investment management, law, media and marketing, nonprofit, real estate, technology, television, and venture capital.

Wetfeet.com is a good site to find information about various types of careers, the latest industry news, and the key players in each area. Wet Feet covers the following industries and professions: accounting, advertising, biotech and pharmaceuticals, brand management and marketing, consulting, entertainment, financial services, health care, human resources, law, manufacturing, information technology, nonprofit and government, oil and gas, and real estate.

Once you have selected tentative industries, you will network to find out issues, trends, and buzzwords, and all this will help you refine your pitch. In addition, networking at this point may uncover other tentative targets, which you may simply add to your list of targets, or you may research them at this time.

While networking, you may find someone who will give you a list of people in a targeted field—perhaps an association membership list. Or perhaps someone will invite you to an association meeting and you can find lists and newsletters there. You may need to spend time in the library to gather the list of organizations. You may use an industry directory or local business publications that provide listings of organizations.

If you think you can work in many industries, get a sense of those that are growing and also fit your needs.

Few executives yet know how to ask:
What information do I need to do my job?
When do I need it?
And from whom should I be getting it?

Peter F. Drucker, "Be Data Literate—Know What to Know," *The Wall Street Journal,* December 1, 1992

Where Else Can You Find Information?

- **Associations.** Almost every profession imaginable has an association—sometimes several—and these are important sources of information. If you don't know anything at all about an industry or field, these groups are often the place to start. They tend to be very helpful, and will assist you in mastering the jargon so you can use the language of the trade. *The Encyclopedia of Associations* is a massive list of professional groups. If you are interested in the rug business, there's a related association. You may also try the Internet. To zero in on key associations, go to Google or Yahoo, key in the field or industry in which you are interested, and the word *association.* For example, key in the words *accounting association* and you'll get a listing of 25 or so. Or try **www.business.com,** which includes links to hundreds of associations.

  Just by their very nature, associations are welcoming—so call them. If they have lots of local chapters, chances are there's one near you, and it will be a great place to network. Contact the headquarters, and ask for information and the name of the person to contact in your area. Then call that person, and say you are interested in the association and would like to attend its next meeting. If there is no local chapter in your area, associations can still send you information.

- **The press.** Read newspapers *with your target in mind,* and you will notice all kinds of things you would not otherwise have seen. Contact the author of an article in a trade magazine. Tell him or her how much you enjoyed the article and what you are trying to do, and ask to get together just to chat. I've made many friends this way.

- **Chambers of commerce.** If you are doing an out-of-town job search, call the chamber of commerce in your targeted area. Ask for a list of industries and organizations in that area.

- **Universities** have libraries or research centers on fields of interest. A professor may be an expert in a field you are interested in. Contact him or her.

- **Networking** is a great research tool. At the beginning of your search, network with peers to find out about a field or industry. When you are in full job search, network with people two levels higher than you are.

- **The Yellow Pages** are a useful source of organizations in your local area. This is so obvious that most people overlook it!

Avoid the crowd. Do your own thinking independently.
Be the chess player, not the chess piece.

Ralph Charell

Get Sophisticated about Using Reference Materials

Research will result in your Personal Marketing Plan, which you will see later in this book and which will guide you through your search. But you'll need more research to construct it.

> **Need more help researching your targets?**
> **Go to the Members Only section**
> **of our website:**
> *www.FiveOClockClub.com.*
> **You will see a 40-page bibliography of**
> **research sources—the best available.**
> **You will also find all of our worksheets,**
> **which you may download.**

CASE STUDY *Denise*
Brainstorming Possible Industries

Developing your list of tentative targets takes creativity as well as research. The worksheet in this book, Brainstorming Possible Jobs, is an important start. Denise was a relatively recent graduate who knew she liked writing and computers, and had her undergraduate degree in agriculture. She had no geographical restrictions, and would actually enjoy relocating. Which industries should she target? The question could be put this way: Who employs people to communicate with the agriculture and farming communities? The world is big, and even though the agriculture market is declining in the U.S., it's a big market internationally. Who knows where this research could take her? Here are a few ideas for starters:

- The government—local, state, and federal—e.g., the U.S. Department of Agriculture (USDA).
- Chemical companies such as Monsanto.
- Financial services companies that specialize in mortgages and loans to farmers.
- Publishers that aim at the agriculture or food market, such as Rodale (*Organic Gardening* magazine).
- Advertising agencies and pubic relations firms that aim at that market.
- United Nations, AID, World Health Organization, and other governmental and quasi-governmental organizations that help farmers in Third World countries.
- Associations, for example, Future Farmers of America. Some may be too small to have paid employees, but other associations are worth exploring.
- Agriculturally focused events, such as World Food Day.
- Denise can go to **www.About.com**, key in *agriculture* or *farming,* and see what comes up.

Denise will next try to come up with a list of specific employers, by industry and subindustry. So, for example, under *government,* she would list all of the government agencies that are appropriate. Under *chemical companies,* she would list as many as possible, and *not* focus only on the big names that make the news every day. If the list contains only *recognized* names that everyone has heard about, Denise did not do a good research job. She must go after the small and midsized firms as well.

If I were Denise, I'd spend *at least* 15 hours researching the market—probably more. We're lucky to have the Internet so we can just sit at home and build the list. Later on, Denise will probably need library research and she'll also have to actually talk to people to find out what's going on. But right now she needs to find out how big her universe of potential employers is.

After Denise has a list of tentative targets, she'll conduct a Preliminary Target Exploration aimed at each of the industries to see which industries/subindustries appeal to her the most. She also needs to know where she might stand the *best chance* of starting her agriculture communications career. For example, she may think that the USDA sounds appealing, but after conducting a preliminary exploration, she may find that her preconception was completely wrong. Or, Denise may think at this point that a large chemical company would be the best place for her. But after meeting with a few people in that industry, she may change her mind and decide that it is the worst place for her.

Salary Information

At **www.Salary.com** you can find job descriptions and salary ranges for hundreds of professions by geographic area. You can get a brief look at various fields. But remember, you have a unique background and bring specific experience to the situation. So what *others* are paid might not reflect what *you* are worth—salary negotiations must be based on many factors—not just standard industry ranges.

Other Sources

50 Cutting-Edge Jobs (Ferguson, Chicago, 2000) presents information on 50 newer careers, plus how to break into a field, a glimpse at the future of the field, and the specific earnings, responsibilities, and locations of the jobs. This is a potpourri of occupations that have been spurred by changes in technology, business, and the makeup of the population. Some listings are: adventure travel specialist, biotechnology patent lawyer, computer and video game designer, forensic psycho-physiologist, fuel cell technician, Internet quality assurance specialist, retirement counselor, and wireless service technician.

On **www.business.com's** home page there is a list of about 25 industries, each broken down into three or more subcategories, i.e., financial services is broken down into banking, insurance, and investment. For banking, the subcategories include: associations, banking institutions, banking law, certificates of deposits, employment, online banking, small business, and software, among others. A section called Popular Searches has links to banking for small business, the banking industry, foreign banking, and sweep accounts, plus more.

JobBank Series (Adams Media, Avon, MA), **www.adamsmedia.com**. You can probably pick up the Job-Bank book for your area at your local bookstore. Just browse through the table of contents and see which industries interest you. Each book contains profiles of local companies in all industries, with up-to-date information including: company descriptions, common professional positions, projected number of hires, educational backgrounds sought, internship information, and benefits. The guides are published on: Atlanta, Austin/San Antonio, Boston, the Carolinas, Chicago, Connecticut, Dallas/Fort Worth, Houston, Los Angeles, New York (which includes New York City, Long Island, Rockland County, Westchester County, and Northern New Jersey), New Jersey, Ohio, Philadelphia, Phoenix, San Francisco Bay Area, Seattle, Virginia, and Washington, DC. You'll still need to find the names of people to contact in each organization, but these books are great for developing your Personal Marketing Plan.

Government websites. Do you want to work for the government? Even at the state level, you will find abundant information. For example, if you want a job in Tennessee, try **www.tennessee.gov** and click on *A to Z Departments and Agencies.* It's exciting to see the list of departments. Starting with "A," the listings include the Appellate Courts, the Department of Agriculture, the Alcoholic Beverage Commission, the Arts Commission, and the Attorney General. Review the various departments and see if there are a few that are of interest to you. At the top of the home page is a link to *employment.* You can search for the jobs and submit an application. But you can also target specific agencies that interest you, send your résumé directly to them, or call them and tell them that you are specifically interested in their agency. If you have a specific agency or two in mind, add them to your target list.

The choice of a career, a spouse, a place to live; we make them casually, at times, because we do not know how to articulate the choices. . . . I believe that people often persuade themselves that their decisions do not matter, because they feel powerless to make the best decision. Some of us feel that, no matter what we do, our decisions won't matter much. . . . But I believe that we know at heart that decisions do matter.

Peter Schwartz, *The Art of the Long View*

A Brief List of Industries To Consider

If you are completely stumped about the industries in which you might like to work, the following list is a starting point. Just say *yes* or *no* to each one, selecting the ones that may hold even a slight interest for you. You will investigate them further. Eliminating industries is just as important as selecting industries.

Of course, if there are no companies in your targeted geographic area for the industries you've chosen, you'll have to change the industries or your targeted geographic area.

Also be sure to look at the bibliography at the back of our *Shortcut Your Job Search* book or in the Members Only section of our website.

Academic and Education
Accounting
Advertising, including Graphic Art and Design
Aging Workers
Apparel, Textiles, Fashion, and Beauty
Art and Design
Associations
Automotive
Aviation and Aerospace
Banking, Finance, Investing, Securities, Trading, Credit, and Other
Biotechnology
Business/College/Liberal Arts/Recent Graduates
Communications Equipment and Services, including Telecommunications
Construction and Building
Consulting
Disabled
Diversity and Minorities (except Gay and Lesbian)
Electronics
Energy, Alternative Energy, and Utilities
Engineering
Entertainment, including Media (Broadcasting and Publishing)
Environmental
Ex-Inmates
Food and Beverages
Franchising
Furniture
Government
Health Care and Medicine
Human Resources
Information Technology/High-Tech (Computers, Technology, and e-Commerce)
Insurance
Law
Law Enforcement and Criminal Justice
Library Science
Manufacturing

Nonprofit
Nursing
Public Relations
Publishing (Books, Magazines, Newspapers, Other)
Real Estate
Retailing
Sales and Marketing
Small Business
Transportation (Shipping, Marine, Freight, Express Delivery, Supply Chain)
Travel, Leisure, and Hospitality (including Hotels, Food Service, Travel Agents, Restaurants, and Airlines)
Veterans
Vocational (no Four-Year College Degree)

Volunteering
Wholesaling and Distributing/Importing and Exporting

Hold fast to your dreams
For if dreams die
Life is a broken-winged bird
That cannot fly.

Hold fast to dreams
For when dreams go
Life is a barren field
Frozen with snow.

Langston Hughes (1902–1967)

The
Five
O'Clock
Club

Research: Developing Your List of Organizations to Contact

Wisdom is the principal thing; therefore get wisdom: and with all thy getting get understanding. Exalt her, and she shall promote thee: she shall bring thee to honour, when thou dost embrace her.

Proverbs 4: 7–8

The entire job search process is a *research* process. After all, if you knew exactly the *right* organization and the *right* person and the *right* job for you, you would not be reading this book, and you would not go to The Five O'Clock Club. You would simply go to the organization that had the right job for you—and get hired!

But that's not the way it is. You'll conduct research throughout your *entire* search. Research will help you *home* in on the right place for you: the right industry, the right *organization,* and the right *kinds* of positions—those where you stand a good chance of getting a job right now. Research will also help you pick the right *job*—the one suiting you best for the long term.

If you've been having little luck answering ads and talking with search firms, you may be ready for an organized, methodical search instead. This means you must conduct research. Once you develop your target list, which we also call your Personal Marketing Plan, the rest of your search will be routine. Then you "simply" contact those organizations, arrange to have meetings, and follow up.

Your **Personal Marketing Plan** will guide you in your search, and it will make your search more efficient. You can directly contact people listed in your plan, and use your list in networking

> **Looking for a place to start your research? Read this chapter and then study the bibliography at the back of this book. Once you have your list of organizations to contact, the rest of your search is clear.**

meetings. You'll be able to show people your plan and ask them, "Are you familiar with any of the organizations on this list? What do you think of them? Who do you think I should contact at each organization? May I use your name?"

If you started with our book, *Targeting a Great Career,* during the assessment phase, you accomplished the following:

- You **brainstormed** *all* of the **targets** that you thought might be of interest to you. Later on, when things seem to be drying up, you'll be glad you did this.

- You conducted your *Preliminary* **Target Investigation** to check out each one. At this point, you were not trying to get a job; instead, you were conducting a little research to see if it made sense to mount a full campaign aimed at each of those targets. You talked to people to see what they thought, and you conducted research at the library or on the Internet. This helped you eliminate some targets.

- Then you **ranked your targets**, and decided which targets to go after first, second, third, and fourth. If you are desperate for a job, you decided to focus first on the target where you were most likely to get hired. If you have time to explore—maybe you're employed right now—maybe your first target is the dream job you've always wanted to explore.

- Then you *measured* **your targets**. If the total number of positions you're going after is fewer than 200, that's not good. Remember that we are not totaling job openings, but *positions*. And it does not matter if the positions are filled right now. You are trying to avoid having a search that is too small. Those searches are doomed from the start.

For example, if you want to be a writer in the corporate communications department of a large corporation, you would ask yourself: "How is this large company *organized*? I wonder to whom *corporate communications* reports. I wonder how many *writers* they have in corporate communications." You'd estimate the number of writers you *think* they have. Just take a guess. They certainly have more than one writer in corporate communications! Might they have 5? Or 10? Just take a guess. Of course, a smaller organization would have fewer writers in corporate communications.

Estimate the number of positions each organization might have and add up all of the positions for the organizations on your target list. If in all of your targets the number does not add up to 200 positions (not *openings* but positions), then brainstorm more targets or more organizations within those targets. If you don't follow this strategy, you're going to have a longer search.

- Next, you **segmented your targets**, and segmented *again* if that was reasonable. In the publishing industry, for example, segments could include book publishing, magazine publishing, and publishing online. Magazine publishing is still too big a target, so you would segment it to better manage your campaign. Within magazine publishing, you would list the *kinds* of magazines of most interest to you—for example, sports magazines, health magazines, women's magazines, men's magazines, and so on. You'll find much more on targeting and segmenting in *Targeting a Great Career*.

Successful people often experience more failures than failures do. But they manage to press on. One good failure can teach you more about success than four years at the best university. Failure just might be the best thing that ever happens to you.

Herb True, super-salesman, as quoted by
Robert Allen in *Creating Wealth*

Most people generally target the well-known organizations—the *top* magazines to work for, the *top* museums, the most prestigious hospitals. They target the organizations that *everybody* has heard of and at which everyone wants to work. It's a better idea to research *lesser-known* organizations. These may be even *better* places to work than some of the top-tier organizations. In the second-tier organizations, you may get to do more, have a chance of being a star, and advance more easily. So don't overlook the second-tier organizations.

Your Personal Marketing Plan allows you to *survey all this at a glance*. It lists the industries you're targeting and the organizations within those industries. Your Personal Marketing Plan is so important that it is one of *three key documents* you should share with your small group, in addition to your résumé and cover letter. Show it to your coach and small-group members even when you have just a rudimentary plan, that is, a *tentative* list of industries and subindustries and perhaps a few organizations within each. You will *refine* your Personal Marketing Plan as you move along in your search. Chances are you will change your mind about your most important targets and the most important organizations within each target.

If your small-group members (or your parents or friends) recognize the names of most of the organizations on your list, *you have not yet begun your research!* Dig in more. You'll have to think hard and do your research to uncover organizations that may be *better* places to work.

Job search is just like any other worthwhile project in life. You *make* your plan and then you *execute* it. At the beginning of your search, you'll have a *tentative* Personal Marketing Plan. As you search—and conduct more research—you'll add more organizations to your list. Your Personal Marketing Plan doesn't have to be 100 percent correct before you start contacting prospective employers.

As you move forward, it's best to divide each target into an **A-list, B-list and C-list.** The A-list includes companies where you would love to work. The companies you would consider *okay* go on the B-list, and the C-list companies are of no interest to you.

Contact your C-list companies first to get your feet wet and use them for practice. Because you don't care that much about them, you will probably be more relaxed and confident and will interview well. You are *practicing*. You will also be testing your market to see if you get a good response from these C-list companies.

> **To get a job within a reasonable time . . . target 200 positions—not *openings*— positions.**

It's important for you to know if the companies on your C-list are *not* interested in you. You need to talk to the people in your small group to find out what you're doing wrong. However, if you are well received by the companies on your C-list, then you can contact the companies on your B-list. You could say something like, "I am already talking to a number of companies in your industry [which is true], but I didn't want to accept a job with any of them [which is also true] until I had a chance to talk with you." This script is just one approach. Be sure to talk to your small group about the right things to say to those on your B-list.

> - **Your A-list: You'd love to work there.**
> - **Your B-list: They're okay.**
> - **Your C-list: They don't interest you.**

Using your Personal Marketing Plan and your A-, B-, and C-lists together *is* the search: It's a search for organizations to contact and the names of people within each of those organizations. This is a vastly superior approach to what you might have done in the past. Your competitors, on the other hand, are out there contacting search firms, scanning ads, and hitting the "send" button on job-search websites. But *you'll* get in to see hiring managers before they even post their jobs. You'll have less competition and you'll find that a job may be created just for you!

This part of your search *must* be combined with the assessment you did in *Targeting a Great Career*. Review that book again and again during your job-search process. You don't want just a job; you want a career. This means you want a job *that positions you best for the long run;* you can achieve this only if you *know* what your long-run vision is.

Now, let's develop your Personal Marketing Plan. This chapter will give you some ideas and your coach and small group will give you others. In addition, you can use the bibliography at the back of this book or the even more extensive bibliography in the Members Only section of our website (www.fiveoclockclub.com).

The choice of a career, a spouse, a place to live; we make them casually, at times, because we do not know how to articulate the choices . . . I believe that people often persuade themselves that their decisions do not matter, because they feel powerless to make the best decision. Some of us feel that, no matter what we do, our decisions won't matter much . . . But I believe that we know at heart that decisions do matter.

Peter Schwartz, *The Art of the Long View*

Few things are impossible to diligence and skill.

Samuel Johnson, *A Dissertation on the Art of Flying*

Using Search Engines to Develop Your List

Many job hunters use Google or Yahoo for industry information, even if they're going after esoteric industries such as social services agencies, ethics, education policy, and think tanks. Key any industry name into Google or Yahoo and see what comes up. You may have to look through a few pages of information, but there will probably be a site that lists what's going on in that industry, or lists other sites for that industry; one or two of those sites will probably list *organizations* in that industry. Luckily, most organizations have a website and contact information, making it much easier to develop your list right from your own home.

It might be helpful to see how a few people have progressed through this process. Let's start with something that is not as easy as it appears. I'll give you a few examples of *junior-level job searchers* because they can have a more difficult time uncovering the names of people to contact: It's usually easier to find the names of senior people in organizations.

Dan had experience as a computer operator, line assembler (computers), data controller, and mail room clerk. He lived in Magnolia, Texas. Where could Dan find prospective employers without simply responding to ads?

To develop a list of companies where Dan could work, I went into Google and simply keyed in "Magnolia, TX businesses." More than 75 *pages* of company listings came up—company name, address, phone number, and distance from Magnolia, TX. Those are a *lot* of companies for Dan to contact. Since Dan's skills are applicable to many industries, he could think about a few industries in which he would enjoy working and focus on those, which would make his job more interesting. How Dan would *contact* those companies is another matter covered in great detail elsewhere in this book.

Jon, a manufacturing engineer/supervisor, had been unemployed quite a while. Manufacturing in Arizona was in a downturn and there were very few jobs. But *some* people were getting hired for jobs that were not advertised. How could Jon find the names of companies to contact so he could become proactive in his search rather than wait for openings? Again, I went into Google. I entered "manufacturers Arizona." It took me to **Addresses.com**, which returned 548 company names. Then I went to company websites to start my research. The first company I looked up was Allied Tool and Die. It's probably too small for Jon, so he could then go on to the next one. Or he could scan the list to see which companies he recognized or found appealing.

Research is the process of going up alleys to see if they are blind.

Marston Bates, *American Zoologist*

CASE STUDY *Julie*
Targeting Professional Services Firms

Let's take it one step further. The Internet can be a great way to develop your target list and also *contact* hundreds of people within a few hours. This technique works when you want to contact small- to mid-sized professional service firms, such as accounting, architecture, or law firms. It also works if you want to contact small businesses in general. It can work for job hunters at all levels—from college students to executives who want to work for a small business.

Julie had just finished her sophomore year at a small college and was having a problem finding a summer job related to her major, which was architecture. If Julie had gone to a major school such as the University of Michigan, she could have contacted alumni who were in her field, used the job-posting boards on the University of Michigan website, or gone to on-campus job fairs where the employers come to the students. But those options were not open to her. Julie's school was small and not especially geared to helping students get placed.

Here's what it took for Julia to get *four terrific concurrent offers.*

Julie lived in a rural area and there were no architectural firms in her town. So she targeted the major metropolitan area that was closest to her (90 minutes away) because that's where most of the firms were located. She also targeted the suburban areas nearer her home.

Julie would be glad to do administrative work in an architectural firm and also work in CAD, a computer program for architects. She had taken a CAD course and worked on CAD a little at a previous job. But she didn't want to get stuck as a CAD operator. Instead, she wanted to learn more about the way small architectural firms work. Doing some administrative work would help her get a feel for the firm. So **Julie had defined her targets The Five O'Clock Club way**:

- Industry: architectural firms
- Position: administration or CAD operator
- Geographic area: large metropolitan area and the suburbs near her home.

A basic Five O'Clock Club tenet is that a job hunter must go after 200 job possibilities to get one good offer! This holds true for students as well as for the most senior executives. So it is important to pay attention to the response rate to your e-mailing. Notice how many people ask you to come in for a meeting. If you send 200 E-mails and get only two calls for meetings you must send out 200 *additional* E-mails. Two meetings are not enough!

Architectural firms are generally small, perhaps employing only one student per firm, so Julie would probably need to contact 200 of them. How could Julie come up with the names of 200 architectural firms—and quickly? She was only a week away from the end of the term and had not yet tried to contact many firms.

> **Julie contacted 200 small firms in less than 10 hours.**

Julie used job-posting sites to make a start on her contact list of 200 firms. First, she went into *www.monster.com*, and selected job postings for *architects* in the major metropolitan area near her. Then she selected job postings for architects in the nearby suburban areas. Julie selected only architectural jobs at *firms* as opposed to jobs in the government or major organizations such as hospitals and hotel chains.

Then Julie clicked on the companies she was interested in—*as if* she were responding to the ad. After all, those organizations were hiring! Her approach was to reach out to the person in each small firm who was likely to handle hiring. (This works for students who want to work in a small firm. A more senior person would need to contact the department or division head in a larger firm, which can

require making a phone call or looking at the company's website.)

When ads are answered automatically like this—through a job-posting site—the "subject" line contains the ad number so the organization will know which ad a person is responding to. Julie changed the subject line to read (see example on the next page):

Administrator/CAD Drafter—Architecture-related—Employment for top student.

Julie contacted about 50 firms this way, but this was not enough. She needed to find at least 150 additional firms.

> **Julie responded to ads for senior architects, but asked for a junior-level job instead. Let them know what *you* want.**

Next she tried the search engines. Julie went into Google and keyed in the word *architect* and the two geographic areas she was interested in one at a time. The American Institute of Architects was one of the results and is a good source, but she also found lots of individual architectural firms listed. In most cases, Julie had to go to the company website to get an appropriate E-mail address. One by one, she came up with 155 additional organizations to contact, bringing her total to 205 firms (including the 50 from *monster.com*).

She sent a mass E-mail. To save time, she stopped e-mailing the firms individually. Instead, she captured the E-mail addresses in a Word document, with one E-mail address per line. After she had gathered 20 or 30 E-mail addresses, Julie sent a "mass E-mail." She didn't put the addresses in the "To" field. She copied all the E-mail addresses into the "bcc" field so the recipients would not be able to tell to which or to how many firms she had mailed. She put the same "subject" as she had for her earlier E-mails, attached her résumé as before, and addressed the E-mail to herself. She did this until she had sent out all 205 E-mails. Then she took her last final exam.

Julie had spent a total of about 10 hours on her research and e-mailing.

> **Using a mass e-mail technique, Julie was able to contact 20 to 30 firms at a time using the "bcc" field.**

Then the calls came in. Within two days, Julie received nine calls for meetings. Interestingly, eight of the calls were from the suburban area and only one call was from the major metropolitan area.

This is the E-mail Julie sent to 205 architectural firms. Her Five O'Clock Club résumé was an attachment.

E-mail

To: julieangelo@udallas.edu
Subject: **Administrator/CAD Drafter—Architecture-Related—Employment for Top Student.**

May 11, 200x
Dear Sir or Madam:
I am writing to you because yours is a prestigious firm in the architecture industry and I am an architectural student interested in summer work at a firm such as yours. I'd like to meet with you or someone else in your firm to find out more about your company and to tell you about myself. Even if you have no openings right now, you never know when you may need someone like me.

I have 10 months' experience with a civil engineering firm. You may be interested in some of the specific things I have done:

* Served as an **assistant office manager**, organizing client proposals and setting up manuals. I also answered an 8-line phone.
* Because of my **basic autoCAD experience**, engineers turned to me when they wanted routine things done.

As an architectural studies major, I tend to **be among the best in my class**, winning contests and doing excellent work. I enjoy client contact, helping architects get ready for meetings, putting proposals together, and assisting with autoCAD work. I would appreciate a meeting and look forward to hearing from you.

With thanks,

Julie Angelo

julieangelo@udallas.edu, University of Dallas Box #3124, 76 North Churchill Rd., Irving, TX 99999, 555-666-4693

angelo555@hotmail.com, 863 Erie Avenue, Brewster, TX 99945

Attachment: JAngelo résumé

Julie had sent 75 percent of her E-mails to firms in the major metropolitan area—that's where most of the firms were. The major metropolitan area was the *obvious* place to look for architectural jobs. That means, of course, that she had far more competitors and, accordingly, lower response.

Firms in the suburban area were more responsive to her because most job hunters were ignoring the suburbs.

The results of *your* search may surprise you. That's why you have to contact so many places. You never know who will respond.

Julie scheduled seven interviews (she immediately ruled out two firms because the travel would have been more than two hours from home, something she would have found acceptable if she had gotten only a few calls).

Julie was thrilled to have seven meetings lined up because a key Five O'Clock Club maxim is to have 6 to 10 job possibilities in the works. It increases the chances of landing something appropriate for you.

Another Five O'Clock Club maxim is, "Don't chase jobs—chase companies." Contact organizations whether or not they have an opening right now. If your search is solely from postings, you will have competition for the jobs you go after. Everyone is chasing those same job openings. So too, most people target the top-tier firms in major metropolitan areas. If Julie had done that, she would have been discouraged by the results, since she got only *one* call from a firm in the major metropolitan area.

> **Even though 75 percent of her E-mails went to firms in the major metropolitan area, Julie received almost no response from them.**

Some firms may *tell* you they have no openings (regardless of your level) but say they would be glad to

107

meet with you anyway. *Meet with them!* Most jobs are created for people and most companies will hire someone if the right person comes along—even though they have no formal opening and were not looking to hire at the moment. Julie overlooked this and turned down two exploratory meetings because she felt such urgency to get a job.

However, Julie did schedule five interviews over three days' time.

> **The Five O'Clock Club**
> **wants you to line up 6 to 10 meetings.**
> **Julie lined up 7.**

Julie prepared for the interview; the full scope of that process is covered in our book, *Mastering the Job Interview and Winning the Money Game*. At the very least, we can say here: **Go to each company's website** before the interview so you know something about the company. Even managers at small companies will ask applicants, "So, have you seen our website? How much do you know about us?" Because of the web, companies expect you to know something about them.

Her offers poured in. In the end, Julie went on **four interviews and got four offers**. As she got offers, she became pickier about the remaining firms on her list, ruling out those requiring more than an hour and a half of travel. In her last job, Julie earned $10 an hour. Her first offer was at $11, two were at $12.50, and one offer had not yet come in.

Julie seemed very desirable *because* she had so many possibilities in the works. Companies were essentially in a bidding war for her. Remember that you need to **see 6 to 10 organizations concurrently to have a good search**.

When Julie interviewed at the last firm, she told them about her other offers, hoping for another offer at $12.50 per hour. They wooed her by promising her she would be able to learn a lot about architecture on the job: She would visit some of the sites where the architects were building, go to client meetings, "shadow" an architect to see what was done all day. They said they would E-mail her an offer later that evening.

Julie would have found it difficult to resist their offer almost regardless of the salary they offered: The experience would have been so extraordinary compared with the others and Julie was trying to keep her long-range future in mind.

However, Julie did not have to choose content over salary. The E-mail came that evening with an offer of $15 per hour!

The last firm knew what it was up against: three other offers. The hiring manager also knew it was difficult to recruit architects in their neck of the woods. But for Julie, the location was perfect: only 45 minutes from her home.

> **Julie increased her pay by 50 percent**
> **because she had so many offers and**
> **she contacted companies that other**
> **job hunters ignored.**

Research is to see what everybody has seen and to think what nobody else has thought.
Albert Szent-Gyorgyi, American biochemist

CASE STUDY *Jack*
A Marketing Executive

You, too, can use search engines to develop your list. Large or even mid-sized organizations are generally easier to research. For example, Jack, a marketing executive, got *all* of the information for his job search online. His targets were pharmaceutical, biotech, and biotech marketing organizations. Jack made lists of companies in all three areas appropriate for him in his geographic area.

You're trying to do the same as Jack. You're trying to make a list of the organizations to contact in each of your targets and find out *whom* to contact at each organization. *Then* Jack started networking and contacting organizations directly. He shortly ended up with four offers—right close to home.

The Internet changes over time. The sites job hunters love and depend on can go out of business or start charging huge fees. So you'll have to find out what's current. Ask your small-group members what they use or check the Members Only area of our website.

However you do it, you'll need a preliminary list of organizations to contact. You'll learn other helpful techniques as you develop your list. Just remember: The list *is* your search. Throughout your search, you refine your target list. That's why they call it a *search*. You have to *search* for the names of people to contact.

For what a business needs the most for its decisions—especially its strategic ones—are data about what goes on outside of it. It is only outside the business where there are results, opportunities and threats.
Peter F. Drucker, "Be Data Literate—Know What to Know," *The Wall Street Journal*, December 1, 1992

Associations

Associations are an important source of information. If you don't know anything at all about an industry or field, associations are often the place to start. Attending their meetings will assist you in getting the jargon down so you can use the language of the trade. If you are interested in the rug business, there's a related association.

Maria, a Five O'Clock Club member, was interested in competitive intelligence. Maria went to her local library to consult the massive *Encyclopedia of Associations* (EOA). There would seem to be an association for almost everything, and, believe it or not, she found the Society of Competitive Intelligence Professionals. She called the headquarters, found out about the local chapter, and went to a meeting. She met a lot of people in the field. She also read the association trade journal and learned enough to sound like an "insider." One of these new contacts led her to the job she later accepted.

You can do what Maria did. Go to *your* library, **ask for the *Encyclopedia of Associations***, and spend a few hours with it. Chances are, you'll find one or more associations related to your field of interest. The EOA usually provides information on the national headquarters of associations (many of which are located in or near Washington, DC). Call and ask for information on the **local chapter**. Then call the local chapter and say that you'd like to attend a meeting as a guest. Associations usually *love* to have guests! You'll meet people in the field, hear lectures that will bring you up-to-date, and find copies of their journals, magazines, or newsletters.

Networking is expected at association meetings. When you meet someone you think may help you, ask if you can meet on a more formal basis for about half an hour. If there is no local chapter in your area, the national office may still be willing to send you information.

Associations usually have **membership directories**, which you will have access to when you join. This directory can become the keystone of your search. You can *contact members directly*. You can write, "As a fellow member of the American Rug Association, I thought you could give me some information that would help me in my search." Fellow members are a great source of information.

Associations often publish **trade magazines and newspapers** you can read to stay up-to-date on the business. By reading these, you'll learn about the important issues facing the industry and find out who's been hired and who's moving; you should try to talk to the people you read about. If an association is large enough, it may even have a library or research department, or a public relations person you can talk to. Associations often sell books related to the field.

An association's **annual convention** is a very quick way to become educated about a field. These conventions are not cheap (they run from hundreds to thousands of dollars), but you will hear speakers on the urgent topics in the field, pick up literature, and meet lots of people. You can network at the conference and later.

If you spend a couple of days at a conference, you'll know more about an industry than many people who are *in* the field right now. You can contact people in the industry (many of whom were *not* at the conference) and say, "Were you at the conference? No? Well, I was and maybe I can give you some of the information that I learned there." This is a chance for you to become an insider! A Five O'Clock Club maxim is, "Only insiders get hired." So share the information you pick up.

Since the EOA is the most complete source of association information, we recommend you use it first. A few websites are also helpful. **Associations on the Net** (www.ipl.org/ref/aon/) lists more than 2000 associations. Simply key in a profession. If you put in "accounting," for instance, you'll find 22 organizations. Also try www.business.com; under each business category, there's a link to "associations." (There are additional sources for associations at the back of this book. Some are in print; some are online.)

On these sites, you'll find links to well-known sites like the one for the National Association of Fund Raising Executives and the Association of Legal Administrators. Or just go to Google, key in the word "association" and an industry or field name (e.g., "accounting"), and you'll come up with leads. But as of this writing, nothing beats the EOA.

Few Americans would lay a large wager that they will be in the same job, working for the same company, ten years hence.

Michael Mandel, *The High-Risk Society*

Alumni Associations

If you went to a prestigious school, you have an advantage over other job hunters because those schools often have great alumni associations. Martin, a graduate of Stanford University, wanted to start a job search. He thought he wanted to target some of the hot technology areas, such as radio frequency identification technology. I told him that his alumni database would be his entire search, and it was. He got a copy of the alumni directory and looked for the names of people who were working in the companies he was interested in. He sent 40 E-mails (which were opened because he put his school's name in the "subject" line) and got responses from 12 alumni who were glad to talk to him about the new technologies and the organizations for which they worked. Martin asked each alumnus about the field, but he also asked for the names of the right person he should contact in each company. Then he used the alumnus's name when he contacted the appropriate manager. To keep up momentum, Martin sent out 40 more E-mails. Needless to say, all his hard work paid off. Martin accepted a one-year assignment in London with his present employer. He plans to stay in touch with his new Stanford network through E-mail to ensure he will be able to find a job quickly when he returns to the United States.

Network with Five O'Clock Club Alumni

Thousands of successful Five O'Clock Club graduates have volunteered to help current job hunters who are attending the Club. The profile of our alumni is impressive: 40 percent of our attendees earn more than $100,000 per year and a growing number earn in excess of $200,000 (60 percent earn under $100,000 a year).

If you are attending the Club, simply go to our website (www.fiveoclockclub.com), to the "Network with Alumni" area. Just key in the name of the industry or field you're interested in and you will get back up to 20 names at a time. You must have attended four group sessions (so we're sure you know how to network properly, The Five O'Clock Club way) and you must be part of the database yourself. Just fill out the form at this link: www.fiveoclockclub.com/exitsurvey.

Be sure you check off that you agree to be contacted yourself (question 26 or 33) and then call us for the code to get in. There is absolutely no risk: After signing up, you will be invited to view, make changes to, or suspend your listing at any time. The only information that will appear will be your name, title, employer, industry, field, and method by which *you select* to be contacted. The information will be available only to graduates and current attendees who have been carefully screened by their career coaches. And of course you have access to the alumni database yourself.

www.linkedin.com

Linkedin.com is a network of professional job seekers. Since members refer each other, it is a network of "trusted professionals." Service is free and people join by being referred online (via E-mail) by a classmate, coworker, colleague, or other professional. Members fill out a profile, which allows them to search the network for contacts by such things as job title, job function, location, etc.; it also allows others to contact them. Members can access via these searches those who are not in their own network, but in the overall database. There are more than 300,000 job listings from more than 1,000 employers worldwide. Jobs are posted directly on the employers' own sites. This network allows users to get needed introductions to a hiring manager or recruiter. For example, a member can call a hiring manager and say, "Joan Smith of Exco recommended that I call you," even if he or she only knows Joan via a network search.

Linkedin.com has been getting rave reviews at The Five O'Clock Club as of this writing. Says one member,

"Linkedin.com is a terrific web-based tool that can help extend a person's network and simplify the process of identifying members of your network in target companies. It's free to join so I've tried to recruit lots of other Five O'Clock Clubbers. As a quick anecdote, I received a cold call this morning from a distant contact in my linkedin network who is looking for help on a number of his projects. I was the perfect fit. A perfect lead! Good luck. And pass it on. If you join, make sure to connect to me; the bigger your network the more effective it will be."

Other Sources

The press. Read newspapers and magazines with *your target in mind,* and you will see all kinds of things you would not otherwise have seen. And don't be afraid to contact the author of an article in a trade magazine. Tell him or her how much you enjoyed the article, what you are trying to do, and ask to get together just to chat. I've made many friends this way. And don't be afraid to contact someone quoted or mentioned in an article.

Mailing lists are not that expensive. You will pay perhaps $100 for several thousand names selected by certain criteria, such as job title, level, industry, size of organization, and so on. You can rent lists from direct-mail houses or magazines. For example, Paul contacted a specialized computer magazine and got the names and addresses by selected zip codes of organizations that owned a specific kind of computer. It was then easy for him to contact all the organizations in his geographic area that could possibly use his skills.

Chambers of Commerce. If you are doing an out-of-town job search, call the local chamber of commerce for a list of organizations in that area. Local business publications can be very helpful as well. In Chicago and New York, for example, *Crain's Business* is a great resource; it publishes annual lists for every industry in the geographic area.

Universities have libraries or research centers on fields of interest. Your research may turn up the name of a professor who is an expert in a field that interests you. Contact him or her.

Networking is a great research tool. At the beginning of your search, network with peers to find out about a field or industry. When you are really ready to get a job, network with people two levels higher than you are.

Don't overlook the obvious! **The Yellow Pages** is a useful source of organizations in your local area. If you're in sales, for example, and you want to know all of the companies within a certain industry with offices in your geographic area, let your fingers do the walking! I can think of no better place than the Yellow Pages. You should look in the hard-copy Yellow Pages, but you could also search in the Yellow Pages online, such as at www.yellowpages.com.

Databases at your library. A CD-ROM database organizes data on a compact disk. This is important because:

1. One disk can hold several volumes' worth of printed material. For example, the *Encyclopedia of Associations* comprises 13 volumes, which would fill a couple of bookshelves. However, all 13 of these volumes are contained on *one* CD!

2. Information can be updated much more frequently on a CD. Publishers can and do release current information on a quarterly basis that is simply "downloaded" onto a disk. Contrast this with print volumes, which can take years to be reprinted and republished. By this time, the new information is often already out of date.

3. You can access and retrieve desired information in a fraction of a second when using CD technology. You simply type the keyword you want to look up. Any information containing the keyword is presented to you almost instantly. When you use printed works, searching for specific pieces of information can be very time consuming.

Libraries. Do not rely only on the Internet for your information. Google cannot replace your local librarian. Libraries have been very enthusiastic adopters of technology. The trend is to continue moving to remote self-service. For example, QuestionPoint is 24-hour live library assistance offered by 1,500 libraries worldwide. Technology inside the libraries themselves is a tremendous source of information for your search, so you may just have to pick yourself up and go there to get the really useful data.

Libraries can often provide you with lists of contacts that will form the basis for your entire search. Many Five O'Clock Clubbers have come into the small-group meetings with disks or computer-printed lists of organizations obtained at the library. See what *your* library has. Many libraries have a system where you can key in the zip codes by which you want to search, the SIC or NAICS codes, and size of the organization. You type, "I'm interested in organizations from $5 million to $10 million in sales," and/or "I want organizations in my geographic area that have between 60 and 200 employees." The system will download or print out the name of the organization, the address, all of the principals (the president, vice president, and other officers), the type of organization (i.e., the product or service), and other information. This could be your entire job-search list! You can look at that list and do some weeding, "Oh, I'm not interested in this organization. Yes, I'm interested in that one." And you'd refine your target list.

How to access the New York Public Library's directories and guides online. You can now search the New York Public Library's directories and guides via the Internet. Go to: www.nypl.org/research/sibl/guides. The page "Research Guides" will appear. There are a limited number of topics on this page, but if one is of interest to you, click

on it; these guides will lead you to a variety of websites, databases, and directories to speed your search.

Also on the "Research Guides" page, click on "Industry Specific Directories," which will open a page **containing links to about 75 industries and professions**. Clicking on one of these will open another page with a list of directories for that topic. Use this list to see if any of these seem helpful and call your local library (or the closest major library in a nearby city or at a nearby college) to see if they have what you want. Join the library online so you can access the databases from your home computer!

These lists are updated regularly. The "Job Targets" section at the back of this book lists the best of these references.

Library-Selected Job Boards—General and Specific

To browse job boards that librarians have researched, go to www.nypl.org/branch. Then access the Mid-Manhattan Library by scrolling down the page and clicking on "Job Information." When the "Job Information Center/Mid-Manhattan Library" page appears, go to "Internet Resources" and click on "Job Search Resources on the Internet." The page titled "Employment" opens. If you click on "Job Searching—General Resources," you will get a listing of job boards with links to all of them. These have been selected by the librarians as the best general job boards. This list is updated every few days.

If you go back to the page marked "Employment," click on "Job Listings—Specific Categories." This will open a page with a list of about 25 categories. Clicking on a specific category will open another page with links for job boards specific to that category. These links are updated regularly by the library staff.

The bibliography in our Members Only area is a great resource containing much more information than is at the back of this book, although in the book it's very handy. Sometimes I meet with a client who says, "I don't know how I can find out the names of organizations in this target area" or "How can I find out about these industries?" I just reach for the *bibliography* at the back of the book and look up the industries in which they're interested. I can point out, "Well, here are five or six sources you might consider—just to find out what's going on in that industry."

Contacting the Company or Organization to Find the Name of the Right Person to Contact

Obviously, it's easy to build lists of *organizations,* but the names of the right people can be more elusive. So, sometimes you just *have* to call the organization and *probe* to find the right person to contact. For example, if you're in customer service, you can call up an organization and say, "May I have the name of the head of customer service?" or "I have to send some correspondence to your head of customer service. Who would that be?" Sometimes you can call and ask for the right person, but sometimes you need to *write* to someone asking for the correct name. (See the chapter, "Handling the Telephone: A Life Skill.")

This can be tough, so brainstorm with your small group to see how you can get the information *you* need for developing your target list. Make sure you get your group to help you. That's why we *have* small groups. You need *other* people's brains to help you in your search. And it's not just enough to get advice from your friends.

Job Postings

Many websites list job postings: Monster.com, AOL, and many field- and industry-specific sites. These sites help you find out who is hiring—even if the postings are not right for you. You don't necessarily need to apply for those jobs, but these sites do give you an idea of what's happening. Consider Businessweek.com, for example. If you click on careers from their home page, you'll find a link entitled, "Who's hiring, looking for an organization?" Clicking there will bring up a huge list of organizations alphabetically with their job postings, a list of the organization job sites, and links to organization websites. See the bibliography of this book for many additional sources.

Classified Ads

Many job hunters place false hopes on the "help wanted" pages. We know most good jobs are never listed in the classified ads and you'll face stiff competitors when you do answer ads. However, studying the ads can be useful. Look at the ads to see *who's hiring*. It doesn't matter whether they list jobs that are appropriate for you. If they're hiring and you're interested in the *organization,* add them to your target list. A Five O'Clock Club maxim is to aim for organizations, not just the jobs. If that industry is not currently on your Personal Marketing Plan, perhaps it's time for you to start a new category.

And no grown-up will ever understand that this is a matter of so much importance!

Antoine de Saint-Exupéry, *The Little Prince*

Additional Resources

Jobvault.com (Vault.com) provides information on more than 1,200 organizations. If you click on "fashion," for example, it will bring up links to articles about the fashion industry and its leading players. You can click on health care, investment banking, and many other major industries. Vault.com doesn't offer information on minor industries; its goal is to provide you with the *inside scoop* on key industries *from a job hunter's point of view*. There are plenty of sites out there where you can find out about an industry from the investor's point of view, but Vault.com offers the *employee* perspective.

Wetfeet.com is a great site for an *introduction* to various industries.

The electric library (elibrary.com) costs about $10 a month and is especially useful for researching small organizations; it often contains full articles on companies that don't catch mainstream attention.

Government websites. Do you want to work for the government? Even at the state level, you will find abundant information. For example, if you wanted a job in Tennessee, try www.tennessee.gov and click on "A to Z Departments and Agencies." It's exciting to see the list of departments. Starting with "A," the listings include the appellate courts, the department of agriculture, the alcoholic beverage commission, the arts commission, and the attorney general. Review the various departments and see if there are a few that are of special interest to you. At the top of the Tennessee.gov home page is a link to "employment." You can search for jobs and submit an application. But you could also target specific agencies that interest you, send your résumé directly to them, call them, and tell them that you are specifically interested in their agency. If you have a specific agency or two in mind, add them to your target list.

Info track, at your library. Info track has full articles and recent stock reports on organizations. On the web, it's **www.Multex.com.** It offers research reports from international brokerage firms and research providers geared to corporate finance specialists, investment bankers, and institutional investors. Stock analyst reports will tell you what's happening in industries as well as in organizations.

PRNewswire.com. When companies and organizations issue press releases, they can also have them listed on prnewswire.com. This is a great way to find out what's going on in any industry you're targeting as well as the major players in that industry.

Nexus, at the library, is a great resource for finding out about a specific *person* to whom you may be talking.

Encyclopedia of Business Information Sources is also a book found at your library. It covers more than *1,000* subjects of interest to business. Select a topic, any topic. If you're interested in "oil," for example, it will tell you the trade journals and books having to do with oil, the associations to join, and helpful websites. If you're interested in rugs, you can find out everything that is happening in the rug industry. The same is true for banking, airlines, or whatever interests you. This is one of my favorite sources.

The "Job Bank" Series of Books

You may live in one of the areas covered by the *Job Bank* series. These are: Atlanta, Austin, Boston, Carolina, Chicago, Colorado, Connecticut, Dallas-Fort Worth, Detroit, Florida, Houston, Indiana, Las Vegas, Los Angeles, Minneapolis, Missouri, New Jersey, Metropolitan New York, Ohio, Philadelphia, Phoenix, Pittsburgh, Portland, San Francisco Bay Area, Seattle, Tennessee, Virginia, Metropolitan Washington, DC. These directories list the industries, as well as the organizations within those industries, and basic contact information. You'll still need to find the names of people to contact in each organization, but these books are great for developing your Personal Marketing Plan.

Not-for-Profits

Business and industry obviously attract a lot of attention and analysis, so it's relatively easy to develop lists of *for-profit* organizations. In the *not-for-profit* arena, you may need to do more digging. It's often helpful to get the annual reports of organizations working with *many* not-for-profits, such as United Way, Catholic Charities, United Jewish Appeal. Look through the annual report and see the agencies they contribute to. If any of them appeal to you, you're on your way to developing your target list.

Also, go to the *Encyclopedia of Associations* to find associations dealing with the not-for-profit areas that interest you. For example, the National Society for Fund Raising Executives is a tremendous organization, as is the Association of Association Executives.

Small and Private Companies

Business Week and *Inc. Magazine* both publish lists of small organizations. *The Encyclopedia of Business Information Sources,* mentioned earlier contains more than 1,000 subjects of interest and reference sources. *Dun & Bradstreet's,* (www.dnb.com), at your local public or business school library, has information on some 160,000 U.S. businesses that have indicated net worths of more than $500,000.

Hoover's Handbook of Private Companies has information on more than 900 nonpublic corporations, such as Milliken & Co. and PricewaterhouseCoopers; hospitals and health care organizations such as Blue Cross; charitable and membership organizations including the Ford Foundation; mutual and cooperative organizations such as IGA; joint ventures such as Motiva; government-owned corporations such as the Postal Service; and major university systems, including The University of Texas system.

Another good source is *Ward's Business Directory of U.S. Private and Public Companies,* which lists more than 114,500 companies, 90 percent of which are private. Locate potential clients and create targeted mailing lists in six volumes, arranged A–Z, geographically, by sales, and SIC or NAICS codes.

You can also use the *Small Business Sourcebook.* It is a guide to sources of information furnished by associations, consultants, educational programs, government agencies, franchisers, trade shows, and venture-capital firms for 100 types of small businesses.

The International Market

One terrific online source is the *Directory of Websites for International Jobs: The Click and Easy Guide (Click & Easy Series),* 2004, Ron and Caryl Krannich, Impact Publications,

www.impactpublications.com. Written by two career and international experts, this 45-page report reveals more than 600 websites for anyone seeking an overseas job.

For a serious search, also take a look at *The Directory of Foreign Firms Operating in the United States,* 2004, Uniworld Business Publications, www.uniworldbp.com. It has information on foreign firms with branches, subsidiaries, or affiliates in the United States. The foreign companies listed have a substantial investment in American operations— wholly or partially owned subsidiaries, affiliates, or branches.

The Directory of American Firms Operating in Foreign Countries, Uniworld Business Publications, www.uniworldbp.com, contains more than 3,600 U.S. firms with nearly 36,500 branches, subsidiaries, and affiliates in 187 countries. Available in hard cover, soft cover, and on CD-ROM, the directory consists of three volumes that encompass alphabetical lists of U.S. firms with operations abroad. Each entry contains the company's U.S. address, phone/fax, NAICS (North American Industrial Codes System) and description of principal product/service, and lists the foreign countries in which it has a branch, subsidiary, or affiliate.

Finally, there is www.ugamedia.com. You can find European consultants via a Google search. The site has links to more than 35 European portals and search engines.

Don't overlook the importance of worldwide thinking. A company that keeps its eye on every Tom, Dick and Harry is going to miss Pierre, Hans and Yoshio.

Al Ries and Jack Trout,
Positioning: The Battle for Your Mind

Two Kinds of Research

There are two kinds of research. *Primary* research means talking to people who are doing the kind of work you're interested in or people who *know* something about those industries or organizations. You can get in touch with such people through networking or by contacting them directly. *Primary research simply means talking to people.*

Secondary research is reading materials in print, at the library, or online. In a sense, secondary research is *removed* from the source—it is information written by and about people and organizations.

It is vital to conduct *both* primary and secondary research and keep a balance between the two. Some job hunters would rather spend their time talking with people during their job search. Others prefer to spend their time in the library or working at their computers. But whichever one you *prefer,* do more of the other. You need balanced sources of information in your search.

So, if you like to stay at home or in the library, get out more and talk to people. If you're a person who *loves* the Internet, don't kid yourself that you'll get hired online! And don't *waste* time online and claim you've spent *hours* on job search! Be careful how you spend your time online. Or if you're the type who likes to meet people and press the flesh, spend some time at your computer or in the library so you will sound intelligent and well informed when you have meetings.

Primary research—talking to people—doesn't just happen in offices. You're researching when you're talking to people on a bus or a plane or at a coffee shop. They ask, "What do *you* do for a living?" You say, "Well, this is what I do and this is what I am interested in doing next." They may be able to tell you something about the industry you're interested in. That's research—and it does happen!

You're researching when you go to an *association* meeting, talk to people there, and find out more about what is happening in the industry. You can research while you're at a *party*. These are all examples of primary research—talking to people.

Time to Move On

If you've researched smartly and thoroughly, your Personal Marketing Plan should have taken shape nicely—at least a rudimentary version of it. Now it's time to start contacting the companies and organizations on your target lists. Maybe you've been itching to do this all along, but it was better to spend time *planning* first. Now you're on your way!

In this high-risk society, each person's main asset will be his or her willingness and ability to take intelligent risks. Those people best able to cope with uncertainty—whether by temperament, by talent, or by initial endowment of wealth—will fare better in the long run than those who cling to security.

Michael Mandel, *The High-Risk Society*

The greatest obstacle to discovery is not ignorance— it is the illusion of knowledge.

Edward Bond, *Washington Post*, January 29, 1984

The
Five
O'Clock
Club

PART FOUR
Knowing the Right People

HOW TO GET INTERVIEWS IN YOUR TARGET AREAS

(If you already have interviews, go to Part Five.)

The
Five
O'Clock
Club

Conducting a Campaign to Get Interviews in Your Target Markets

The codfish lays ten thousand eggs,
The homely hen lays one.
The codfish never cackles
To tell you what she's done.
And so we scorn the codfish,
While the humble hen we prize,
Which only goes to show you
That it pays to advertise.

Anonymous

An Overview of the Strategy for Your First Campaign

If the only tool you have is a hammer,
you tend to see every problem as a nail.

Abraham Maslow

B y now, you have developed preliminary job targets and conducted a Preliminary Target Investigation (through networking, the Internet, and the library) to see which targets are worth pursuing.

Then you selected those you think are worth a full campaign and ranked them in the order in which you want to conduct those campaigns. You are ready to conduct a campaign to contact every organization in your first target. When you are busy meeting with people in Target 1, you will start the campaign preparation for Target 2.

Do not expect to get a job through:

- **Networking**
- **Direct contact**
- **Search firms**
- **Ads (even on the Internet)**

These are techniques for getting *meetings*, **not jobs.**

After you get the meeting, you can think about what to do next to *perhaps* **turn it into a job. (See the chapters on Follow-Up in our book** *Mastering the Job Interview and Winning the Money Game*.**)**

A Personal Marketing Plan, which you may show to your networking contacts, contains your list of targets, including the organizations in each of those targets. This plan forms the overview of your search.

For Target 1 you will now:

1. **Research to develop a list of all the organizations,** if you have not already done so. Find out—through networking, the Internet, or other research—the names of the people you should contact in the appropriate departments in each of those organizations.

2. **Develop your cover letter.** Paragraph 1 is the opening; Paragraph 2 is a summary about yourself appropriate for this target; Paragraph 3 contains your bulleted accomplishments ("You may be interested in some of the things I've done"); Paragraph 4 is the close. (Many sample letters appear later in this book.)

3. **Develop your plan for getting a large number of meetings in this target.** There are four basic techniques for meeting people in each of the areas you have targeted for a full campaign. In the following chapters, you will learn more about them. They are:

- networking,
- direct contact (direct mail, targeted mail, walk-in, cold call),
- search firms, and
- ads (both print and online).

Do not think of these as techniques for getting *jobs*, but as techniques for getting *meetings*. After the meeting, think about what to do next to keep the relationship going or perhaps to turn the interview into a job offer.

Organize the names of the people you want to contact, and develop strategies for contacting them.

Only 5 to 10 percent of all job leads are through search firms, and another 5 to 10 percent are through ads. You do not have much control over these leads: you have to *wait* for an ad to appear, and *wait* for a search firm to send you on an interview. Both networking and direct contact are *proactive* techniques you can use to get meetings in your target market. In networking, you contact someone simply by using someone else's name. In direct contact, you contact someone directly—usually after you have done some research and know something about him or her. Networking and direct contact complement each other and gain added effectiveness when used together. You may start your campaign either with direct contact (if you know your target area very well) or with networking (to research an area you don't know well or find a way to contact people), and introduce the other technique as your campaign progresses.

Consider all four techniques for getting meetings, but spend most of your energy and brainpower on networking and direct contact.

Selecting the Techniques

> *Do not be too timid and squeamish about your actions. All life is an experiment.*
> Ralph Waldo Emerson

Select the techniques most appropriate for the industry or profession you are targeting, as well as for your own personality. Each technique can work, but the strength of your campaign lies in your ability to use what is best for your particular situation. Contact as many potential employers as possible and then *campaign* to keep your name in front of them.

Use all of the techniques to:

- Learn more about your target area.
- Test what you are offering.
- Let people know you are looking.
- Contact people in a position to hire you.

> *Opportunities are multiplied as they are seized.*
> Sun Tzu, *The Art of War*

The Myth of How to Get Interviews: Consider Contacting Organizations Directly

Search firms. Ads. Networking. Ask most people how to get interviews, and they'll mention those ways. But The Five O'Clock Club wanted to find out what really works. Its survey of professionals, managers, and executives clearly shows that *job hunters get more meetings for the time spent through "direct contact" than through any other single technique.*

Articles abound to prove the importance of networking. However, Five O'Clock Club research shows that direct contact is a more efficient way to generate meetings.

Networking means using someone else's name to get a meeting. *Direct contact* means aggressively pursuing people whom you may have known in the past or people you have never met. These might include association members or people identified on the Internet, through newspaper or magazine articles, or from library research. (For entry-level people, direct contact even includes going from one human resources office to another in an office center.) Here are the survey results:

- **Direct contact is the most time-efficient way to get meetings.** Surveyed job hunters spent 45 percent of their time networking, yet networking accounted for only 35 percent of their meetings. On the other hand, surveyed job hunters spent 24 percent of their time on direct contact, resulting in 27 percent of their meetings. Networking is very time-consuming. You have to find people who are willing to let you use their names. With direct contact, there is no middle person.

- **Even executives got almost 1/3 of their meetings through direct contact.** It's a myth that executives must rely on networking to get in to see people more senior than they are. Our surveyed senior executives did in fact get 62 percent of their meetings through networking, but almost 30 percent of their meetings resulted from their contacting executives to whom they had not been referred. Executives should not overlook direct contact.

- **People making a career continuation relied on direct contact even more than networking.** People looking to stay in the same industry or field got about one-third of their meetings through direct contact and a little less by using someone else's name to get a meeting. The job searchers contacted strangers, and got meetings because of their accomplishments—and their discipline in working follow-up phone calls.

- **Even career changers (42 percent of those surveyed) got 20 percent of their meetings through direct contact.** Career changers often feel they should network to meet people in new fields or industries. However, direct contact can also result in meetings.

- **Search firms accounted for only 8 percent of meetings; newspaper ads accounted for 7 percent; online job boards accounted for 13 percent.** Everyone makes the mistake of placing too much emphasis on published openings. Contact organizations that don't publicize openings now, and stay in touch with them. This increases the chance they'll hire *you*, rather than post the job, when they need help.

We want our job hunters to consider all four techniques for getting meetings in their target markets. See what's working for you.

Using Search Firms

If you are looking for a position that naturally follows your most recent one, you can immediately contact search firms. As I've mentioned, only about 5 to 10 percent of all professional and managerial positions are filled by search firms, so it would seem logical to spend only 5 percent of your effort on them. However, certain professions use search firms more than others do.

Contact reputable search firms that handle positions in your target area. If you don't already have relationships with search firms, find the good ones by asking managers which search firms they use or recommend. Remember, search firms are rarely able to help career changers.

Answering Ads

Five to 10 percent of all jobs are filled through ads—both print and Internet. The odds are against you, so don't spend too much thought or energy on them. And don't sit home hoping for a response. Just answer the ad—as long as it sounds close to what you have to offer—and get on with your search. Maybe you'll hear from them—maybe you won't. (See the chapters in this book on "How to Answer Ads" and "What to Do When You Know There's a Job Opening.")

You must call each thing by its proper name, or that which must get done will not.

A. Harvey Block, President, Bokenon Systems

Networking

Studies show that about 60 to 70 percent of all positions are filled through networking. This is partly because most job hunters mistakenly refer to talking to people as "networking," no matter *how* they wound up talking to them. For example, Pete just found a job. I asked how he got the initial meeting. He said, "Through networking." When I asked him to tell me more, he said, "I'm an accountant,

originally from Australia. There is an association here of accountants from Australia. I sent for a list of all the members, and wrote to all of them. That's how I got the job."

Pete got the job lead through a direct-mail campaign, *not* through networking. That's why the survey numbers are off, and that's why you should consider using every technique for getting meetings in your target market. You never know where your leads will come from.

Networking simply means getting to see someone by using another person's name. You are using a contact to get in. You want to see the person *whether or not they have a job for you.* This technique is essential if you want to change careers, because you can get in to see people even if you are not qualified in the traditional sense. To stay in the same field, you can network to get information on which organizations are hiring, which are the best ones to work for, and so on.

Networking can lead you in directions you had not considered and can open up new targets to pursue. You can network to explore even if you are not sure you want to change jobs right now. What's more, it's a technique you can use *after* you land that new job, whenever you get stuck and need advice.

Networking is more popular today than ever before and it is effective when used properly. But, depending on your target, it is not always the most *efficient* way to get meetings. Furthermore, it sometimes gets a bad name because even though people are constantly networking, they often are doing it incorrectly. Learn how to network correctly (see the chapters on networking), but combine targeted mailings (a direct-contact technique) with your networking when you are aiming at small organizations or ones with very few jobs appropriate for you. Networking your way into all of them could take forever. Also, directly contact other people when you would have great trouble getting a networking contact. If the direct contact doesn't work, you can always network in later.

When you combine direct mailing with networking, you can cover the market with a direct-mail campaign and then network certain sections of that market. Or you can network in to see someone, and then perhaps get a list of names you can use for further networking or a direct-mail campaign.

If you do not cover your market, you risk losing out. You may find out later that they "just filled a job a few months ago—too bad we didn't know you were looking." Be thorough. Let *everyone* in your target market know that you are looking.

The beginning of wisdom is to call things by their right names.

Chinese proverb

Direct-Contact Campaigns

Writing directly to executives is a consistently effective technique for generating meetings. Twenty to 40 percent of all jobs are found this way and more jobs would result from this technique if more job hunters knew about it. You can write to lots of organizations (direct mail) or a few (targeted mail). The techniques are quite different.

Direct contact can save time. You can quickly test your target to see if there are job possibilities for someone like you. If you are familiar with your target area, you can develop your list, compose your letter, send it out, and start on your next target, all within a matter of weeks. Most job hunters contact larger corporations, ignoring smaller firms. Yet new jobs are being created in smaller organizations, so don't overlook them.

Direct contact is also the only technique that allows you to quickly contact *every* employer in the area of interest to you. You are essentially blanketing the market. Networking, on the other hand, is spotty by nature: You get to see only those organizations where your contact knows someone. Direct contact is effective for an out-of-town job search. And this technique works whether you are employed or unemployed. It works for all job levels.

This technique is an effective one for career changers. You can state all the positive things you offer and leave out anything not helpful to your case. Those things can be handled at the meeting.

Direct contact can help you get in to see someone you know you cannot network in to see. Shelli, for example, wanted to see someone very senior in an industry in which she had no experience. But she knew the field would be a good fit for her—she researched the industry and figured out how her background could fit in. She targeted six organizations and was able to network into two of them. She knew she would not be able to network into the other four organizations within a reasonable time frame: It would take her months to find someone who could only *possibly* help her get in to see the people she'd need to see.

Instead of networking, she researched each of the four organizations, wrote to the senior people she was targeting at each one, and followed up with a phone call. Because of her presentation, three of the executives agreed to see her. This saved her many months in her search. Sometimes a targeted mailing can be *more* effective than networking in getting in to see important people. It takes more brainpower than networking, but you already have that.

Direct contact primarily involves targeted and direct mailing, but a junior person can also go from organization to organization to talk to personnel departments or store managers. As long as job hunters follow up, this technique can work. An executive client of mine used this technique effectively by walking into a small, privately owned, prestigious store, speaking with the store manager to find out the name of the president, and then calling the president. It led to an executive position with that company. This was "direct contact" because he did not use someone's name

to get in to see the store manager or the president. Even when I was very young, I used direct contact to get in to see virtually anyone I wanted.

Sometimes I had trouble getting in, but people eventually saw me because I usually had a good reason, did my homework, didn't waste their time, was sincere about why I wanted to see them, and was gently persistent. It suits my personality because I am shy about using someone else's name for the core of my effort, I am comfortable about putting my effort into research and writing, and I don't have the time it takes to see a lot of people who may not be right on target for me. As I go along, I network when appropriate.

Direct contact also includes cold calls, which can work for some personalities in some industries.

We will now focus on targeted mail and direct mail:

Targeted mailings are similar to networking. You target a relatively small number of people (e.g., fewer than 20 or 30) and try to see all of them, *whether or not they have a job for you.* Instead of already having a person to contact, you *establish* your own contact through the research you do. The meeting is handled exactly the same as a networking meeting.

Direct mail is used when you have a large number of organizations to contact (e.g., 200 or more). You mail a brilliant package to all of them and expect seven or eight meetings from the mailing.

---

*If I had eight hours to chop down a tree,
I'd spend six sharpening my ax.*

Abraham Lincoln

Using All of the Techniques

A good campaign usually relies on more than one technique to get meetings. Think of how you can divide up your target list. For example, if you have a list of 200 organizations in your target area, you may decide you can network into 20 of them, do a targeted mailing (with follow-up phone calls) to another 20 or 30, and do a direct-mail campaign to the rest. This way you have both blanketed your market and used the most appropriate technique to reach each organization in your target area. In addition, you could also contact search firms and answer ads.

Networking vs. Direct Mail

Let's use the banking industry as an example.

You could easily network your way into a large bank. You could find someone who knew someone at a number of them. Each contact you'd make at a large bank could refer you to other people within the same bank, which would increase your chances of getting a job there. Since one person knows others within that organization, networking is efficient. You can meet many potential hiring managers within one organization.

On the other hand, it may be difficult to network into smaller banks. Fewer of your friends are likely to know someone there, because each small bank has far fewer employees. Each networking meeting would represent fewer jobs and fewer referrals within each bank. Referrals to other small banks would also generally represent fewer jobs than the larger banks have. It could take forever to network to the same number of potential jobs at hundreds of small banks that could easily be covered by networking at large banks. Networking can be inefficient with smaller organizations and you may find that you can't put a dent in the market.

You could contact smaller banks directly. They do not expect you to know someone who works there, so they are more open to intelligent mailings. They tend to get fewer contacts from job hunters. You could categorize the smaller banks in a way that makes sense to you—those strong in international banking, for example, or those strong in lending. Or you could categorize banks by nationality—grouping the Japanese banks, European banks, South American banks, and so on. Then you could *target each segment* with a cover letter customized for that market.

Decide which techniques are best for you. Think about how people tend to get hired within your target industry and profession. Also consider your own circumstances, such as whether you are currently employed, how much freedom you have to go on networking meetings, how much use you can make of the phone, and so on. You can always network your way into a few specific organizations, but networking into a great number is sometimes not possible.

Remember, networking requires a great deal of time and travel. Direct mail is often appealing to those who are working and must ration their meeting and travel time.

A word of caution to very senior executives: Because of your extensive networks, you may be tempted to rely exclusively on them to find your next position. As extensive as they are, your contacts are probably spotty. You may be reluctant to do research because you are used to having others do such things for you. Do your research anyway. Define your targets. List all of the organizations in your target areas that are appropriate for you and the names of the people you need to see in each of these organizations. Most very senior executives skip this step and get their next position serendipitously. That's just fine—if the position is right for you. But many senior executives in their eagerness to land something quickly may land something inappropriate, beneath what they deserve, or nothing at all. If you have listed all of the people you should see in your target areas, you increase your chances of having a thorough campaign and you will not miss out on a good possibility for yourself.

If you can network in to see the people you should see in your target market, fine. But if you can think of no way

to network in, contact them directly. You will get plenty of serendipitous leads and meet plenty of people who have business ideas and want to form partnerships with you. These opportunities may be fine, but they are better if you can compare them with those you uncover through an organized search.

Things which matter most must never be at the mercy of things which matter least.

Goethe

In Summary

Make a list of all the people you should meet in *each* of your target areas or, at the very least, make a list of all the organizations in your target areas. Intend to contact all of them. Get meetings with people in your target area through networking, direct contact, search firms, and ads (print and online). Do not think of these as techniques for getting *jobs,* but as techniques for getting *meetings.* Plan how you can contact or meet the *right* people in *every* organization in each of your target areas as quickly as possible.

After the meeting, either keep in touch with networking-type contacts (regardless of how you met them) or think about what you can do next to *perhaps* turn the interview into a job offer.

Getting Polished for a Full Campaign

Although action is typical of the American style, thought and planning are not; it is considered heresy to state that some problems are not immediately or easily solvable.

Daniel Bell, sociologist, *Daedalus*

Before the meeting, be prepared: know exactly what you want and what you have to offer. In the next chapter, you will prepare your pitch to organizations. Have your pitch ready even *before* you contact anyone—just so you are prepared. Read the chapters on interviewing in our book *Mastering the Job Interview and Winning the Money Game,* and *practice.* Be a polished interviewer. Remember the cliché: "You don't get a second chance to make a good first impression."

After you have practiced interviewing, contact the people on your "hit list." Start with those who are less important to you, so you can practice and learn more about your target area. You will want to know, for example, your chances in that market and how you should position yourself.

After you have met with someone, follow up. This method works. Read the chapters on following up. Once you have contacted a target area, contact it again a few months later. Keep following up with the people you meet.

121

Read magazines and newspapers. Attend organizational meetings. Keep abreast of what is happening in the field. Keep on networking.

Begin at the beginning . . . and go on
till you come to the end: then stop.

Lewis Carroll

A Promotional Campaign to Get Meetings

Sometimes I say to a client who is shy, "So far, you and I are the only ones who know you are looking for a job." Get your name out there. Get on the inside track. You must conduct a promotional campaign to contact as many potential employers as possible. *Campaign* to make sure they remember you.

Make a lot of contacts with people in a position to hire or recommend you. If there are sparks between you, and if you help them remember you, you will be the one they call when a job comes up. Or they can give you the names of others to contact. They may even create a job for you if it makes sense.

The goal of your promotional campaign is to let the *right* people know what you are seeking. Some discussions will become job interviews, which will lead to offers. Get a lot of meetings so you will have a number of offers to consider. You want options.

Focus on getting *meetings* in your target area. People who focus on *getting a job* can get uptight when they have a meeting. They do not think of themselves as *looking around* or *finding out what is out there.* They act as if they are in a display case hoping someone will buy them. They may accept the first offer that comes along—even when they know it is inappropriate—because they think they will never get another one.

If you aim to make lots of contacts and get lots of meetings, you are more likely to keep your perspective. If you are an inexperienced job hunter, talk to some people who are not in a position to hire you. Practice your lines and your techniques. Get experience in talking about yourself, and learn more about your target market. Then you will be more relaxed in important meetings and will be able to let your personality come through.

Labor not as one who is wretched, nor yet as one who would be
pitied or admired. Direct yourself to one thing only, to put
yourself in motion and to check yourself at all times.

Marcus Aurelius Antonius, *Meditations*

You Are the Manager of This Campaign

You are in control of this promotional campaign. After reading this book you will know what to say, how to say it, and to whom. You will select which promotional

techniques to use and when and learn how to measure the effectiveness of your campaign.

You will also decide on your image. You can present any picture of yourself you like. You present your image and credentials in your written communications—résumé, cover letters, and follow-up notes. You have *complete* control over what you put in them and how you present yourself.

How you act and dress are also important to your image. Look like you're worth the money you would like. Watch your posture—sit up straight. *Smile!* Decide to feel good and to feel confident. Smile some more. Smile again. Smiling makes you look confident and competent and gives you extra energy. It is difficult to smile and continue being down. Even when you are at home working on your search, smile every once in a while to give yourself energy and the right attitude to help you move ahead. This is true no matter what your level. Even executives are better off doing this as they go through their searches. The ones who cannot do this tend to do less well than those who can.

Whether direct contact or networking, search firms or ads, choose techniques most likely to result in a good response from your target—techniques appropriate to your situation. When you become an expert, change a technique to suit yourself.

Modify your approach or even abandon an effort that is ineffective. You want a good response from your promotional efforts. A *response* is a meeting. A polite rejection letter does not count as a response. Some organizations have a policy of sending letters and some have a policy against them. Rejection letters have nothing to do with you. They do not count. Only meetings count.

This is a campaign to generate meetings. Your competition is likely to have polished presentations. Decide on the message you want to get across in the meeting, and practice it. There are two kinds of meetings: information-gathering (networking) meetings and actual job interviews. Do not try to turn every meeting into a job interview. You will turn people off—and lessen the chances of getting a job. *In the beginning, you are aiming for contact or networking meetings.* (See the chapters on networking meetings, as well as information on handling the job interview, in our book *Mastering the Job Interview and Winning the Money Game.*)

When things do not work, there is a reason. Be aware and correct the situation. There is no point in continuing an unsuccessful campaign. Remember, when things go wrong—as they will—it is not personal. This is strictly business. It is a project. With experience, you will become better at managing your promotional campaigns to get meetings.

Why Stagger Your Campaigns?

Why is it unwise to start all of your campaigns at once? Let's pretend your first target is the telephone industry, and your second target is the environmental industry. If one day you talk to a telephone company and the next day you talk to an environmental organization, you will not sound credible. When you meet with the environmental organization, it does you no good to mention that you met with the telephone company.

If, however, you talk to someone in a telephone company, and then another person in the same or another telephone company, you can say, "I'm talking to four different divisions of your firm right now and I'm also talking to other phone companies." Then it sounds as if you really want to work in their industry.

Similarly, when you want to talk to an environmental organization, you can mention you are talking to a lot of environmental organizations. The information you learn at one organization will make you sound smarter with the next.

As you research and meet with people in a target area, the target becomes richer and less superficial. In the beginning of a search, for example, you may be interested in health care, which is too broad a target. Later, however, you may find that the field is more complex than you thought and learn that people's jobs are not at all what an outsider would expect.

You are an insider when you give back non-proprietary information, such as: "Do you know that Southern Bell has a fulfillment system very similar to yours?"

Or you can say to an environmental organization: "I've been talking to a lot of environmental organizations and it seems that a trend in this industry right now is _____. Do you agree?"

This methodical search is the only smart way to do it because you gain momentum. Most job hunters simply "go on interviews," but that's not enough in this economy. Organizations expect you to know something about them.

On the following page is one Club member's Personal Marketing Plan. There are additional plans in our book *Targeting a Great Career.* You may want to use them as a model for your own.

Sample Personal Marketing Plan

Personal Marketing Plan: Joe Doakes

TARGET FUNCTIONS: VICE PRESIDENT/DIRECTOR/MANAGER

- Management Information Services
- Applications Development
- Information Systems
- Information Systems Technology
- Systems Development
- Business Reengineering

RESPONSIBILITIES:

- Identification of new information systems technologies and how they could affect the profitability of a company.
- Management of projects for the implementation of information systems or new technologies.
- Providing for and managing a business partner relationship between the information systems department and the internal company departments that use their services.
- Implementing and managing a business partner relationship among the company and its primary vendors and its customers using systems technologies, such as EDI (Electronic Data Interchange).

TARGET COMPANIES:

Attributes

- People-oriented
- Growth-minded through increased sales, acquisitions, or new products
- Committed to quality customer service
- Receptive to new ideas on how to do business or using new technologies

Location

- Primary—Northern New Jersey or Westchester/Orange/Rockland Counties in New York
- Secondary—New York City, Central New Jersey, Southern Connecticut, Eastern Pennsylvania
- Other—anywhere along the Eastern Seaboard

TARGET INDUSTRIES:

Consumer Products:	Pharmaceuticals:	Food/Beverage:	Chemicals:	Other:
Unilever	Merck	Pepsico	Castrol	Medco
Kimberly-Clark	Schering-Plough	T.J. Lipton	Witco	Toys-R-Us
Avon	Warner-Lambert	Kraft/General Foods	Allied Chemical	Computer Associates
Carter Wallace	American Home Products	Nabisco	Olin Corp.	Becton Dickinson
Sony	Bristol-Myers Squibb	Hartz Mountain	Union Carbide	Dialogic
Minolta	Pfizer	Continental Baking	Air Products	Siemens
Boyle Midway	Jannsen Pharmaceutica	Nestlé	General Chemical	Automatic Data Proc.
Revlon	Hoffmann-LaRoche	Häagen-Dazs	Englehard Corp.	Vital Signs
L&F Products	Ciba-Geigy	Tuscan Dairies	BASF Corp.	Benjamin Moore
Houbigant	Sandoz	Dannon Co.	Degussa Corp.	
Mem	A.L. Laboratories	BSN Foods	GAF Corp.	
Chanel	Smith Kline Beecham	Campbell Soup	Lonza Inc.	
Airwick	American Cyanamid	Cadbury Beverages	Sun Chemical	
Church & Dwight	Boeringer Ingelheim	Labatt		
Johnson & Johnson	Roberts Pharmaceuticals	Arnold Foods		
Reckitt & Colman	Winthrop Pharmaceuticals	S. B. Thomas		
Philip Morris	Glaxo	Sunshine Biscuits		
Clairol	Block Drug			
Estée Lauder	Hoechst Celanese			
Cosmair	Ethicon			

Campaign Checklist

Aim for a critical mass of activity that will make things happen, help you determine your true place in this market, and give you a strong bargaining position.

I plan to approach this target using the following techniques:

1. Do research (gather information at the library and through the Internet).
2. Network (gather information through people).
3. Conduct a direct-mail or targeted-mail campaign.
4. Contact selected search firms.
5. Join one or two relevant trade organizations.
6. Regularly read trade magazines and newspapers.
7. Follow up with "influence" notes.
8. Follow up with key contacts on a monthly basis.
9. Answer ads.
10. Aim to give out as much information as I get.

The best techniques for you to use to get meetings depend on your personality and your target market.

For certain targets, search firms may be the most important technique for getting meetings. In other fields, my own for example, people *rarely* get job leads through search firms. When you are networking in your target market, ask people: "Are there certain search firms you tend to use? How do you go about hiring people?"

If I insist that my work be rewarding, that it mustn't be tedious or monotonous, I'm in trouble. . . . Time after time it fails to become so. So I get more agitated about it, I fight with people about it, I make more demands about it. . . . It's ridiculous to demand that work always be pleasurable, because work is not necessarily pleasing; sometimes it is, sometimes it isn't. If we're detached and simply pick up the job we have to do and go ahead and do it, it's usually fairly satisfying. Even jobs that are repugnant or dull or tedious tend to be quite satisfying, once we get right down to doing them. . . . One of the routine jobs I get every once in a while comes from putting out a little magazine. You have to sort the pages. It's a simple, routine, mechanical sort of job. . . . I never realized that this would be one of the most satisfying parts of the whole thing, just standing there sorting pages. This happens when we just do what we have to do.

Thomas Merton, *The Springs of Contemplation*

Information on Research; Additional Personal Marketing Plans

See our book *Targeting a Great Career* for a thorough discussion of how to research your targets (four chapters on research and a 50-page annotated bibliography on the subject, the best on the market). You will also find additional examples of Personal Marketing Plans, including an extensive write-up for targeting the Internet job market.

The
Five
O'Clock
Club

Your Two-Minute Pitch:
The Keystone of Your Search

If I venture to displace, by even the billionth part of an inch, the microscopical speck of dust which lies now upon the point of my finger, what is the character of that act upon which I have adventured? I have done a deed which shakes the Moon in her path, which causes the Sun to be no longer the Sun, and which alters forever the destiny of the multitudinous myriads of stars that roll and glow in the majestic presence of their Creator.

Edgar Allen Poe, *An Essay on the Material and Spiritual Universe*

> **If your pitch—the way you position yourself—is wrong, everything else about your search is wrong.**

Navigating the Minefield

The *Two-Minute Pitch* is the answer to the question, "So, tell me about yourself." With a great pitch, people are more likely to see you as *appropriate* for the kind of job you're going after. However, as we say at The Five O'Clock Club, "If your pitch is wrong, everything is wrong." You may have an interview every day and be absolutely brilliant in those meetings, but employers will not see you as appropriate for their jobs if your pitch is wrong.

The top of your résumé is the *written* positioning of yourself. The Two-Minute Pitch is the *verbal* positioning of yourself. And they must correspond. So, the top of Wally's résumé reads:

**Web Press Supervisor
with 20 years' experience
and an emphasis on quality and productivity**

In an interview, when an employer says, "So, tell me about yourself," Wally could start out with the verbal version of that same pitch, such as, "I'm a web press supervisor with over 20 years' experience. I've always emphasized

quality and productivity. For example . . ." And then he would go into examples of his accomplishments, which may even correspond to some of the bulleted accomplishments at the top of his résumé.

If your résumé is done well, *I should be able to pick it up and recite a pretty good Two-Minute Pitch right from your summary.* For example, here's a pitch right from Elliott's new résumé: "I'm a marketing manager with 15 years in the leisure and sporting good industry" and so on. Test your own résumé and see if your pitch is that clear.

People tend to pitch themselves incorrectly unless they're thinking clearly about their positioning. Here's a typical example. I was chatting with Kathy before the start of a Five O'Clock Club meeting. Here's the way the conversation went:

Kate: So, what field are you in, Kathy?
Kathy: Banking.
Kate (sensing her positioning was incorrect): Well, I doubt that. What do you *do* in banking?
Kathy: Customer service.

Kathy worked in customer service, not banking. She was positioning herself incorrectly. This doesn't matter so much when she's talking to *me,* but it does matter when she's trying to get a customer service job.

Many job hunters have to reposition themselves, if only to emphasize certain parts of their backgrounds and downplay others. Figure out the kind of job you want to have next, and make sure that your résumé—and your verbal pitch—make you look appropriate to that target market.

Sugar, Sugar, Sugar: Use the Jargon of the Industry You Are Targeting

Cheryl had been in a sales position in the *sugar* business. In her small group, Cheryl talked about bulk sugar, liquid sugar, brown sugar, white sugar, sugar cubes, truckloads of sugar, and train-car-loads of sugar. Everything was sugar, sugar, sugar! Yet Cheryl wanted a job in the bulk food business.

It's easy for an outsider to see that Cheryl simply needs to say *bulk food* instead of *sugar.* But when it's happening to you, it can be much more difficult to see that *you are positioning yourself incorrectly.*

Use the jargon and the words of your new industry. If you don't *know* the new jargon, then you must learn it. You cannot pass the translation responsibility on to the people who will be interviewing you.

Cheryl may think, "If I can sell sugar, they should be able to *see* that I can sell food." But they think Cheryl's committed to the sugar industry. It is *her* responsibility to show them that she understands and can fit into the new target industry by using their jargon.

Eventually Cheryl learned to say *food* instead of *sugar.* She soon got a terrific job in the food industry. A few years later, she repositioned herself again and got a terrific job in the computer software industry!

Where Your Pitch Is Used

Your Two-Minute Pitch is the backbone of your search. You'll use it in job and networking interviews, and in your cover letters. You'll be ready when someone calls and says, "So tell me about yourself."

Your résumé summary statement could serve as the starting point for your pitch. Keep in mind:

- to whom you are pitching;
- what they are interested in;
- who your likely competitors are; and
- what you bring to the party that your competitors do not.

Think about your target audience and what you want to say to them. Examine your background to find things that fit.

All managers establish relationships over their careers . . . the unsavvy [managers] form fewer of those relationships. They are also more likely to let relationships fade when they move on to new positions. . . . The savvy managers . . . consistently seek to build relationships and then keep them up once they move on. It doesn't take much time, just a phone call now and then to ask, How are you doing?

Joel M. DeLuca, Ph.D., *Political Savvy*

Your Pitch in a Networking Meeting

The format for a networking meeting is covered in much more detail elsewhere. Use this same format whether you get in to see someone through a targeted mailing or by using someone else's name. They are both networking meetings. Here is the format, briefly, so you can see where your pitch fits in:

1. Exchange pleasantries—so the manager will focus on you.

2. Tell the manager why you're there, such as, "Jane suggested I contact you because she thought that you could give me the information I need. I'm interested in moving into the sports marketing field."

3. Then the manager will say, "Fine. What questions would you like to ask me?" Rather than ask questions at this point, say, "I do have questions, but first I'd like to tell you a little about myself." And then you give your Two-Minute Pitch: "I'm an accounting manager with strong Lotus Notes background," and so on.

That's how the Two-Minute Pitch fits into the networking meeting.

Your Pitch in a Job Interview

When you have a job interview, you are likely to be asked, "So Jane, tell me a little bit about yourself." If you have not done your homework and you know nothing about the company, you will be in trouble. Find out something about them *before* you give your pitch. Otherwise, you will not know how to position yourself.

So, for example, you could say, "There are a lot of things I have to say about myself, but I'd like to keep it relevant to your situation. What do you see as your needs right now?" Or say, "I can tell you a lot about myself, but first I'd like to know what it was about my cover letter or résumé that made you call me in."

Once they tell you something about what is going on in the organization, then you will be able to position yourself appropriately. Know something about them before you give your Two-Minute Pitch.

Your Pitch in the Cover Letter

Your cover letters will be much more effective if you use The Five O'Clock Club format.

1. Paragraph one is your introduction. You might say, "I have been following Apex Chemicals for some time and admire your emphasis on tight controls. I, too, focus on the close monitoring of business units and would like to work in a place like yours. I think we should meet because you never know when you may need someone like me." Your opening paragraph is generally *specific to the company.*

2. Paragraph two contains your summary. *That is your pitch.* "I am a senior accountant with over five years' experience in Lotus Notes."

3. Paragraph three contains the bulleted accomplishments you think would be of most interest to this target market. "You may be interested in some of the specific things I've done:
   - Reduced expenses in 4 units, saving the company over $200,000. And so on.

4. Paragraph four is the close, where you ask for a meeting, such as: "I will call you in a few days to set up a mutually convenient time to meet." Then you'll follow up with a few phone calls.

The heights by great men reached and kept
Were not attained by sudden flight,
But they, while their companions slept,
Were toiling upward in the night.

Henry Wadsworth Longfellow

What's Wrong with This Pitch?

Take a look at the beginning of my client Joshua's pitch, and see if you can tell what's wrong: "I have 18 years' experience in education and training: in developing training programs, in running training centers, etc."

What's wrong with this pitch? We can't know for sure until we know *to whom he is talking.* It turned out that the pitch was wrong because the interviewer was not interested in training but in personal computers. How much did Joshua know about PCs? A lot. "Why, I can make PCs dance," he said. "The only problem is that the hiring manager would probably want someone who could network them together, and I've never done that."

"*Can* you do that?" I asked.

"Of course, I can do it," Joshua replied.

"Then go *do* it," I said, "so you can tell her you have already done it. Network together the computers you have at home. And join a group that specializes in that. Ask one of the people if you can go along and help him or her network computers together."

Here's the pitch one week later: "I have 18 years' experience in computers, specializing in PCs. I have built PCs from scratch, and I've done software and applications programming on PCs. I also understand how important networking is. I've even networked together the PCs I have at home, and I belong to a group of PC experts, so I always know whom to talk to when tricky things come up."

But Joshua was feeling some frustration because he was an older guy aiming at a field full of mostly young people. He said to me, almost pleadingly, "I can do *anything* that has to do with PCs. Kate, I can make PCs dance!"

Joshua is speaking out of his *passion* and his love of PCs. I said, "Joshua, you have to *say* that in your Two-Minute Pitch." So, then Joshua's pitch ended on this note: "I can do anything, *anything* that needs to be done with PCs. I can make PCs dance. And I am very excited about talking to you today because I know that your shop relies on PCs. Maybe you can tell me more about that." Of course, Joshua got the job.

You, too, have to convey your passion, if indeed you're feeling any. Your passion will *dramatically* separate you from your competitors.

The Outline of Your Pitch

When developing your own pitch, first ask yourself, "What is the most important thing that I want them to know about me?" No, it's not that you're a hard worker and dedicated. That doesn't separate you from your competition, and it's a useless thing to say. Your opening statement should be a *positioning* statement having to do with the field you're in or the one you're going after. For example, "I'm an international marketing manager."

Now what's the *second* most important thing you want them to know about you? This thought should separate you from all the other international marketing managers, such as "with a strong operations background." What is the third most important thing? This statement usually supports the first two and may be an overarching statement that introduces the *accomplishments* that will follow, such as "My experience includes strategic planning, business generation, and people development. On the strategy side, I wrote the business plan for the division, which encompassed . . ." Here you would give concrete examples of your accomplishments—but not *too* detailed because you can give the details later. You don't have to cover your entire career in two minutes. Give them an overview, and you can interject, "I can tell you more about that later."

The final statement in your pitch could be something like, "I'm excited about talking to you today because of the strong international component of your business."

That is how you can think through the formulation of your pitch. It has an overarching statement with organized details to enable the listener to grasp the key points you are trying to make.

Courage is doing what you are afraid to do.
There can be no courage unless you're scared.

Eddie Rickenbacker

Repositioning Yourself in Your Pitch

Remember, *most* people have to reposition themselves based on the kind of job that they want to go after next. For example, when we asked Janie to "tell us a little bit about yourself," Janie said, "I've worked for big consulting firms my entire life."

If Janie still wanted to work for a big consulting firm, *then* her pitch would have been okay. However, Janie now wanted to work in international communications. In fact, when we dug into her background, we could see that she had been *doing* international communications with the big consulting firms.

So Janie had to reposition the top of her résumé to read, "Communications Executive—with 10 years of international experience."

Here's the start of Janie's revised verbal pitch, which now matches her résumé: "I'm a communications executive with 10 years of international experience." Now, notice how you *feel* about the next sentence of her pitch: "I have 10 years of international experience [now pay attention] in Europe, Latin America, South Africa, the Far East, Eastern Europe, and Russia." See how much more *interesting* it is with the geographic details rather than if she had said only, "I have 10 years of international experience." That would have been boring!

> **The richness of a pitch is in the details. You need to include details about yourself, too.**

Otherwise, yours will be a generic pitch, and it will not capture the imagination of your listeners.

And so Janie went on. "In fact, I was based in Amsterdam for three years." That adds even more interest.

And then: "I am known for getting new business. I've trained people all over the world in proposal writing and 50 percent of their pitches have resulted in new business." Now pay attention to this next part:

". . . These pitches were aimed at companies such as IBM, Philips, Natwest and GE." Again, see how the details add interest to Janie's pitch. You have to do that too.

So decide on a *key statement* about yourself. Janie's pitch was "I am a communications executive." What's yours? Then, what's your subpitch? Janie's subpitch is "with 10 years of international experience including the following countries." And then, what are the most important additional points that you want to make about yourself that would be of interest to your target market? Janie added a few accomplishments that had to do with international communications, and this is the pattern you should follow.

Interviewers Need to Know Your Level

One final word about the beginning of your pitch. Prospective employers need to be able to tell what your level is. So if, for example, you say, "I install computer systems," they can't tell if you're making $25,000, $50,000, or $200,000 a year installing computer systems. So that's not a good pitch.

The listener needs to be able to identify your level quickly, within the first two or three lines on your résumé, and in the first few words of your pitch.

More Customization

In your pitch, do not tell your whole life story. Instead, say things that are relevant. Position yourself, and tell accomplishments that would be of interest to the organization. You *memorize* your pitch, and then *modify* it depending on whom you are talking to.

Philip, for example, was in marketing and specialized in developing new products. He interviewed at one company that already had dozens of new products. They wanted their products taken to market. Philip had to change his pitch. Instead of saying, "I develop new products," he said, "I'm an expert at taking products to market."

Be sensitive about your target market. Find out their needs, what they're missing, and their problem areas. Then position yourself accordingly.

Practice Your Pitch

Most people write out their Two-Minute Pitch, or the key points, and rehearse it in front of a mirror or with their small group.

Alice, a senior human resources executive, landed a prestigious job with a large company. When she reported on her successful job search at the Club, she said that she had met with the president of the company as well as with people on the board of directors and other very senior people. Alice said that she had practiced so much that she felt as though she were having an out-of-body experience when she gave her Two-Minute Pitch: The words just flowed out of her mouth! You want to get to where the words just flow. And that takes practice.

There are a lot of surprises during the interview process, but some things are *certain*. "Tell me about yourself" is *not* a surprise question. The answer to that question is your Two-Minute Pitch.

If you're following The Five O'Clock Club technique, you have highlighted certain accomplishments on your résumé, and the hiring team is going to ask you about them! You know these questions are coming. Make sure your answers are smooth; make sure they flow.

You have complete control over this aspect of the interview. If you do it The Five O'Clock Club way, your résumé will help to guide the interview process and make it more likely that the hiring team will ask you about certain accomplishments.

I know you are asking today, "How long will it take?" I come to say to you this afternoon, however difficult the moment, however frustrating the hour, it will not be long, because truth pressed to earth will rise again.

. . . How long? Not long, because you still reap what you sow. How long? Not long, because the arm of the moral universe is long but it bends towards justice.

Reverend Martin Luther King, Jr., at the end of his
march from Selma (last lines of his speech)

What Point Are You Trying to Make?

When you rehearse your Two-Minute Pitch, ask yourself: What *point* am I trying to make? What impression do I hope people will get about me?

I was listening to a client's pitch, and could not understand the point this executive woman was trying to make. After she had finished:

Kate: I don't get it. What point are you trying to make?
Client: Look, I want them to know that I have 20 years' experience in capital markets, whether it's in aerospace or petroleum, metals and mining, or real estate. *My experience is in capital markets.*
Kate: That's a great pitch. Why don't you just tell them exactly that up front?

They Won't "Get It" on Their Own, So Just Tell Them.

Most job hunters think: I'll just tell them my background, and they'll see how it fits in with their needs. But they probably won't see.

> **Don't expect the hiring team to figure out something about you. If you have a conclusion you'd like them to reach about you, tell them what it is.**

If you want them to see how all of your jobs have somehow been involved in international, say, "All of my jobs have somehow been involved in international." Isn't that easy?

If you want them to notice that you have always been willing to move wherever the company wanted you to move, then say just that. If you want them to know that you have done things treasury executives rarely do, then tell them that.

If you want them to see that you have developed intensive product knowledge while handling various operations areas, tell them that. Do you want them to know that FORTRAN is your favorite language? Then don't say, "I have five years of FORTRAN experience." That's not your point. Do you want them to know that you can make computers dance? Tell them. Don't make them figure it out for themselves. They won't.

Don't think to yourself, "I thought that if I told them that I had done 12 years of programming, they would just understand that I also know how to manage project teams." No! *Tell* them what you want them to know and how your background fits in with their needs.

Make your message so clear that if someone says, "Tell me about John," they will know what to tell the other person about you.

What Will They Say about You When You're Gone?

If you're an accounting manager and your résumé says *Accounting Manager* in the summary, and you're applying for an accounting manager job, chances are good that everyone else they're interviewing is also an accounting manager. When you leave, the hiring manager is not going to say, "Oh, my gosh! I just met an accounting manager." Instead, you want them to say, "Oh, my gosh. I just met somebody who is an expert in developing new accounting systems. And he worked on a project in our industry doing exactly what we're trying to do."

What do you want them to say about *you* when you're gone? *That's* your pitch. Repeat it enough during the interview so that you know how they'll position you to *other* people after you leave.

Communicating Your Pitch

Many job hunters try to cram everything they can into their Two-Minute Pitch, but when your pitch is too densely packed, people won't hear what you want them to hear. Think about those who are considered the great communicators today. We judge communicators very differently from the way we did in the past, when the Winston Churchill type was ideal.

Today, our standards are based on the medium of TV. The best communicators speak on a personal level—the way people talk on TV. Whether you are addressing a big audience or are on a job interview, cultivate a TV style—a friendly, one-on-one conversational style, not a *listing of what I've done* style. Speak the way you would normally speak.

The interviewer is assessing what it would be like to work with you. Make your pitch understandable. Before people go on TV, they decide the three major points they want to make—what they want the audience *to remember*. For example, don't say, "I started out in this job as a trainer, where I traveled to x and y and worked on special projects, etc.," if what you *really* want them to know is "That was a great assignment. My programs accounted for more than two thirds of the company's revenue."

Many job hunters have pitches that are too heavy in content. Let's return to the woman executive we were discussing: "I have 20 years' experience in capital markets in airlines, real estate and petroleum, metals and mining—assessing customers' and prospects' financial requirements based on the industry's point within the business cycle as well as the specific company's. I assess client credit, etc."

People can't listen to that. It's too dense. It needs some filler around the important words to resemble the way people really talk: "I have 20 years' experience in capital markets—capital markets has always been my chief interest. I had this experience in three different areas, but the area where I spent the most time was in the airlines. I was also most recently involved in petroleum, metals and mining, and earlier on in my career, I was involved in real estate."

The new pitch is more *conversational* than a list and will be more effective than simply getting all the facts out.

Vary Your Pitch by Organization

Change your pitch for every organization with which you meet. If you're pitching yourself to a large organization, you will probably have a different pitch than if you are pitching to a small organization. When you know something about the organization that you're interviewing with, you should be able to modify your pitch. Now, this does not contradict what I said earlier about having your pitch down pat. You *can* have it down pat, then you can ad lib a bit and modify it to suit this target market. Know your main point and your subordinate points, and modify those for each organization.

Emphasis and Tempo

When you say something important, emphasize it by slowing down. For example, in the sentence "I worked on that project for over nine months," you could slow down on "nine months" to give it emphasis. Like this: "I worked on that project for over [slowly] *nine months.*" That's what TV announcers do. They speed up background words and slow down on the important words. Then your listener will not miss what you consider important.

I speak quickly, but when I am on an interview with somebody who is laid back and casual, even *I* can change tempo and slow myself down a little bit so that I match their pace.

But if I were meeting with somebody who is more fast-paced and chop-chop, then I can operate at the fast-paced end of my spectrum. If you speak very slowly to someone who is fast-paced, they'll think you're slow and won't fit in.

More about Filler Words and Pointer Words

As indicated earlier, filler words can be useful. They help *engage* your listener. Words can highlight important points that are coming up. You might say, for example, "One of

the most interesting things that I've ever done was . . ." Those are highlight words. They point to whatever you're going to tell them next. You're saying, "What I'm about to say will be important." And then you may name an accomplishment. You may want to follow that (or a different accomplishment) with "That was one of the most satisfying things I have ever done because [slowly] I was in charge and I was able to operate on my own." That phrase points *back* to what you just said, so they don't miss it.

Smile

When I rehearse people for interviews, I find that I commonly tell people to *smile.* When you smile, it has an impact on the viewer. Even if you're on the phone, when you are smiling, it impacts the listener.

When you smile, people see you as more competent and more self-confident. If you do not smile, then you look worried and you look less qualified than you really are.

When you smile, the other person has a *visceral reaction* to you. Their tendency, unless the person is a brick wall, is to smile back. A good healthy smile helps you during the interview, and the hiring manager is more likely to think that there is good chemistry between you.

Use your hands as you would in a normal conversation. Don't sit there like a rock. Pay attention to the hiring manager's style. Take a look at the things around their room. Is the person more formal or more laid back? You can adjust your presentation accordingly.

Two Minutes Is a Long Time, So Show Enthusiasm

In this TV society, people are used to 15-second sound bites on the news. As the communicator, you have to engage the listener. Reinforce your main points. Don't say too many things.

Show *enthusiasm* during those two minutes. If you're an introvert and a low-key person, force yourself to sit *forward* in your chair. Sit almost on the edge of your seat. It will thrust your body forward and make you look more energetic. And using your hands a little will also give much more energy to your presentation. The interview process is an extroverted process, and low-key people are at a disadvantage. So, *act* a little extroverted on the interview; whether you're extroverted or not, you have to act that way more than you normally would. Otherwise, people may doubt that you have the energy to get work done. The good news is that you do not have to act that way on the job!

I once did a magazine article on who got jobs and who got to keep them. I talked to the deans of business and engineering schools.

I learned that the person most likely to get the job was the one who sounded enthusiastic. And the one who got to keep the job was the enthusiastic one—even more than people who were more qualified. Employers decided to keep someone who was willing to pitch in and do anything to help the company.

Even more interesting to me is that this same thing is true for senior executives. In my line of work, I sometimes have the opportunity to follow up with organizations when someone doesn't get a job. I am amazed by the number of times I am told (about people making from $150,000 to $600,000) that the applicant lacked enthusiasm: "He was managing 1,300 people, and I don't know how he did it. He just doesn't sound enthusiastic. How could he motivate his troops if he can't motivate me? Anyway, I don't know that he really wants the job. He didn't sound interested."

If you're in the interview thinking, "I don't know whether or not I want to do this job," that's the wrong attitude. The safest route is to be enthusiastic and act as *if* you want the job anyway. Later on, you can decide that you don't want it. But if you act unenthusiastically during the interview process and decide later that you're indeed interested, it's usually too late. So, when you go in for that interview, try to make it work. Try to get that next meeting. Whether you want the job or not, *act* like you do. Enthusiasm from start to finish, by the way, gives you the advantage when salary negotiation gets under way.

Depend on Your Small Group

Your group is terrific at giving feedback on the Two-Minute Pitch. Tell the other people in the group who they should pretend to be. That is, should they pretend that they are the marketing manager, accounting manager, or operations manager? Then they say to you, "So tell us about yourself." Then you say your pitch—you can refer to your notes—and ask them for their comments. Your group can comment on both the delivery and the content. They can tell if your pitch is clear, if you're being too modest about your accomplishments, or if your pitch is too general. Then refine your pitch and practice it again in your group the following week. Keep practicing it until you get it right. (Sometimes people use tape recorders to record the pitch.) It may take you three or four weeks to get it perfect, but that's what your small group is for.

Remember: The Two-Minute Pitch is one of the most important parts of the entire Five O'Clock Club job-search process. Most successful Five O'Clock clubbers said that once they got their pitch down, things seemed to work out better in their search. So practice your Two-Minute Pitch in your small group and take it to the world!

A very large amount of human suffering and frustration is caused by the fact that many men and women are not content to be the sort of beings that God had made them, but try to persuade themselves that they are really beings of some different kind.

Eric Mascall, *The Importance of Being Human*

Summary of What I Have/Want to Offer—Target 1

To Help Me Develop My Pitch to That Target

You must know:

- to whom you are pitching; you have to know something about them.
- what they ideally would want in a candidate.
- what they are interested in.
- who your likely competitors are.
- what you bring to the party that your competitors do not.

For Target 1:   Geographic area _____

Industry or company size: _____

Position/function: _____

1. What is the most important thing I want this target to know about me? (If they know nothing else about you, this is what you want them to know.)

2. What is the second most important thing I want this target to know about me? (This could support and/or broaden your introductory statement.)

3. Key selling points: statements/accomplishments that support/**prove** the first two statements:

   1. _____
   2. _____
   3. _____
   4. _____
   5. _____

4. Why they should be interested in me/what separates me from my competition:

   _____

   _____

5. Other key points that may apply even indirectly to this industry or position:

   _____

   _____

6. Any objection I'm afraid the interviewer may bring up, and how I will handle it:

   _____

Summary of What I Have/Want to Offer—Target 2

To Help Me Develop My Pitch to That Target

You must know:

- to whom you are pitching; you have to know something about them.
- what they ideally would want in a candidate.
- what they are interested in.
- who your likely competitors are.
- what you bring to the party that your competitors do not.

For Target 2:   Geographic area: _____

Industry or company size: _____

Position/function: _____

1. What is the most important thing I want this target to know about me? (If they know nothing else about you, this is what you want them to know.)

2. What is the second most important thing I want this target to know about me? (This could support and/or broaden your introductory statement.)

3. Key selling points: statements/accomplishments that support/**prove** the first two statements:

   1. _____
   2. _____
   3. _____
   4. _____
   5. _____

4. Why they should be interested in me/what separates me from my competition:

   _____

   _____

5. Other key points that may apply even indirectly to this industry or position:

   _____

   _____

6. Any objection I'm afraid the interviewer may bring up, and how I will handle it:

   _____

Summary of What I Have/Want to Offer—Target 3

To Help Me Develop My Pitch to That Target

You must know:

- to whom you are pitching; you have to know something about them.
- what they ideally would want in a candidate.
- what they are interested in.
- who your likely competitors are.
- what you bring to the party that your competitors do not.

For Target 3:   Geographic area: _____

                     Industry or company size: _____

                     Position/function: _____

1. What is the most important thing I want this target to know about me? (If they know nothing else about you, this is what you want them to know.)

2. What is the second most important thing I want this target to know about me? (This could support and/or broaden your introductory statement.)

3. Key selling points: statements/accomplishments that support/**prove** the first two statements:

    1. _____
    2. _____
    3. _____
    4. _____
    5. _____

4. Why they should be interested in me/what separates me from my competition:

_____

_____

5. Other key points that may apply even indirectly to this industry or position:

_____

_____

6. Any objection I'm afraid the interviewer may bring up, and how I will handle it:

_____

Getting Interviews and Building Relationships

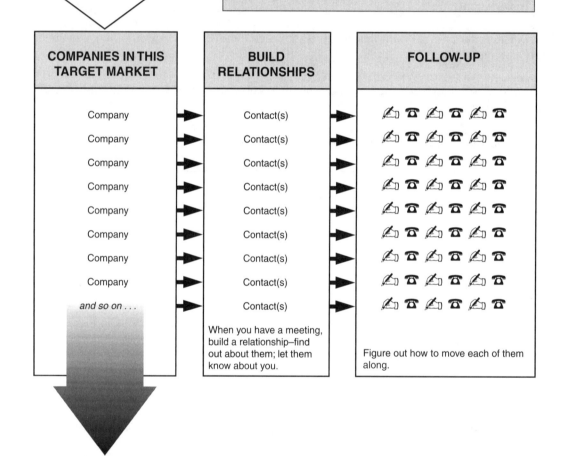

Four ways to get interviews in your target market

1. Search Firms
2. Ads
3. Networking
4. Direct Contact:
   - *Targeted Mailing*
   - *Direct-Mail Campaign*
   - *Cold Calls*

Plan to contact or meet the *right* people in *every* company in each of your target areas—as quickly as possible.

Get meetings with people in your target areas through:
- Search Firms
- Ads
- Networking
- Direct Contact

Do not think of these as techniques for getting *jobs,* but as techniques for getting *interviews.*

- After a networking meeting, be sure to keep in touch with the person you met.

- After a job interview, think about what you can do next to turn the situation into a job offer.

COMPANIES IN THIS TARGET MARKET	BUILD RELATIONSHIPS	FOLLOW-UP
Company	Contact(s)	
Company	Contact(s)	
Company	Contact(s)	
Company	Contact(s)	
Company	Contact(s)	
Company	Contact(s)	
Company	Contact(s)	
Company	Contact(s)	
and so on . . .	Contact(s)	

When you have a meeting, build a relationship—find out about them; let them know about you.

Figure out how to move each of them along.

The Five O'Clock Club

How to Network Your Way In

I use not only all the brains I have,
but all I can borrow.

Woodrow Wilson

In the old days, networking was a great technique. We job hunters were appreciative of the help we got and treated those we met with respect and courtesy. We targeted a field and then used networking to meet people, form lifelong relationships with them, and gather information about the area. We called it "information gathering," but it also often led to jobs.

Today, stressed-out, aggressive, demanding job hunters want a job quickly and expect their "contacts" to hire them, refer them to someone important (obviously not the person with whom they are speaking), or tell them where the jobs are. The old way worked; this new attitude does not. This chapter tells you how to network correctly.

Network informally by talking to acquaintances who may know something about your target area. **Network formally** by contacting people at their jobs to get information about their organization or industry. Networking is one way to find out what skills are needed where, what jobs may be opening up, and where you might be able to fit in. Use the networking—or information-gathering—process *to gather information and to build new relationships.*

Gather Information

Networking is one way to find out what skills are needed where, what jobs may be opening up, and where you may be able to fit in. Talking to people because "they might know of something for me" rarely works.

Build Lifelong Relationships

You are also trying to build lifelong relationships. If a target area interests you, get to know the people in it and let them get to know you. It is unreasonable to expect them to have something for you just because you decided to con-

tact them right now. Some of the most important people in your search may provide you with information and no contacts. Be sincerely grateful for the help you get, form a relationship that will last a lifetime, and plan to **recontact regularly the people you meet**.

Remember, you are not talking to people assuming they have heard of job openings. That approach rarely works. For example, if someone asked you if you happen to know of a position in the purchasing department in your old organization, your answer would be no. But if they said, "I'm really interested in your former organization. Do you happen to know *anyone* I could talk to there?" you could certainly give them the name of someone.

This is how people find jobs through networking. As time passes, the people you've met hear of things or develop needs themselves. If you keep in touch, they will tell you what's happening. It is a long-term process, but an effective one.

As you talk to more and more people, you will gather more and more information about business situations and careers in which you think you are interested. And the more people you meet and tell about your career search, the more people are out there to consider you for a job or a referral to a job when they know of one. But, remember, they have to know you first. Networking allows you to meet people without asking them for a job and putting them on the spot. And the fact is, **if they like you and happen to have a job that's appropriate for you, they will *tell* you about it—you will not have to ask.**

People *like* to talk to sincere, bright people and send on those who impress them. People will not send you on if you are not skilled at presenting yourself or asking good questions.

CASE STUDY *Monica*
Networking when You Don't Know Anyone

Monica moved to Manhattan from a rural area because she wanted to work in publishing. She found a temporary job and then thought of ways to network in a city where she knew no one. She told everyone she had always wanted to work in publishing and would like to meet with people who worked in that industry. She told people at bus stops, church, and restaurants. She read *Publishers Weekly*, the publishing trade magazine, to find out who was doing what in the industry and contacted some people directly. She also joined an association of people in the publishing industry. At meetings, she asked for people's business cards and said she would contact them later. She then wrote to them and met with them at their offices.

Monica found that one of the best contacts she made during her search was a man close to retirement who was on a special assignment with no staff. There was no possibility of her ever working for him, but he gave her great insights into the industry and told her the best people to work for. He saved her from wasting many hours of her time and she felt free to call him to ask about specific people she was meeting.

Over time, lots of people got to know Monica and Monica got to know the publishing industry. She eventually heard of a number of openings and was able to tell which ones were better than others. Monica is off to a good start in her new profession because she made lifelong friends she can contact *after* she is in her new job.

Using the networking technique correctly takes:

- time (because setting up meetings, going on them, and following up takes time);
- a sincere desire for information and building long-term relationships; and
- preparation.

You Are the Interviewer

In an information-gathering meeting, *you* are conducting the meeting. The worst thing you can do is to sit, expecting to be interviewed. The manager, thinking you honestly wanted information, agreed to see you. Have your questions ready. After all, you called the meeting.

Our plans miscarry because they have no aim. When a man does not know what harbor he is making for, no wind is the right wind.

Seneca the Younger, Roman statesman

Questions You May Want to Ask

To repeat: People will be more willing to help you than you think *if* you are sincere about your interest in getting information from them *and* if you are asking them appropriate questions to which you could not get answers through library research or from lower-level people.

If what you really want from them is a job, you will not do as well. At this point, you don't want a job, you want a meeting. You want to **develop a relationship with them,** ask them for information, tell them about yourself, see if they can recommend others for you to talk to, and build a basis for contacting them later.

Before each meeting, write down the questions you sincerely want to ask *this specific person.* (If you find you are asking each person exactly the same thing, you are not using this technique properly.) Some examples:

The Industry

- How large is this industry?
- How is the industry changing now? What are the most important trends or problems? Which parts of the industry will probably grow (or decline) at what rates over the next few years?
- What are the industry's most important characteristics?
- What do you see as the future of this industry 5 or 10 years from now?
- What do you think of the organizations I have listed on this sheet? Which ones are you familiar with? Who are the major players in this industry? Which are the better organizations?

The Company or Organization

- How old is the organization and what are the most important events in its history? How large is the organization? What goods and services does it produce? How does it produce these goods and services?
- Does the organization have any particular clients, customers, regulators, etc.? If so, what are they like and what is their relationship to the organization?

- Who are your major competitors?
- How is the company organized? What are the growing areas? The problem areas? Which areas do you think would be good for me given my background?
- What important technologies does this organization use?
- What is the organizational culture like? Who tends to get ahead here?
- What important challenges is the organization facing right now or in the near future?

The Job or Function

- What are the major tasks involved in this job? What skills are needed to perform these tasks?
- How is this department structured? Who reports to whom? Who interacts with whom?
- What is it like to work here? What is the organization's reputation?
- What kinds of people are normally hired for this kind of position?
- What kind of salary and other rewards would a new hire usually get for this kind of job?
- What are the advancement opportunities?
- What skills are absolutely essential for a person in this field?

The Person with Whom You Are Meeting

- Could you tell me a little about what you do in your job?
- How does your position relate to the bottom line?
- What is the most challenging aspect of your job?
- What is the most frustrating aspect of your job?
- What advice would you give to someone in my position?
- What are some of the intermediate steps necessary for a person to reach your position?
- What do you like or dislike about your job?
- How did you get into this profession or industry?
- What major problems are you facing right now in this department or position?

The Information-Gathering or Networking Process

1. **Determine your purpose.** Decide what information you want or what contacts you want to build. Early on in your job search, networking with people at your own level helps you research the field you have targeted. At this point in your search, you are not trying to get hired. Later, meet with more senior people. *They* are in a position to hire you someday.

2. **Make a list of people you know.** In the research phase, you made a list of the organizations you thought you should contact in each of your target areas. You need lists of important people or organizations you want to contact. Then, when you meet someone who tends to know people, you can ask if he or she knows anyone on your list.

    Now make a list of all the people you already know (relatives, former bosses and coworkers, your dentist, people at your church or synagogue, former classmates, those with whom you play baseball). Don't say you do not know enough appropriate people. If you know one person, that's enough for a start.

    Don't discard the names of potential contacts because they are not in a position to hire you. Remember, you are not going to meet people to ask for a job, but to ask for information. These contacts can be helpful, provide information, and most likely have other friends or contacts who will move you closer and closer to your targets.

People to Contact in Each Target Area

In the chapter "Research: Developing Your List of Organizations to Contact," you made a list of organizations you want to contact in each of your target areas. Then you used the "Sample Personal Marketing Plan" as a model for your own complete list. Now you want to get in to see the people at these and other organizations.

For each target, list on the following page the names of people you know, or know of, or even generic names (such as "lawyers who deal with emerging businesses") who can help you in each target. Whether you contact them through networking or a targeted mailing, the meetings will all be networking meetings.

You will not be idly chatting with these people. Instead, you will have your pitch ready (see the chapter on the Two-Minute Pitch in our book *Mastering the Job Interview and Winning the Money Game*) and will tell them the target you have in mind. The target will include the industry or organization size, the kind of position you would like, and the geographic area. For example:

"I'm interested in entrepreneurially driven, medium-sized private organizations in the Chicago area. I would do well as a chief financial or chief administrative officer in that kind of organization. Can you suggest the names of people who might have contact with those kinds of organizations or do you know anyone who works at such an organization or an organization on my list?"

Tell *everyone* the target you are going after—including people you meet on the train and at the barbershop or beauty salon. You never know who knows somebody.

---

*If you have always done it that way,
it is probably wrong.*

Charles Kettering

---

3. **Contact the people you want to meet.** Chances are, you will simply call (rather than write to) people you already know—those on your "People to Contact" list. In the beginning of your search, practice on people who know you well. If you say a few things wrong, it won't matter. You can see them again later.

    But as you progress in your search, most of the people you meet should not be people you know well. Extend your network beyond those people with whom you are comfortable. (See the worksheet on the next page.)

People to Contact in Each Target Area

You made a list of organizations to contact in each of your target areas. Now you will show your list to those with whom you network because you want to get in to see those on your list and other organizations as well.

For each target, list below the names of people you know, or know of, or even generic names, such as "lawyers who deal with emerging businesses." You will contact them through networking or a targeted mailing. The meetings you set up will be networking meetings. However, you will not be idly chatting with people. Instead, you will have your "pitch" ready (See Two-Minute Pitch in our book *Mastering the Job Interview and Winning the Money Game*) and will tell them the target you have in mind. The target will contain the industry or organization size, the kind of position you would like, and the geographic area. For example:

"I'm interested in entrepreneurially driven, medium-sized private organizations in the Chicago area. I would do well as a chief financial or chief administrative officer in such an organization. Can you suggest the names of people who might have contact with those kinds of organizations, or do you know anyone who works at such an organization?"

You will tell *everyone* the target you are going after—including people you meet on the train and at the barbershop or beauty salon. You never know who knows somebody.

Target 1	Target 2	Target 3	Target 4	Other Names
				such as: dentist, hairdresser, neighbors

As you build your network of contacts (people you know refer you to people you don't know and they refer you to others), you will get further away from those people with whom you originally began. But as you go further out, you are generally getting closer to where the jobs are. Be willing to go to even further networking levels. Many people report that they got their jobs through someone six or seven levels removed from where they started.

You will probably want to contact people you do not know personally by letter. Force yourself to write that letter and then follow up. People who are busy are more likely to spend time with you if you have put some effort into your attempt to see them. Busy people can read your note when they want rather than having to be dragged away from their jobs to receive your phone call. Often, people who receive your note will schedule an appointment for you through their secretary and you will get in to see them without ever having spoken to them. (On the other hand, some job hunters are in fields where people are used to picking up the phone. "Cold calling" can work for them.)

- Identify the link between you and the person you wish to meet; state why you are interested in talking to her or him.

- Give your summary and two short examples of achievements of possible interest to him or her.

- Indicate that you will call in a few days to see when you can meet briefly.

"I'm sorry, but Mr. Roberts no longer takes meetings, phone calls, cell calls, faxes, snail mail, e-mail, messages, notes or appointments. Is there anything else we can do for you?"

A Sample Note for Information Gathering

Dear Mr. Brown:

Penny Webb suggested I contact you because she thought you could give me the information I need.

I'm interested in heading my career in a different direction. I have been with Acme Corporation for seven years and I could stay here forever, but the growth possibilities in the areas of interest to me are extremely limited. I want to make a move during the next year, but I want it to be the right move. Penny thought you could give me some ideas.

I'm interested in human resources management. My seven years' experience includes the development of an executive compensation system that measures complex human resource variables. For the past two years, I have been the main liaison with our unions and am now the head of the labor relations section. In this position, I managed the negotiation of six union contracts—and accomplished that feat in only 90 days.

I'd like some solid information from you on the job possibilities for someone like me. I'd greatly appreciate a half hour of your time and insight. I'll call you in a few days to see when you can spare the time.

Sincerely,

Enclose your résumé if it supports your case. Do not enclose it if your letter is enough or if your résumé hurts your case.

. . . we know that suffering produces perseverance; perseverance character; and character hope.

Romans 5: 3–4

4. **Call to set up the appointment** (first, build up your courage). When you call, you will probably have to start at the beginning. Do not expect the person to remember anything in your letter. Don't even expect him to remember that you wrote at all. Say, for example, "I sent you a letter recently. Did you receive it?"

Remind him of the reason you wrote. Have your letter in front of you—to serve as your script—because you may again have to summarize your background and state some of your accomplishments.

If the person says the organization has no openings at this time, that is okay with you—you were not necessarily looking for a job; you were looking for information or advice about the job possibilities for someone like you or you wanted to know what is happening in the profession, organization, or industry.

If the person says he is busy, say, "I'd like to accommodate your schedule. If you like, I could meet you in the early morning or late evening." If he or she is still too busy, say, "Is it okay if we set something up for a month from now? I would call you to confirm so you could reschedule our meeting if it's still not a good time for you. And I assure you I won't take up more than 20 minutes of your time." Do your best to get on his calendar—even if the date is a month away. (Remember: You are trying to form lifelong relationships. Don't force yourself on people, but do get in to see them.)

Don't let the manager interview you over the phone. You want to meet in person. You need face-to-face contact to build the relationship and be remembered by the manager.

Rather than leave a message, keep calling back to maintain control. If no one returns your call, you will feel rejected. But be friendly with the secretary; apologize for calling so often. An example: "Hello, Joan. This is Louise DiSclafani again. I'm sorry to bother you, but is Mr. Johnson free now?"

"No, Ms. DiSclafani, he hasn't returned yet. May I have him call you?"

"Thanks, Joan, but that will be difficult. I'll be in and out a lot, so I'll have to call him back. When is a good time to call?"

Expect to call 7 or 8 times. Accept it as normal business. It is not personal. (See the section, "How to Use the Telephone.")

5. **Prepare for the meeting.** Plan for a networking meeting as thoroughly as you would for any other business meeting. Follow the agenda listed in step 6. **Remember: It is _your_ meeting. You are the one running it.** Beforehand:

- Set goals for yourself (information and contacts).

- Jot down the questions you want answered.

- Find out all you can about the person, and the person's responsibilities, and areas of operations.

- Rehearse your Two-Minute Pitch and accomplishments.

Develop good questions, tailoring them to get the information you need. Make sure what you ask is appropriate for the person with whom you are meeting. You wouldn't, for example, say to a senior vice president of marketing, "So, tell me how marketing works." That question is too general. Instead, do your research—both in the library and by talking with more junior people.

Decide what information you want or what contacts you want to build. Early on in your job search, networking with people at your own level helps you research the field you have targeted. At this point in your search, you are not trying to get hired. Later, meet with more senior people—the ones who are in a position to hire you someday.

Then when you meet the senior vice president, ask questions that are more appropriate for someone of that level. You may want to ask about the rewards of that particular business, the frustrations, the type of people who succeed there, the group values, the long-range plans for the business. Prepare 3 to 5 open-ended questions about the business or organization that the person will be able to answer.

If you find you are asking each person the same questions, think harder about the information you need or do more library research. The quality of your questions should change over time as you become more knowledgeable, more of an insider, and more desirable as a prospective employee. In addition, you should be giving information back. If you are truly an insider, you must have information to give.

If you think education is expensive, try ignorance.
Derek Bok

6. **Conduct the meeting.** If this is important to you, you will continually do better. Sometimes people network forever. They talk to people, but there is no flame inside them. Then one day something happens: They get angry or just fed up with all of this talking to people. They interview better because they have grown more serious. Their time seems more important to them. They stop going through the motions and get the information they need. They interview harder. They feel as though their future is at stake. They don't want to chat with people. They are hungrier. They truly want to work in that industry or that organization. And the manager they are talking to can sense their seriousness and react accordingly.

Nothing great was ever achieved without enthusiasm.
Ralph Waldo Emerson, *Circles*

*Business is a game, the greatest game
in the world if you know how to play it.*
Thomas J. Watson Jr., former CEO of IBM

Format of a Networking Meeting

Prepare for each meeting. The questions you want to ask and the way you want to "pitch" or position yourself will vary from one meeting to another. Think it all through.

Be sure to read this chapter in detail for more information on the networking, or information-gathering, process.

The Format of the Meeting

- **Pleasantries**—this is a chance to size up the other person and allow the other person to size you up. It's a chance to settle down. Just two or three sentences of small talk are enough.

- **Why am I here?** For example: "Thanks so much for agreeing to meet with me. Ruth Robbins thought you could give me the advice I need. I'm trying to talk to CEOs in the Chicago area because I want to relocate here." Remind the person of how you got his or her name and why you are there.

- **Establish credibility with your Two-Minute Pitch.** After you tell the person why you are there, they are likely to say something like: "Well, how can I help you?" Then you can respond, for example: "I wanted to ask you a few things, but first let me give you an idea of who I am." There are a number of reasons for doing this:

  1. The person will be in a better position to help you if she knows something about you.

  2. It's impolite to ask a lot of questions without telling the person who you are.

  3. You are trying to form a relationship with this person—to get to know each other a bit.

- **Ask questions** that are appropriate for this person. Really think through what you want to ask. For example, you wouldn't say to the marketing manager: "So what's it like to be in marketing?" You would ask that of a more junior person. Consider having your list of questions in front of you so you will look serious and keep on track.

- As the person is answering your questions, **tell him or her more about yourself if appropriate**. For example, you might say: "That's interesting. When I was at XYZ Company, we handled a similar problem in an unusual way. In fact, I headed up the project . . ."

- **Ask for referrals if appropriate.** For example: "I'm trying to get in to see people at the organizations on this list. Do you happen to know anyone at these organizations ? . . . May I use your name?"

- **Gather more information about the referrals** (such as: "What is Ellis Chase like?").

- **Formal expression of gratitude.** Thank the person for the time he or she spent with you.

- **Offer to stay in touch.** Remember that making a lot of new contacts is not as effective as making fewer contacts and then *recontacting* those people later (see Follow-Up).

- **Write a follow-up note and be sure to follow up again later.**

Remember:

- **You are *not* there simply to get names. You may get excellent information but no names of others to contact. That's fine.**

- **Be grateful for whatever help people give you and assume they are doing their best.**

- **Remember too that this is *your* meeting and you must try to get all you can out of it.**

- **This is not a job interview. In a job interview, you are being interviewed. In a networking meeting, *you* are conducting the meeting.**

Networking Cover Letter

Asking for advice is appropriate early on in your search.

PHIL GITTINGS
20 Trinity Place
New York, New York 10000
(222) 555-2231
PGittings@earthlink.net

March 10, 200X

Mr. Max McCreery
Executive Vice President
Young & Rubicam
285 Madison Avenue
New York, New York 10017

Dear Mr. McCreery:

I am following up on the suggestion of Nancy Abramson, who refers to herself as a fan of yours, and am writing to ask for your counsel on my current career plans.

I have recently decided to leave my present company, McGraw-Hill Publishing, and continue my career elsewhere. Nancy thought you could give me the advice I need.

I have targeted the advertising industry as part of my search strategy because I believe that my skills in financial planning and problem solving, combined with my international experience, I could make an important contribution to good business management. In addition, I believe I would enjoy working in the dynamic and creative environment of most agencies.

Nancy suggested I ask for your response to my thoughts on how my experience in financial management in the publishing industry can be productively applied in advertising.

Briefly, my experience includes commercial banking (1977–1979) followed by financial analysis at CBS (1979–1981). The largest part of my career was with Time, Inc. (1981–1993), where I served in a variety of financial and administrative assignments, including tours as International Finance Manager, Financial Director of Time's fully independent Mexico subsidiary, and an assignment in the direct marketing group. Following Time, I became a principal in a small publishing company and since 1994 have been Vice President, Administration, at McGraw-Hill Book Clubs.

I look forward to speaking with you and will call in a few days to see when we can meet.

Sincerely,

Phil Gittings

The
Five
O'Clock
Club

Are You Conducting a Good Campaign?

The thing is to never deal yourself out . . . Opt for the best possible hand. Play with verve and sometimes with abandon, but at all times with calculation.

L. Douglas Wilder, in "Virginia's Lieutenant Governor: L. Douglas Wilder Is First Black to Win Office," *Ebony,* April 1986

How You Know You Are in a *Campaign*

You feel as though you know a critical mass of people within that industry. When you go on "interviews," you contribute as much as you take away. You have gained a certain amount of information about the industry that puts you on par with the interviewer—and you are willing to share that information. You are a contributor. An insider.

You know what's going on. You feel some urgency and are more serious about this industry.

You are no longer simply "looking around"—playing it cool. You are more intense. You don't want anything to stand in your way because you know this is what you want. You become more aware of any little thing that can help you get in. Your judgment becomes more finely tuned. Things seem to fall into place.

You are working harder at this than you ever could have imagined. You read everything there is to read. You write proposals almost overnight and hand-deliver them.

Your campaign is taking on a life of its own.

At industry meetings, you seem to know everybody. They know you are one of them and are simply waiting for the right break.

When someone mentions a name, you have already met that person and are keeping in touch with him or her. The basic job-hunting "techniques" no longer apply.

You are in a different realm and you feel it.

This is a real campaign.

The Quality of Your Campaign

Getting a job offer is not the way to test the quality of your campaign. A real test is when people say they'd want you—but not right now. When you are networking, do people say, "Boy, I wish I had an opening. I'd sure like to have someone like you here"? Then you know you are interviewing well with the right people. All you need now are luck and timing to help you contact or recontact the right people when they also have a need.

If people are not saying they want you, find out why. Are you inappropriate for this target? Or perhaps you seem like an outsider and outsiders are rarely given a break.

During the beginning of your search, you are gathering information to find out how things work.

Why should someone hire a person who does not already work in the field? Lots of competent people have the experience and can prove they will do a good job.

There is a test to see if you are perceived as an insider. If you think you are in the right target, talking to people at the right level, and are not early on in your search, you need feedback. Ask people, "If you had an opening, would you consider hiring someone like me?"

Become an insider—a competent person who can prove he or she has somehow already done what the interviewer needs. Prove you can do the job and that the interviewer is not taking a chance by hiring you.

The Quantity of Your Campaign

You need to find a lot of people who would hire you if they could. You know by now that you should **have 6 to 10 things in the works at all times**. This is the only true measure of the effectiveness of your campaign to get meetings in your target area. If you have fewer than this, get more. You will be more attractive to the manager, will interview better, and will lower the chances of losing momentum if your best lead falls apart.

Use the worksheet "Current List of My Active Contacts by Target." At the beginning of your search, these will simply be networking contacts with whom you want to keep in touch. At this stage, your goal is to come up with 6 to 10 contacts you want to recontact later, perhaps every two months. In the middle of your search, the quality of your list will change. The names will be of the right people at the right level in the right organizations. Finally, the 6 to 10 names will represent prospective job possibilities you are trying to move along.

If you have 6 to 10 job possibilities in the works, a good number of them will fall away through no fault of your own (job freezes or hiring managers changing their minds about the kind of person they want). Then you'll need to get more possibilities in the works. With this critical mass of ongoing possible positions, you stand a chance of getting a number of offers and landing the kind of job you want.

There is a tide in the affairs of men, Which, taken at the flood, leads on to fortune; . . . On such a sea we are now afloat; And we must take the current when it serves, Or lose our ventures.

Shakespeare, *Julius Caesar*

Developing Momentum in Your Search

A campaign builds to a pitch. The parts begin to help one another. You focus less on making a particular technique work and more on the situation you happen to be in. This chapter gives you a feel for a real campaign.

In your promotional campaign to get meetings, you see people who are in a position to hire you or recommend you. Keep in touch with them so they will . . .

- think of you when a job opens up,
- invite you to create a job for yourself,
- upgrade an opening to better suit you, and
- give you information to help you in your search.

When you are in the heat of a real campaign, a critical mass of activity builds, so you start:

- hearing the same names,
- seeing the same people,
- contributing as much as you are getting,
- writing proposals,
- getting back to people quickly,

- feeling a sense of urgency about this industry; and
- writing follow-up letters and making follow-up phone calls.

. . . the secret is to have the courage to live. If you have that, everything will sooner or later change.

James Salter, *Light Years*

Eventually, and often after the survival of a long and profound crisis, often after the painful shedding of one skin and the gradual growth of another, comes the realization that the world is essentially neutral. The world doesn't care, and is responsible neither for one's spiritual failures nor for one's successes. This discovery can come as a profound relief, because it is no longer necessary to spend so much energy shoring up the self, and because the world emerges as a broader, more interesting, sweeter place through which to move. The fog lifts, as it were.

Frank Conroy, *The New York Times Book Review,* January 1, 1989

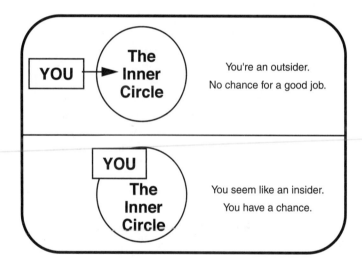

Targeted Mailings: Just Like Networking

The Five O'Clock Club

There's nothing to writing. All you do is sit down at a typewriter and open a vein.

Walter ("Red") Smith, in *Reader's Digest,* July 1982

Networking is not the only way to job hunt. Consider targeted mailings when:

- You want to see a particular person but have no formal contact. You must think of how you can create some tie-in to that person and contact him or her directly.

- You have selected 20 to 30 organizations in your target market that you really want to get in to see, and there are only a few jobs that would be appropriate for you in each company. For the 20 or 30 organizations you have chosen, research the appropriate person to contact in each one. Ask each for a meeting—whether or not they have a job for you. You want to get in to see them *all* because your target is very small.

There is no way of writing well and also of writing easily.

Anthony Trollope, *Barchester Towers*

The Letter

- **Paragraph 1:** The opening paragraph for a targeted mailing would follow the format for a networking letter: State the reason you are writing and **establish the contact** you have with the reader.

> Congratulations on your new position! I know you are extremely busy (I've heard about it from others). After you are settled in, I would be interested in meeting with you. I think it would be mutually beneficial for us to meet, although I have no fixed idea of what could come of it.

After you have found out something about the person or the organization, pretend you are sitting with that person right now. What would you *say* to him or her? Here's what one job hunter wrote to an executive:

> I agree. Your position *is* truly enviable.

> With the merger of AT&T and United Telecom completed, AT&T is now positioned to become an even greater force in shaping telecommunications for the future, both domestically and internationally. However, with all the challenges comes the inevitable need for control, resolution of legal and regulatory issues, competitive threats, pricing issues, and reexamination of both the positioning and global packaging of AT&T. Clear, focused strategic and business plans become essential for success. I believe I can help you in these areas.

See the next chapter, "Targeted Mailing Cover Letter: A Case Study," for the rest of this letter. Here's another letter that reflects a great deal of thought:

> As the banks look back on their risky involvement with groups like Campeau, it is clear that a better understanding of the retail business would have saved them from considerable losses. As a result, I'm sure many banks and lending institutions have gone to the opposite extreme. Another solution, however, would be to have an unbiased expert merchant involved in evaluating their retail plans.

Your opening should reflect whatever you know about the organization or the person:

> Whenever people talk about organizations with excellent internal temporary services departments, Schaeffer's name always comes up. In fact, the people who run the Amalgamated Center, where I am now assigned, speak often of the quality of your work. I am interested in becoming a consultant in this field and I hope to meet with you.

- **Paragraph 2:**

Give a **summary about yourself**.

- **Paragraph 3:**

  Note a few **key accomplishments that would be of interest to this target.**

- **Paragraph 4:**

  Ask for **half an hour** of his time, and say you will **call him in a few days**. For example:

  > I am sure a brief meeting will be fruitful for us both. I will call your new secretary in a week or so to see when I can get on your calendar.

  or

  > I hope you will allow me half an hour of your time and insight to explore this area. I will call you in a few days to set up a mutually agreeable time.

  If you plan to follow up with a phone call, say so. (But if you say so, do it—or you may get no response while they wait for your call.)

Life is like playing a violin solo in public and learning the instrument as one goes on.

Samuel Butler

Out-of-Town Search

For an *out-of-town search* (perhaps placed next to the last paragraph):

> As a result of many years' travel to Seattle, I would prefer to live and work in that area. In fact, I am in Seattle frequently on business and can arrange to meet with you at your office.

Who has begun has half done.
Have the courage to be wise. Begin!

Horace, Epistles

Scannable Letters

As we have seen, other variations include the use of **underlining key points,** which can increase your response rate. This helps the busy reader scan the letter, be drawn in, and want to read the rest. Underlining makes certain key points pop out at the reader—anywhere in your text. Underline parts of sentences in no more than five places. Read the underlined parts to make sure they sound sensible when read together, have a flow, and make your point.

Even when I look at my own letters, I sometimes don't want to read them before I make them scannable. I rephrase my letters, underlining in a way that will make sense to the reader. People will read the salutation, then the first few words of your letter, and then the parts you have underlined. If they find these things compelling, they'll go back and read the rest of your letter.

Underlining should make sense. Don't underline the word "developed," for instance, which doesn't make sense. Underline *what* you developed, because that's probably the compelling part.

Take calculated risks. That is quite different from being rash.

Gen. George S. Patton, letter to his son, June 6, 1944

Do What Is Appropriate

Strange as it may seem, **sometimes it can be very effective to ignore all of this.** Do what works in your target area. Nat, who was interested in Japanese banks, wrote to 40 banks with a four-line cover letter along these lines: "Enclosed please find my résumé. I have had 20 years of banking experience, am mature, . . ."

Nat knew his market. He thought the Japanese would be put off by the typically aggressive American approach. He got an excellent response rate—and the kind of job he wanted.

Remember, it is sometimes better to follow your instincts rather than listen to the experts. You're smart. You know your market better than we do. Make up your own mind.

The Follow-Up Call (after a Targeted Mailing)

When you call, you will probably have to **start again from the beginning.** Do not expect them to remember anything in your letter. Do not even expect them to remember that you wrote to them. For example, when you phone:

- Say, "I sent you a letter recently. Did you receive it?"
- Remind them of the reason you wrote. You may again have to summarize your background and state some of your accomplishments.
- If they say they have no job openings at this time, that is okay with you—you were not necessarily looking for a job *with them;* you were looking for information or advice about the job possibilities for someone like you, or perhaps you wanted to know what is happening in the profession, organization, or industry.

Leave messages that you called, but do not ask to have them call you back. Chances are, they won't and you will feel rejected. However, be friendly with the secretary and apologize for calling so often. If she would like to have her boss call you back, tell her thanks, but you will be in and out and her boss will be unable to reach you: You will have to call again. After the first call, try not to leave your name again. **Expect to call seven or eight times.** Do not become discouraged. It is not personal.

The way to get good ideas is to get lots of ideas and throw the bad ones away.

Linus Pauling, American chemist

The Meeting

When you go in for your meeting, **handle it as you would a networking meeting** (unless the manager turns it into a job interview):

- Exchange pleasantries.
- State the reason you are there and why you wanted to see this particular person.
- Give your Two-Minute Pitch.
- Tell the manager how he or she can help you. Get the information you want, as well as a few names of other people to whom you should be talking.

As we have said, **be grateful for whatever help people give you.** They are helping you the best they can. If they do not give you the names of others to contact, perhaps they cannot because of a feeling of insecurity in their own jobs. Appreciate whatever they do give you.

For a more detailed description of how to handle the meeting, refer to the chapter "What to Do When Your Networking Isn't Working."

Form a Relationship

Take notes during your meeting. Your follow-up notes will be more appropriate and then you will feel free to contact this person later. Keep in touch with people on a regular basis. Those who know you well will be more likely to help you.

A targeted mailing is a very powerful technique for hitting *every* organization in a small target area. A direct-mail campaign hits every organization in a large target. Both can dramatically move your job hunt along. Try them!

Follow Up

Follow up with a customized note specifically acknowledging the help you received. These notes follow the same concept as follow-ups to networking meetings.

Final Thoughts

You will strike sparks with certain people you meet. They will develop a true interest in you and will surprise you with their help. I have had people invite me to luncheons to introduce me to important people, or call me when they heard news they thought would be of interest to me. I have even made new friends this way.

Of course, I have done my part too by keeping in touch to let them know how my campaign was going. If you are sincere about your search, you will find that the people you meet will also be sincere and will help. It can be a very heartwarming experience.

Without effort we cannot attain any of our goals in life, no matter what the advertisements may claim to the contrary. Anyone who fears effort, anyone who backs off from frustration and possibly even pain will never get anywhere. . . .

Erich Fromm, *For the Love of Life*

CASE STUDY *Ahmed*
Research and Focus

Ahmed had just moved to the United States from Turkey, so he had no contacts here. He had a background in international sales and trading.

He targeted nine major employers and did extensive research on each one. Then he wrote to the head of international sales at each of the nine companies. In his introductory paragraph, he said things like "I notice that your international sales have declined from 6 percent to 3 percent over the last year. I find that very disturbing. I was wondering why that is happening, given the state of the market now . . ."

Paragraph two was his summary. Paragraph three listed his bulleted accomplishments. Paragraph four was the close: "I would really appreciate meeting you . . ."

He called only two of them—because the other seven called him before he had a chance. This targeted mailing resulted in nine meetings and three job offers.

Direct Contact Requires Research and Excellent Writing Skills

Targeted mail works only if you've done your research and if you're a good writer. Furthermore, you must target the right person and have something interesting to say to each person you are contacting. That's why direct contact works best for job hunters who clearly understand their target markets and the important issues in them. And that's also why most people do not attempt direct contact until after they have done their research—through preliminary networking or the library.

Are You Sincere?

It's not enough to write to people and expect to get in to see them. They are probably busy with their own jobs and may be contacted by quite a few people.

Unless you sincerely want to see a person, you won't develop strategies to figure out how to get in to see him or her. You won't do your research. You won't do the follow-up phone calls required to prove your sincerity. You won't prevail when someone doesn't return your phone calls.

If you really want to see this person, you'll persevere. And you won't mind asking for an appointment one month from now if he or she is too busy to see you now. You may even say, "I know you're busy now. How about if we schedule something for a month from now and I'll call you in advance to confirm?"

To Enclose Your Résumé or Not?

A cover story in *Time* magazine was titled "Junk Mail." People said, "Why do junk-mail companies enclose so many things in these envelopes we get? They're wasting paper." In the Letters to the Editor, junk-mail companies said they had no choice because the response rate increased so dramatically with the number of additional enclosures carrying the same message. If they have fewer enclosures, their response rate decreases dramatically.

The same is true for the mailings you are sending. Some people say, "If they see my résumé, they'll know I'm job hunting." But they'll probably know it anyway from your letter. People are very sophisticated today.

My rule of thumb is this: If it supports your case and it has a message that complements your cover letter, then enclose your résumé. You can say, "I've enclosed my résumé to let you know more about me." If you have a brilliant résumé, why not enclose it?

On the other hand, if you want to make a career change, you probably do not want to enclose your résumé because you can probably make a stronger case without it.

Do what is appropriate for you. Try it both ways and see which works better for you and your situation.

Unless you call out, who will open the door?
African proverb

Stating Your Accomplishments in Your Cover Letter

Think of which of your accomplishments are of interest to your target market. You may want to list different accomplishments for the different industries to which you are writing.

Rank your bulleted accomplishments generally in order of importance to the reader, as opposed to chronologically or alphabetically. If some other order would be more appropriate in your case, then do that.

CASE STUDY *Rick*
Out-of-Town Search

A Five O'Clock Club job hunter was looking for a job in Denver. He conducted research by getting a listing of companies from the Denver Chamber of Commerce. He called each company and asked for the name of the department head for the area in which he was interested. He wrote to each one and followed up with a phone call.

He was employed at the time. Yet most of his effort did not take time away from his job. He did his research and wrote his letters evenings and weekends. Networking would have been an impossible way for him to start his search, especially in another part of the country. But after he had made these initial contacts and had traveled to Denver, he could network around.

He wound up with 80 companies to contact—too many for follow-up phone calls. Even 20 is a lot. He followed up with 20 companies and scheduled a three-day trip to Denver. Before he went, he had set up eight meetings for the first two days of his trip. When he met with those first eight, he networked into four additional companies and held those meetings on the third day of his trip.

He didn't have a lot of money, so he couldn't stay long in Denver. But this is also the best way to conduct an out-of-town search—a few days at a time.

When job hunters visit a city for two weeks and hope that something will happen, they usually come home empty-handed. It's better to do your research, contact all of the organizations ahead of time, and go there with meetings already set up. The meetings could be with search firms, in response to ads, or through networking or direct contact.

Go for three days. Tell the people you meet that you are planning to be in town again in a few weeks and would like to meet with other people in their organization or in other organizations. Go back home, do more work, return in another three or four weeks, and stay for another three days. This is how you develop momentum in your out-of-town campaign. A one-time visit rarely works.

Rick went back again six weeks later. It took a few more visits to land the job he wanted, but he did it all with direct and targeted mail as the basis for his campaign, supplemented by networking.

The following pages contain case studies of people who have been successful with targeted mailings. Rather than simply copying their letters, **think of *one* actual individual on your list to whom you are writing and the compelling things you should say to make that person want to meet with you.** Even if you write exactly that same kind of letter to 20 people, it will sound more sincere and have more life if you write that first letter with a particular person in mind.

Targeted Mailing Cover Letter: A Case Study

Faint heart never won fair lady.

Cervantes, *Don Quixote*

Terry was very interested in AT&T. She researched the company and decided to write to the vice chairman of the board. This was an appropriate person for her to write to because he was head of strategic planning, her area of expertise.

She wrote a cover letter using our standard format. The cover letter started out by saying, "I agree with you completely . . ." Then she quoted from an article in which he was mentioned. She was attempting to establish a business relationship with him.

Paragraph two was her summary paragraph. Paragraph three contained her bulleted accomplishments. Paragraph four was her close.

Before sending the letter, she called the company to find out the name of his secretary. It was Kim. Then she called to say that she was writing a letter to Mr. Chase and would Kim please look out for it?

In the last paragraph of her letter, she said, "I would very much appreciate the opportunity to meet with you for half an hour to introduce myself . . . I'll call Kim next week to set up an appointment."

She wound up meeting with the vice chairman, and four other very senior people at AT&T. But the company had a hiring freeze and she ended up working elsewhere.

Was Terry's targeted mailing successful? The answer is yes! Did you forget? Mailings, networking, search firms, and ads are techniques for getting *meetings*. If she got a meeting, the technique was successful. Terry got the meeting she had wanted and more.

By the way, she enclosed her résumé. She was careful not to mention the business she had been in because it was very different from the one at AT&T. But she knew her skills were transferable because she had done so much research on AT&T and could prove it in her letter. She could talk about her background without emphasizing the exact product or service with which she had been involved.

Why Not Network Instead?

When Terry wrote to the vice chairman of the board, she really wanted to see him. If she had decided to network in, it would have taken her a very long time to meet someone who would be willing to introduce her to such an important person. Instead, she did her homework: extensive research and intensive follow-up. Be sure to include targeted mailing in *your* bag of tricks.

Note: Do not necessarily aim for a person at the top of the organization. See people who are appropriate for your level. As a rule of thumb, you want to see people who are two levels higher than you are.

TERRY PILE
Greenwich, CT 02555
212-555-1212 (day)
tpile@trusite.net

August 1, 200X

Mr. Ellis Chase, Vice Chairman
AT&T Corporation
Corporate Planning and Development
One Stamford Forum
Stamford, CT 06904

Dear Mr. Chase:

I agree. Your position *is* truly enviable.

With the merger of AT&T and United Telecom completed, AT&T is now in a position to become an even greater force in shaping telecommunications for the future both domestically and internationally. However, with all the challenges comes the inevitable need for control, resolution of legal and regulatory issues, competitive threats, pricing issues, and reexamination of both positioning and global packaging of AT&T. Clear, focused strategic and business plans become essential for success. I believe I can help you in these areas.

I offer 20 years' experience in management and marketing with more than half that time focused on international markets. In addition, having been primarily involved in start-up and turnaround ventures, I was directly responsible for developing both five- and 10-year strategic plans and one-year operating plans.

Other areas where my experience could assist your corporate planning and development area:

• Established and implemented a global marketing and sales strategy that ensured consistency of message and product delivery to customers.
• Developed an "insider" approach in the local markets for the products and services sold while adhering to corporate values.
• Instituted a global program aimed at ensuring zero defects for multinational clients. Given AT&T's product mix and its strategy for global expansion, superior-quality service is essential for success.
• Developed, installed, and managed a centralized core system for the business noted as the best in the industry.
• Hosted quarterly global sales and marketing conferences and training sessions to cement team spirit and ensure product, corporate and local communications were current and correct.
• Developed a global risk management program to control risk with "common sense" procedures to ensure compliance and support.
• Traveled globally at an 80% level. Focused on visiting/selling/cheerleading clients, prospects, industry leaders, and staff.
• Created and implemented a global promotion and advertising campaign to establish an image of a global yet local player.

I would very much appreciate the opportunity to meet with you for half an hour to introduce myself, discuss the AT&T environment, and identify any areas of your organization or the corporation that may need someone with my background and experience. I have the maturity and sophistication to deal with the wide variety of personalities, problems, and opportunities presented by the international markets plus the persistence to see things through to meet your goals.

I'll call Kim next week to set up an appointment. I look forward to meeting you.

Sincerely,

Terry Pile

The
Five
O'Clock
Club

What to Do When You Know
There's a Job Opening

*To paraphrase Peter Drucker, effective people are
not problem-minded; they're opportunity-minded.
They feed opportunities and starve problems.*

Stephen R. Covey, *The Seven Habits of Highly Effective People*

You've heard about a job opening from someone, or you've seen an ad in the paper. Answer that ad. But to increase your chances of getting a meeting, find an additional way in besides the ad (through networking or through directly contacting the organization).

When using networking or direct contact, most job hunters aim for the hiring manager. After all, he or she is the one with the job, so why would you contact anyone else?

But consider contacting someone other than the hiring manager. He or she is being inundated with requests for meetings by people who have heard about the job. To the hiring manager, those who network in may seem just like those who responded to the ad: another job hunter who knows there is a job opening.

But you are different. You're not a grubby job hunter. You're sincerely interested in this organization, aren't you? You want to meet with someone regardless of whether or not he or she has an opening, don't you? In fact, you are so interested in this organization you would be glad to speak with other people there, not just the hiring manager.

If you first meet with others, you will learn a lot about the hiring manager, the organization, its needs, and the kinds of people who work there. They can refer you in to the hiring manager—with their recommendations. You will be much better prepared than those who got in through the ad. After the formal job interview, you will have advocates in the organization who can coach you and speak to the hiring manager on your behalf.

Some job hunters worry that the job may be filled before they get to the hiring manager. That's possible, but unlikely. Most jobs take a long time to fill. Résumés may sit for weeks before anyone even looks at them. In most cases, you will have time to meet with other people first.

To gather basic information, it's okay to meet with people junior to you or at your level to gather information. But it is sometimes difficult for those lower in the organiza-

tion to refer you up to the boss. Those at your boss's level, or perhaps higher, are in a better position to refer you up, so make sure you aim to meet with them.

CASE STUDY *Madge*
I've Followed Your Organization

Jean, a participant at The Five O'Clock Club, met with five people at Conference Associates and received an offer. It was an interesting place, but she decided the job was too low-level and took another job.

When Jean announced at The Five O'Clock Club that she had turned down an offer from Conference Associates, Madge became very interested in the position.

Jean and Madge had dinner so Madge could learn more about the organization, the job, and the people with whom Jean met. Madge also did library research on the organization. Since she knew exactly who all the players were, she could easily have contacted the hiring manager. In fact, she could have networked in through Jean. But that's not what she did.

In this case, we decided Madge should write directly to the president, who was three-up in the chain of command (the person who would be her boss's boss's boss). In her letter, she said she had long been interested in Conference Associates and she referred to issues Jean had told her were important. **She did not refer to the fact that she knew there was a job opening.**

The cover letter Madge wrote (with a résumé enclosed) is on the next page. The president suggested Madge meet with human resources, the hiring manager, and others. By the way, **this is not networking. This is a targeted mailing.**

Through this technique, Madge got the meeting she wanted. Through her follow-up, she got the job. Read about follow-up in our book *Mastering the Job Interview and Winning the Money Game.*

---

*Let your own discretion be your tutor:
Suit the action to the word,
The word to the action.*

William Shakespeare, *Hamlet*

This is the cover letter Madge sent. She also enclosed her résumé.

MADGE WRIGLEY
345 East Ball Park Avenue
Scottsdale, AZ 44555
(555) 555-0121

July 3, 200X

Ms. Phyllis Rosen, President
Conference Associates
5637 Columbus Avenue
Phoenix, AZ 44555

Dear Ms. Rosen:

These days, the last thing an executive looking to improve profitability probably wants to hear is, "Go to a conference." But that is precisely what he or she may need to find ideas to solve problems back home. I am writing because Conference Associates' goal of encouraging interaction and furthering the exchange of knowledge is one I would like to promote.

I'm currently a manager at AT&T marketing directly to credit-card customers. I manage about $32 million in revenue annually. I've been successful in building a market for expensive products, some, such as life insurance, with negative connotations to overcome.

The key has been twofold: (1) setting clear-cut goals and guiding both the creative and managerial processes to see them realized and (2) carefully researching and identifying a target market, then developing compelling communications to reach them. Now, though, I would like to put my 10 years of business development and marketing experience to work for Conference Associates, specifically in order to take a broader, and global view, of business.

Several aspects of Conference Associates' activities are particularly aligned with my interests and skills:

- The customer orientation: I would like to make companies my customer, evaluating their needs and delivering the services to meet them.
- The Associates' stated goals for expansion in Europe: I firmly believe my international experience could prove beneficial. I'm fluent in French and Spanish, and have worked in France and Sweden.
- I'm an educator at heart: I enjoy managing and developing staff and making connections among people and ideas.

In sum, I believe I could offer a trained and critical eye to understand the need and persuasive marketing programs to communicate the service.

At your convenience, I would be most interested in having a chance to speak with you. I'll call your office shortly to see if that may be possible.

Sincerely,

Madge Wrigley

After each meeting, Madge followed up with a letter that addressed the person's issues. Three of her five letters, slightly abridged to fit on one page, are reprinted here and on the next two pages. For more information on turning job interviews into offers, see the chapters on follow-up in our book *Mastering the Job Interview and Winning the Money Game*.

MADGE WRIGLEY
345 East Ball Park Avenue
Scottsdale, AZ 44555

August 17, 200X

Mr. Charles Conlon
Director, Personnel
Conference Associates
5637 Columbus Avenue
Phoenix, AZ 44555

Dear Chip:

First of all, it was a pleasure to meet you last Wednesday. I enjoyed hearing your assessment of the potential that exists for C.A., and seeing your commitment and enthusiasm for the organization.

You spoke of the unique position of C.A. as a nonprofit service organization run more and more like any business in a competitive environment. The role of a new marketing director, then, would be to develop a strategy for the business to position C.A. for the next level of growth. It's fortunate that C.A. has a solid base to grow from, including a reputation for quality and service. The challenge would be to enhance that reputation while building new markets and customers.

One of the things we spoke about was the need for the marketing director to work closely and productively with other departments. Ellis Chase and I spoke about that as well. I feel particularly motivated by that type of challenge and have been successful in working with diverse groups. For example, recently at AT&T a major new segmentation strategy and methodology for my product line required tying in systems, finance, and new products, in addition to marketing. It wasn't easy, but the reward is a successful expansion of our business and a precedent set for productive cross-departmental projects.

Getting a business built depends a lot on people who don't report to you and buying them into the goals and the process is the only way of getting the job done well. It requires using a balance of sensitivity and toughness and relating to colleagues with flexibility and creativity. If C.A.'s marketing department is going to become a vital and integral part of the operation, it has to establish itself as responsive, knowledgeable, and resourceful.

I truly believe this position is a solid match with my experience and interests, both for the specific skill base required and the opportunity to build a comprehensive marketing program. I've developed marketing plans for organizations ranging from small nonprofits to AT&T and achieved positive results with the implementation.

The common thread in that success has been what you called "ownership." In both my professional experience and my community volunteer work, I tend to approach the task at hand with energy and commitment. After all, the most effective marketer is the one who can combine strategic development and proven skills with genuine product enthusiasm. I would be most interested in putting that same experience and enthusiasm to work for C.A..

Looking forward to speaking with you again soon.

Best,

Madge Wrigley

MADGE WRIGLEY
345 East Ball Park Avenue
Scottsdale, AZ 44555

August 18, 200X

Mr. Ellis Chase
Senior Vice President, Development
Conference Associates
5637 Columbus Avenue
Phoenix, AZ 44555

Dear Ellis:

It was good meeting with you last Wednesday. I got a clear picture of the requirements of the marketing director position and the kind of challenges to be met.

First and foremost, you expressed a need going forward for someone who can develop a comprehensive, integrated marketing strategy and can communicate that plan effectively and appropriately in all facets of its implementation.

That requires the skills of listener, evaluator and diagnostician, coupled with an ability to generate and harness ideas and turn them into positive results. The goal would be to establish C.A. as a leading source of business intelligence and creativity for corporations and their executives.

I've had a chance to think about some of the ways we discussed to accomplish that goal. It seems that both the stated mission of C.A. and its profitability center on building and enhancing its relationship with members, working to have members' resources and activities become a more familiar and integral part of corporate life. One of the priorities you outlined was devising ways to package existing products and services, maximizing both internal marketing efficiency and external perception of value. That would include targeting different people within the same organization with relevant services, as well as determining the right level of pricing.

You also mentioned C.A.'s global objective, trying to serve both U.S. companies competing internationally and many of their foreign competitors. Although I understand the Paris affiliate handles much of the activity in Europe, one of the components of an integrated marketing plan would be defining the optimum balance between a U.S. and global emphasis.

I firmly believe my experience and personality fit the job at hand and that the skills required play to my strengths. I have demonstrated success in strategic and creative planning, researching, and identifying target markets, then developing compelling and appropriate communications to reach them. At both AT&T and previously at RCA, I have developed new businesses and products, including pricing, positioning, and packaging existing services. Efforts I've directed include advertising that increased response from 58% to 93%, and market expansion of 30% with new targeting programs.

I've found ways to run marketing activities more efficiently, saving on both fixed overhead and variable production costs. Finally, as I mentioned, I'm in charge of all writing for the business unit, working closely with each area to communicate group and corporate monthly results as well as the five-year and annual strategic plans.

From my conversations with you and Deborah, the goals for the position, the products of C.A., and its environment seem to represent a strong match with my background and interests. I look forward to speaking with you again soon and having a chance to discuss the position further.

Sincerely,

Madge Wrigley

MADGE WRIGLEY
345 East Ball Park Avenue
Scottsdale, AZ 44555

October 18, 200X

Ms. Phyllis Rosen
President and CEO
Conference Associates
5637 Columbus Avenue
Phoenix, AZ 44555

Dear Phyllis:

While everything is now official and I'll be starting Thursday, October 24th, I wanted to let you know what a pleasure it was to finally meet with you and how delighted I am to be joining C.A.

When we met, you spoke of approaching the task of marketing C.A. with an eye to challenges and opportunities, building on a strong foundation to find better ways to position ourselves in an increasingly competitive market. That includes keeping the focus on senior-level executives. Your outline of the process you've undertaken to evaluate C.A.'s activities was extremely helpful, as well as your expectations for staff to initiate and persuade, even without direct-line responsibility. I particularly appreciated your straightforward review of the financial position.

You also spoke specifically of the need for someone to bring to the position not only marketing expertise but also an enjoyment of your intellectual, knowledge-based product. I firmly believe in that genuine product combination. I'm looking forward to working with that combination and with colleagues who are clearly committed to the organization.

One of them is certainly Melanie. We had a terrific meeting, reviewing everything from general history to specific programs. Particular attention was paid to the strategic plan and development of C.A. over the past few years and the challenge of communicating that strategy both internally and to our customer base. I'm very much looking forward to working with her on integrating a marketing strategy into the overall planning process and new product development, and incorporating that strategy into marketing the programs. I'll also be able to meet with Aaron before I start.

Over the past few weeks, I've had a chance both to think about my conversations with you and others with whom I've met and to review some of C.A.'s materials (50th anniversary history, last year's annual report, etc.). I believe there is enormous potential to spread the word—and the work—of C.A. to a wider audience and to enhance the value of the organization to its current customers. A major component of the task is communication—defining those characteristics that differentiate us in the marketplace and translating them into language that sells. Your commitment to testing new approaches is welcome, understanding the need for moving thoughtfully and with careful planning.

I look forward to the 24th and to a wonderful association at my new home.

Very best,

Madge Wrigley

The
Five
O'Clock
Club

How to Contact Organizations Directly

I don't know anything about luck. I've never banked on it and I'm afraid of people who do. Luck to me is something else: hard work and realizing what is opportunity and what is not.

Lucille Ball

Beth conducted 5 direct-mail campaigns. She selected 5 clear targets and developed lists of names for each, ranging in size from 50 to 200 names. She mailed a cover letter and résumé to her first list. When she started to get calls for meetings, she mailed to her second list. At approximately 2-week intervals, Beth would send out another mailing. She received an excellent response (calls for meetings) from 3 of her 5 mailings.

To develop her interviewing skills and investigate each target area, Beth first had meetings at firms she did not care about. She treated these meetings as networking meetings. Beth probed, for example, to find out what the manager thought of other organizations on her list. If the comments were generally negative, she dropped those organizations. If the comments were positive, she asked if the manager might know someone in the organization whom she could contact. She got a lot of mileage out of her campaign because she combined direct mail with networking and worked the system with great energy.

The entire process took only one-and-a-half months. Beth had clear targets, followed the process, and prepared thoroughly for her meetings. She explored career possibilities in which she had been somewhat interested and refined her career direction. She turned down a number of job offers before she accepted a high-level position that allowed her to combine her strongest skill area with something that was new to her and satisfied her long-range motivated skills. Beth took a two-week vacation before she started that job. She deserved it.

Jack's campaign strategy was very different. Jack is intelligent, articulate, research oriented—and also very shy. He targeted an industry that would result in a career change for him. He had read a lot about this industry and wanted to find out the job possibilities within it.

Jack meticulously researched organizations and selected 20 in which he was seriously interested. They were huge corporations, which made it relatively easy to get the names of people to contact. If he had simply mailed to that list, however, he might have gotten no response. As you will see later, 20 names is generally not enough for a direct-mail campaign. The effort would have been even more futile in Jack's case because he had, essentially, no hands-on experience in that field.

Jack did a targeted mailing—that is, he wrote to the 20 people and *followed up with phone calls* to all of them. His well-written and convincing letter proved his sincere interest in and knowledge of the field. He sent it without a résumé, because he was making a major career change, and told each of the 20 he would call him or her. He sent all the letters at once and called every person. It was quite an effort. Jack got in to see just about every person on his list and—as usually happens—some of them took a personal interest in his case. They gave him the names of others and told him how to break into the field. Two of his contacts volunteered to sponsor him in their organization's training program.

How It Works

Approximately 20 to 40 percent of all jobs are found through direct mail campaigns. This technique is even more effective when you combine it with networking—as both Beth and Jack did.

You will do better in your direct-mail campaign when you:

- have clearly identified your target market;
- are familiar with the problems faced by organizations in that market; and
- know what you have to offer to solve its problems.

Know enough about your target market to compose an appropriate cover letter and to hold your own in a meeting. If you don't know enough, learn more through library

"I'm sorry, but Mr. Taylor no longer engages in human interaction. He does check his E-mail once a week, though."

research or networking. If you feel you may be caught off-guard in a meeting because of a lack of knowledge of your target market, do not use this technique until you have gained at least some knowledge.

These are not job interviews, but exploratory meetings that may lead to:

- more information;
- names of other people to contact; and/or
- a job interview.

Conduct the meeting using the same format as that of a networking meeting.

Don't let the interviewer know you blanketed the market. If an organization wants to see you, quickly do a little research on it. Tell the manager you wrote to him as a result of your research and name something specific about the organization of interest to you.

It doesn't matter if your meetings come from a direct contact or from networking. What matters is that you get in to see people who are in a position to hire you.

Benefits of This Technique

Direct mail blankets the market. In one fell swoop, you can find out the chances for someone like you in the market. You

"market test" what you have to offer and also get your name out quickly to prospective employers. This technique is fast and as complete as you want it to be, as opposed to networking, which is slower and hits your target in a spotty manner.

What Is a Targeted Mailing?

A targeted mailing is direct mail followed by a phone call. Use it when you would like to see every person on your small list. Research so you can write customized letters (you may want to call for annual reports, for example, or talk to people to get information about an organization). Follow the process for networking, paying special attention to the follow-up call, which requires a great deal of persistence. As with networking, you want to meet with people whether or not they have a job to offer.

An Easy Way to Contact Lots of People

Typically, job hunters do not contact many people. Either the job hunter is unemployed and has the time to contact lots of people but may be suffering from low self-esteem—or is employed and simply does not have the time to contact people during the day. The direct-mail campaign allows a person to contact lots of potential employers despite reluctance or a lack of time.

Sometimes job hunters hit a slump and find networking overly stressful. Direct mail can help you get unstuck. You can hide away for a short while and grind out a mailing. You can sound more self-confident on paper than you actually feel and get your act together before you go out and talk to people. A direct-mail campaign can be a way out of a bind. But eventually you must talk to people. You cannot get a job through the mail. Don't use this technique to avoid people forever. Remember, you are writing so you can get in to see them.

The man without purpose is like a ship without a rudder—a waif, a nothing, a no man. Have a purpose in life, and, having it, throw such strength of mind and muscle into your work as God has given you.

Thomas Carlyle

The Numbers You'll Need

In a small industry, your list will be smaller. In a larger industry, your list may be so large you'll want to hit only a portion of it as a test and then hit another portion later.

The "response rate" is measured by the number of meetings you get divided by the number of pieces you mailed. Meetings count as responses; rejection letters do not. Meetings count because there is the possibility of continuing your job search in that direction. Rejection letters, no matter how flattering, have ended your search in that particular direction.

In direct mailing, a 4 percent response rate is considered very good. The basic rule of thumb is this:

A mailing of 200 good names results in

- seven or eight meetings, which result in
- one job offer.

If your list is smaller, you may still do okay if you are well suited to that target and if there is a need for your services. If, however, your list has only 10 names, you must network in, or use a targeted mailing with a follow-up phone call.

Another factor that affects your response rate is the industry to which you are writing. Certain industries are very people oriented and are more likely to talk to you. Targeting industries that have a great demand for your service should result in a lot of responses.

Assuming that the job you are seeking is reasonable (i.e., you have the appropriate qualifications and there are positions of that type available in the geographic area you are targeting), persistent inquiries will eventually turn up some openings.

What makes men happy is liking what they have to do.
This is a principle on which society is not founded.

Claude Adrien Helvetius

Should You Enclose Your Résumé?

If your résumé helps your case, enclose it. Beth enclosed her résumé; Jack did not. Direct-mail experts have proved that the more enclosures, the greater the response rate. You never know what may "grab" the reader and the reader is likely to glance at each enclosure. Your résumé, if it supports your case and is enticing, is another piece to capture the reader's attention. I have been called for meetings because of what was on page three of my résumé.

If, however, your résumé hurts your case, change it or leave it out altogether. A résumé may hurt your case when you are attempting a dramatic career change, as Jack was. (Read the chapter "How to Change Careers" to get more ideas on how you can support your case.)

Cover Letters

The format you follow for your cover letter essentially can be the same whether you enclose your résumé or not. Your cover letter focuses your pitch more precisely than your résumé does and makes the reader see your résumé in that light. You can pitch to a very precise segment of the market by making only minor changes in the letter. The format for your cover letter is:

Paragraph 1—The grabber. Start with the point of greatest interest to your target market. This is the equivalent of a headline in an ad.

If your background is enough of a grabber for the target market to which you are writing, use it. For example, if you want a job in sales and have an excellent track record in that area, then open with a terrific sales accomplishment. Or if your expertise is in turnaround management, your cover letter might start like this:

As vice president of a $250 million organization, I directed the turnaround of an organization in serious financial difficulty. As a result, this year was more profitable than the previous 10 profitable years combined.

On the other hand, you can open your letter with a statement that shows you understand the problems faced by the industry to which you are selling your services. A successful letter to advertising agencies started like this:

Many ad agencies are coping with these difficult times by hiring the best creative and sales people available. While this may maintain a competitive edge, many agencies find their bottom line is slipping. The usual response is to send in the accountants. These agencies, and perhaps your own, need more than accounting help. As vice president of operations, I . . .

Here's a variation on the same theme aimed at organizations probably doing well financially:

I know this is a time of rapid growth and high activity for technology-based firms. I believe this is also a time when technology-based firms must be as effective as possible to maintain their competitive edge. If you are looking for new developers—either on an ad hoc or a permanent basis—consider a person like me.

If you work for a well-known organization in an area that would be of interest to your target market, you could start your letter like this:

I am at present with X Company in a position where I . . .

Perhaps your background itself would be your key selling point:

I started out in computers in 1976 and have been involved with them ever since. I am now at . . .

If you are targeting a small number of organizations, mention your specific interest in each one:

I have been interested in [your organization] for a number of years because of . . .

Paragraph 2—A summary of your background aimed at a target, perhaps taken from the summary statement on your résumé.

Paragraph 3—Your key accomplishments of interest to this target market. These can be written in a bulleted or paragraph format. Make them lively and interesting.

Paragraph 4 (optional)—Additional information. This could include references to your education or personality, or other relevant information, such as:

> I am high in energy and integrity—persuasive, thorough, and self-confident—a highly motivated self-starter accustomed to working independently within the framework of an organization's policies and goals. I thrive on long hours of work, and enjoy an atmosphere where I am measured by my results, where compensation is directly related to my ability to produce, and where the job is what I make it.

Final paragraph—The close. Such as:

> I would prefer working in an environment where my leadership and problem-solving abilities are needed and would be pleased to meet with you to discuss the contribution I could make to your organization.

Or use a statement like this one, which excludes those who may want to hire someone at a lower salary level:

> Hiring me would be an investment in the mid-$70,000 range, but the return will be impressive. I would be pleased to meet with you to discuss the contribution I could make to the performance of your organization.

Or use this statement for a direct-mail campaign where you will not be making follow-up phone calls, especially to a list to which you have some relationship, such as that of an organization of which you are a member:

> I can understand how busy you must be and therefore do not want to bother you with a follow-up phone call. However, I trust that you will give me a call if you come across information that would be helpful to me in my search.

You gain strength, courage and confidence by every experience in which you really stop to look fear in the face. You are able to say to yourself: "I lived through this horror. I can take the next thing that comes along." . . . *You must do the thing you think you cannot do.*

Eleanor Roosevelt

We African-American women have always worked outside of our homes, in slavery or in freedom—in the fields, in the kitchen, or in the nursery.

Frederica J. Balzano, Ph.D., "And Ar'nt I a Woman?" *The Five O'Clock News,* September 1995

Happiness is not a matter of events; it depends upon the tides of the mind.

Alice Meynell

Pain: an uncomfortable frame of mind that may have a physical basis in something that is being done to the body, or may be purely mental, caused by the good fortune of others.

Ambrose Bierce

The Five O'Clock Club

Direct-Mail Campaigns

Perfection of means and confusion of goals seem, in my opinion, to characterize our age.

Albert Einstein

Does Direct Mail Work?

A technique "works" if it helps you get meetings in your target market. When you are mounting a full campaign, your goal is to have the organizations in your target market know about you as quickly as possible. You can supplement your networking by using search firms and answering ads, but you will still not have hit most of the organizations in your market. Regardless of how you get in, if you find you are being well received by some organizations in your target market, consider direct mail and/or targeted mail for the rest.

If you use direct mail, consider mounting campaigns to a number of targets. Out of four campaigns, for example, maybe two will be effective and result in meetings and two won't work at all. Part of it is selecting a target likely to be interested in you. Another part is being able to express yourself clearly and compellingly in writing. And a third part is a numbers game. If you get no response when you mail to a very small number, that mailing was not a good test.

Most job hunters expect every letter they write to result in a meeting, which is unreasonable. They don't expect every search-firm contact or every ad to result in a meeting. The same is true for direct contact.

CASE STUDY *Diane*
Getting More Job Possibilities in the Works

Last week, Diane accepted a job offer. She had uncovered two job possibilities through networking, but she wanted to have the requisite "6 to 10 things in the works." So she did a mailing of 250 letters, which resulted in four more job leads. Admittedly, that's a very small response rate from a mailing, but she wound up with four more job interviews than she would have had exclusively through networking.

Act As If This Company Is Important to You

One time I wrote a direct-mail letter to 200 companies. A manager at one company said to me, "How did you hear of us? No one ever writes to us." I said, "Oh, a number of people have mentioned your company." "Really. Who?" I said, "Pierre Charbonneau and Lillian Bisset-Farrell, to name two [making up the first two names that came to my mind]." The manager said, "I don't know them." "Well," I replied, "they've heard of you!"

If they take your letter personally, you cannot tell them you sent that same letter to 200 people.

> **For direct-mail campaigns using the Internet, see "Using Search Engines to Develop Your List" in the chapter, "Research: Developing Your List of Organizations to Contact."**

Helen: Making It Sound Personal

*Out there things can happen to people as
brainy and footsy as you.*

*And when things start to happen don't worry. Don't
stew. Just go right along. You'll start happening too.*

Dr. Seuss, *Oh, the Places You'll Go!*

Helen is an organizational-development person. She
wrote a letter to 60 fellow members of the Organization Development Network, saying: "As a fellow
member of the OD Network, I thought perhaps you might
come across information to help me in my job search. I am
interested in making a career move and I sure would
appreciate hearing from you." Paragraph two was her summary. In paragraph three, she listed her accomplishments.

Paragraph four was very clever because she had no
intention of calling these people, and she didn't want to
make it sound like a mass mailing, so she said a variation
of "I don't want to bother you with phone calls, but I trust
you will give me a call if you come across information that
would help me in my search."

She got six calls back about real job openings. She did
another mailing to another 60 people in the same organization, got another six meetings, and eventually wound up
with a job offer.

Which technique did she use? It was a direct-mail
campaign.

If you have an association list, consider using it for a
direct-mail campaign, and be sure to mention your membership in that association in your opening paragraph.

---

*Results! Why, man, I have gotten a lot of results. I
know several thousand things that won't work.*

Thomas A. Edison

> **If you are not going to follow up your
> letter with a phone call, here's one way to
> end your letter (if this is appropriate in
> your situation):**
>
> **"I don't want to bother you with a
> follow-up phone call. However, I am very
> interested in meeting with you. If you
> feel the same, I hope you will give me a
> call so we can set up a time to meet."**

AURORA BRITO
2421 Maindays Boulevard
Columbus, Ohio 43700
231-555-1212

April 6, 200X

Name
Position
Company
Address
City, State, ZIP

Dear _____:

As a fellow member of the Organization Development Network, I am writing to explore with you potential opportunities in your organization.

Currently with Bell South as an internal corporate human resources consultant, I am seeking an opportunity in organization and management development. Perhaps it would facilitate this process if I share key highlights of my background:

- Management development specialist with more than **6 years of experience** developing and making presentations.
- At **Bell South**, I am responsible for designing and implementing projects to enhance the professionalism of more than 2,000 managers worldwide. This involves:
  — **Executive and high-potential development**—Assessing and identifying top performers to meet specific business talent needs, attend Executive University programs, and facilitate succession planning.
  — **Needs analysis**—Running focus groups throughout the United States and Europe for the purpose of creating and designing training programs.
  — **Organizational research**—Using statistical and research design (SPSSX) to conduct surveys, climate studies, and turnover studies.
- Experience in Asia as a process consultant to an American-based company. **Fluent in Japanese.**
- Hold **2 master's degrees from Columbia University** in organizational and counseling psychology.

What do you think? Are there any possibilities within your purview for someone with my skills and experience base? I realize you are busy and I don't want to be intrusive by phoning; however, if you are interested or would just like to discuss some ideas, please contact me at 231-555-1212. Attached is my résumé. I look forward to your input. Thank you.

Sincerely,

The Five O'Clock Club

How to Answer Ads

Of all sad words
Of tongue and pen
The saddest are these:
"It Might Have Been."

Let's add this thought
unto this verse:
"It Might Have Been
A Good Deal Worse."

Anonymous

Some people get excited when they see an ad in the paper or on the Internet. They *know* this is the job for them and their hopes soar.

But try to keep things in perspective. Don't be surprised if you answer 30, 50, or more ads and *get no meetings*. Your résumé is one of perhaps hundreds or even thousands of responses. What's more, your résumé is not being screened by the hiring manager.

Chances are, your cover letter and résumé will be screened by a computer or by a junior clerk. I once met a 20-year-old woman who reviewed résumés on behalf of blue-chip companies, screening thousands of professionals and managers in the $40,000 to $100,000 range. *She* decided who would get interviewed. This young woman was good at her job and often took a personal interest in the people whose résumés she saw—but she was only 20 years old. Writing a cover letter to intrigue or strike a responsive chord in her wouldn't have worked.

While writing creative cover letters will work for targeted- and direct-mail campaigns, stick to the basics in answering ads. If the ad asks for specific qualifications and experience, highlight those areas from your background. Respond point by point to each item mentioned. Show how you have everything they want. Keep your cover letter crystal clear. Remember, the reader of your letter may be 20 years old. If you don't fit exactly, you will probably be screened out.

Fewer than 10 percent of all jobs are found through ads, including both print and online ads. At The Five O'Clock Club, we say you should consider *all four* tech-niques for getting interviews in your target market—search firms, ads, networking, and direct contact—and then *notice* which techniques are working for you. "Working for you" means that a technique results in *meetings*. You don't measure the effectiveness of a technique by whether or not you got a *job*. You measure the effectiveness of a technique by whether or not it's resulting in *meetings* for you.

If an average ad in *The Wall Street Journal* or *The New York Times* gets a 1,000 responses, you have 999 competitors. Websites for large corporations can get one million résumés a year. Many people sit at their computers for hours on end, hitting that "send" button and wondering why no one is responding to them. Everyone else is doing

"Actually, we're not hiring. We hold lots of interviews like this one so our competition thinks we're busy."

the same thing. We frequently hear hiring managers say they don't even consider this accumulating database of résumés. It's a rare job hunter who even includes a cover letter in response to an Internet ad. Yet, the cover letter is the piece that can most significantly increase the chances you'll be called in.

The Cover Letter for Answering Ads

It's unlikely the hiring manager will be the one who does the screening. Instead, some junior-level person (or a computer) reviews the hundreds or thousands of responses. You can be sure the person wants to get through those résumés as quickly as possible. Their job is to get rid of all but 10 or 20 of them! So make it easy for them to screen you *in*. All you want is to be in the "*include*" pile.

You must **_personalize_ the cover letter when answering an ad.** Sometimes when we're looking for people to work in The Five O'Clock Club office, we may post jobs on the Internet and we are deluged with responses. Often we can't tell which job the person is applying for: an accounting job or a public relations job. People just unthinkingly hit the send button without a thoughtful cover letter.

So even when you respond to an Internet ad, be sure to use The Five O'Clock Club's four-paragraph approach. Make your cover letter very clear, very short, very readable. Show a strong match between you and the position they've posted. Then the résumé screener will at least know which pile to place you in. Here's our formula for the cover letter:

In paragraph one, be sure to mention the *position* for which you are applying, as well as the newspaper or Internet site where you saw the ad, and the date of the ad.

Paragraph two contains your *summary* about you *as it relates to this position*. Such as, "I have 10 years of international marketing experience in the chemical and pharmaceutical industries."

For paragraph three, if you *think* you're qualified for the job, use The Five O'Clock Club's two-column approach when mailing or e-mailing in the response. Your response will definitely stand out compared with all the other responses.

The first column says "You are looking for . . ." or "Your requirements," under which you list everything they've mentioned in the ad. In column two, you say "I have this to offer" or "My experience," and match up what you have to offer to what they're looking for. Of course, make sure what you have to offer seems better than what they're looking for.

List your points in the order in which they're listed in the ad. Most hiring managers will list first in an ad the requirements that are most important to them. So you want to list first those things that are most important to the hiring team. That way, the junior-level person who is screening all of these cover letters (even the ones the computer selected) will have an easier time *including* you rather than *excluding* you.

Use _their_ terminology not yours. When answering an ad, make sure you use *their* terminology and not the terminology from your last position. If they say they're looking for a *trainer* and you've been a *teacher,* then just say you've had 12 years of *training* experience. Don't use a word that's inappropriate for their industry or their firm.

Use The Five O'Clock Club's two-column approach if you think you're a good match for the job. On the other hand, if you feel you're *not* a strong match and still want to answer the ad, *don't* use the two-column approach, which would highlight the fact that you're not a strong match. Instead, clearly state what you have to offer and *say* you think you're an ideal candidate and why.

In paragraph four, list any additional information about yourself that you think would be of interest to the hiring company.

Finally, as far as salary in concerned, *say nothing*. Many ads include the words, "Please tell us your salary requirements," yet savvy job hunters decline to mention salary because it increases the chance they'll be *excluded*.

What are the chances you're going to match whatever salary they have in mind? You'll name a number that's too high for them, too low—but rarely just right. The odds are against you. So it's a disadvantage for you to list your salary.

Therefore, job hunters generally say, "I'd be glad to discuss salary requirements upon mutual interest. I look forward to meeting with you to further discuss the position." That way, you're not ignoring their request for salary information.

Sometimes you'll see an ad stating, "You will absolutely not be considered for this job unless you provide your salary history." Those ads are usually placed by academic institutions or by the government. If an ad says you *must* name your salary history, the best approach is to provide *limited information;* don't disclose your *entire* salary history, because you reduce your chance of being called in *and* you reduce your chance of negotiating an appropriate salary. However, you *can* mention a broad range of what you're looking for. Be sure to think strategically. Research the industry you're targeting and its standard procedures and play it accordingly. No matter what the industry, don't disclose too much about yourself before you even get an interview.

By the way, these are the issues and details you should discuss with your small group. That's why we *have* a small group. You may face unusual situations, so be sure to use your group for guidance.

Surround the Hiring Manager

An ad for a job is as good as a flashing neon sign: The company is telling the world it has an opening! Your strategic thinking should go into high gear—if it's a company or a job that *really* interests you. Don't wait to get in by just responding to the ad. Network into the company or contact someone there directly, but not the person mentioned in the ad. "Surrounding the hiring manager" is a very effective technique. Get in to see someone—almost *anyone* other than the hiring manager. An insider can become an advocate for you and refer you in to the hiring manager. You'll have a better chance of standing out from your competitors—because you were referred in and will know more—and you'll do better in the meeting. You're no longer one more grubby job hunter who is simply responding to an ad—you're now someone who is sincerely interested in this company and knows how to go the extra mile. The hiring manager will get to know you in a different way from the other applicants and he or she *may* consider you even though you don't have all of the qualifications they listed. For more information on this technique, see the chapter "What to Do When You Know There's a Job Opening."

Bottom line: **If it's a good ad for you, answer the ad, then forget about the ad and try to get in some other way—without mentioning the ad**.

> **If you meet all the requirements of the job, then make it very clear to the screener that you should *not* be screened out. Be sure to read "What to Do When You Know There's a Job Opening" in this book.**

CIRO DISCLAFANI
38 Cicily Place
West Hamstart, MO 59684
CiroDisc@worldwidenet.com

March 23, 200X

Terry Pile
Employment Manager
National Data Labs
22 Parns Avenue
East Hamstart, MO 59684

Dear Ms. Pile:

I believe I am a good fit for the Assistant Controller position advertised in the *Hamstart Times* on March 20, 20xx.

Having been continually challenged and rapidly promoted at Toronto Dominion Bank, I have a proven track record in controllership functions. I've headed the controllership function in every major area of the company, including credit cards, travelers checks, and private banking. As you may be aware, Toronto Dominion has a rigorous budgeting, financial analysis, and cost-accounting process, similar to National Data Labs, and this has contributed to the success of the organization.

Here is a breakdown of my experience vs. your requirements:

Your Requirements	**My Experience**
• 12+ years experience in private accounting/ management	• 14+ years experience in financial management
• BBA, MBA a plus.	• BBA in finance MBA in financial management
• Financial analysis/cost-accounting skills	• Strong financial analysis skills—controllership functions
	• Strong cost-accounting skills—designed cost-accounting/unit-cost methodologies

I consider myself a sophisticated management professional with a significant number of business accomplishments, coupled with excellent ability to communicate both orally and in writing.

I would welcome an interview with you to review my experience in financial management.

Sincerely,

Ciro Disclafani

Blind Ads

If you are considering a blind ad, be careful. Blind ads don't include the name of the organization seeking to hire someone. It could be placed by a search firm or by the company itself with just a box number. You don't know to whom you're sending your résumé. Be *especially* careful if you're currently employed. That ad could have been placed by your employer or by a search firm who works with your employer. Employed job hunters often respond with just a letter and no résumé. Their letter states why they're a match, but they don't mention their present place of employment. But even this can be risky. If you're employed, you may want to skip those blind ads.

If They Call You

If you do answer an ad, be prepared for a phone call, just in case. Someone may actually respond to your letter! So make sure your message machine doesn't have something silly on it, such as all three of your children saying, "Hi, this is Janet and this is Jim and this is Karen and we all live here." Your message should be professional or you may turn off prospective employers with a silly message or strange music. They may simply hang up and you won't even know they called. Job hunters need to be hypersensitive about *impressions*—and this includes the outgoing message on your answering machine.

If you *do* get a phone call, the first thing you may be asked is your salary range. And that's the *last* thing you want to talk about. So make sure you're ready to handle that. Read our book, *Mastering the Job Interview and Winning the Money Game*. You might say, "I think it's a little early to discuss salary. I'm sure salary is *not* going to be a problem." You want a *meeting*—in person—and you want to be prepared. It's certainly too early to discuss salary.

Remember, however: Most job seekers who respond to ads will never get a call. So don't expect to hear back and get on with your search. Don't spend too much time trying to figure out how ads work. Figure out how *else* to get in.

Rejection Letters

If you get a rejection letter when you've answered an ad, try not to give it a second thought. That letter is not personal. They don't even *know* you. They're just sending letters out routinely. So ignore the letter, but don't necessarily ignore the *company*! One Five O'Clock Club coach has on his office wall *three* framed rejection letters from the *same company,* which eventually hired him! He put these on public display so his clients could see that rejection letters *don't count*.

If there's a name on the rejection letter, you may want to respond to the letter—especially if you're interested in the company. Remember the person who "rejected" you

may be the junior-level person who's going through all those résumés. So you may want to write to the *manager* saying you're disappointed and think you're a great match for the company—if not now, maybe in the future. Be sure to enclose your résumé: Remember that this person may never have even *seen* your résumé! We say at The Five O'Clock Club, "The ball is always in your court"—so a rejection letter may *still* be an opportunity!

Where to Find Ads

Where can you find ads? In your local paper, in the national papers, in association journals having to do with your field or industry. If you have very well-defined targets, association journals, association websites, and other websites having to do with your field or industry can be a terrific place for ads.

> If the ad gives a fax number, use the fax number to respond. But *also* respond through snail mail—and perhaps E-mail—if possible. You never know which method may get their attention.

Refining Your Response

Of course, ads point you toward current openings. But remember that ads—whether Internet or print—are great for *research*. Ads tell you who's hiring, what they're looking for, and the jargon they use. You may be able to spot trends by tracking the ads week after week. You can modify the approach to your entire search based on what you find out through this research. And ads give you the names of additional companies to target. Then you can try to get in to see people by contacting them directly or through networking.

Being Effective with Internet Postings

José was a Five O'Clock Clubber who had an e-commerce background. He'd been searching for *four* months before he came to the club, but with slim results—not even one interview. When the small group looked at José's résumé, they couldn't even *see* his e-commerce background. He was positioned incorrectly. So José's small group suggested changes for the top of his résumé. Instead of saying, "international marketing executive," the group suggested that he change it to say, "E-commerce executive with strong marketing background." They suggested he follow *that* headline with bulleted accomplishments related to his e-commerce background, followed by his international background.

José was comfortable with posting his résumé on the web because he was not employed at this time. He got a tremendous number of responses. However, most of them were inappropriate because the person (or machine) saw the words "E-commerce executive" and saw him as a technology person. So his small group suggested he refine his résumé one more time. They suggested he change it to "E-commerce *marketing* executive." *Now* José got called in just for e-commerce *marketing* positions.

José was with The Five O'Clock Club only six weeks. He got four offers. He accepted a job with a terrific firm and his group suggested he *not* close off conversations with the other companies until he had been in the new firm for about two weeks—just to try it out. But it was the *repositioning* that made the Internet work for him.

On the Internet, sometimes *people* are not looking at your résumé. *Computers* are looking at it. So the words you use, and *where* you use them are very important. Because José did not have the word "marketing" in the *first* line of his résumé, but had it in the *second* line, the results he got from the machine were completely different. So you owe it to yourself to think things through: The words on *your* résumé must be carefully chosen.

When you answer Internet ads or post your résumé on an organization's website, don't use esoteric words that were used only in your last firm. Use words that would be *generally* used. If you're *employed, never post* your résumé on the Internet. Respond to ads posted by specific identified organizations. After all, you wouldn't post your résumé on the bulletin board in your local grocery store, would you? You don't want to put your résumé out there for *anybody* to see. Treat your résumé as a confidential document.

For an electronic résumé, put key words at the top. Depending on the software the hiring organization is using, you may need to repeat certain words. For example, certain software packages will rate a résumé higher if it has the word JAVA in it 13 times as opposed to one or two times. Ironically, somebody who may be more qualified but have the word JAVA in the résumé only once may be disqualified. So you might have to be very aware of these things until the software is upgraded. Pay attention to what is working in the market.

Our next chapters cover more about writing an electronic résumé and using the Internet as a job-search tool. And don't forget the bibliography at the back of this book, and a more extensive one in the Members Only section of our website.

SHANA L. KINGSLEY

883 Ledger Lane, Minneapolis, MN 88888
(555) 555-2268
skingsley@msn.com

July 19, 2000X

Mr. Theobold J. Yegerlehner
Vice President, Tax
United Telecom Corporation
United Telecom Building
Minneapolis, MN 88801

Dr. Mr. Yegerlehner,

Could United Telecom benefit from a hands-on tax director and counsel with international expertise and the ability to drive strategic initiatives?

I have designed and implemented tax strategies for businesses in the United States and more than 35 other countries.

I know how to work with operations, finance, and legal people to deliver tailored solutions that get results. I have managed cross-functional teams in North America, Europe, Latin America, and the Asia–Pacific region in complex projects, including

- Executing a **$4 billion U.S. recapitalization**.
- Refinancing global operations to **extract cash from overseas** without crippling operations or paying significant taxes.
- Implementing a global trading company to streamline production, increase sales, and **reduce the global effective tax rate by 50%**.
- Reconfiguring a global sales organization to isolate and manage an estimated **$100 million foreign tax exposure**.

I am very interested in meeting with you. I believe you will find even a brief meeting beneficial. I will call your office in the next few days to see when I can get on your calendar.

Sincerely,

Although hers is a narrow field, when Shana wrote to 20 executives who had no advertised positions, 6 of them contacted *her* immediately for an exploratory meeting.

The Five O'Clock Club

How to Work with Search Firms

Once-in-a-lifetime opportunities come along all the time—just about every week or so.

Garrison Keillor, *A Prairie Home Companion*

If you understand how search firms work, your expectations will be more reasonable and you will better understand how to approach them.

Contrary to what some people think, a recruiter in a search firm does not place hundreds of managerial and professional people per year. Their search assignments are very specific and require extensive research, networking, and screening prior to presenting qualified individuals to their client organizations. Therefore, **the average recruiter places one or two people a month.** This is the most important statistic for you to know about search firms and this information will affect your entire thought process about search firms.

Recruiters who deal with junior-level people need to place two people a month. Recruiters who deal with the very highest-level people may place only *six people a year!* So search firms are not filling as many jobs as you think. It's actually *unlikely* that a search firm and a specific recruiter will be able to place you. Should you talk to search firms? Absolutely. But for goodness' sake don't *count* on them. The numbers are not on your side. Agencies may have lots of openings, but they are usually given the toughest positions to fill: Companies are willing to pay high agency fees to get candidates who walk on water. Agency recruiters would be the first to admit they don't have great hit ratios: Typically only *1* out of every 10 people they send on interviews is hired!.

The work recruiters do is in some respects similar to the work done by realtors. Recruiters "represent" positions that need to be filled (the equivalent of houses for sale), and they recruit qualified people to fill those positions (house hunters). They match qualified candidates with their job opportunities, just as realtors match house hunters with the houses on their lists. The realtor is trying to get buyer and seller to come together on price, and the realtor wants to stay in the middle of the transaction. In both fields, possibilities are sometimes presented as "once-in-a-lifetime" opportunities. And often, the actual matches are just as rare!

Recruiting is basically a sales profession and recruiters are interested in working with individuals who are marketable—just as realtors prefer houses that are marketable. Therefore, the more marketable you are, the more likely a search firm will be interested in handling you. If you are too difficult to categorize, are trying to make a major career change, require an unreasonable compensation, or have other drawbacks, search firms will balk at working with you (although they may not be totally honest about it).

You can increase your odds by *making it easy* for search firms to market you. Here are a few suggestions:

- Summarize your marketable characteristics in your cover letter. Recruiters need to categorize you anyway, so make it easy for them.

- Clearly state your target market (geographic area, industry, and position) and your salary range. For example: "I'm interested in a financial position in the direct-marketing industry in the New York or Chicago areas. I'm looking for a salary in the $65,000 to $70,000 range."

- Next, state your key selling points—your summary and accomplishments. Recruiters present your *accomplishments* to client organizations—not your job description. *Tell them what to say to sell you.* It will make their jobs easier and thus make them more likely to want to handle you.

- Be honest. Assume the search firm will check references and verify whatever information you give to them. Their reputations are based on the caliber of individuals they represent. If you misrepresent information, it could cost you the perfect career opportunity. Even if you get past the search firm, your employer could fire you later if falsehoods are uncovered.

To Redo Your Résumé—or Not

If recruiters want you to redo your résumé, follow their suggestions only if you think you're interested in the job about which they're talking to you. Sometimes customization is appropriate for a specific position, but some recruiters simply want résumés done their own way based on their own habits and biases—and their way may not be *better* at all. They forget that you got in to see *them* with your present résumé. They also forget that their technique "works" not because of their *résumé* approach but because they get on the phone and talk about you to someone. It's okay to change your résumé for them to meet a particular circumstance, but don't change your résumé *for the rest of your search* just because of what a recruiter wanted. Believe it or not, recruiters are *not* résumé experts. Listen instead to your coach and small group.

Sample Search-Firm Cover Letter

Search firms need to know your target: the kind of job you want and where. Your cover letter can give you a boost here. They also need to know your salary requirements, so you might as well include a range in your cover letter. The letter on the following page uses our formula for cover letters presented earlier.

A Typical Search-Firm Marketing Call

Here's what may happen if you have made it easy for the recruiter by positioning yourself in your cover letter. They place a few phone calls. "Joe," they say, "I've got someone you may be interested in. He's a highly skilled individual who has the exact profile you have hired through me before." And then they may read from your cover letter. "He's got 15 years of financial experience in the direct-marketing industry. [Then they will stress your accomplishments, especially those that saved a past employer time or money.] He's an energetic, ambitious person—a real self-starter. When would it be convenient for us to set up a meeting? He's available next Tuesday or Wednesday morning . . . Oh, I know you don't have any positions currently available. After I met him, I just thought of you. I really think he'd be worth your time to interview."

Should You Keep in Regular Touch with Agencies?

The short answer is no. Recruiters are very aware of the positions they are trying to fill at the moment, and they are very aware of the candidates in their database. All of their energies are going into finding good matches for their client organizations. If they have a position that is appropriate for you and if they are not already too far along with the search, they will call you in. A follow-up phone call from you will do no good and just cuts into their busy day. We advise job hunters to send their résumés to search firms and then *get on with other aspects of their searches.*

It is better to form long-term relationships with reputable search firms. You can do this by helping them when they have an assignment they are trying to fill—even though it is not right for you. Perhaps you could suggest the names of other people they should call. Then when you are ready to make a move, they are already aware of you and your character, and are more likely to consider you when they have an opening that *is* right for you.

Life will give you what you ask of her if only you ask long enough and plainly enough.

E. Nesbitt

Which Organizations Use Search Firms?

Search firms are used by small- to mid-sized organizations with limited personnel departments. The search firm acts as an extension of their human resources staff. In addition, smaller organizations often must use search firms because applicants don't contact them as often as they do larger organizations.

Search firms are also used by major organizations with specific needs. Major organizations expect the search firm to identify the best individual in their industry nationwide—and usually in a very short period of time. Search firms are expected to know—or be able to find out quickly—the important players in a specialty.

Search firms are also used to fill jobs when there is a labor shortage. This could be for a specialty that is much in demand at the moment or for an executive-level position in a field so unusual that the search firm may have to look outside the organization's normal geographic area. Common positions may also be difficult to fill on occasion, leading organizations to turn to agencies.

How to Find Good Agencies and Recruiters

1. One of the best ways to identify good recruiters is by asking hiring managers or other job hunters—that is, through *networking.* When you meet with people during your search, ask them, "Are there any search firms you've used or you think I should talk to?"

2. A primary source of good information is the *Directory of Executive Recruiters.* Despite its title, this book lists firms for most job levels and job categories and also by geographic area. It is found in many libraries, or you can get your own copy from Kennedy Publications, Templeton Road, Fitzwilliam, NH 03447. However, don't contact contingency search firms blindly. (See below for the definition of contingency firms.) Instead, have a targeted list of search firms to contact rather than giving your résumé to everybody.

Search-Firm Cover Letter

Search firms need to know your target: the kind of job you want and where. They also need to know your salary requirements. This letter follows our formula format: Paragraph 2—Summary. Paragraph 3—Bulleted accomplishments.

Dear Ms. Bruno:

In the course of your search assignments, you may have a requirement for a technically knowledgeable IBM AS400—System 38 professional.

I have been both a "planner" and a "doer" of the phases of the System Development Life Cycle at companies such as General Motors and Proctor & Gamble, where I have spent most of my career. My accomplishments span the gamut, including the following:

- Evaluation of application and system software and hardware,
- Installation/setup of a new computer site,
- Conversion of RPG and COBOL programs,
- Requirements for and design of applications,
- Development and programming,
- Quality assurance and testing, and
- Optimization of performance for applications and systems.

At this juncture, after many years of commuting to Manhattan, I'm interested in seeking permanent employment in New Jersey, where I live.

The enclosed résumé briefly outlines my experience over the past 15 years. My base is now in the $70,000 range plus the usual fringes.

If it appears my qualifications meet the needs of one of your clients, I would be happy to further discuss my background in a meeting with you.

Yours truly,

Enclosure

Do not send your résumé to search firms unless you know their reputation. A disreputable agency could "blanket" the market with your résumé and cheapen your value. Make sure the search firm tells you *before* they send your résumé to anyone.

3. Look for search firms in the want ads in newspapers or trade journals. It's easy to identify those that handle the kinds of jobs for which you're looking. You can find out who specializes in your field or industry.

   Just be aware of the game that may be going on here. Not every ad you see in the paper represents a real job. Sometimes, contingency firms need a fresh batch of résumés: The people in their files have already moved on to new jobs. The next time you see an ad in the paper or on the Internet and you think *that job's too good to be true*. It probably *isn't* true. They placed a great, generalized ad to pull in a lot of résumés. Contact those search firms, but not necessarily for the job they have listed in the paper. When you call, they'll say, "That job is filled; let me talk to you about *other* jobs that may be right for you." Working with agencies really is a game.

4. If you're leaving a company because of a downsizing and you plan to stay in the same field, ask your human resources department which search firms *they* use. That will give you some *clout* because you can say that "Jane Doe in human resources at Databank, Inc. suggested I call you." Since Databank, Inc. pays the search firm for placements, its search firm is likely to try to help you.

Retainer vs. Contingency Search Firms

The "search-firm" field has become more complex in recent years. It now includes new services, such as temporary-service firms.

"One of those head-hunters called about you today, but it's not what you think. They have offered to pay us to keep you here."

Whether retainer or contingency, search firms are hired by organizations to fill positions. Organizations pay search firms about one-third of the new person's annual salary. Retainer firms receive an exclusive assignment to fill a position and get paid whether or not they find the person for it. Even if the employer finds a new person through another source, the retainer search firm keeps the fee. Contingency firms are paid only if they fill the position and several contingency firms could be working to fill the *same* position. The one that fills it gets the fee.

Do not send your résumé to contingency search firms unless you know their reputation. A disreputable agency could blanket the market with your résumé, cheapen your value, and even cripple your job search. A careless agency may even send your résumé to your present employer by accident—it's been known to happen!

Aim for a collaborative relationship with the agencies with which you decide to work. Insist on ground rules that will ensure you stay in control. Make sure, for example, that the search firm asks you before it sends your résumé to anyone. A search firm might want to send your résumé to an organization you're trying to get into on your own.

Search firms can help you, but some can actually harm you. For example, a firm—even one that's normally a retainer search firm—could say to you: "Oh, don't worry about your search. I'll take care of it for you." Then they blanket the market with your résumé—or contact employers *you* would have contacted on your own anyway. Now the hiring employer *cannot* consider ever hiring you unless they want to pay a fee. The employer may tell you they already have your résumé from a search firm and "We don't want to pay a fee." Therefore, the search firm becomes your competitor. They got into the organization before you did.

If the employer *is* willing to pay a fee, but two (or more) search firms have sent in your résumé, the organization will not hire you because it does not want to get into an argument about which search firm to pay.

The moral to the story: Yes, use search firms judiciously, but the far better approach is to contact prospective employers on your own wherever possible. If the search firm offers to market you around, this may sound like a gift, **but don't agree to this**. Market *yourself* around. Remember: When an agency represents you, there's a price on your head. You may end up being in competition with a candidate who submitted a résumé directly. Being able to hire without paying a fee may influence the organization's decision.

So tell the search firm, "Don't send out my résumé without calling me first." Keep control of where your résumé is going. Keep control of your search.

For God sake hold your tongue.
John Donne, *The Canonization*

Can I Get the Search Firm to Increase the Salary Being Offered?

The answer is: In most cases, you can't. A search firm is hired by a client organization to fill a certain position at a certain salary. A search firm needs to know your salary requirements. The salary cap can sometimes be negotiated based on the level or experience of the candidate. However, if the search firm does not put you in for the job because your salary requirements are too high, contact the firm directly. Read the chapter "What to Do When You Know There's a Job Opening."

Let's remember the purpose of search firms: They cannot get you a job. Search firms can help you get *meetings* in your target market. You can also get meetings through ads, networking, and direct contact. When a search firm tells you about a specific job at a specific salary, decide if you want the *meeting*. Once they get you a meeting, you have to do the rest yourself.

Also remember our basic principle regarding salary negotiation: Do not negotiate the salary until you have received an offer. After you have had the interview, turn it into an offer by following up with the organization itself. Once you have the offer, get involved in the negotiating process yourself. There are some search firms that are excellent at negotiating on your behalf if the organization really wants you. In general, however, you will want to do the deal yourself. And you may have to stand up to the search firm if it tries to exclude you from the process.

Who naught suspects is easily deceived.

Petrarch, 1304–1374, Italian poet, *Sonnets*

Develop Long-Term Relationships: Become a Referral Source

Of course, there are always the headhunters who contact you. Establish a rapport with them. Their current job opening may not be appropriate for you, but if they sense that you are cooperative and know what you will accept, they will contact you when the right opportunity crosses their desk. Become a referral source—someone who recommends candidates—and you will receive calls on a regular basis.

In addition, keep the good firms regularly apprised of your situation—over the long term. For your current search, send a letter or E-mail to those with whom you already have a relationship: "It has been a while since we last spoke and I wanted to send you an updated résumé for your files." But be sure to develop a letter that helps the recruiter position you to clients.

When you accept a new position, send each organization with whom you have a relationship the same kind of note and an updated résumé. Good career management is a matter of staying in touch with key people.

Why a Retainer Recruiter May Not Put You in for a Job

Jim, a Five O'Clock Club member and marketer by profession, was one of the best networkers—and researchers—who has ever come to the Club. During the course of his search—through direct contact and networking—he uncovered *52 job openings for marketing management positions.* Jim had first contacted all of the retainer search firms appropriate for him, but he got very few employer meetings. When he networked into or directly contacted prospective hiring organizations themselves, the hiring managers said, "We really like you and we have a job that's out for search right now. Call the recruiter and *use my name.*" But Jim had *already* contacted those firms and they had told him nothing about those openings! (Of those 52 openings he uncovered, 48 were being handled by retainer search firms.)

Jim called the recruiters again, restrained himself from being impolite, got the meetings using the names of the hiring manager, and ended up with at least five offers. *Many Five O'Clock Clubbers have had similar experiences landing interviews and jobs after they had been rejected by a search firm.* So a recruiter with a retainer search firm might *not* put you in for a job even though you may be perfect. What's going on here? Several factors are at work. Search firms are hired by the organization to go out and "search" for the right person. Recruiters with retainer firms are supposed to know their markets inside out. So, let's say a retainer search firm has conducted a search and said to the hiring organization, "These are the three best candidates for the job." Then *you* come along. It would be difficult for them to then say, "Oops, by the way Ms. Hiring Manager, I've found another person for you."

There are other reasons why you may not be put in. In large search firms, there may be one recruiter who is handling that search, but you contacted a different recruiter. Perhaps the one you're talking to doesn't refer you to the recruiter who is handling that search. They're busy working on their own searches or recruiters may be in competition for the most placements that month! They're not going to pass you on to one of their competitors. So they tell you they don't have any appropriate openings right now.

Finally, if a retainer firm fills jobs for your *present* employer, they cannot help you leave your present employer! In fact, some major organizations will actually put a search firm *on* retainer just so the search firm *cannot* recruit from them.

You can see how easy it is for search-firm people not to put you in for a job even if you're the right person: You might make them look bad if they have said their search is complete, they may not be the actual recruiter who is handling the search, or they may have a contract with your present employer.

To take it one step further, a retainer search firm may tell you a hiring manager is not interested in you when they haven't even *told* the manager about you. Because the search firm has already rejected you, *you* contact the organization directly and find the organization has never even heard about you! That's because the search firm was pushing somebody else. They just don't want to tell you they were not going to put you in for the job. Don't be upset by any of this. It's just business and they really can't tell you the truth. They won't say, "I can't put you in for this job because I've already told the client company I've found them the perfect person." So they tell you a white lie. It's business. It's a game. So it's easy to see you shouldn't *depend* on search firms for your search.

But here's the key point: If a search firm refuses to submit your résumé or claims that you were rejected, *pretend you never contacted the search firm at all.* Instead, arrange to have a networking meeting with someone, *anyone* in the firm—not necessarily the hiring manager. After all, you're interested in working there, even if this job is not appropriate for you. **Contact the organization on your own.** However, don't mention you heard about an opening from a search firm. Instead, take the interview as you would with any organization in which you're interested—whether or not they have an opening right now.

The wise man avoids evil by anticipating it.

Publilius Syrus, c. 42 B.C., Roman writer, *Maxims*

Other Points about Salespeople

- Sometimes recruiters may tell you you're a strong candidate for the job when they really see you as *weak* or perhaps as a first or second runner-up. That's because they don't want you to drop out of the picture. They want to have you "in the pipeline." If *you* drop out of the picture, they might have to dig up somebody else. Don't be scandalized by these tactics. It's like any salesman who tells you this is your last chance to buy his product or the price will go up tomorrow. Recruiters are *sales*-people.

- Remember: Recruiters are paid *well* if they place you. They get between 25 to 33 percent of your first year's salary when you land. The more money you make, the more money they make. *But* a recruiter may not necessarily be interested in getting you the highest salary possible. It's just like a realtor who wants to make that sale. The realtor gets a percentage, but doesn't mind cutting the price tag $10,000 if it means closing the deal. The recruiter would rather get the placement at a *lower* salary and with a *lower* fee instead of losing the placement. What's more, the recruiter can brag to the employer about the great job he did: "Have I found a bargain for you!" Remember, recruiters work for the *hiring* organization, not for you!

- Be wary of other aspects of the agency business. A contingency recruiter may ask you where else you've interviewed and who you have talked to there. She says, "I really need to know the kind of positions you're looking for. And who have you talked to? I want to know where you're seeing people so I don't send your résumé to the same places." But this may be a fishing expedition. Recruiters need to find *job openings*. As soon as you leave their office, an unethical contingency recruiter could be on the phone to the hiring manager you interviewed with telling him he has the *ideal* candidate for the job—and it *won't be you*! He'll put one of his other clients in for the job to have a shot at getting the fee.

- Be suspicious of recruiters who ask for names of references the first time they meet you. They may be looking for other people to add to their database and recruit for jobs. They shouldn't need references right away anyway. Protect your references.

After the Interview—Back to Five O'Clock Club Basics

When you go on interviews through agencies, be prepared for a tug-of-war concerning follow-up. Chances are, agencies will want you to step out of the way and let them "handle everything." But this is not in your best interests. Remember: The ball should always be in *your* court. Once you have met with the hiring team at the employer's organization, write your follow-up proposals directly to the *hiring* organization, *not to the recruiter.* When we talk about following up after a job interview, we mean **the follow-up you do with the organization itself, not the follow-up with the search firm**.

Most recruiters get nervous when Five O'Clock Clubbers say, "I'm writing a proposal for the employer," because they're afraid you'll ruin the hard work they put in. Most job hunters are not very savvy and might like the idea of letting the agency run the show. But Five O'Clock Clubbers are actually *better* at this process than most search-firm recruiters are. Do your follow-up with the prospective employer. In general, you should *not* copy the recruiter on the follow-up you're doing. Obviously call your recruiter after the interview to find out his impressions—weighing the possibility that what he tells you may not be completely truthful. Then deal with the hiring organization. This is where your small group is invaluable. Ask their advice.

Be courteous to all, but intimate with few; and let those few be well tried before you give them your confidence.

George Washington, 1721–1799,
Letter to Bushrod Washington

A Final Word about Search Firms

Some search firms give the industry a bad name. If you are belittled or badgered by a search firm, do not take it personally, but *do move on*. The possible damage to your ego isn't worth it. A recruiter may, for example, hurt your ego so you will accept a position that is rather low in salary.

If you refuse a job offer, a search firm will still present you to their other client organizations. Getting an offer proves you are marketable. If you've received one offer, most will conclude you can get another. They will drop you, however, if they feel you are just shopping the market and are not interested in making a move. After all, they are running a business. So don't be frivolous in refusing offers.

But don't be afraid to turn down an offer if it is not appropriate for you. It is important that you not be talked into accepting an offer you don't want by a recruiter who is trying to satisfy the needs of the client organization. Recruiters are just trying to do their job: selling the benefits of the client organization's position.

Most recruiters are ethical and care about job hunters as well as the employers who pay them. But be smart and be on your guard against those firms that may use tactics that are not in your best interests. When times are good, search firms may be less likely to resort to these tactics. But when times get tough and business is more difficult to come by, firms are more likely to do things you need to guard against. Should you use search firms? Absolutely! Contact a number of search firms in your specialty. Depending on your target market, they may be a very important tool for getting meetings. But should you rely on search firms? Absolutely not! They should represent only a fraction of your job-hunt focus.

---

*Pain: an uncomfortable frame of mind that may
have a physical basis in something that is being
done to the body, or may be purely mental, caused
by the good fortune of others.*

Ambrose Bierce

The Five O'Clock Club

Following Up When There Is No Immediate Job

Contrary to the cliché, genuinely nice guys most often finish first, or very near it.

Malcolm Forbes

During each meeting, you have taken up the time of someone who sincerely tried to help you. Writing a note is the only polite thing to do. Since the person has gone to some effort for you, go to some effort in return. A phone call to thank a person can be an intrusion and shows little effort on your part.

In addition to being polite, there are good business reasons for writing notes and otherwise keeping in touch with people who have helped you. For one thing, few people keep in touch so you will stand out. Second, it gives you a chance to sell yourself again and to overcome any misunderstandings that may have occurred. Third, this is a promotional campaign and any good promoter knows that a message reinforced soon after a first message results in added recall.

If you meet someone through a networking meeting, for example, he or she will almost certainly forget about you the minute you leave and just go back to business. Sorry, but you were an interruption.

If you write to people almost immediately after your meeting, this will dramatically increase the chance they will remember you. If you wait two weeks before writing, they may remember meeting someone but not remember you specifically. If you wait longer than two weeks, they probably won't remember meeting anyone—let alone you.

So promptly follow the meeting with a note. It is important to remind those to whom you write who you are and when they talked to you. Give some highlight of the meeting. Contact them again within a month or two. It is just like an advertising campaign. Advertisers will often place their ads at least every four weeks in the same publication. If they advertised less often, few people would remember the ad.

What Michael Did

This is a classic—and it worked on me. I wanted to hire one junior accountant for a very important project and had the search narrowed down to two people. I asked my boss for his input. We made up a list of what we were seeking and we each rated the candidates on 20 criteria. The final scores came in very close, but I hired Judy instead of Michael.

In response to my rejection, Michael wrote me a note telling me how much he still wanted to work for our organization and how he hoped I would keep him in mind if

"I'm sorry, but Mr. Konklin is extremely busy today. Can I take a message and have him get back to you?"

something else should come up. He turned the rejection into a positive contact. Notes are so unusual and this one was so personable, that I showed it to my boss.

A few months later, Michael wrote again saying he had taken a position with another firm. He was still very much interested in us and he hoped to work for us someday. He promised to keep in touch, which he did. Each time he wrote, I showed the note to my boss. Each time, we were sorry we couldn't hire him.

After about seven months, I needed another helping hand. Whom do you think I called? Do you think I interviewed other people? Do you think I had to sell Michael to my boss? Michael came to work for us and we never regretted it. Persistence pays off.

---

*We make a living by what we get, but
we make a life by what we give.*
Winston Churchill

What to Say in Your Follow-Up Note

Depending on the content of your note, you may type or write it. Generally use standard business-size stationery, but sometimes Monarch or other note-size stationery, ivory or white, will do. A *job* interview follow-up should almost always be typed on standard business-size ivory or white stationery.

Sample Follow-Up to a Networking Meeting

PETER SCHAEFER

To: Alexandra Duran

Thanks again for contacting Brendan for me and for providing all those excellent contact names.

There's such a wealth of good ideas in that list that it will take me a while to follow up on all of them, but I'm working hard at it and will let you know what develops.

Again, thanks for your extraordinary effort. (By the way, should you ever want to "review your career options," I would be delighted to share a few names, or more than a few, with you.)

Stay tuned!

Peter

After an information-gathering meeting, play back some of the advice you received, any you intend to follow, and so on. Simply be sincere. What did you appreciate about the time the person spent with you? Did you get good advice that you intend to follow? Say so. Were you inspired? Encouraged? Awakened? Say so.

If you think there were sparks between you and the person with whom you met, be sure to say you will keep in touch. Then do it. Follow-up letters don't have to be long, but they do have to be personal. Make sure the letters you write could not be sent to someone else on your list.

To keep in touch, simply let interviewers/network contacts know how you are doing. Tell them whom you are seeing and what your plans are. Some people, seeing your sincerity, will keep sending you leads or other information.

It's never too late to follow up. For example: "I met you a year ago and am still impressed by . . . Since then I have . . . and would be interested in getting together with you again to discuss these new developments." Make new contacts. Recontact old ones by writing a "status report" every two months telling them how well you are doing in your search. **Keeping up with old networking contacts is as important as making new ones.**

Some job hunters use this as an opportunity to write a proposal. During the meeting, you may have learned something about the organization's problems. Writing a proposal to solve them may create a job for you. Patricia had a networking meeting with a small company where she learned that it wanted to expand the business from $5 million to $50 million. She came up with lots of ideas about how that could be done—with her help, of course—and called to set up a meeting to review her ideas. She went over the proposal with them and they created a position for her.

However, you are not trying to turn every networking meeting into a job possibility. You *are* trying to form life-long relationships with people. Experts say most successful employees form solid relationships with lots of people and keep in touch regularly throughout their careers. These people will keep you up-to-date in a changing economy, tell you about changes or openings in your field, and generally be your long-term ally. And you will do the same for them.

Has a man gained anything who has received a hundred favors and rendered none? He is great who confers the most benefits.

Ralph Waldo Emerson, "Essay on Compensation"

Following Up after a Networking/ Direct-Contact Meeting

The
Five
O'Clock
Club

*Opportunities are usually disguised as hard work,
so most people don't recognize them.*

Ann Landers, syndicated advice columnist,
Rowes, *The Book of Quotes*

The follow-up after a networking meeting—or a meeting resulting from having directly contacted an organization (through a direct-mail campaign or a targeted mailing)—is very different from the way you follow up after a job interview.

Analyze the meeting. In your letter, thank the interviewer. State the *specific* advice and leads you were given. Be personable. Say you will keep in touch. *Do* keep in touch.

Follow up every few months with a "status report" on how your search is going, an article, or news of interest to the manager.

Make sure people are thinking about you. You may contact the manager just as he or she has heard of something of importance to you.

Recontact those you met earlier in your search. Otherwise, you're like a salesman who works to get new leads while ignoring his old relationships. Get new leads but also keep in touch with people you've already met.

It's never too late to follow up. For example: "I met you three years ago and am still impressed by____. Since then I have_____and would be interested in getting together with you again to discuss these new developments." Make new contacts. Recontact old ones. It's never too late.

If you know anything that will make a brother's heart glad, run quick and tell it; and if it is something that will only cause a sigh, bottle it up, bottle it up.

Old Farmer's Almanac, 1854

Trouble getting started? What would you say to the person if he or she were sitting across from you right now? Consider that as the opening of your follow-up letter.

*In differentiation, not in uniformity,
lies the path of progress.*

Louis Brandeis, U.S. Supreme Court Justice,
Business—A Profession

Job hunters make a mistake when they fail to *recontact* people with whom they have formed relationships earlier in their search. Keep in touch on a regular basis so you increase your chances of contacting them just at a time when they have heard of something that may interest you—or may have a new need themselves.

Follow up with a customized note specifically acknowledging the help you received.

JOHN WEITING
163 York Avenue—12B
New York, New York 10000
(212) 555-2231 (day)
(212) 555-1674 (message)
jweiting@attnet.net

June 25, 200X

Ms. Rachel Tepfer
Director of Outplacement
Time-Warner Communications
8 Pine Street
New York, NY 10001

Dear Ms. Tepfer:

Thanks so much for seeing me. Your center is very impressive and seems very well run. But of course, I had heard that before I met you.

As you suggested, I sent for information on ASTD and was pleasantly surprised to see your name in there! It sounds like a great organization and I can't wait until they start to have meetings again in the fall.

I will definitely follow up with both Max McCreery and Marilyn Kaufman, and appreciate your giving me their names. I've called them each a few times, but they and I are very busy people.

After I left your place, I wished I had asked you more about your own career. Only at the very end did you bring up the interesting way you got your job. I had wrongly assumed you came up through the ranks at Time-Warner Communications. Perhaps some other time I can hear the rest of the story. You certainly seem to know your stuff.

I've enclosed The Five O'Clock Club calendar for June, July, and August. In addition, I'll be speaking at The New School in a few weeks and have a lot planned for myself for the fall. I will keep you posted regarding my activities and perhaps I'll even run into you at ASTD meetings.

Thanks again for your time and insight. Till we meet again.

Cordially,

John Weiting

GREGORY BOARDMAN

August 24, 20xx

Dear Mary Ann:

Just a quick note to thank you for taking the time to meet with me yesterday. Even though it seems I've located most of the places that could use my skill set, it's always nice to revalidate that opinion.

I was interested to learn of your new position in national product engineering. Although I understand your current situation, I'm always excited to discover new possibilities for becoming involved in Big Red's national campaign. I've long believed this effort is paramount to Big Red's continued dominance in the industry. In fact I expressed just such an opinion to Julie Ward on Tuesday. Julie is involved in Big Red's advertising program to develop a national brand image and I commented to her how much I liked the concept.

I am very flattered, too, that you would consider involving me in your developing organization. As I mentioned to you, I am quite good at "start-up" positions requiring a great amount of vision to allow for working in an indeterminate environment. Clearly my marketing liaison and consulting activities would be a natural for your charter as well. If I can help you in any way as you define your area, I would be happy to offer you my assistance.

I would like very much to contact you again in a few weeks to learn more about your progress. In the meantime I am going to try to contact Lou Fleming and others involved in the National Marketing effort to keep abreast of this exciting new area.

Thanks again for your time—hope to see you again soon.

Sincerely,

Gregory

Follow-up letters don't have to be long, but they *do* have to be personal. Make sure the letters you write could not be sent to anyone else on your list.

SYLVAN VON BERG

To: Judy Acord

I enjoyed our conversation, which I found most helpful.

I will meet with Betsy Austin when she returns from overseas, and will talk to Jim about seeing Susan Geisenheimer. I'll also contact Bob Potvin and Clive Murray, per your suggestion.

Again, thanks for your help. I'll let you know how things develop.

Sylvan

CARL ARMBRUSTER

To: Nancy Abramson

Thanks again for contacting Brendan for me and for providing all those excellent contact names.

There's such a wealth of good ideas in the list it will take me a while to follow up with all of them, but I'm working hard at it and will let you know what develops.

Again, thanks for your extraordinary effort. (By the way, should you ever want to "review your career options," I would be delighted to share a few names, or more than a few, with you.)

Stay tuned!

Carl

Mr. Miguel Villarin
President
Commerce and Industry Association
Street Address
City, State

Dear Miguel:

Thank you for the time from your busy schedule. I enjoyed our discussion and appreciated your suggestions about marketing myself in the northern part of the state. Your idea on using the Big 8 firms as pivot points in networking is an excellent one. As you requested, I have enclosed copies of my résumé. I plan to call you next week, Miguel, so that I can obtain the names of the firms to which you sent my résumé.

I have been thinking about using Robert Dobbs (Dobbs & Firth) in my networking efforts. Since he is a past president of Commerce and Industry, I would be foolish not to tap such a source. Thanks again, Miguel.

Sincerely,

Janet Vitalis

Enclosures

The
Five
O'Clock
Club

How to Control Your Campaign

Do not fear death so much,
but rather the inadequate life.

Bertolt Brecht

Your overall campaign can be managed with just a few important worksheets:

- Use the **Interview Record** for *every* meeting—both networking and job. (See our book *Mastering the Job Interview and Winning the Money Game*.)

- The most important worksheet for controlling your search is the **Current List of My Active Contacts by Target**. At the beginning of your search, these will simply be networking contacts with whom you want to keep in touch. At that stage, your goal is to come up with 6 to 10 contacts you want to recontact later.

   Later, the quality of your list will change. Then the names will be prospective job possibilities that you are trying to move along.

   If you have 6 to 10 job possibilities "in the works," five of them will fall away through no fault of your own (because of job freezes or the hiring manager changing his or her mind about the kind of person wanted). Then you'll need to get more things in the works. With this critical mass of ongoing possible positions, you stand a chance of landing the kind of job you want.

Other Worksheets

The worksheets mentioned above are critical to the management of your search. Other worksheets guide specific parts of your search.

- In the beginning, the **Seven Stories Exercise** and **Your Forty-Year Vision** will help you select job targets appropriate for you (see our book *Targeting a Great Career*).

- **Measuring Your Targets** will assure that you have targets of a size that have a reasonable chance of working.

- The **Summary of What I Have/Want to Offer** will help you "position" yourself appropriately to each of your targets.

- **People to Contact in Each Target Area** is a way to get your search off to a quick start through networking or targeted mailings.

- The **Format of a Networking Meeting** is your guide to properly managing the networking-type meetings you get through networking, targeted or direct mailings, or cold calls.

- The **Summary of Search Progress** and **How to Assess Your Campaign** help you clearly assess how you are doing with regard to each of your targets.

- **The Follow-Up Checklist: Turning Job Interviews into Offers** (in our book *Mastering the Job Interview and Winning the Money Game*) will help you assess the interview and decide what to do next. Your goal, after all, is to move the process along and see if you can create a job for yourself.

- Assessing whether you are at **Stage 1, 2, or 3** of your search will help you see where you really stand, rather than you hoping for a job offer too soon.

Four-Step Salary Negotiation (from our book *Mastering the Job Interview and Winning the Money Game)*:

- Are you keeping all four steps in mind?
   — Negotiate the job
   — Outshine and outlast your competition
   — Get the offer
   — Negotiate the compensation package

- Are you **negotiating the job** to make it appropriate for you and for the hiring manager?

- Are you **paying attention to your competition**, what they have to offer, and what you must do to outshine and outlast them? Are you aware that your competitors may not be real people, but may be in the mind of the hiring manager?

- Are you trying to postpone discussion of salary until after you **get the offer**?

Current List of My Active Contacts by Target

Make copies of this page for each target and keep track of your active contacts in each target area. To see how well you are penetrating each target market, compare the total number of appropriate contacts in your market with the number you have actually contacted. Keep adding names to your list. Certain people will become inappropriate. Cross their names off. You should probably have some contact once every month or two with the people who remain on your list.

After your search is up and running, keep track of your contacts by the stage you are in for each one. This will tell you how well you are doing in your search and will give you some idea of how likely it is for you to get an offer.

For Target _____:

Geographic area: _____

Industry or company size: _____

Position/function: _____

	Name of Contact	Company	Position	Date of Last Contact	Targeted Date of Next Contact
1.					
2.					
3.					
4.					
5.					
6.					
7.					
8.					
9.					
10.					
11.					
12.					
13.					
14.					
15.					
16.					
17.					
18.					
19.					
20.					
21.					
22.					
23.					
24.					
25.					

Current List of Active Stage-1 Contacts
Networking Contacts With Whom You Want To Keep in Touch

The Beginning of a Search

Measure the effectiveness of your search by listing the number of people with whom you are currently in contact on an ongoing basis, either by phone or mail, who are in a position to hire you or recommend that you be hired. The rule of thumb: If you are seriously job hunting, **you should have 6 to 10 active contacts going at one time. At the beginning of your search, these will simply be networking contacts with whom you want to keep in touch.** You are unlikely to get an offer at this stage. You are gathering information to find out how things work—getting your feet wet. You look like an outsider and outsiders are rarely given a break. Keep adding names to your list because certain people will become inappropriate. Cross their names off. You should probably have some contact once a month with the people who remain on your list.

Because you have already developed targets for your search, please note below the target area for each contact or note it is serendipitous and does not fit in with any of your organized targets. This will help you see the progress you are making in each target area.

Name of Contact	Company	Position	Date of Last Contact	Targeted Date of Next Contact	Target Area
1.					
2.					
3.					
4.					
5.					
6.					
7.					
8.					
9.					
10.					
11.					
12.					
13.					
14.					
15.					
16.					
17.					
18.					
19.					
20.					
21.					
22.					
23.					
24.					
25.					

Current List of Active Stage-2 Contacts

The Right People at the Right Levels in the Right Organizations

The Middle of a Search

The nature of your "6 to 10 things in the works" changes over time. Instead of simply finding networking contacts to get your search started, you meet people who are closer to what you want.

Getting a job offer is not the way to test the quality of your campaign. A real test is when people say they'd want you—but not now. Do some people say: **<u>"Boy, I wish I had an opening. I'd sure like to have someone like you here"</u>**? Then you are interviewing well with the right people. All you need now are luck and timing to help you contact (and recontact) the right people when they also have a need.

If people are *not* saying they want you, find out why not. If you think you are in the right targets talking to people at the right level and are not early on in your search, you need feedback. Ask: "If you had an opening, would you consider hiring someone like me?" Find out what is wrong.

Become an insider—a competent person who can prove he or she has somehow already done what the interviewer needs. *Prove* you can do the job and that the interviewer is *not* taking a chance on you.

You still need 6 to 10 contacts at this level whom you will recontact later. Keep adding names to your list because certain people will become inappropriate. Cross their names off. You should probably have some contact once a month with the people who remain on your list.

Name of Contact	Company	Position	Date of Last Contact	Targeted Date of Next Contact	Target Area
1.					
2.					
3.					
4.					
5.					
6.					
7.					
8.					
9.					
10.					
11.					
12.					
13.					
14.					
15.					
16.					
17.					
18.					
19.					
20.					
21.					
22.					
23.					
24.					
25.					

Current List of Active Stage-3 Contacts
Moving Along Actual Jobs or the Possibility of Creating a Job

The Final Stages of a Search

In this stage, you **uncover 6 to 10 actual jobs (or the possibility of creating a job) to move along**. These job possibilities could come from *any* of your target areas or from serendipitous leads. Find a *lot* of people who would hire you if they could. If you have only one lead that could turn into an offer, you are likely to try to close too soon. Get more leads. You will be more attractive to the manager, will interview better, and will not lose momentum if your best lead falls apart. A good number of your job possibilities will fall away through no fault of your own (such as job freezes or major changes in the job requirements).

To get more leads, notice which targets are working and which are not. Make *additional* contacts in the targets that seem to be working or develop new targets. **Recontact just about everyone you met earlier in your search.** You want to develop more offers.

Aim for three offers: This is the stage of your search when you want them. When an offer comes during Stage 1 or Stage 2, you probably have not had a chance to develop momentum so you can get a number of offers. When choosing among offers, **select the job that positions you best for the long term**.

Name of Contact	Company	Position	Date of Last Contact	Targeted Date of Next Contact	Target Area
1.					
2.					
3.					
4.					
5.					
6.					
7.					
8.					
9.					
10.					
11.					
12.					
13.					
14.					
15.					
16.					
17.					
18.					
19.					
20.					
21.					
22.					
23.					
24.					
25.					

The
Five
O'Clock
Club

Stuck in Your Job Search?
What to Do Next

Drive thy business, or it will drive thee.

Benjamin Franklin

How to Measure the Effectiveness of Your Search

Most job hunters say, "I'll know my search was good when I get a job." That's not a very good way to measure your search. You need to be able to tell as you go along whether you are heading in the right direction. There are a number of hints you can pick up along the way.

What Stage Are You In?

As you go along, the basic measurement tool to use in your search is this: Do you have 6 to 10 things in the works? That is, are you talking to 6 to 10 people on an ongoing basis who are in a position to hire you or recommend that you be hired?

The quality of your contacts varies with where you are in your search.

- In the beginning of your search, you will speak to as many people as possible in your target market—regardless of the organization for which they work. At this stage, you simply want market information. If you plan to stay in touch with them on an ongoing basis, they are Stage-1 contacts. To have any momentum going in the beginning of your search, keep in touch with 6 to 10 people on an ongoing basis (every few months).

  Over time, you will talk to more and more people who are Stage-1 contacts—perhaps 60 to 100 people during the course of your search. Some of those contacts will bubble up and become Stage-2 contacts.

- Stage-2 contacts are people who are the right people at the right level in the right jobs in the right organizations in your targeted areas. They are senior to you, perhaps future hiring managers. Your goal is to have contact with 6 to 10 of the right people on an ongoing basis. Then you have a full Stage-2 search going: You are in the middle of your search.

  However, you will rarely get a good job offer at Stage 2. You aren't even talking to these people about real jobs at this point. You just want the right people to know you and remember you. And if one later happens to have a job opening, you still need to go after 6 to 10 other job possibilities, because 5 will fall away through no fault of your own. If you do get an offer at Stage 2, you won't have many others with which to compare it. Keep in touch with your current Stage-1 contacts (using *networking* follow-ups), and develop additional Stage-1 contacts so more will bubble up to Stage 2. Some of those will bubble up to Stage 3 (real job possibilities)—and then you're really cooking.

- You are in a full Stage-3 search when you are talking to 6 to 10 people on an ongoing basis who actually have a job opening or who have the possibility of creating a job for you. Then you have a number of opportunities that you can move along (using *job* follow-ups), and are in the best possible position to get the right job for you: the one that positions you best for the long term and the one that pays you what you are worth.

  If you have 6 to 10 possibilities in Stage 3, you have the chance of getting 3 offers. Remember, these do not have to be ideal jobs—some may even be disgusting. But an offer is an offer and makes you more desirable in the market. You don't have to want to work at each of these places, but at least you will have a fallback position and can honestly say, if appropriate, "I have a number of job offers, but there's no place I'd rather work than yours." With a number of offers in hand, you are less likely to be taken advantage of by a prospective employer who thinks you are desperate.

Life moves on, whether we act as cowards or heroes. Life has no other discipline to impose, if we would but realize it, than to accept life unquestioningly. Everything we shut our eyes to, everything we run away from, everything we deny, denigrate or despise, serves to defeat us in the end. What seems nasty, painful, evil, can become a source of beauty, joy and strength, if faced with an open mind. Every moment is a golden one for him who has the vision to recognize it as such.

Henry Miller

How's Your Search Going?

When I ask you how your search is going, I don't want to hear that a prospective employer really likes you. That's not a good measure of how well your search is going, because one prospect could easily fall away: They may decide to hire no one or they may decide they want an accounting person instead of a marketing person. A lot can happen that is beyond your control.

Instead I expect you to tell me how many things you have in the works. You would say, for example, "My search is going great. I have five Stage-1 contacts in the works. I'm just getting started."

Or you might say, "I have nine Stage-2 contacts and three contacts in Stage 3." If you are expert at this, you may even add: "I want more Stage-3 contacts, so my goal is to get 30 more in Stage 2. Right now, I'm digging up lots of new contacts and keeping the other ones going. With my Stage-2 contacts, I'm generally doing networking follow-ups and with my Stage-3 contacts, I'm generally doing job follow-ups."

That kind of talk is music to my ears.

It usually takes very little effort to get a few more things "in the works." Simply recontact your network, network into someone you haven't met with yet, directly contact someone, talk to a search firm, answer an ad. You will soon have more activity in your search.

I know God will not give me anything I can't handle. I just wish He didn't trust me so much.

Mother Teresa

What Job Hunters Do Wrong

In addition to looking at the *stage* of your overall search, it is also helpful to look at what can go wrong in each *phase* of your campaigns. Some job hunters err in their overall search approach or attitude. Then things can go wrong in the assessment phase or in the other parts of your campaigns (the planning, interviewing, or follow-up phases). We'll examine each of these to determine what you may be doing wrong, if anything.

The Overall Search: What Can Go Wrong?

Here are some problems that are general to the entire search:

- **Not spending enough time** on your search. If you are unemployed, you should be spending 35 hours a week on your search. If you are employed, spend 15 hours a week to get some momentum going. If you spend only two or three hours a week on your job search, you may complain that you have been searching forever, when actually you have not even begun. If you are employed, you can do most of your work in the evenings and on weekends—researching, writing cover letters and follow-up letters. You can even schedule your meetings in the evenings or early mornings.

- **Not having enough fun.** Some job hunters—especially those who are unemployed—say they will start having fun after they get a job. But your search may take many months and you are more likely to come across as desperate if you are not allowing yourself to have some fun. Having fun will make you seem like a more normal person in your meetings and you'll feel better about yourself. The Five O'Clock Club formula is that you *must* have at least three hours of fun a week.

- **Not having 6 to 10 things in the works.** See the beginning of this chapter about Stages 1, 2, and 3 of your search.

- **Talking to people who are at the wrong level.** At the beginning of your search, talk to peers just to gather information to decide whether a prospective target is worth a full campaign. When you have selected a few good targets, talk to those who are at a higher level.

- **Trying to bypass the system.** Some job hunters feel they don't have time for this and simply want to go on job interviews (usually through search firms or answering ads). Others want to skip the assessment process (see our book *Targeting a Great Career*) or don't even do the Seven Stories Exercise. Their campaigns are weaker because they have no foundation.

  At least touch on every step in the process. You will have a quicker and more productive search.

- **Lowering your salary expectations just because you have been unemployed a while.** Even those who have been unemployed a year or two land jobs at market rates. They get what they are worth in the market because they have followed the system.

  At The Five O'Clock Club, half the people who attend are employed; half are unemployed. Many of those who are unemployed have been out of work for a year or two. Usually, they have been doing something wrong in their searches, and the counselor and their group can help them figure out what it is. When they get a job (which they almost certainly will if they stick with the system), they usually wind up getting something appropriate at an appropriate salary level.

Sometimes, if people really need money, we suggest they take something inappropriate to earn some money and continue to search while they are working.

The world is moving so fast these days that the man who says it can't be done is generally interrupted by someone doing it.

Harry Emerson Fosdick

- **Getting discouraged.** Half the battle is controlling your emotions. Jack had been unemployed one-and-a-half years when he joined us. He seemed very agitated— almost angry—which happens when a person has been working at a job search for so long. I told him I was afraid he might come across that way during meetings. He assured me (with irritation in his voice) that he was completely pleasant during meetings but was simply letting his hair down in the group.

In career coaching, we have nothing to go on but the way the person acts in the group: The way you are in the group probably bears some resemblance to the way you are in the interview. We would recognize you as being the same person. Anyway, it's all we have to go on, so we have to point out to you what we see.

The next week, Jack still seemed angry. I asked the group what they thought and of course they could see it too. It was easier for him to hear it from his peers, and, because he was a mature person, Jack listened to them.

The third week, Jack laughingly announced that he had had a lobotomy and was a completely different person. He said he had changed his attitude and that his meetings reflected this change.

The fourth week he announced that he had had another lobotomy because he felt he still had room for improvement. He was a noticeably different person and did not seem at all like someone who had been out of work a long time. Every day Jack read the books we use at The Five O'Clock Club and provided very good insights to the other job hunters in our small group.

By the fifth week, Jack was almost acting like a cocounselor in the group. He had made great strides in his own search (with three Stage-3 contacts and lots of contacts in Stage 2) and was able to astutely analyze the problems others were having. He was a wonderful contributor.

By the seventh week, Jack was close to a number of offers and in the eighth week, Jack proudly addressed the large group and reported on his successful search. We were sorry to see him go.

By the way, Jack did not have to take a pay cut or a job that was beneath him. His prolonged search did not affect his salary negotiation.

Do what you need to do to keep your spirits up. Don't ask yourself if you feel like searching. Of course you don't. Just do it anyway. And act as if you enjoy it.

- **Not having support.** Looking for a job is a lonely business. You may want to "buddy" with another job hunter. You can call each other every morning to talk about what you are each going to do that day and to review what you each accomplished the day before. You could also join free emotional-support groups at places of worship. You may find you need such help in addition to the job-search strategy you get at The Five O'Clock Club. Or you may find you would like to see a counselor privately to help you with specifics having to do with your search, such as your résumé, a review of your search, salary negotiation, or the follow-up to a very important job interview. Get the help you need.

- **Inflating in your own mind the time you have actually been searching.** You may feel as though you've been searching forever. But if you are searching only three hours a week, you have not yet begun. If at the end of a year, you finally start to put in the required 15 to 35 hours a week, you have just really started to search. Then when people ask how long you have been searching, the correct answer is "a few weeks." It's good to be honest with yourself about how long you have actually been searching.

Procrastination is the fear of success. People procrastinate because they are afraid of the success that they know will result if they move ahead now. Because success is heavy, carries a responsibility with it, it is much easier to procrastinate and live on the "someday I'll" philosophy.

Denis Waitley

During the Assessment Phase: What Can Go Wrong?

In the assessment phase you use our book, *Targeting a Great Career*, to go through the exercises (Seven Stories, Values, Forty-Year Vision, and so on) and select job targets (industries or organizations of a certain size and the position you would like in each target and geographic area).

If you are not sure what you should do with your life, assessment is a time to explore—perhaps with the help of a career coach. What can go wrong in this phase?

- **Selecting 1 or 2 targets too quickly.** Rather than exploring, a job hunter may pick a target, go after it, find out it doesn't work, and then not know what to do next. Instead, brainstorm as many targets as you can at the beginning of your search, rank them, and go after them in a methodical way.

- **Not being specific in selecting a target.** Some job hunters say, "I just want a job. I don't care what it is." You may not care, but the hiring team wants someone who cares about their specific industry and organization. In the beginning of your search, you want to explore and stay calm while you are doing your research to find out

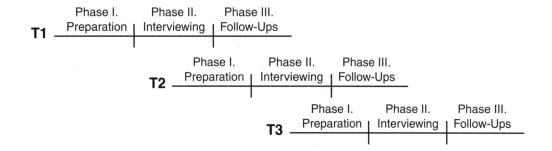

what the likely targets are for you. If you don't have targets defined (such as "being a COBOL computer programmer in a medium-sized organization in the Albuquerque area"), then you are still exploring and that's okay. But it is not an organized search. And even when your search is organized and targeted, you will still have plenty of room for serendipitous leads.

- **Not doing the right research.** Read the chapter on research, including the bibliography at the back of this book. Research is critical throughout your search and separates those who follow The Five O'Clock Club method from other job hunters. Instead of just *doing* research, why not learn to enjoy it and make it part of your life?

   The better your research, the richer your targets will become—well defined rather than superficial—and the more knowledgeable you will sound to prospective employers. In addition, you will save a lot of time as you discover where the markets are and which ones are the best fit for you.

- **Not ranking your targets.** Some job hunters go after everything at once. For a more organized search, overlap your targets, but still conduct a condensed search focusing on each target and keeping them separate in your mind.

   Take a look at the chart above, which shows a campaign aimed at each target (T1, T2, and T3). Yet the targets overlap to speed up the search.

   Next, let's look at what can go wrong in the various phases of the campaign aimed at each target.

Quit now, you'll never make it. If you disregard this advice, you'll be halfway there.

David Zucker

During the Preparation Phase: What Can Go Wrong?

- **Relying on only one technique for getting meetings.** Consider using all four techniques for getting meetings: networking, direct contact, search firms, and ads (in print and on-line). Even in fields where people like to talk to people, such as sales or human resources, though networking is easier, it is not thorough. It is a scattered approach.

Make a list of all the organizations in your target area—say, 120.

— Perhaps network into 20 of them;

— Do a targeted mailing into 20—it's just like networking: use a letter with a follow-up phone call. Remember that you want to see this person whether or not he or she has a job opening;

— Talk to search firms (if appropriate); and

— Answer ads.

— Do a direct-mail campaign (no follow-up phone call) to the remaining 80 organizations—just to be thorough so all the organizations in your target area know that you exist and are looking.

- **Contacting the wrong person.** The human resources person is the wrong one unless you want a job in human resources. The right person is one or two levels higher than you are in the department or division in which you want to work. If you are very senior and want to work for the president, the right person for you to contact is the president or perhaps someone on the board. If you want to be the president, the right person is someone on the board, or whoever may influence the selection of the president.

- **Being positioned improperly.** If you are not positioned properly, you will not be able to get meetings. Write out your Two-Minute Pitch. In your small group, be sure to practice your pitch. Try role-playing. Tell the group who they are pretending to be, and ask them to critique you. You want to make sure you have your pitch down pat. Write it out.

- **Using skimpy cover letters.** We use a four-paragraph approach that is thorough. Most job hunters write paragraphs one and four and skip the meat.

- **Having a weak or inappropriate résumé.** If your résumé doesn't speak for you in your absence and tell them exactly who you are, your level, and what you bring to the party, develop one that helps you. We have a whole book on this topic—along with case studies of real live people.

"Mr. Billings realizes you traveled a long way to meet with him. However, he decided to change the meeting until next week."

- **Skipping the research phase to develop a good list of target organizations.** If you have a good list, you will get more out of every one of your networking contacts. Show your list of prospective organizations to your contacts, ask them what they think of the organizations on the list, who they suggest you should contact at the good organizations, and ask, "May I use your name?"

The thing always happens that you believe in; and the belief in a thing makes it happen.

Frank Lloyd Wright

If you want a quality, act as if you already had it. Try the "as if" technique.

William James

To laugh often and much; to win the respect and the affection of children; to earn the appreciation of honest critics and endure the betrayal of false friends; to appreciate beauty; to find the best in others; to leave the world a bit better—whether by a healthy child, a garden patch or a redeemed social condition; to know even one life has breathed easier because you have lived. This is to have succeeded.

Ralph Waldo Emerson

If you are distressed by anything external, the pain is not due to the thing itself, but to your estimate of it; and this you have the power to revoke at any moment.

Marcus Aurelius

During the Interviewing Phase: What Can Go Wrong?

- **Trying to close too soon.** When a company is interested in you, you may have the tendency, like most job hunters, to focus on that one possibility and hope you get an offer. Because everything depends on that one possibility, chances are that you will do something wrong—trying to force them to decide before they are ready.

  Instead, get other things going while you keep an eye on the company you are already interested in. Ease the pressure on yourself and that company. Get your 6 to 10 things in the works and you'll have a balanced search.

- **Being seen as an outsider.** It's okay to be an outsider when it's early in your search. However, to get offers, you must be seen as an insider. When you are an insider, higher-level networking contacts say, "I really wish I had an opening because I would love to have someone like you on board." You are being well received, and this person counts as a Stage-2 contact. Keep in touch with him or her. Find lots more. It's only a matter of time until you get a job if the target you picked is a good one, if you contact more and more people who say the same thing, and if you keep in touch with those you already met.

- **Not using the worksheets.** Fill out What I Have/Want to Offer. This will help you position yourself to each targeted area. Use one for each of your targets. Make a zillion copies of the Interview Record. Fill one out every time you go on an interview. Note to whom you spoke, to whom they referred you, their important issues, and so on. Two weeks later, you may not remember what you discussed.

  If you are having a terrific search, you may meet with 5 to 15 people each week. Keep track of them with your Interview Record. Some people keep the records in a three-ring binder, alphabetically or by industry or target. Every time they write a follow-up letter, they attach a copy of that letter to the Interview Record. They cross-reference the information and become very methodical.

  That way, when you conduct your networking follow-ups every two months, you will have the notes from your last discussion, and copies of the letters you had sent earlier.

Other things that can go wrong in the Interviewing Phase include:

- Not thinking like a consultant.
- Not looking or acting like the level for which you are searching.
- Not seeing the interview as only the beginning of the process.
- Not getting information/giving information to move it along. "Where are you in the hiring process?" "How many other people are you talking to?" "How do I compare with them?" Be impersonal in the way you ask these questions so you can find out about your competition.
- Not preparing for the interview by having a 3x5 card or finding out with whom you will be meeting.
- Not being in sync with their timing (trying to close too soon or not moving quickly enough).
- Not listening to what's really going on.

During the Follow-Up Phase: What Can Go Wrong?

In addition to targeting, follow-up is the most important reason Five O'Clock Clubbers land jobs quickly. This is the brainiest part of the process. Notice that the earlier diagram showed the three parts as equal: Preparation, Interviewing, and Follow-Ups. Spend an equal amount of time on each.

Study thoroughly those parts of this book. Some of the obvious things that go wrong include:

- **Taking the first offer.** Try to get three offers at the same time. Then select the one that positions you best for the long run.

- **Not recontacting your contacts.** If you have been in search awhile, the most important action you can take to

develop new momentum is to recontact those with whom you have already met—perhaps every two to three months. That way they have a better chance of thinking of you when they come across news that may help you in your search.

Tell them, "It's been a while since we've met, and I am having a very interesting time. My search has taken a different direction, and I now find there is a lot of activity in the roof-repair market, which I am currently exploring. You were such a help to me before that I would like to call you again to find out what is going on at your end, and to tell you a little about what I've been doing." However you do it, recontact your contacts.

- **Not studying the books.** Follow-up is covered in great detail in this book. Study it and spend the time it takes to think through what you can do next to move along the *job* contacts you have made. While those you have networked with should be contacted every few months, job follow-up is more complicated.

- **Stating your salary requirements too soon.** The discussion of salary negotiation in this book is another thing you should read thoroughly *at the beginning of your search*. Salary negotiation starts with the way you position yourself at your very first meeting.

- **Not reassessing where you stand in your search.** Let's say you have been in search awhile and would like to know where you stand. Take all of the contacts you have in the works (people you are in touch with on a regular basis), and divide them up into Stage-1, Stage-2, or Stage-3 contacts. You will probably have a ratio of 60 Stage 1 to 20 Stage 2 to 6 Stage 3. Therefore, to increase the number of contacts you have in Stage 3, your only recourse is to increase the number of contacts you have in Stage 1. Some will bubble up to Stage 2, and others to Stage 3.

Now that we've taken a break from your search to assess how you are doing, it's time to get back to work. Read on!

Sample Summary of Search Progress

	# of companies in this target	# contacted	# met with	Quality/Status of Contacts
For Target 1: Geog. area: Chicago metro Ind. or org. size: Consumer goods companies Pos./function: Director of direct mail	10 Note: Not a great target. Keep in touch with same 5 people.	10	3	Stage 3: 1 job lead Stage 2: 2 Stage 1: 2
For Target 2: Geog. area: Chicago metro Ind. or org. size: Direct marketing service cos. Pos./function: Director of direct mail	200 Note: I'll aim to get 80 Stage-1 contacts; 30 Stage-2 contacts.	70	30	Stage 3: 3, 1 close to offer Stage 2: 9 Stage 1: 16
For Target 3: Geog. area: Chicago metro Ind. or org. size: Direct marketing—based co. Pos./function: Vice pres., marketing	120 Note: I need to do a lot more work in this target.	11	4	Stage 3: 0 Stage 2: 0 Stage 1: 4
For Target 4: Geog. area: Chicago metro Ind. or org. size: Advertising agencies Pos./function: Director of direct mail	15 Note: This is the field I'm in now, but I want to get out of it.	15	4	Stage 3: 0 Stage 2: 0 Stage 1: 2

Note: In the far right column, **note those contacts you are keeping in touch with on an ongoing basis**:
Stage 1 contacts: People with whom I want to keep in touch—regardless of level or ability to hire.
Stage 2 contacts: The right people at the right levels in the right organizations. (Potential hiring managers with whom I am keeping in touch. They may be telling me: I wish I had an opening; If I did, I'd like to hire someone like you.)
Stage 3 contacts: Moving along actual jobs or the possibility of creating a job.

Summary of Search Progress

	# of companies in this target	# contacted	# met with	Quality/Status of Contacts
For Target 1:				
Geog. area: _____				Stage 3:
Ind. or org. size: _____				Stage 2:
Pos./function:				Stage 1:
For Target 2:				
Geog. area: _____				Stage 3:
Ind. or org. size: _____				Stage 2:
Pos./function:				Stage 1:
For Target 3:				
Geog. area: _____				Stage 3:
Ind. or org. size: _____				Stage 2:
Pos./function:				Stage 1:
For Target 4:				
Geog. area: _____				Stage 3:
Ind. or org. size: _____				Stage 2:
Pos./function:				Stage 1:

Note: In the far right column, **note those contacts you are keeping in touch with on an ongoing basis**:

Stage 1 contacts: People with whom I want to keep in touch—regardless of level or ability to hire.

Stage 2 contacts: The right people at the right levels in the right organizations. (Potential hiring managers with whom I am keeping in touch. They may be telling me: I wish I had an opening. If I did, I'd like to hire someone like you.)

Stage 3 contacts: Moving along actual jobs or the possibility of creating a job. (I aim to have a total of 6 to 10 when I am in Stage 3 of my search.)

How to Handle Your References

In an exploratory meeting, the ball ends up in the savvy manager's court, which is exactly the intent. An observant manager also gains valuable information about the political lay of the land from such a meeting. The manager should come out with a good sense of how hard a sell the idea is going to be. A great number of objections indicate a tough road but still can be used to develop strategy. Every objection or reservation shows a concern that needs to be taken into account or an agenda item of the manager who is objecting.

Joel M. DeLuca, Ph.D., *Political Savvy*

Navigating the Minefield

When you reach the reference-checking stage, two opposing forces are at work: prospective employers (sometimes) want to find out as *much* as possible about you, while previous employers (usually) want to say as *little* as possible about you—and all *you* want, when the dust has settled, is that a *few nice things* have been said about you. You must play a role in achieving this, and it requires strategy and savvy. Leave as little as possible to chance.

Companies need to protect themselves against lawsuits and tend to clam up when they are asked for references. Their policy, officially, is to give out your dates of employment and title—that is, name, rank and serial number—only. In some cases, this could work to your advantage, but actually it would not be good if your prospective employer makes inquiries and *everybody* pleads the fifth. Your future boss would worry that something was wrong. Of course, everyone expects that the HR people at your former employer will be sticklers for policy and disclose almost nothing. But, as we all know, that's not really how business works. That's not the way the game is played: people will find a way to find out about you—if they want to. And you can't afford to be passive.

Thus, it's best if prospective employers are able to get *good* information about you, and you have some control over that. *You* need to be prepared to provide the names of

good references and be *thorough* in preparing for this part of the search process.

What commonly happens, however? You go through the entire interview process, and then they ask for references. The dot.com you worked for has gone out of business. They loved you there. Too bad you don't know where to find your old boss. The previous manager you worked for didn't like you all that much, and you didn't like him either. And you forgot to ask any of your coworkers to serve as a reference for you, and now it's job-offer time.

Don't wait until you get a job offer to think about your references. Take care of them now. Take care of them always.

Here's some advice to help get you through this important process.

1. **Make a list of people you want to use as references.** Depending on the relationships you've forged over the years, former bosses, your boss's boss, and even former coworkers or clients can be used as references. If you are in a consulting or part-time job, be sure to add your current boss to the list. If there is no way you can risk giving your *former* boss's name as a reference, be prepared with names of peers, subordinates, your former boss's boss, or boss's peers as backup references.

Come up with a list of names appropriate for the position you're going after. For example, the prospective employer may be interested in hearing from a few former clients of yours, as well as one boss and one peer. Of course, you would rarely use your *present* place of employment as a reference. If you confide in your boss that you are looking, chances are strong that you will be shut out and forced out—or maybe even fired on the spot.

2. **Next, get permission.** Ask the people on your list if they would serve as a reference for you. Get the agreement of three or four people, at least one of whom should be a boss or former boss. Tell everyone about the kinds of jobs you are looking at, and remind them of the good things you did for them—things you would like them to tell

others about you. In other words, help people with the reference process. For more about this, see Point 4.

You can say to the prospective reference: "I was hoping to use your name as a reference in my job search. Do you think you would feel comfortable providing a strong reference for me?" If you sense that a person is lukewarm (that is, not inclined to give you a *great* reference), you don't want to use that person. If the person promises to be "very fair" and "provide a balanced picture," get someone else. Hiring managers *expect* you to give them the names of people who will have glowing reports about you. Remember: This is a game—it's a game when an interviewer asks you why you left your last two jobs (she doesn't want to hear all the gory details!)—she wants to hear positive things. If a reference talks frankly to a prospective employer about your good and bad points, you may not stack up well against the other applicants.

3. **Do your best to make sure that the hiring company talks to your best references first.** For example, tell any interviewer who asks for your references that you would like to call them first, as a courtesy, and you'll let them know which ones you have contacted. Your best reference may be from five years ago—and you'll be positioned better if this is the first reference checked. Say, "I was able to reach George Duke and Agnes Forrest, so you can contact them now." This is just another aspect of staying in control of the process. Ask George and Agnes to get back to you when they have spoken to your prospective employer (see Point 7). Then you'll know it's okay to release a few more names, saving the weakest till last.

Give a little warning about the weak references. Be sure to say, "You can call Jacob now, but don't expect to hear great things. He was very upset at my leaving, (or he tends not to give good references)." Get your two cents' worth in before they contact that person. That way, if they do hear something negative about you, they'll think to themselves, "Oh, that's what Kevin said they would say." You don't want people to be surprised by what they hear.

4. **Help your references to help you.** Some time ago, I received a call from a prospective employer checking on Bessie, a woman who had worked for me and used to head the accounting department. The caller asked, "Is Bessie the type who was happiest heading the accounting department?" I raved about Bessie's managerial and organizational skills. The caller said, "That's just what I was afraid of. We were considering her for an analytical position." So I had to backtrack and praise Bessie's analytical skills and ability to work alone. Call your references and tell them the kind of job you are applying for and what you would like them to say about you. Help them help you. You can even put some points in writing so the references can refer to your sheet when they get a call about you. This leaves little to chance. It may sound pushy to prompt your references this way, but they'll usually appreciate having a script to follow.

Sometimes, after you receive an offer, you will be asked to sign a statement releasing your former employers from liability about anything they may say about you. This means that your former employers can feel free to tell the truth about you as they see it. So then it's especially important to guide who they call about you, if possible.

5. **Keep in touch with your references on an ongoing basis.** People change jobs a lot, and that includes your former bosses; you don't want to discover that you can't find your favorite old boss. If a company looks as though it is folding, get the home address and phone numbers of those you would like to use as references. Send these people a holiday card each year—just so you can keep tabs. If the card is returned by the post office, you need to make calls right away before the trail goes really cold.

I've run The Five O'Clock Club for 20 years now, so I don't need references anymore, but I still have on my mailing list a boss I had 20 years ago. I never want to lose touch with him.

Work hard to eliminate the problem of not being able to locate someone who could provide the perfect reference when you need it. Of course, if you don't want anyone to contact a boss from five years ago who didn't like you, then let the guy disappear. Then you can honestly say you can't locate them.

6. **Protect your references from too many phone calls.** If lots of prospective employers call the same person, your references will get annoyed and you will look like a loser: "I wonder why Joe is having such a hard time finding a job." So don't give out your references too soon or too freely. If an employer asks for references before you've even had a meeting, that is too soon—except in academia, where it is more standard to give references up front.

Don't let people call your references unless they are on the verge of making you an offer that's acceptable to you. Just say, "My references are very important to me, and I don't want to bother them with phone calls until we're really sure we want to work together."

7. **Ask your references to follow up with you.** You need to know when a reference has actually been called, so ask your references to let you know when they are contacted. Then debrief them. Remember, the ball is always in your court. Your references may be able to shed some light on how a prospective employer feels about you, and you may get information to help you with more follow-up.

Also, if you have given out three names and none of them has been called within a week or two, you are probably not as close to an offer as you think. Call the hiring company and try to uncover any possible hidden objections.

8. **Thank your references.** After you get a job, let them know what happened and thank them for their help. Keep Point 5 in mind: These are people who have helped you; keep in touch on an ongoing basis.

199

If You Left Under Bad Circumstances

Think of it this way: Many of the people we meet at The Five O'Clock Club have had a recent problem despite an otherwise fine career. Yet they get new jobs.

In the case of an unhappy departure, it's best if you and your former manager can settle on a mutually agreeable story. If this is impossible, think of a substitute reference, such as someone who used to be your boss, even if it was a while back. Then say, "I worked for Jane for five years, so she knows me better than my most recent boss."

If they *still* insist on speaking with your former boss, it's time for a preemptive strike to warn them that they might not hear good things. You might want to say something like this: "I'll be happy to give you Jonathan's phone number. I'm sure he'll be able to tell you details about the work I did. But I wanted to become part of a productive and organized team, which was not the case in my last position. Jonathan's style is more flamboyant and seat-of-the-pants, so please keep that in mind when you speak with him. And definitely do give him a call. But I really want you to hear about a special project I worked on when Jane was my boss, so be sure to call her as well. . . ."

If you've been at one place for a long time but had problems only with your most recent boss, then you have a long track record of success with that employer. If you'd been there a short time, then you probably had a long track record of success elsewhere. Focus on your past successes, not on your most recent failure.

For example, if you worked for your last employer only 6 months but worked for the prior one for 10 years, you would obviously prefer that they contact the employer for whom you worked for 10 years. Then you need to say to your prospective employer, "I worked at that place for only 6 months, and it didn't work out. You'd get better information about me if you contacted the employer where I worked for 10 years."

You need a rationale for why interviewers should *not* contact your most recent employer. Don't fabricate a story. Chances are, you have a good reason. Just BRIEFLY state your reason. Don't go on and on about it. If it's true, you could say, for example, "I had four bosses in two years." Or perhaps your style is more like the style of the company where you are now interviewing. Or point out where you have learned from your past about the kind of firm where you would work best, and that's why you're so excited about this new opportunity.

Or my favorite, which I used in my own search: "Everyone makes one mistake in his or her career, and going to that firm was mine. If you would like a more balanced feedback of my performance, it would be better if your contacted Bob Johnson at Acme instead, and here's why." Remember this is a game. People who have decided to hire you want to hear positive things about you, so get good at positioning your strengths during the reference-checking stage.

If You Work in a Field Where Everyone Knows Everyone Else

In a very small, tight field where everyone knows the people where you used to work, you may not have a chance to give out references. Prospective employers simply pick up the phone and call people where you used to work—even if HR has a strict policy against such informal reference checking. You will have to develop a strategy about how to handle this in your particular case. Often, there are key players in the industry—people whom everyone calls. Try to make sure those people think well of you. If that's not possible, do a preemptive strike and suggest names of people the prospective employer can call. One good rule that flows out of this reality of "reference by reputation" is: Work to establish a sterling reputation. Become known as a great boss and peer. There are consequences when you don't; if you are difficult to get along with, your reputation will precede you.

Gaining Leverage in the Reference Game

What if things did not work out well in your last job, and you're afraid prospective employers will want to call them as a reference? Get on with your search, line up some other references—perhaps someone you worked with earlier or someone at your last organization who liked you—and *have three or four job possibilities in the works*. When you're in demand, your prospective employers won't care so much about a few bumps in your past. They'll care more about beating out the other companies that are interested in you.

By the way, if you're talking to a small-to mid-sized company, and you have 6 to 10 things in the works, they are less likely to do a reference check. And if they do, it's likely to be perfunctory, because they're influenced by your marketability.

If a Former Boss Is Sabotaging You

If you're getting interviews everywhere, second interviews, and then no job offers, then your references may be suspect.

If you think a former boss is doing you in, you could have a friend call your former employer and pretend to be interested in hiring you. Your friend can probe to see what your former boss says about you. If it really is a problem, you could approach your former boss and say that you are having a problem getting a job and think that it's because of his references. Ask him directly what he is saying about you. Tell him what you'd like him to say, and negotiate with him. Focus on whatever you did well in that organization, not on your most recent failure. As we said earlier, job hunters can write out a script for a former employer, listing the good things you think the former employer might be willing to say. Then, when your former employer gets a call, he or she can just refer to the script.

If he *insists* on saying bad things:

- Figure out a way not to use him as a reference.
- Bring your concerns to human resources. Believe me, they *will* care (see below).
- Or tell prospective employers that you've been working for 20 years and have lots of great references, but your latest employer is unlikely to give you a good reference because he (for example) tends to say negative things about everyone. That way, when they call him, they will not expect to hear good things and will somewhat discount what he says.

A former employer should not have the power to derail your career. In fact, employers are not allowed to say whatever they want, and human resources above all will be sensitive to this. Terminated employees can sue for defamation if they think they have been *wrongly* maligned by a former employer. A former employee can sue for what a former employer tells prospective employers who seek a reference, and they can sue for what a former employer tells former coworkers about the termination. (Amy DelPo, *Dealing With Problem Employees: A Legal Guide,* Nolo Press, 2003).

We're not suggesting you sue your former employer. On the contrary, lawsuits are usually a bad idea. These cases are difficult to win, even though your employer can say only things he can prove are true. However, knowing that your employer is not allowed to say just any old thing about you gives you some clout. Most employers know they should be careful when giving out references; they know there's a reason why many companies have a strict policy about giving out only your title and dates of employment. But if your former boss doesn't use judgment when giving references, go to human resources and tell them that someone ought to talk to your former boss because he is ruining your chances of getting another job. Then give them your evidence of this (such as "I had a friend call and my former boss said . . .").

One final note on lawsuits. Not only are they difficult to win but also they are a huge distraction. *You should be focusing on your job search.* Furthermore, if word gets out that you're suing your former boss, prospective employers are likely to lose interest in you—*fast.*

Asking for a Written Reference

It's more common for young people, but even seasoned professionals may ask an employer for a written reference. While a letter of reference may not be considered as good as a reference done via the phone—which allows for probing during the give-and-take of conversation—enthusiastic praise captured forever in a letter can be valuable. And if you do lose contact with the reference, you've always got the letter.

But make it easy for your reference to provide the letter. Don't be like Jeff, who was young, naive—and just a little bit lazy. Jeff was about two years out of college, working for a company whose president had great influence in the industry. Jeff thought a letter of reference would help him tremendously as he applied for positions in the future.

Jeff sent an e-mail to the company president asking for a written letter of recommendation. The president said he would help Jeff in any way he could, but Jeff was aghast when "he wanted *me* to write the letter, and then pass it along to him for editing."

Jeff should count his blessings. You can only imagine how many requests for references the president of a company gets. He cannot spend his time writing references—he has to manage the company. Yet, what a nice guy he is for offering to "help in any way he could."

But Jeff has to make the president's job easier. He has to put in a little effort if he wants a reference. I often ask employees to give me a draft when they want a reference from me. Then I know what aspects of their personalities and their jobs they want to have emphasized. They are also reminding me of what they have done. If I'm trying to help them, the last thing I need is someone complaining that I left out an important project he or she worked on!

So, if you want a written reference, ask your boss and volunteer to write a draft. You'll see how difficult it is to do.

Writing is easy. All you have to do is stare at a blank sheet of paper till drops of blood form on your forehead.

Gene Fowler (writer)

How to Write a Reference Letter (Also Called a "Letter of Commendation")

The following guidelines can be used as a template:

- Put "To Whom It May Concern" at the top, then use the first sentence to place you in context: "Jeff worked with us for two years in the capacity of. . . ."
- Next, give a general appraisal ("Throughout his time with the company he was a top-notch employee and . . .").
- Follow with some details of what you've accomplished. Don't be afraid to brag a little.
- Finally, you could conclude with something like "I would highly recommend Jeff for whatever position he believes is appropriate."

Then your manager will modify your letter to suit her style and perhaps include things she knows about you.

Then, Keep Up the Good Work

Don't forget you've got to live up to the letter of recommendation!

I once wrote a terrific letter of reference for Stan, an employee who was also a student, about to graduate and move on (of course, at my request, he first wrote a draft). Once Stan had that letter in his hot little hands, he slacked off; he missed days and showed up late. He figured he had what he needed.

Au contraire! A few weeks later, I received a phone call from a vice president of a venture capital firm who asked about Stan. This would be a plum opportunity for a recent graduate. Stan would be the assistant to the president of an organization. He would travel with the president and help him get ready for meetings. All of the other students who worked there did copying and stuffing envelopes but were glad just to be in that firm.

I urged them to hire Stan but mentioned that he sometimes had to take off from work for personal reasons, although I thought those reasons were behind him (this was true). I was trying to give them a hint that he may have problems, although I didn't want to ruin his chances of getting this great job.

A few months later, the venture capital firm called me again to say that they *had* hired Stan—but they had just *fired* him, too! He routinely missed work and gave very lame excuses. The vice president said to me, "He must have thought we were stupid!"

Developing Your Character

Young people can get away with character flaws: arrogance, pettiness, impatience, recklessness, impulsiveness, distractedness (to name a few suggested by the students in our office!). Managers excuse them because of their youth, and they expect that young people will grow out of it. But as employees get older, managers are less tolerant—they figure you ought to know better. When you are older, you are likely to *lose* your job because of your arrogance—and other character flaws.

I once coached Jane, whose reputation preceded her. She was brilliant but irritating and unpopular with her bosses and peers. By her mid-40s, she had chewed up so many relationships that she couldn't find a job. I explained to her that she had achieved her previous high level not because of her personality but in spite of it. Like so many obnoxious people, she mistook being difficult for being strong and committed. When she was younger, she could get away with being arrogant, but managers expect mature behavior from adult employees. After all, there are *lots* of bright people around, and employers can choose the *nice ones*. Many studies have shown that managers prefer ability to get along over high IQ.

Jane decided to reform. She went to those she had offended and apologized. Did she turn into a charmer? No. But she learned a little humility and how to bite her tongue. She realized that if she couldn't keep a job, maybe she wasn't so bright after all! She's now been with her present employer seven years.

If You've Made a Big Mistake

Here's a sticky one, and I'm sure some readers (especially older ones) will not agree with me on this case. I received an E-mail from the mother of Julian. Her 16-year-old son and three other teenage boys were fired from their jobs at a local grocery store because they stole soda, candy, and/or money. Julian made restitution, wrote a letter of apology, and asked the owner for forgiveness. The owner said he'd forgive him but could not give him a job reference.

People of all ages make mistakes. Julian seemed to have learned his lesson. Here's the sticky part—and remember that the topic right now is protecting your references. If Julian were my son, I would advise him *not* to put the grocery job on his record. Just pretend this part of his life never happened, resolve to do better in the future, and get a fresh start at age 16½.

Now, what if you're older and have had a problem? According to the National WorkRights Institute, a nonprofit human rights organization (and reported in the *New York Times*), "Forty-six million people in the United States have been convicted of something sometime in their lives and our economy would collapse if none of them could get jobs. . . . That figure includes everybody in the FBI's criminal records database, which includes people convicted of a relatively minor misdemeanor." Where would we be without forgiveness and fresh starts?

Remember that George W. Bush was convicted of driving while intoxicated quite a long time ago, but he was still considered for a very important job. Generally speaking, everyone should have a chance at redemption. I asked a few human resources people for their thoughts, and I heard that companies are only supposed to ask about felonies. But I've seen applications that ask if you have ever been arrested. That's outrageous. And even when someone has been convicted of a crime, hiring systems should be flexible. People should not be branded for life. One woman who e-mailed me said she was convicted of battery years ago after hitting a woman she found in bed with her husband. It's unfair that she should be punished for life. None of us is perfect, after all. We're supposed to believe in second chances.

If your record includes an arrest, misdemeanor, or felony, stay away from large corporations, which are more likely to have more rigid policies and more thorough background checks. Go after the smaller firms (fewer than 1,000 employees) and not-for-profit organizations. Certain convictions will limit a person from entering fields such as banking, health careers, and computer information systems. Work hard at getting letters of reference or introductions from previous employers. As a matter of routine, attach these to your resume. This may help move the hiring team past the reference issue.

Some people have been able to have their convictions expunged (erased). This varies from state to state, and the laws are changing all the times, so see an attorney.

If you have made mistakes in your past, don't let your fears run away with you. References may seem like an impossible mountain to climb. But are they? If you perfect your interviewing skills, you may win people over. They may not care all that much about references. Don't believe me? A survey for the *New York Times* advertising department found that two-thirds of hiring managers thought interviews were the most effective way to judge job candidates, while "fewer than one in six hiring managers said that references are an effective manner of determining whether to hire a candidate."

In closing, I want to point out that the job-search process is a research process: finding out where you fit in and who will accept you. Your life might have to change—but life goes on, often for the better. I have been inspired by former New York State Court of Appeals Judge Sol Wachtler, who was on his way to becoming governor. He spent 15 months in prison for stalking an ex-lover (while self-medicating at the rate of 5,000 pills in an 18-month period while serving on the bench). After his astonishing fall, Wachtler, now rehabilitated, teaches at a small college and lectures to keep others off unprescribed drugs. Of his long, dark period when his life fell apart, Wachtler says, "It's true that when one door closes, another opens, but the hallways are hell."

At no point in the job search should you go it alone, and references are no exception, because references can be a complicated matter. Every individual has a unique situation, all the more reason to get help in brainstorming what to do. That's why we have small groups, so you can discuss your reference strategies with your small group and your coach.

Being entirely honest with oneself is a good exercise.
Dr. Sigmund Freud

The
Five
O'Clock
Club

PART FIVE

Getting What You Want
HOW TO INTERVIEW AND NEGOTIATE

The Five O'Clock Club

Basic Interviewing Techniques

Just know your lines and don't bump into the furniture.
Spencer Tracy's advice on acting

Most people think of the interview as the *end* of the job-search process. They think: "Thank goodness. I finally got an interview!" But at The Five O'Clock Club, we think of the interview as the *beginning* of the process. So far, you've searched to line up *meetings,* but your *job* search is just beginning.

What an Interview *Really* Is— and What It Isn't

An interview is a business meeting—a time to exchange information between an organization's representative and a person, namely you. As many Five O'Clock Club coaches suggest, it is helpful to your self-esteem to think of interviews as *meetings* and even refer to them that way.

The purpose of the interview *is not* to get a job. Perhaps you find this shocking, but the purpose of the interview is to *get* information and *give* information—**so you'll get another meeting**.

Most job hunters try to close too soon. They're under a lot of pressure. When they're going in for their first meeting, everyone says: "I hope you get the job!" At The Five O'Clock Club, we hope you *don't*. We hope you get the next *meeting*. It is unlikely that you will get an offer for a *good* job after just one meeting. I would wonder what's wrong with the company: Is it the type that hires easily and fires easily?

Instead of trying to land a job immediately, conduct yourself at the first interview so that they will want you back for a second one. Get enough information so that you can follow up intelligently. It is not uncommon in today's market to have 12 to 15 meetings at one company for one job. You may have fewer, but don't count on it. Instead, plan to be in this for the long haul with each company, perhaps with 6 to 10 meetings.

The *primary* purpose of the first meeting is to start to uncover information about

- the organization
- the job
- the environment
- the opportunity
- the boss
- your prospective peers

Another purpose of your interview is to uncover their objections—to find out if there's any reason they might be *reluctant* to bring someone like you on board. Any salesperson will tell you that the sale begins *after* the customer reveals the reason for his or her reluctance to buy. Once this is done, you have a chance of *overcoming* objections. Later, we'll tell you how to uncover this information and increase your chances of turning a job interview into a job offer.

With Whom Will You Meet?

If you were invited to a business meeting—especially one where you were going to be the topic of discussion—you would naturally want to know who else would be there, and you might want to know something about them, such as

- their names and job titles
- the issues important to each of them
- their personalities
- their ages
- the length of time they have been with the company

Yet most job hunters go into interviews—which, of course, are business meetings—unprepared, knowing little about the people.

At The Five O'Clock Club, we work to change your thinking on this issue. Matt, for example, was going to be screened by telephone by *five* recruiters from an out-of-town search firm. All five would be on the phone at the same time. He told his Five O'Clock Club group about his upcoming meeting and said, "Wish me luck." And we thought, wish me luck? *Nobody* trained The Five O'Clock Club way says, "I'm going in blindly to a meeting with five other people. I don't even know who they are and just wish me luck." So we told him, "Call the search firm and get some information."

Even though Matt was talking to search firm people and not members of the hiring team, he needed to prepare as he would prepare for any other business meeting by simply asking about *each* of the people who'd be on the phone. What were their names? Their titles? What issues tended to be important to each of them?

Frankly, it's also nice to know a person's age beforehand. *You* know that it's very different if you're in a meeting with a 28-year-old versus, say, a 58-year-old. You can't ask directly for a person's age, but you can get a feel for it. How long has the person been in the industry? How long in this organization? Those answers will give you a hint.

By the way, we also told Matt that he should ask the people to identify themselves as they spoke so he would know who said what during the call, and he should take notes so he can analyze the meeting later.

The meeting of two personalities is like the contact of two chemical substances; if there is any reaction, both are transformed.

Carl Jung, *Modern Man in Search of a Soul*

The people you want to reach, whether they're your coworkers, your boss, or an organizational president, should be viewed as distinct target audiences that require different approaches and strategies.

Jeffrey P. Davidson, *Management World,* September/October 1987

Develop Your Script

This is a basic, but important, Five O'Clock Club technique. Prepare a 3x5 card for *each* organization with which you'll meet. Write the following on it:

- Your pitch—your summary about yourself for this particular organization. "I'm an international marketing manager."

- Then write the headlines of three or four accomplishments you want to tell this specific company. "Increased sales 17% average per year over three years."

- Also write the question *you're most afraid they're going to ask you* at this specific company and how you're going to handle it.

- An answer to what you think might be the employer's main objection to you, if any.

- A statement of why you would want to work for this company.

Keep your 3x5 card in your pocket or purse and review it just before going in for the interview so that you will know your lines.

Questions You Might Ask in an Interview

You are there not only to answer the interviewer's questions, but also to make sure you get the information you need. Ask questions that are appropriate. What do you really want to know? Here are a few possibilities to get you thinking in the right direction:

Questions to Ask Personnel

- Can you tell me more about the responsibilities of the job?
- What skills do you think would be most critical for this job?
- Is there a current organization chart available for this area?
- What happened to the person who held this job before?
- What kinds of people are most successful in this area?
- What do you see as the department's strengths and weaknesses?

Questions to Ask Managers (and Perhaps Peers)

- What are the key responsibilities of the job?
- What is the most important part of the job?
- What is the first problem that would need the attention of the person you hire?
- What other problems need attention now? Over the next six months?
- How has this job been performed in the past?
- Are there other things you would like someone to do that are not a formal part of the job?
- What would you like to be able to say about the new hire one year from now?
- What significant changes do you see in the future?
- May I ask what your background is?
- What do you find most satisfying about working here? Most frustrating?
- How would you describe your management style?
- How is the department organized?
- May I meet the other people who work in the area?
- How is one's performance evaluated? By whom? How often?
- What skills are in short supply here?

You can never enslave somebody who knows who he is.

Alex Haley

Don't ask: "Is there anything I can do to convince you that I'm the right person?" The answer is always no. Decide for *yourself* what you must do to convince them.

The
Five
O'Clock
Club

Research: Preparing for the Interview

There is no knowledge that is not power.

Ralph Waldo Emerson, *Old Age*

Do Your Homework

Before the meeting, research the company and the industry. There's no excuse for going into an interview without knowing something about the organization. Interviewers expect you to know, at the very least, basic information available on the company website. They also expect you to know what has been written in the press about them. If you're asked why you are interested in the organization, you will have your answer if you've done this kind of homework. So do your research—through the library or the Internet and also through friends or contacts you may have in associations you belong to.

You don't want to look foolish. The hiring manager will probably ask, "So why would you like to work here at Smithfield Labs?" Often, the job hunter looks at the person as if to say, "Oh, is that where I am? I forgot what company I was interviewing with."

In most cases, of course, you will have plenty of time for research—but here's what one job hunter did when an interview came up with almost no warning. She knew she couldn't go in without research. Denise had a job interview scheduled at a major company—for a position in which she had no direct experience. The job had to do with organizational development.

But before she went on the interview, she went on the Internet. She had only about 45 minutes before the meeting, and she spent it doing research. She found what had been written about this company in the press in the last 6 months to a year, as well as other information having to do with the organizational development field. She found out when organizational development started and what company had developed it first. With this *quick and dirty* research under her belt, she ran over to the company for her interview. She had to meet with 18 people that one day! Interviewers followed her into the ladies' room asking her questions.

But when she met with person after person, all of this Internet information was fresh in her mind. She was able to speak knowledgably about the trends in the company and also the trends in the profession. She got the job—and she credits it 100 percent to the research she did ahead of time.

The ability to learn faster than your competitors may be the only sustainable competitive advantage.

Arie P. de Geus, *Harvard Business Review*, March/April 1988

In our book, *Shortcut Your Job Search*, read the chapter on research and study the bibliography at the back of the book.

Make yourself necessary to someone.

Ralph Waldo Emerson

The will to persevere is often the difference between failure and success.

David Sarnoff, *Wisdom of Sarnoff and the World of RCA*

Two Kinds of Research

There are two kinds of research. *Primary* research means talking to people who are doing the kind of work you're interested in or people who *know* something about those industries or organizations. You can get in touch with those people through networking or by contacting them directly.

Secondary research is materials in print, generally at the library or information online. Secondary research is removed from the source—removed from the people themselves.

Conduct both primary and secondary research, and keep a balance between the two. Some job hunters would rather spend their time talking with people during their job search. They need to do more library and Internet research. Others prefer to spend their time in the library or working on their computers. They need to get out more and talk to people. Whichever *you* prefer, do more of the other. You need a balanced source of information in your search.

Primary research—talking to people—doesn't just happen in an office. You're researching when you're talking to a person on a plane or at a bus stop. Someone asks, "What do *you* do for a living?" You say, "This is what I do, and this is what I am interested in doing next." They may be able to tell you something about the industry you're interested in. That's research!

You're researching when you go to an *association* meeting, talk to people there, and find out more about what's happening in your target industry. You can research while you're at a party. Those are all examples of primary research—talking to people.

You're also researching when you go to a website that has to do with the organization that you're targeting. That, of course, is secondary research. But be honest. Job hunters often waste time on the Internet. They start exploring and go off on side journeys that may not be relevant to their search. Be careful about how you spend your time online.

Before your interview, you need information on the organization—and the people in it—so you can go in prepared. In addition to the sources listed in the *Shortcut Your Job Search* book, here are a few other research resources that are helpful specifically before an interview.

- Study the **organization's website**. Even for very low-level jobs, a hiring manager is likely to ask, "So how much do you *know* about us?"

- Often, they'll expect you to know the information in their **annual report**, which may appear on their website. Or you can call and ask investor relations or public relations to send you a copy of their annual report.

- Many organizations have a **press release** section on their websites. Or you can go to **prnewswire.com**. Organizations will expect you to know *whatever* they have made public. You may go on an interview, and they may say, "Oh, don't worry about having to work in the Acme building." Maybe they've put out a lot of press releases announcing that they are moving a lot of employees to the Acme building in a remote part of town. If you're interested in this organization, they expect you to know about the things that are of most interest to them.

- **Former and current employees.** One Five O'Clock Clubber met with a former employee before he went on an interview. The employee told him all about the projects the department was working on and gave him great information about the personalities of all the managers he would be dealing with. Dig in before you go on interviews. The more senior you are, the more research you must do before the interview.

- **Journalists** are another source, especially trade journalists. If they cover the industry you're targeting, they can probably tell you a lot about this organization.

  If you're reading a trade journal having to do with health care, banking, opera, association management, or whatever you're targeting, find an article that interests you, and write to that journalist. Nobody writes to them—except you, of course.

  Just follow the standard Five O'Clock Club format for cover letters. Paragraph one is your introduction. You can say, "I was reading your article in *Association Management* magazine and I thought it was interesting. I'd like to talk to you because I'm conducting a job search aimed at that industry." Paragraph two is your summary about yourself. Paragraph three in a standard Five O'Clock Club letter contains three or four bulleted accomplishments. Paragraph four is the close, where you ask for a meeting.

- **www.linkedin.com** is a network of professional-level job seekers. The idea behind this site is that since members refer each other, it is a network of *trusted professionals.* Service is free, and people join by being referred online (via E-mail) by a classmate, coworker, colleague, or other professional. Members fill out a profile, which allows others to contact them, as well as search the network for contacts by such things as job title, job function, or location. Members can access those who are not in their own network but are in the overall database via these searches. There are over 300,000 job listings from over 1,000 employers worldwide. Jobs are posted directly on the employers' own sites. This network allows users to get needed introductions to a hiring manager or recruiter. For example, a member can call a hiring manager and say, "Joan Smith of Exco recommended that I call you"—even if the member knows Joan only via a network search.

- **Association members.** Another important part of your research into specific organizations is deciding whether you actually want to *work* there. Ask about this organization at association meetings. Say to everyone you meet: "I'm going on an interview at XYZ organization. What do you know about them? Do you think this is a good organization or a bad organization? What are they like in our field? Are they ahead in the field or are they behind in the field? What's going on there?"

- **www.edgar-online.com** provides all of the 10-Ks for corporations. A 10-K is the information that a corporation legally *has* to reveal about their business. This includes, for example, the salaries an organization pays their senior officers. That information may be of interest to you. www.motleyfool.com contains investment information, but you may be able to get some inside information on those organizations in their discussion boards. Yahoo is interesting for organization information. On their message boards and in their financial section, you can find very good organization information—including a lot of gossip.

- **Discussion boards** helped George, a Five O'Clock Clubber. George was going on an interview at a rather small organization, and when he searched online, he found information and gossip about the *president* of the organization. People were saying that she was difficult to work with and that she was not willing to move to the next stage in the growth in the organization.

    Often, online gossip is untrue. Disgruntled current or former employees may be trying to hurt the organization. But when George met with the president, the way she acted reflected what he had read online. He landed a very significant-sized contract with that organization because he knew a lot about their weaknesses, and he also felt that he knew how to talk to the president.

    (Many more sources are covered in our book *Shortcut Your Job Search*.)

Every exit is an entry somewhere else.

Tom Stoppard

- Research for the **follow-up phase** is covered in great detail in the chapter on follow-up in this book. However, I'll mention some of the more important points here. In the follow-up phase, consider the *issues* that came up in the meeting and think of how you can address those issues. For example, if the hiring team is concerned that you have no experience in mergers, you may have to talk to a few people who work in mergers and ask them how *they* would handle the meeting. Then you would get back to the organization and say, "I've been giving some thought to how I would handle mergers in this job and would like to meet with you again to discuss it."

    So, depending on what happened in the meeting and what reservations they may have about you, you're likely to have to do some kind of research *after* the interview. It may be that you talk to others in the field, research on-line or at the library, or simply think hard to *develop a plan* of what you could do for them. Whatever you're considering, mull it over with your small group. This phase of the process is too difficult to go alone. You want to turn that job interview into an offer!

    After the interview, you may need to conduct primary as well as secondary research so you can write a proposal. You may have to talk to people in the field, read trade journals, or search the Internet. Then you'd get back to the organization and say, "I've been giving this some thought and here is what I think I would do if I got this job with your organization."

- Finally, you'll need to research **salary information** to find out what you're worth in the market. You can go to websites such as salary.com or look at the salary surveys on yahoo.com—or find sites having to do with your field. Or you can look at job postings for your field and see what's being offered. But the best source of information for what *you're* worth in *this* market is to talk to people.

    When you're talking to hiring managers who have no openings right now, say to them, "If you had an opening right now for someone like me, what kind of salary range would you bring that person in at?" You're worth different amounts in different fields, different industries, and different geographic markets, so you have to test yourself in various markets.

The crisis consists precisely in the fact that the old is dying and the new cannot be born. In this interregnum, a great variety of morbid symptoms appear.

Antonio Gramsci

How to Handle Those Difficult Interview Questions

A sudden, bold, and unexpected question doth many times surprise a man and lay him open.

Francis Bacon, "Of Cunning"

It doesn't help you to read those books that say, "Here are a thousand interview questions and here are a thousand answers." The Five O'Clock Club takes a *strategic* approach to this issue. Remember the strategies—not the memorized answers you find in those books.

Have the Right Attitude: Business Is a Game

When an interviewer asks you a question, don't ask yourself, "I wonder what the answer to that question is?" Instead, ask yourself, "I wonder how I should *play* it?" Because *job hunting* is a game. *Interviewing* is a game. So be a little light-hearted, have a lot of meetings, and get good at playing the game.

But when an answer isn't working for you, change your answer! Don't use a bad answer on dozens of interviews, hoping you will find someone who values you. Find another way to answer the question.

Have positive answers to everything. If people ask about your former boss or your former place of employment, the game is to see how positive you can keep it. Don't tell the gory, irrelevant truth. If someone says, "Tell me about your former boss," what will they think if you say, "My boss didn't have a lot of time for us"? They'll wonder what's wrong with you that you needed a lot of your boss's time. You'll leave a negative impression if you say negative things.

Keep your answers brief. Pay attention—to keep from rambling when you're trying to explain something. Others don't care. *You* care. This is probably your sensitive spot. You're probably trying to explain exactly where you were in the hierarchy or exactly why you left your last job. *They don't care.* Keep your answers brief. Practice in your small group. Decide how you want to *play* this.

Most often, when interviewers ask you a question, they're hopeful about your answer. They want to find the right person, and they're hopeful that you're the one! Sometimes I have the opportunity to talk to prospective employers, and they say to me, "Why did he have to tell me that? I didn't want to know so many details about why he left that job."

Don't be like a little kid who mindlessly says, "I'm just going to tell them the truth." I don't want someone working for *me* who's obsessed with the truth. Because somebody is going to call my office and ask, "Where's Kate?" "Kate's out bowling." Even if something like that were the truth, it's not the right answer. I need people who are business savvy rather than obsessively truthful.

I worked with David, a senior person, and I asked him what he told people on interviews when they asked, "Why did you lose your last job?" David said, "I tell them I lost my job because I did my boss in. I really killed him. I even ruined his marriage. Later on, when he had the chance, he did me in. That's why." You've *got* to have a better answer than that.

Don't take questions so literally. This is not like a discussion with a friend. For example, if the interviewer asks you why you didn't finish college, should you tell the truth? Should you say, for example:

- I couldn't decide on a major.
- My mother died and I had to help out.
- I ran out of money.

These answers are not wise because they're negative, and they also take you both away from what should be the main discussion: the company's needs and how you can help.

The interviewer is not interested in you and your mother. There is a job to fill. Talking about certain subjects weakens your position—regardless of who brought them up. Keep the interview positive, and try not to discuss subjects that detract from your case. Many times hiring managers say to me, "Why did Joe (the applicant) have to tell

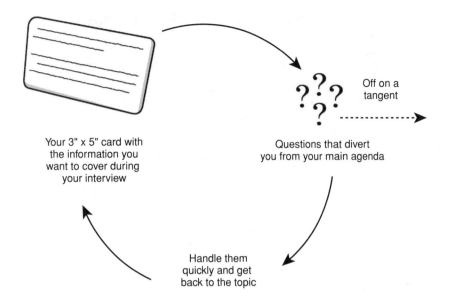

Your 3" x 5" card with the information you want to cover during your interview

Off on a tangent

Questions that divert you from your main agenda

Handle them quickly and get back to the topic

Do not allow the interview to get off track. When the interviewer brings up something that takes you in a direction in which you don't want to go, briefly give a response that satisfies the interviewer, and then get back on track. Give your answer, and then say, for example, "But I really wanted to tell you about a special project I worked on." It is your responsibility to get the conversation back on track.

me that? I was ready to hire him, but now I'm not so sure. When my boss confronts me about Joe's lack of college, I don't have a good answer."

As I mentioned earlier, some job hunters insist on being *honest.* They think, "I'll just tell them the way it is, and if they don't hire me, then so be it." These job hunters are putting the responsibility on the interviewer. We've all had problems. The interviewer doesn't have to hear about them.

A businesslike answer, however, moves the interview along. Let's try the question again, keeping the goal of the interview in mind.

Why Didn't You Finish College?

"I like to be out there doing things. I finished several semesters, but I wanted to get more done. And that's what my bosses have always said about me: I'm someone who gets things done. They've all been happy with me."

Do not go into long discussions. *Briefly and politely* handle those questions that might take you off course, then smoothly move the conversation back to the company's needs or your abilities—the things on your 3x5 card that you had planned to cover. Give your answer, and then say, for example, "but I really wanted to tell you about a special

project I worked on." It is your responsibility to get the conversation back on track.

Lettice: Let me play the interviewer for once: you be the victim.

Peter Schaffer, *Lettice & Lovage*

There are no hopeless situations. There are only men who have grown hopeless about them.

Clare Booth Luce, *Europe in the Spring*

Be Prepared

Your 3x5 card will become your little bible. At the top of your 3x5 card, write your summary about yourself. That's your Two-Minute Pitch. You'll have three to five accomplishments you want to talk about, and you'll have the answer to what you consider a tough question. Master these. Carry your 3x5 card in your pocket or purse, and before you go into your interview, look at the card. This is what you want to tell people—regardless of what they ask you. It's like a politician: It doesn't matter what reporters ask the president, for example. He knows what he wants to talk about.

Difficult interview questions are *any* questions that take you off course—that get you away from what you should be talking about during the interview. So, if the interviewer says, "How's your tennis game?" get the conversation back on course: "Well, I don't know about tennis, but it reminds me of my last job. One of the things I did there is. . . ." And talk about an accomplishment you have listed on your 3x5 card.

When anyone asks you a question that takes you off course, don't simply handle it and let those words hang out there. If *you* also talk about tennis, that's where the conversation will go. Later, you'll say to yourself, "How did we get on this?" Tennis is an innocuous example. But normally, it's something you really *don't* want to talk about, such as what happened in your last job, or the one assignment you didn't do well in. Then you wind up thinking that one assignment is killing your interviews, but it's not that at all. It's *your* fault because you didn't handle it briefly enough. Give enough of an answer, and then *get back to information on your card.* "You know another job I had that's even more interesting is. . . ." Get back to your card.

If you've been unemployed for a long while, be prepared. You may be asked, "What have you been doing these last two years?" Employers don't want to hear that you've been a stay-at-home dad, regardless of how proud you are of it. That has nothing to do with business. Instead, say you've been taking care of a family situation and you've also been studying cost accounting via the Internet. And now you've become an expert in cost accounting, you've been going to accounting meetings, and you've done some cost accounting as a volunteer for a friend's business. If you haven't been doing anything, *do* something.

Before you start answering questions, know something about the employer's needs. So, for example, Angie's been an accounting manager and is great at managing a staff. But *this* employer wants a troubleshooter who can solve some of their long-term accounting problems. Angie can't stick with her regular pitch, which is "I'm great at managing the accounting staff and keeping the work reconciled." They'll say, "Too bad. We need someone who can help us analyze the business—and also manage a staff." So, probe first. If you don't know where the interview is headed, you can say, "There are a lot of different ways I can answer this, but can you tell me a little about your situation? What are your goals? What are you trying to do? What are the problems that keep you up at night?" Find out *something* so you'll know how to position yourself.

Remember that you're talking to a specific company, so do your research ahead of time. Then you can say what interests you about this organization, as opposed to "Oh, I'm at Xerox, is that where I am today?" Organizations want to hire people who want to work for them.

Midway in our life's journey, I went astray from the straight road and woke to find myself alone in a dark wood.

Dante, *The Inferno*

Sample Questions

Let's try some sample questions, but remember that you must find your own answers, depending on your situation.

Tell me about yourself.

See Your Two-Minute Pitch.

Why are you looking? Why are you leaving?

You can count on being asked this because it's their job to ask it. Have your answer ready and then move back to the topics on your 3x5 card. They're just checking off items on a list to make sure there are no problems. Keep it brief. You are the only one who cares about the gory details.

Some job hunters have very solid reasons for being out of a job. One Five O'Clock Clubber, a PR executive in his mid-50s, lost the best job of his life when his boss died and the new president brought in her own person. He was out through no fault of his own, and there was no better answer than what really happened to him.

Other than a story like that one, the best strategy is to describe your job loss as something you were proactive about—as if you had some say in the matter—and are also glad about. At the very least, do not describe your job loss as having to do with your own performance. Here are a few examples of positive responses:

"My company is going through a reorganization. I had the option of taking another job internally, but I decided to look elsewhere."

"X company has been great for me, but the career possibilities in the areas that interest me are extremely limited."

"Perhaps you heard that the _____ industry has been going through a major restructuring. I was caught, along with 3,000 others."

- If you're still employed, or if you're in outplacement and are allowed to look for a job back in your old firm:
"I don't know that I *am* leaving. I'm talking to people around the company. They sure would like me to take another job there, but I feel like I want to look outside as well."

- If you lost your job and received even a little severance, you can say:
"I had the opportunity to grab a package and I took it. I'm so lucky. I was not growing as much as I would have liked, and now I can move my career along. That's why I'm glad to be talking to you today. I understand that your department is very involved in the new technologies."

They'll rarely ask how long you will be getting paid, and it's none of their business anyway.

Do what's appropriate for you and for your comfort level. Talk it over with your counselor or with those in your small group. Maybe there's a variation of these answers that's right for you.

- If you had been working long hours: "I decided I couldn't work 75 hours a week and also look for a job. I couldn't do justice to my staff or to my former employer. I left the company so I could conduct a proper search."

- If you didn't get along with your boss:
Generally speaking, it's not a good idea to say that you left because of personality conflict. People may suspect that *you* are a difficult person. Sometimes those at very senior levels can get away with the *personality clash* excuse, but even then it's better to say, "We have differences on strategic issues."

When you're tempted to talk about conflict with a boss, it's best to say instead:

"I want to move my career in a different direction. My expertise is not the most important thing at my present company, and I want to move to a company where my skills will be put to better use."

What are you looking for?

It takes a lot of thinking to be ready for this question. Nothing turns off interviewers more than candidates who don't know what they want. So don't speak in generalities: "I'm looking for a job that excites me" or, even worse, "I'm not sure." This amounts to asking the interviewer to come up with ideas for you! You shouldn't be going on job interviews if you're not hungry and *focused*.

Be prepared to name the kinds of positions you think would be appropriate for you. If your Two-Minute Pitch is polished, you will be able to talk persuasively about the kind of things you can do for the company.

How long have you been unemployed?

If you've been unemployed for a long time, and you answer, "26 months," how likely are you to be hired? I have run job-hunt groups of people who have been unemployed 2 years or more. The first thing we work on is an answer to this question.

From a moral point of view, I must help these people develop a good story so they can get back to work. It would be cruel for me to insist that they tell the truth. Who will hire an applicant who says, "When I was fired, I got depressed for 6 months and couldn't move, and then my mother got sick and I had to help. By then, I had been unemployed 11 months, and no one would hire me. I'm hoping you will give me a chance."

Very few people are willing to give this person a chance, and you can't fault them for that. After all, the "truthful" job hunter is saying, "I've had all these problems, but I'm better now. Will you risk your organization for me?" It's not fair to burden the interviewer. All the interviewer wants to do is fill a job—not save lives.

The solution is to develop a good answer you can live with. Think of what you have actually been doing. Have you been working on your computer? Helping at your church or synagogue? Helping friends with their businesses? Most people can think of something they've been doing—even something little—that they can build a story around.

If you really haven't been doing anything at all, then *go do something.* You are unlikely to interview well if you haven't been out there at all. Get your adrenaline going. Walk dogs, pick strawberries, usher at church. Get active.

Better yet, learn a new skill. Master new software. Take refresher courses. Volunteer your skills, or get paid something nominally. You might even consider saying you were paid for volunteer work, if you think they would back you up. Then think up a good story:

1. "I've actually been *looking* only a month or so. After I left X company, I spent some time working on a special project for a small company."

2. "I've been looking only a few weeks now. After working for more than 20 years, this was my first time off, and I took advantage of the time to (fix up my house, take care of a sick family member, learn tax accounting, etc.). I was glad to have the opportunity to (help out, learn something new, etc.). But now I'm ready to get back to work and put in another 20 years."

3. Take the work you've done:
   "I've been doing public relations work for a small firm. I thought it would be fun to try after so many years with a big corporation, but now I know I like corporate life and I want to get back."

If your answers aren't working—if you're not getting second interviews or job offers—change your answers. Be creative, brainstorm with family and friends, and try new approaches. Positioning is everything; things won't go well until you've positioned yourself correctly.

How would you handle this?

The interviewer describes a problem situation and asks how you would handle it. You can't think that quickly.

"I'd have to give it some thought. I'm the type who likes to think things through. I've been up against problems like this before, such as when we were behind schedule at X company. I thought about the problem, and quickly decided we should do a, b, c. This reduced our processing time and everyone was happy."

"Everywhere I've worked, I've been able to assess situations and resolve them, and I'd do the same for you. I don't know how to answer your question at the moment, but I know I would handle the problem the way I have handled things in the past. I have a good track record."

What are your greatest weaknesses?

After taking time to mull it over:

"Actually, I can't think of any work-related weakness. My bosses have always thought I was great. I'm the kind not only to do my own job but also to notice what else needed to be done in other areas and pitch in to help."

Or name a weakness and show how you have dealt with it, such as:

"Sometimes I get impatient with people because I want the job to get done, but I make sure I find out what's going on and help them with whatever may be stopping them."

The Five O'Clock Club

Advanced Interviewing Techniques

If you don't go, you'll never know. You have to not look at it like a rejection. There are so many reasons you're not picked that you can't even worry about it.

Robert DeNiro, actor

Think and Act Like a Consultant

Pretend for a minute that you own a small consulting company. When you first meet a prospective client, you'll probe to better understand the problems this person is facing.

> **If the manager has no problems, or if you cannot solve them, there is no place for you.**

You are also there to sell your company. Therefore, as the manager talks about company problems, you reveal your own company's experience and credentials by asking questions or by telling how you have handled similar situations. You want to see how *your* company fits in with *this* company.

If the conversation goes astray, as a consultant you would lead it back to the topics on your 3x5 card—the work you would do for them and your abilities. That way, you can make your points in context.

It is your responsibility, as a consultant, to reassure the hiring manager that everything will work out. The manager does not want to be embarrassed later by discovering he's made a hiring mistake. It is almost as if you are patting the manager on the arm and saying, "Everything will be just fine. You can count on me."

You must display self-confidence in your ability to handle the position. If you are not confident, why should the hiring manager take a chance on you? If you want the job, take a stand and say that you believe it will work.

If you are asked how you would handle a situation, there are several approaches you can use to reassure the manager.

- It won't be a problem. I'm good at these things. I can figure it out.
- I'm very resourceful. Here's what I did as company controller . . .
- I've been in that situation before. I can handle your situation even though I don't know the specifics (since I'm not on the job yet).

Let the manager air doubts about you. If you are told what these reservations are, you can reassure the manager on the spot or you can mull it over later and reassure the manager in writing.

Do not appear to be *shopping around.* Be sincerely interested in this particular company, at least during the interview.

Follow up on your meetings. Address the important issues, stress your interest and enthusiasm for the job, and state your major selling points—especially since you now know what is of interest to the interviewer.

> **Thoughtful follow-up will dramatically increase the number of job offers you get. It is one of the most powerful tools you have to influence the situation.**

We've been preaching the consultative approach for decades. It will make you much more powerful and calmer during the interview process—instead of sitting there like a grubby job hunter pleading, hoping that they'll hire you, and passively trying to answer the questions correctly so that you'll win the big prize.

With the consultant mentality, you'll be much more proactive. A consultant is trying to land an assignment—an assignment that pays $40,000, $60,000, $100,000—whatever your salary is. You know that a consultant doesn't expect to breeze through one meeting and then get handed a $100,000 or a $40,000 consulting assignment.

What do consultants do at a first meeting? Imagine me right now, holding an 8½ x 11 pad of paper. I've got my pen in hand and I'm thinking—thinking really hard. I'm thinking the way a consultant thinks. They're not just sitting there answering questions as if they were on a quiz show. They're trying to understand the situation and what the organization's needs might be, maybe even squinting because they're thinking so hard. They're thinking and asking questions that reveal:

- What's going on with this organization?
- What's the flow of work? Who does what exactly?
- And what's handled by this department versus what's handled by that department?
- Have you thought about perhaps needing a person who can handle *this* thing and *that* thing?

Let's be more specific. Pretend that you really are a consultant on the job truly trying to advise this manager. *Pretend you have no stake in the outcome of this meeting. That is, you're not trying to land an assignment.* You're just trying to think about what is right for this organization, not what's right for you. What do they need to have done—*whether it includes you or not?* What's the political situation in the organization? What are the things that are holding them up? You may ask the hiring manager, "What's your vision for this department going forward? What's keeping you from having this department work the way that you want it to work?" Ask questions that help you to help this organization.

The secret of science is to ask the right question, and it is the choice of problem more than anything that marks the man of genius in the scientific world.

Henry Tizard

Let's pretend, for example, that they have an opening for a marketing management position in a subsidiary of a company. You may want to ask:

- Exactly what's your *relationship* with the parent company?
- Do any of their marketing people get involved in the marketing efforts here?
- Are you forced to use any of the marketing solutions that they might have at the parent company?
- Are you allowed to do pretty much whatever you want to do here?
- What's this division's sales volume right now?
- What sales volume would you like it to be?
- What do you think is stopping the division from getting there?
- What is your time frame for getting the sales volume to that new level?
- Is there a problem with your marketing literature, or are you satisfied with it?
- Is there a problem with your sales force? Are you satisfied with that?

- Who exactly on staff is doing whatever affects marketing right now?
- Do you feel like you're understaffed or overstaffed? (What do you think is going on?)
- Do you think your employees are stars or not stars?
- Who are your major competitors? How do you see them in comparison to you?
- Have you been gaining ground or losing ground?

These are not the standard interview questions you might find in some other interview books. These are real questions—as if I was working with a job-hunter client who was preparing for a meeting. I'm thinking, "Well, what are some of the things that *I'd* like to know if I were meeting with these people, if I wanted to get a good feel for what's going on?"

> **Ask yourself what you would *really* like to know if you were actually about to get a job there—rather than repeating generalized questions job hunters always ask in interviews.**

Now, don't just shoot all those questions out one after another. Write them on your notepad, and as interviewers are answering, make comments and tell them something about your experience. "Gee, that's interesting, because when I worked with ABC International, we had the same kind of problem with the parent, and here's what we did about it." Or you say, "The staffing problems seem to be an important issue here. Let me give some thought to how jobs could be combined." Ask questions that are appropriate to the job you're going after. Give them ideas and suggestions that are appropriate to the job. All this gives you a chance to talk about yourself. Have a **consultative mind-set**—probe to really understand what's going on so you can figure out the kind of solutions they need.

What convinces is conviction. Believe in the argument you're advancing. If you don't, you're as good as dead. The other person will sense that something isn't there, and no chain of reasoning, no matter how logical or brilliant, will win your case for you.

Lyndon Baines Johnson

Now what does a consultant do *to follow up?*

> **Consultants ask questions, they take notes, and then they go away and they work on the problems.**

They don't just ask questions and shoot the breeze as if it doesn't take any brainpower. It takes brainpower. After the meeting, you'll do your homework. We'll cover this in depth later in *Turning Job Interviews into Offers*, but at the very least, your homework includes doing Internet research on other organizations that are in the same situation and finding out what they're doing. In the case of one Five O'Clock Clubber, it meant going far beyond that. He visited all of the company's car dealerships and talked to the manager of each about the insurance coverage they had, then went back to the hiring manager and said, "Since I last met with you, I've stopped by a lot of your dealerships and I talked to each manager to uncover their attitudes about the insurance they use. Here's what I learned."

Of course, he got the job. He was able to do intelligent follow-up because he found out during the interview what was of concern to the hiring manager and others with whom he was meeting. He had a consultative mentality.

Help hiring managers define the job: Remember that most jobs are created for people. Some job hunters come away from a meeting and say, "They don't even know what kind of job they want filled here." *Most* companies don't know. You're the consultant. Help them! Of course, don't be an arrogant know-it-all. Show some humility in your suggestions. After all, you couldn't possibly know as an outsider what they know as insiders, and you can admit that to them.

Uncover any political problems. It may affect whether or not you want to work with them. Get the offer, and then decide later if you want to take the job.

That is the essence of science: ask an impertinent question, and you are on the way to a pertinent answer.

Jacob Bronowski

Consultants also find out about their competitors. Consultants know that others are being considered. So, a consultant asks,

- How many other consulting firms are you talking to?
- How far along are you with them?
- How do you see our firm comparing with the other firms you're talking to?

Consultants try to measure how they stack up against their competitors. You, too, need to find out how you stack up against your competitors. Otherwise, you go away dumb and happy, thinking, "They liked me, they really liked me." Well, they liked you, but are they going to hire you? And how do they see you versus your competition? So you have to ask,

- Where are you in the hiring process?
- How many others are you talking to?
- Now that you've met with some of these other people, how do you see me compared with them?
- What kind of person might you be tending toward hiring and why?
- Can you think of any reason why you *wouldn't* want to have someone like me on board?

You could also ask, "What kind of person would be your ideal candidate, and how do you see me in comparison with your ideal?"

Interview Practice

Even experienced job hunters need practice. Each interview smooths out your presentation and responses. As you get better, your self-confidence grows.

By now, you've had networking or information-gathering interviews. You will have practiced talking about yourself and will have information about your area of interest and the possibilities for someone like you.

When I was unemployed, I had lots of interviews, but I was not doing well. I was under so much stress that I kept talking about what *I* wanted to do rather than what I could do *for the company*. I knew better, but I could not think straight. An old friend, who belongs to The Five O'Clock Club, helped me *develop my lines* for my 3x5 card. Then we practiced. After that, my interviews went well.

"Jenkins and I worked it out. He can have the office with the window."

> **Be sure to record every networking and job interview on the Interview Record.**

People who are in Five O'Clock Club small groups do better on interviews for a number of reasons. One is that they get to hear the experiences and the blunders of those who are ahead of them in the job search so they don't make those same mistakes later. But another reason is that they're practicing every week how to speak, keep things concise, and get to the point. When it's your turn in the small group, you tell other people what is happening in your search and what you need help with.

The way you seem in the small group bears some resemblance to the way you are in interviews. It's better to get feedback from friendly peers and your career coach rather than lose one job offer after another and not know why. Every Five O'Clock Club session gets you more ready for your meetings with prospective employers.

Do Your Best, Then Let It Go

You are trying to find a match between yourself and a company. You are not going to click with everyone, any more than everyone is going to click with you. Don't expect every interview to turn into a job offer. The more interviews you have, the better you will do at each one.

And don't punish yourself later. Do your best, and then do your best again.

Hang in there. Get a lot of interviews. Know your lines. And don't bump into the furniture. You will find the right job. As M. H. Anderson said: "If at first you don't succeed, you are running about average."

It may sound like a contradiction, but you achieve spontaneity on the set through preparation of the dialogue at home. As you prepare, find ways of making your responses seem newly minted, not preprogrammed.

Michael Caine, *Acting in Film*

The
Five
O'Clock
Club

How to Use the Interview Record

Obviously the way you move will be affected by the character you are playing; but natural movement comes from your "center," from the same place as a natural voice. When you walk from your center, you will project a solid perspective of yourself. Walk with that certainty and ease, and your path becomes a center of gravity. Your force pulls all eyes to you. Slouch or poke your head forward, or pull your shoulders back uncomfortably, and that power seeps away. Only a relaxed, centered walk creates a sense of strength. A centered walk can be very menacing, too. Even if you don't get film work on the basis of this advice, follow it and you'll never get mugged, either. Mind you, if you look like I do you'll never get mugged anyway because people generally think
I have just been mugged.

Michael Caine, *Acting in Film*

On the next page is a very important worksheet: the Interview Record. Make a lot of copies of this page for your own personal search. Every time you have a meeting—**whether a networking meeting or a job interview**—fill it out. Make note of with whom you met, to whom they referred you, and what happened in the meeting. Attach to the Interview Record a copy of your notes from the meeting, the follow-up letter you sent, and perhaps the letter that led to the meeting.

Two weeks after the meeting, you may not remember what you discussed. If you are having a productive search and you are meeting with 10 to 15 people each week, you will not be able to remember what each person said, let alone how you met that person. To keep track of your meetings, maintain a record of each one.

Some job hunters use a three-ring binder, and arrange all of the Interview Records alphabetically or by industry or in some other logical order, with their letters attached.

Some job hunters methodically cross-reference the names by noting who referred whom.

At the beginning of your search, you may think you will be searching for a short time. But part of a good search is to follow up with your contacts at least every two months. You can have a more intelligent follow-up if you have an Interview Record to refer to.

Interview Record

Name: _____

Position: _____

Company: _____

Address: _____

_____

_____

Phone: Business:_____

　　　　Home:_____

E-mail:_____

Referred by:_____

Link to referral: _____

People spoken to (may require separate sheets):

_____

Issues (advice, problems, plans, etc.): _____

_____

_____

Key points to remember: _____

_____

_____

Referrals (write additional names on back):

Name: _____

Position:_____

Company: _____

Address: _____

_____

_____

Phone: Business:_____

　　　　Home:_____

Date of initial contact: _____

Method used: _____
　　　　　　　(if letter, copy and attach to this sheet)

Planned date of follow-up call to set up

　　appointment: _____
　　　　　　　(also record date on job-hunting calendar)

Actual dates of calls to set up appointment:

_____

_____

_____

_____

Appointment: _____

Follow-up note mailed: _____
　　　　　　　　　　　(copy attached)

Follow-up 2: _____

Follow-up 3: _____

Follow-up 4: _____

Follow-up 5: _____

Follow-up 6: _____
　　　　　　　　　　　(copy attached)

Other comments:

- tone of the meeting
- positives about you
- objections to you
- key issues to address
- logical next steps
- influencers
- your feelings about the job

The
Five
O'Clock
Club

Follow-Up after a Job Interview: Consider Your Competition

Bullock shrugged. He'd been thinking about Bill that afternoon, trying to decide how to fit him into Deadwood Brickworks, Inc. It wasn't a question he could be useful. Anybody could be useful when you decided where they fit. That was what business was.

Pete Dexter, *Deadwood*

So far in the interview process, we have considered you and the hiring manager. By acting like a consultant, you can negotiate a job that's right for both you and him or her. But there are other players and other complexities in this drama. First, there are all the other people you meet during the hiring process. They are influencers and, in fact, may influence the hiring decision more than the hiring manager does. These are people the hiring manager trusts and on whose opinions he relies. In addition, there are complexities such as outside influencers, the timing of the hiring decision, and salary considerations. Finally, you have competitors. They may be other people the interviewer is seeing, or your competition can be an ideal candidate in the interviewer's mind.

This chapter contains case studies of how some people considered and dealt with their competition. In the next chapter, we'll give you the guidelines they followed, which helped them decide what they could do to win the job. Remember, the job hunt really starts after the interview. What can you do to turn the interview into an offer? This is the part of the process that requires the most analysis and strategic thinking. Think *objectively* about the needs of the organization and of everyone you met, and think about what you can do to influence *each* person.

If you're in a seller's market, however, you may not need to follow up: You'll be brought back for more meetings before you have a chance to breathe. *If you're in a buyer's market,* you will probably have to do thoughtful follow-up to get the job.

Because effective follow-up is a lot of work, your first decision should be: Do I want to get an offer for this job? Do I want to *go for it*? If you are ambivalent, and are in a competitive market, you will probably *not* get the job. Someone else will do what he or she needs to do to get it.

Follow-ups will not guarantee you a specific job, but extensive follow-ups on a number of possibilities increase the number and quality of your offers. If you focus too much on one specific situation and how you can *make* them hire you, that won't work. You need both breadth and depth in your job hunt: You have both when you are in contact on a regular basis with 6 to 10 people who are in a position to hire you or recommend that you be hired. You must have 6 to 10 of these contacts in the works, *each* of whom you are trying to move along.

Ideally, you will get to a point where you are moving them along together, slowing certain ones down and speeding others up, so you wind up with 3 concurrent job offers. Then you can select the one that is best for you. This will usually be the job that positions you best for the long run—the one that fits best into your Forty-Year Vision. It will rarely be sensible to make a decision based on money alone.

Therefore, if one situation is taking all of your energy, stop right now for 10 minutes and think of how you can quickly contact other people in your target area (through networking, direct contact, search firms, or ads). It will take the pressure off and prevent you from trying to close too soon on this one possibility.

CASE STUDY *The Artist*
Status Checks Rarely Work

Most people think follow-up means calling for the status of the search. This is not the case:

At Citibank, a project I managed needed an artist. I interviewed 20 and came up with two piles: one of 17 rejects and another of the 3 I would present to my boss and my boss's boss. A few people called to *follow up.* Here's one:

Artist: "I'm calling to find out the procedure and the status. Do you mind?"

Me: "Not at all. I interviewed 20 people. I'll select 3 and present them to my boss and my boss's boss."

Artist: "Thanks a lot. Do you mind if I call back later?"
Me: "No, I don't mind."

The artist called every couple of weeks for three months, asked the same thing, and stayed in the reject pile. To move out, he could have said things like:

- Is there more information I can give you?
- I've been giving a lot of thought to your project and have some new ideas. I'd like to show them to you.
- Where do I stand? How does my work compare with the work others presented?

If all you're doing is finding out where you are in the process, that's rarely enough. *The ball is always in your court.* It is your responsibility to figure out what the next step should be. Job hunters view the whole process as if it were a tennis game where—*thwack*—the ball is in the hiring manager's court. Wrong.

Me to job hunter: "How's it going?"
Job hunter to Kate: (*Thwack!*) "The ball's in their court now. They're going to call me."

When they call, it will probably be to say, "You are not included." If you wait, not many of your interviews will turn into offers.

CASE STUDY *Rachel*

Trust Me

Rachel had been unemployed for nine months. This was her first Five O'Clock Club meeting. She was disgusted. "I had an interview," she said. "I know what will happen: I'll be a finalist and they'll hire the other person."

Rachel was nice, enthusiastic, and smart: She was always a finalist. Yet the more experienced person was always hired.

Here's the story. Rachel, a lobbyist, was interviewing at a law firm. The firm liked her background, but it needed some public relations help and perhaps an internal newsletter. Rachel did not have experience in either of those areas, though she knew she could do those things. She wrote a typical thank-you note playing up her strengths, playing down her weaknesses, but essentially ignoring the firm's objections. She highlighted the lobbying and said that PR and a newsletter would not be a problem. She could do it. She was asking the firm to *trust her.*

A man is not finished when he's defeated; he's finished when he quits.

Richard Milhous Nixon

Lots of Job Hunters Take the *Trust Me* Approach

The following occurred during a group meeting at The Five O'Clock Club:

Me: "Do you want this job? Are you willing to go through a brick wall to get it?"
Rachel: "Yes. I am. I really want this job."
Me: "Let's think about overcoming their objections. If you can write a PR plan after you get hired, why not do it now? Why ask them to trust you?"

Two people in the group had old PR plans, which they lent her. Remember: The proposals or ideas you write will probably be wrong. That's okay. You're showing the company you can think the problem through and actually come up with solutions.

Rachel's lack of experience with newsletters was also an objection. We suggested Rachel call law firms in other cities and get their newsletters.

After doing research, Rachel sent a very different note. In this one she said she had been giving it more thought and was very excited about working for the firm. She had put together a PR plan, *which she would like to review with them,* and had gotten copies of newsletters from other law firms, which gave her ideas of what she could do in a newsletter for them. Of course, she got the job.

Mediocrity obtains more with application than superiority without it.

Baltasar Gracian, *Oraculo Manual*

Uncovering Their Objections

Rachel got the job because she overcame the objections of the hiring committee. Start thinking about how you can overcome objections. This will change the way you interview, and you will become more attuned to picking up valid objections rather than quashing them. Then you can even solicit negatives. For example, you can ask:

- Who else is being considered?
- What do they have to offer?
- How do I stand in comparison with them?
- What kind of person would be considered an ideal candidate?
- What would you like to say about a new hire one year from now?

Get good at interviewing so you can solicit valid objections to hiring you.

Without competitors there would be no need for strategy.

Kenichi Ohmae, *The Mind of the Strategist*

Act Like a Consultant

Since most jobs are created for people, find out what the manager needs. Hiring managers often decide to structure the job differently depending on who they hire. Why not influence the hiring manager to structure the job for you?

Probe—and don't expect anything to happen in the first meeting. If you were a consultant trying to sell a $30,000 or $130,000 project (your salary), you wouldn't expect someone to immediately say, "Fine. Start working." Yet job hunters often expect to get an offer during the first meeting.

Forget about job hunting. This is regular business. You're selling an expensive package. Do what a consultant or a salesperson does: Ask about the company's problems and its situation; think how you could get back to the interviewer later. Get enough information so you can follow up and give the interviewer enough information so he'll want to see you again. Move the process along: Suggest you meet with more people there. Do research. Have someone influence the interviewer on your behalf. Then get back to him again. That's what a consultant does. Remember to move the process along; outshine and outlast your competition.

What Happens as Time Passes

Most jobs are *created* for people: Most interviewers don't know clearly what they will want the new person to do. Yet job hunters expect the hiring manager to tell them exactly what the job will be like and get annoyed when the manager can't tell them.

Generally, the job description depends on who will be in the job. Therefore, help the hiring manager figure out what the new person should do. If you don't help him, another job hunter will. This is called "negotiating the job." You are trying to remove all of the company's objections to hiring you, as well as all of *your* objections to working for them. Try to make it work for both of you. But time is your enemy. Imagine what happens in the hiring process as time passes.

You have an interview. When I, your counselor, ask how it went, you tell me how great it was: The two of you hit it off, and you are sure you will be called back. You see this interview as something frozen in time, and you wait for the magical phone call.

But after you left, the manager met with someone else, who brought up new issues. Now his criteria for what he wants have changed somewhat, and consequently, his impression of you has also changed. He was honest when he said he liked you, but things look different to him now. Perhaps you have what he needs to meet his new criteria, or perhaps you could convince him that his new direction is wrong, but you don't know what is now on his mind.

You call to find out "how things are going." He says he is still interviewing and will call you later when he has decided. Actually, then it will probably be too late for you.

His thinking is constantly evolving as he meets with people. You were already out of the running. *Your call did nothing to influence his thinking:* You did not address his new concerns. You asked for a status report of where he was in the hiring process, and that's what you got. You did nothing to get back into the loop of people he might consider or to find out the new issues that are now on his mind.

Oh I could show my prowess, be a lion not a mou-esse, if I only had the nerve.

The Cowardly Lion in the movie *The Wizard of Oz* (from the book by L. Frank Baum) by E. Y. Harburg and Harold Arlen

---

The manager meets more people and further defines the position. Interviewing helps him decide what he wants. You are getting further and further away from his new requirements.

You are not aware of this. You remember the great meeting you two had. You remind me that he said he really liked you. You insist on freezing that moment in time. You don't want to do anything to rock the boat or appear desperate. You hope it works out. "The ball is in his court," you say. "I gave it my best. There's nothing I can do but wait." So you decide to give it more time . . . time to go wrong.

Annie: . . . you want to give it time—
Henry: Yes—
Annie: . . . time to go wrong, change, spoil. Then you'll know it wasn't the real thing.

Tom Stoppard, *The Real Thing*

You have to imagine what is going on as time passes. Perhaps the hiring manager is simply very busy and is not working on this at all. Or perhaps things are moving along without you. Statistics prove that the person who is interviewed last has the best chance of being hired. That's because the last person benefits from all the thinking the manager has done. The manager is able to discuss all of the issues of concern with this final applicant.

He had made a fortune in business and owed it to being able to see the truth in any situation.

Ethan Canin, *Emperor of the Air*

What You Can Do during the Interview

If you go into an interview with the goal of getting a job, you are putting too much pressure on yourself to come to closure. When you walk away without an offer, you feel discouraged. When you walk away without even knowing what the job is, you feel confused and lost.

Boone smiled and nodded. The muscles in his jaw hurt. "What I meant was did you ever shoot anybody but your own self. Not that that don't count."

Pete Dexter, *Deadwood*

Instead of criticizing managers who don't know what they want, try to understand them: "It seems that there are a number of ways you can structure this position. Let's talk about your problems and your needs. Perhaps I can help."

Your goal is not to get an offer but to build a relationship with the manager. You are on the manager's side, assessing the situation and figuring out how to move the process along so you can continue to help define the job.

Pay Attention to Your Competition

Most job hunters think only about themselves and the hiring manager. They don't think about the others being considered for the position. But you are different. You are acutely aware at all times that you have competition. Your goal is to get rid of them.

As you move the process along, you can see your competitors dropping away because you are doing a better job of addressing the hiring manager's needs, coming up with solutions to her problems, and showing more interest and more competence than they are.

You are in a problem-solving mode. Here's the way you think: "My goal isn't to get a job immediately but to build a relationship. How can I build a relationship so that someday when this person decides what he or she wants, it'll be me?" You have hung in there. You have eliminated your competition. You have helped define the job in a way that suits both you and the hiring manager. You have the option of saying, "Do I want this job or don't I?"

He who knows only his own side of the case, knows little of that.

John Stuart Mill, *On Liberty*

The
Five
O'Clock
Club

Follow-Up Checklist: Turning Job Interviews into Offers

Biblical waiting, the kind of waiting Abram and Sarai did, and which you and I must learn to do, is a very active kind of waiting. It's a faith-journey; the waiting of a pilgrimage. We can only wait for God to give us what we cannot do ourselves; but, paradoxically, we must move toward it in faith as we wait, asking, seeking and knocking. . . .

Ben Patterson, *Waiting*

Do you want a job? Follow-up is the only technique that influences the person who interviewed you. You may think you can get a job through a search firm, answering an ad, networking, or directly contacting a company. But what you are getting is interviews in your target area. You are not job hunting yet. You prove your mettle by seeing how—over the long run—you can turn each interview into a job. Now you're job hunting. And that's where follow-up comes in. Remember, you generally don't want a job offer at that first meeting. An easy hire decision may mean an easy fire decision later. Instead, establish a long-term relationship. It is not unusual to be brought in for three to nine or more interviews.

In the last chapter, you read a few examples of job hunters turning job interviews into offers. They had to think hard about what to do next. They objectively and methodically analyzed *all* the interviews they had and developed strategies for addressing every issue for *each* person with whom they met. They thought about who their likely competitors were and what the hiring managers probably preferred. Who are your likely competitors? How do you stack up against them? Prove you're better than they are, or you won't get the job.

Follow-up will dramatically increase the number of job offers you get. It is one of the most powerful tools you have to influence the situation.

Why Bother with Follow-Up?

Follow-up can be used:

- to influence both the decision makers and the influencers
- to move things along
- to show interest and competence
- to knock out your competition
- to reassure the hiring manager
- to turn a losing situation into a winning one
- to make it difficult for them to reject you
- to set the right tone/buy yourself time after you are hired

In a tight market, follow-up helps. But still *strive to have 6 to 10 contacts in the works at all times.* The job you are interviewing for may vanish: The manager may decide not to hire at all or hire a finance instead of a marketing person. There may be a hiring freeze or a major reorganization. Follow-up techniques will generally not help in these situations. If you are in a competitive market, put extra effort into those job possibilities that are still alive.

Nothing is more dangerous than an idea when it is the only one you have.

Emile Chartier

And if you have lots of other contacts in the works, you will be less likely to allow yourself to be abused by hiring managers trying to take advantage of *desperate* job hunters. You can assess ridiculous requests and be more willing to walk away.

The Interview Record is a checklist of items to consider in assessing your interviews and planning your follow-up. Try to remember everything that happened at each of your meetings. Many job hunters take notes during the interviews so they will do a better follow-up. After all, wouldn't a consultant take notes during a meeting? How else can you remember all the important issues that come up? At the very least, take notes immediately after the meeting. Some job hunters keep track of every person with whom they meet by using the Interview Record. Make plenty of copies of the form for your job search. Keep them in a folder or a three-ring binder, in alphabetical order within a target area.

Waiting is not just the thing we have to do until we get what we hoped for. Waiting is part of the process of becoming what we hope for.

Ben Patterson, *Waiting*

Assess the Interview(s)

Effective follow-up depends on knowing what happened in the interview. In fact, you will begin to interview very differently now. You now know you are there to gather enough information so you can follow up, and to give enough information back so the interviewer will be willing to meet with you again. As your counselor, I'd want the following background information:

- How did it go? What did they say? What did you say?
- How many people did you see?
- How much time did you spend with each?
- What role does each of them play?
- Who is important?
- Who is the hiring manager?
- Who is the decision maker?
- Who most *influences* the decision?
- Who else did you meet (secretaries, receptionists, bosses from other areas)? How influential might they be? (Do not dismiss them too readily. They may be more influential than you think. A trusted secretary, for example, has a lot of influence. She had better want you there.)
- How quickly do they want to decide? A year? Months? Next week?
- What do you have to offer that your competition doesn't?
- What problems did the interviewer have? Do you have any solutions to those problems?
- How badly do you want this job? (If you want it a lot, you will be more likely to do what you need to do to get it. Or perhaps someone wants it more than you. *That* person will do the things he or she needs to do to get the job.)

The key to being a strategic player is to be in play, working on a significant level.

Thomas Krens, director, the Guggenheim Museum, *The New York Times*, May 29, 1988

Anyone who fears effort, anyone who backs off from frustration and possibly even pain will never get anywhere.

Erich Fromm

Anyone who listens well takes notes.

Dante

Follow Up with *Each* Person

For *each* person with whom you interviewed, analyze and craft a follow-up note that takes into account

- **The tone of the conversation.** Was it friendly? Formal? Familylike? Follow up with a similar tone.

- **The positives about you.** Why would this person want you there? If you interviewed with peers, why would they want you on the team? In the interview, it is *your* job to make sure each person you meet can see the benefit of having you on board.

- **The objections to you**—for *each* person you met, whether or not these objections were expressed. For example, you may know that the company typically hires someone with a background that is different from yours, or you may not have certain experience it is looking for, or your past salary may be too high, or it may see you as overqualified. A future peer may see you as a threat (let that peer know you are not) or think you will not fit in. You may be seen as too old or too young or too something else. If you think the company is worried about having you on board for some reason, address that reason. For example, if someone sees you as too old, think of the benefits that come with age. Then you might say, "I hope you are interested in hiring someone with maturity and a broad base of experience."

Even in a highly controlled meeting, there is a lot . . . going on. The real process of making decisions, of gathering support, of developing opinions, happens before the meeting—or after.

Terrence E. Deal and Allan A. Kennedy, *Corporate Cultures*

Many job hunters want to ignore or gloss over the objections; instead, pay attention to why *each* person may not want you there. Joel DeLuca, author of *Political Savvy*, noted that if you are observant, you should come out of a meeting with a good sense of how hard a sell this is going to be, as well as some idea of the political lay of the land.

"Why yes, we are interviewing. But we now charge the applicant $18 an hour for the interview."

If [a man] is brusque in his manner, others will not cooperate. If he is agitated in his words, they will awaken no echo in others. If he asks for something without having first established a proper relationship, it will not be given to him.

I Ching

- **The key issues.** Was the interviewer concerned about interdepartmental relationships? Work overload? The political situation with a key vendor? How you will support people in other areas? How you can make his or her job easier? What makes you different from your competition? Identify those issues that are key to the interviewer(s).

- **Your feelings about the job.** If this is the one place you really want to work, say so. If you would enjoy working with your prospective manager and peers, say so. **At the executive level, most decisions are based on fit.** In addition to competence, people want someone they'd *like* to work with and someone who *wants* to work with them. Write with enthusiasm. Let your personality come through.

- **The next steps.** Regardless of *who* should take the next steps, what exactly are the next logical steps? What will move the process along?

The average sale is made after the prospect has said "no" six times.

Jeffrey P. Davidson, marketing consultant, *The Washington Post*

For example, the next step could be:

- another meeting to discuss something in greater detail
- meeting(s) with other people
- another meeting after the other candidates have been interviewed

- an in-depth review of documents
- discussing a few of your ideas with them
- drafting a proposal about how you would handle a certain area

Let him who wants to move and convince others be first moved and convinced himself.

Thomas Carlyle

State the "next steps" in your follow-up note. For example, "I'd like to get together with you to discuss my ideas on . . ." or "If I don't hear from George in a week or so, I'll give you a call."

If you were the first person interviewed, try to be interviewed again. "As you interview others, you may more clearly define what you want. I would appreciate the opportunity to address the new issues that may arise."

There is a tide in the affairs of men,
Which, taken at the flood, leads on to fortune;
Omitted, all the voyage of their life
Is bound in shallows and in miseries.

William Shakespeare *Julius Caesar*, IV, iii

Influence the Influencers

Most job hunters pay attention to the hiring manager and ignore everyone else. However, most hiring managers want the input of others. You may be rejected if a future peer or subordinate says that you seem difficult to work with or the receptionist complains that you were rude. Remember that everyone is an influencer. *Follow up with everyone you met formally.* Cultivate as many advocates as you can. Have people inside rooting for you. It's better if your future peers, for example, say that you would be great to have on the team. You can influence the influencers with a letter or phone call.

Who might *influence* the hiring decision? **If they are future coworkers, follow the analysis in the preceding section "Follow Up with *Each* Person."** Tell outside influencers the position in which you are interested, why, and how they can help you.

Joe, a well-known top-level executive, felt one of his interviews went very well, but he was afraid the interviewer would tap into the corporate pipeline and hear untrue negative rumors about him. Joe has two choices: He can hope the interviewer doesn't hear the rumors, or he can fight for the job he deserves.

Joe has to try to control the pipeline—the key influencers in this situation. First, Joe called some influential people who thought well of him and would be respected by the hiring manager. He stated why he wanted this job and asked them to put in a good word for him. Second, Joe thought of the people the hiring manager was most likely to run into or call for information. Joe called them next and did his best to influence them to support him. Joe successfully fended off bad reports and landed the job he wanted.

Progress always involves risk.
You can't steal second base and
keep your foot on first.

Frederick B. Wilcox

Success seems to be largely a matter of
hanging on after others have let go.

William Feather

Be in Sync with Their Timing

Move the process along to the next step, but at *the interviewer's* pace, not yours. The timing depends on the personality of the interviewer and his or her sense of urgency.

If the situation is urgent, write your letter overnight and hand-deliver it in the morning. If the manager is laid back, an urgent delivery is inappropriate.

Use your judgment. If things are going along at a good clip, and you are being brought in every other day, you may want to let it ride *if* you think you have no competition.

Also be aware that if things are *not* moving along quickly, it may have nothing to do with you. It may well be that the interviewer is not doing *anything* about filling the position—he or she may be busy with other business. If you were the hiring manager, you would find that you can't work on the hire every minute, because you have your regular job to do, and emergencies come up as well.

If you have no idea what is going on, it would help if you've formed a good relationship with the hiring manager's secretary. Then you could call and say, "Hi, Jane. This is Joe. I was wondering if you could help me with something. I haven't heard from Ellis [her boss] for two weeks and I had expected to hear something by now. I was going

to drop him a note, but I didn't want to bother him if he's really busy. I was wondering if he's still interviewing other people or if he's just been tied up, or what." Who knows what she'll say? But if she says he had a death in the family and has been out of town, that gives you some idea of what is happening. He is not sitting around talking about you all day long. He is doing other things, and the hiring process often moves more slowly than you think.

Understanding is a wellspring of life to him that hath it.
Proverbs 16:22

Even if you're on the right track, you'll get
run over if you just sit there.
Will Rogers

How Can You Tell If a Follow-Up Letter Is a Good One?

A good letter is *tailored* to the situation. It would be impossible to send it to someone other than the addressee. *It sells you, separates you from your competition, addresses all issues and objections, and states a next step.* Finally, its tone *replicates* the tone of the interview (or creates a good tone if the interview wasn't so good). For example, John's various follow-up notes to those he met at the Kennedy Foundation addressed each manager's issues.

Your letters to some people will be very detailed and meticulous. These may take you half a day to write. For others, you will write a simple letter saying that you thought they would be great to work with and addressing the issues they brought up.

Most job hunters err, however, when they assume someone at a lower level has no influence. Be careful about whom you dismiss. During the interview, try to pick up on the relationships between people. In brief, remember to influence the influencers. Write notes to prospective peers you have met. They have some say in the hiring decision—maybe a lot of say. If they don't want you, you might not get hired. For each person you met, think of why he or she would want you there. What do you bring to the party? Make sure you are not a threat. Overcome his or her objections. Address any issues raised. Use the tone set in the interview.

A job hunter, Philip, put a lot of thought into his follow-up with *a prospective peer*, Jonathan. Philip considered Jonathan an important influencer and had noted the following from their meeting:

- Philip sensed that Jonathan was worried about losing his standing as the second in command to George, the hiring manager, when the new person came in.

- He was also concerned that the new person might not be a team player or a hard worker or might not be willing to help out with his special projects, which involved computer simulations.

- He was concerned about losing the camaraderie in the department and hoped the new person would have a good sense of humor to offset the stress of working under deadline.
- He was obviously trying to conduct a very professional interview and asked Philip a number of times what he thought of the questions.
- He was relieved when Philip said he would enjoy developing materials for the department, although it was not central to the job. This is a project none of the other competitors would be able to handle.
- He wondered about the department's reputation outside the company.

The conversation had been light and friendly. Philip considered Jonathan to be the key influencer, and thought George, the hiring manager, would be making the decision with Jonathan. Philip wrote to each of his prospective peers and also to George. This is the letter he wrote to Jonathan:

Dear Jonathan:

I was glad finally to have a chance to meet you. George had spoken of you so proudly, I knew you had earned everything you've gotten at Bluekill and have worked very hard. I, too, am a hard worker, and I know we would complement each other.

I liked your professional approach to the interview and found your questions and direction quite interesting. I hope I "did okay." I believe I could work out a schedule to accommodate your many projects—and one thing you can count on is that I'm good at developing computer simulations. In my last position, I was considered the best, and would enjoy doing the same for you. I work very hard at it, and it pays off.

My impression is that George depends on you a lot, and perhaps I could help out also. I think I could develop materials that could be used both inside and with customers, and I will be glad to hear your ideas on the matter. I've developed a great deal of material in the past that I will be happy to show you.

All things considered, I think I would make a good addition to the group, and I believe you and I would enjoy working together. As I said to you when we met, I've worked in a few companies, and I do my best to make every place I work as enjoyable as it can be. Your sense of humor surely helps, and I'm sure mine will also.

Cordially,
Philip Johnson

Time passed. Philip met again with George and with other peers. But he was concerned about whether Jonathan would still be in favor of him in light of the number of additional applicants Jonathan had met by then. Philip decided to contact Jonathan again, this time more informally. In reviewing his notes, he fixed on what Jonathan had said about the reputation of the department. Philip then arranged a networking meeting with an important person in the industry so he would have something to contact Jonathan about. The information would also help him make up his mind in case he received a job offer. Then he wrote on informal stationery:

Dear Jonathan,

In our meeting, you wondered about the reputation of your department. I'm sure you will be happy to hear, as I was, that your department is thought of as the best in the industry. I met with Cheryl Jenkins yesterday, and she raved about each person in your group—including you. You should be proud of her commendation, and I admit that I was proud as well because I sincerely hope I wind up working with you.

I mentioned to you that I would be happy to show you the computer simulation materials I have developed in the past. I have finally put them together and will call you to see if you still want to look at them. It shouldn't take more than 15 minutes of your time.

Hope all is well.
Best regards,
Philip

Sometimes an important influencer is the best way to sway the hiring manager. Philip got the job, but he got much more: He started the job with a very good relationship with each of the people with whom he would be working. When you analyze what is important to each person, you not only increase your chances of getting the job but also increase your chances of having the new job go smoothly.

We are what we repeatedly do. Excellence, then, is not an act, but a habit.

Aristotle

Discuss your follow-up problems with your private Five O'Clock Club coach or at Five O'Clock Club meetings. Make the effort required to develop strategies for your follow-up moves. It's worth the trouble.
As one Five O'Clock Clubber advised, "Make sure the follow-up letter you write is absolutely the best the company will see—or don't write it." Be sure to read the follow-up case studies in this book.

There is no such thing as "soft sell" or "hard sell." There is only "smart sell" and "stupid sell."

Charles Bower, President, BBD&O, *Editor & Publisher*

Job Interview Follow-Up: Sample Letters

Influence belongs to men of action, and for purposes of action nothing is more useful than narrowness of thought combined with energy of will.

Henri Frédéric Amiel, *Journal intime*

> **Job follow-ups are not merely *thank you* notes. Your primary goal is not to *thank* the interviewer but to *influence* him or her.**

How Can You Tell Whether a Follow-Up Letter Is a Good One?

A good letter is **tailored** to the situation. It would be impossible to send it to someone other than the addressee. It **sells the writer, separates the writer from the competition, addresses all issues and objections, and states a next step.** Finally, its **tone replicates the tone of the interview** (or creates a good tone if the interview wasn't so good).

Look at the follow-up letter on the next page.

Paragraph 1
- talks about the next steps
- separates me from the competition: They're talking about counseling, but I'm trying to offer something additional—the development of program materials

Paragraph 2
- handles an objection: Would I enjoy working with this kind of client?

Paragraphs 3 & 4
- another objection: Would I be too independent in the job (or would I listen to my boss)?

Paragraph 5
- another objection: Why hire a strong, older person when someone with less experience would do?

Paragraph 6
- recalls the camaraderie of the interview
Note: Most objections are unstated. You have to notice them for yourself based on the questions at the interview or your assessment of who your competition is likely to be. Also be aware of tone, facial expression, and body language.

Follow-Up after a Job Interview

M. Catherine Wendleton
163 York Avenue—12B
New York, New York 10000
(212) 555-2231 (day)
(212) 555-1674 (message)

July 18, 2005

Ms. Joy Muench
Director of Outplacement
RightBank
100 Madison Avenue
New York, NY 10000

Dear Joy:

Now I've met everyone in your group, and I'll be glad to get together with you again. I can see how carefully you have parceled out your assignments to each person. I can also see where I would fit in—something we can discuss in more detail when we get together. I certainly am expert in developing program materials and will be happy to show you things I have done in that area.

In general, I enjoy the type of client you get at RightBank because a good deal of my approach is business oriented and based on business systems and logic. That is essentially the way I operate with people from other banks, as well as from the big accounting firms. These people tend to be self-motivated and direct, and I like that. They tend to not want to be psychoanalyzed too much, and that's fine with me. I'm all for getting on with it.

On the other hand, I believe I can learn a lot from you, and am looking forward to the opportunity to do so. I am even planning to join the Jung Foundation, and visited there for the first time today.

I know you are in a delicate position dealing with the RightBank corporate problems, and I do understand the difficulties of your job. For most of my career, I have worked for senior management. All of my bosses have been able to count on me to see what needs to be done, to do it, and to work smoothly with the rest of the organization. I have a lot of ideas, but I also follow through on them and know how to get the willing cooperation of others.

I hope you are looking to hire a strong person—one you can depend on to carry out your vision as well as add to it—a person with maturity and strong corporate experience as well as one who is a solid counselor and good at running a small business—which is what you are trying to do. I look forward to helping you and will do more than my share to support you.

I hope you have a wonderful vacation, and I can't tell you how jealous I am. I've never had two weeks together in my life. I'll see you when you get back. Don't think about all of this.

Cheers,

Follow-Up after a Job Interview

Influence the Influencers

These are *notes to prospective peers* for the job on the preceding page.

They have some say in the hiring decision, maybe a *lot* of say. Make sure your follow-up letters influence them. If they don't want you, you might not get hired. Write to *each* person with whom you interviewed. For each, think of <u>why they would want you there.</u>

What's in it for them?

What do you bring to the party? Make sure you are not a threat to them. Overcome their objections.

Address any issues raised.

Use the tone set in the interview.

M. Catherine Wendleton

July 18, 2005

Dear Peter:

It certainly was a pleasure meeting you. You add a lot of humor and a lot of ability to the place. All things considered, I think I would make a happy addition to the group, and I believe you and I would enjoy working together. I believe you are a person I would turn to to broaden my expertise in the area of evaluation. I would also help you out with the reception area, as I can see that is one of your major duties. (Just kidding.)

Sandy said she would like me to concentrate on the area of materials development—something I have some experience in and would enjoy doing.

I hope you and I will have the opportunity to work together.

Cordially,
Kate

M. Catherine Wendleton

Dear Carolyn:

I was glad to finally have a chance to meet you. Sandy had spoken of you so proudly, she made me proud too. I can see that you've earned everything you've gotten at RightBank and have worked very hard. I too am a hard worker, and I know we would complement each other.

I liked your professional approach to the interview, and your questions and direction were quite interesting to me as a professional. I hope I "did OK." I believe I could work out a schedule to accommodate your needs in the group training area—and one thing you can count on is that I'm <u>good</u> at it. I believe I was the favorite counselor at JC Penney—which was essentially all group work. I put a lot of effort into it, and I got rave reviews.

My impression is that Sandy depends on you a lot, and perhaps I could help out also. I could develop materials that could be used in the group as well as in the individual program, and I will be glad to hear your ideas on the matter. I've developed a great deal of material in the past that I will be happy to show you.

All things considered, I think I would make a happy addition to the group, and I believe you and I would enjoy working together. As I said to you when we met, I've been around, and I certainly do my best to make every place I work as enjoyable as it can be. Your sense of humor surely helps, and I'm sure mine will also.

Cordially,
Kate Wendleton

M. Catherine Wendleton

Dear Alan:

I'm glad to have met you. Your smile seems to soften things in the office, and I'm sure we would enjoy working together. I believe I could learn from each person in the group, and I also think I bring a lot to the party. My special assignment from Sandy would be in developing program materials—something that is right up my alley.

All things considered, I think I would make a happy addition to the group. As I said to you when we met, I certainly do my best to make every place I work as enjoyable as possible. Your attitude surely helps in that area, and I'm sure mine will also.

Cordially,
Kate Wendleton

Follow-Up after a Job Interview

The most overlooked part of job follow-up is the statement of next steps. It is *your* responsibility to make sure the process is moved along to the next step.

For example, if they say they'll call you in a week, you can say: "If I don't hear from you in a week or so, I'll give you a call."

Don't be surprised if they don't call: Everyone is very busy, and you are probably not at the top of their list. Gently move them along—within *their* time frame—in your follow-up note.

Psalm 23

The Lord is my shepherd, I shall not want.
He makes me lie down in green pastures;
He leads me beside quiet waters.
He restores my soul;
He guides me in the paths of righteousness
For His name's sake.

Even though I walk through the valley of the
shadow of death, I fear no evil; for Thou art with me;
Thy rod and Thy staff, they comfort me.

Thou dost prepare a table before me
in the presence of my enemies;
Thou hast anointed my head with oil;
My cup overflows.

Surely goodness and loving kindness will follow me
all the days of my life,
And I will dwell in the house of the Lord forever.

Although this note is short, it still contains a strategy for moving this process along to the next step.

Penelope Webb

To: Wally Dobbs

I enjoyed our conversation last week. Your need to modernize and integrate existing systems, and to make them flexible enough to accommodate future opportunities such as the repeal of Act 27, certainly sounds like an intriguing challenge.

I appreciate your suggestion that I meet with some of the people in your group and would like very much to talk with you further. I'll call you in a few days to set something up.

Best regards,
Penny

Four-Step Salary Negotiation Strategy

The
Five
O'Clock
Club

---

*I've got all the money I'll ever need
if I die by four o'clock.*

Henny Youngman

There arises from the hearts of busy [people] a love of variety, a yearning for relaxation of thought as well as of body, and a craving for a generous and spontaneous fraternity.

J. Hampton Moore, *History of the Five
O'Clock Club,* written in the 1890s

Now you know you have to impress not only the hiring manager but also other influencers so they will want to have you on board. In addition, you have to think about your likely competitors and how you can convince everyone you meet that you are the best choice. During the interview, a job hunter may also think about salary.

When job hunters ask about salary negotiation, they usually want to know how to answer the questions, What are you making now? and What are you looking for? We'll cover these issues in detail a little later, but it is more important to first look at salary negotiation from a strategic point of view. From the very first meeting, you can set the stage for compensation discussions later.

Most job hunters think about salary—unconsciously and anxiously—during their first meeting. They think, I'm making $50,000 now (or $150,000), but I know this person won't pay more than $35,000 (or $135,000). Most job hunters try to get rid of the anxiety. They don't want to waste their time if this person isn't going to pay them fairly. So when the hiring manager mentions money, the job hunter is relieved to talk about it.

Hiring manager: How much are you making now?
Job hunter: I'm making $50,000.
Hiring manager: That's a little rich for us. We were thinking about $35,000.
Job hunter: I couldn't possibly take $35,000.

End of discussion. Another wasted interview. But there is a better way. Intend to turn every job interview into an appropriate offer. Overcome the company's objections to hiring you, and overcome your own objections to working there. If the salary or something else bothers you about the job, think about how you can change it.

Think more consciously and more strategically. Intend to negotiate. Most job hunters don't negotiate at all.

- They don't negotiate the job. They listen passively to what the job is and try to fit themselves into it—or reject it.

- They certainly don't negotiate the salary. They listen to the offer and then decide whether they want to take it.

> **Don't accept or reject a job until it is offered to you.**

Job hunters decide whether or not they want the job without negotiating to make it more appropriate—and without even getting an offer! Career counselors have a maxim: Don't accept or reject a job until it is offered to you.

We'll see how you can be more proactive rather than passive. The following guidelines will allow you to take more control and more responsibility for what happens to you. Following these steps will not guarantee you the compensation you want, but you will certainly do much better than if you do not follow them. Remember the four steps you will learn here—and pay attention to where you are in those steps.

> **If you can remember these four steps with regard to a particular company, you will do better in your salary negotiation— and in your entire search as well.**

Step 1: Negotiate the Job

By now, you have already negotiated the job. You have created a job that suits both you and the hiring manager. Make sure it is at an appropriate level for you. If the job is too low-level, don't ask about the salary—*upgrade the job*. Add responsibilities until the job is worth your while. Make sure the hiring manager agrees that this new job is what he or she wants. Don't negotiate the salary yet.

If your ship doesn't come in, swim out to it.

Jonathan Winters

Step 2: Outshine and Outlast Your Competition

By now, you have already killed off your competition. You have kept in the running by offering to do more than your competitors. You have paid more attention to the progress made in your meetings, and you have moved the process along. You have satisfied every need and responded to every objection. For some jobs, it can take five interviews before the subject of salary is discussed. All the while, your competitors have been dropping out. It is best to postpone the discussion of salary until they are all gone.

Step 3: Get the Offer

Once a manager has decided that you are the right person, you are in a better position to negotiate a package that is appropriate for you. Until you actually get the offer, postpone the discussion of salary.

The moment you feel foolish, you look foolish. Concentrate, block it out, and relax. Of course, that's not always easy.

Michael Caine, *Acting in Film*

Step 4: Negotiate Your Compensation Package

Most job hunters hear the offer and then either accept or reject it. This is not negotiating. If you have never negotiated a package for yourself, you need to practice. Why not try to get some offers that don't even interest you, just so you can practice negotiating the salary? Here are some hints to get you started:

- Know the company's and the industry's pay scales.
- Know what you want in a negotiation session, and know what you are willing to do without. Negotiate one point at a time. Negotiate base pay first and then the points the employer would easily agree to. Save for last the issues of conflict. Be prepared to back off, or not even bring up, issues that are not important to you.
- You are both on the same side. Each of you should want a deal that works now and works later—not one that will make either of you resentful.
- Care—but not too much. If you desperately want the job—at any cost—you will not do a good job of negotiating. You must convince yourself, at least for the time you are interviewing, that you have alternatives.
- Try to get them to state the first bid. If they say: "How much do you want?" You say: "How much are you offering?" If pressed about your prior salary, either say instead what you are looking for or be sure to include bonus and perks. Some include an expected bonus or increase in salary.
- If the manager makes you an unacceptable offer, *talk about the job*. Look disappointed and say how enthusiastic you are about the position, the company, and the possibility of doing great things for this manager. Say everything is great, and you can't wait to start—but your only reservation is the compensation. Ask what can be done about this.

Be reasonable. As the saying goes: Bulls win, and bears win, but pigs never win.

It Works at All Levels

Once I did a salary-negotiation seminar for low-level corporate people. One person had been a paper-burster for 25 years: He tore the sheets of paper as they came off the computer. But because he had been at the company for 25 years, his salary was at the top of the range of paper-bursters. He had the same kind of salary problem a lot of us have.

The four steps worked for him, too. He told the hiring managers, "Not only can I burst the paper, but I can fix the machines. This will save you on machine downtime and machine repair costs. And I can train people, which will also save you money."

He was:

1. **Negotiating the job**

And:

2. **Outshining and outlasting his competition**

And after he:

3. **Gets the offer**

He'll have no trouble:

4. **Negotiating the salary.**

Know where you are in the four steps. If you have not yet done steps one, two, and three, try to postpone step four.

CASE STUDY *Bessie*
It Can Even Work against <u>Me</u>

Once when I was a CFO for a small firm, I wanted to hire an accounting manager who would supervise a staff of four.

I told an excellent search firm exactly what I wanted and the salary range I was looking for: "someone in the $50,000 range."

I received lots of résumés—all of which the search firm had marked at the top: "Asking for $50,000." I interviewed a lot of people, but Bessie stood out from the crowd. I had Bessie meet with a peer of mine and also with the company president. Everyone loved her.

Finally, I told Bessie that we were pleased to offer her the $50,000 she wanted. Bessie said, "I would love to work here, but I would not be happy with $50,000. I didn't put that there."

I was stunned, but I was also stuck. We had made an investment in Bessie. Everyone had met her and loved her, and she wisely stayed mum about the money until she received the offer. A more anxious job hunter might have said early on, "I see that it says $50,000 at the top of my résumé, but I just want you to know that I am already making more than that." That would have been admirable honesty, but the person would have been out of the running.

Bessie wound up with $55,000, which is what she was worth—and we wound up with an excellent employee. Bessie had followed the four steps exactly.

1. Negotiate the job.
2. Outshine and outlast your competition.
3. Get the offer.
4. Negotiate your package.

> **Be sure the person with whom you are negotiating is at the right level. If you find yourself constantly bumping up against the salary level of the people with whom you are negotiating, the problem is not your salary negotiation technique. The problem is that you are talking to people who are at the wrong level.**

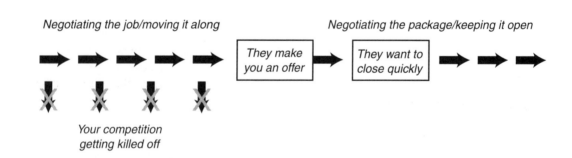

Negotiating the job/moving it along   Negotiating the package/keeping it open

They make you an offer

They want to close quickly

Your competition getting killed off

The Five O'Clock Club

Answering the Tactical Questions

We're all in this alone.

Lily Tomlin

By now, you know where you are in the four steps. In fact, for each company with whom you are meeting, you know exactly where you are in the process. If you are conscious of where you are, you will do much better than if you simply do what seems reasonable without regard to where you are in the process.

In addition, the more experienced you become in negotiating your compensation, the more you can assess what is appropriate for a given situation and deviate from the rules. However, until you are an experienced negotiator, it is best to play by the rules.

What Are You Making Now? What Are You Looking For?

Now we'll look at the questions you've been waiting for. But we'll look at them strategically—so you can *plan* an appropriate answer depending on your situation. First, you need to develop some background information before you can plan your strategy for answering the questions. The strategy will also give you hints for postponing the discussion of salary until you have an offer.

Background Information: Figure Out What You Really Make

Start with your base salary but also include your bonus and any perks, such as a company car, a savings plan, deferred compensation, company lunches, and company contribu-

Are you presently at market rates? Below market? Above market? Knowing where you stand will help you answer the questions: "What are you making now?" and "What are you looking for?"

tion to insurance plans. That's what you really make—but that may not be what you will tell the prospective employer.

Background Information: Figure Out What You Are Worth in the Market

Talk to search firms, ask people at association meetings, look at ads in the paper, and—most of all—network. At networking meetings, ask, "What kind of salary could someone like me expect at your company?" A few networking meetings will give you a good idea of the market rates for someone like you.

However, you must remember that you are worth different amounts in different markets. You may be worth a certain amount in one industry, field, or geographic area, and a different amount in other industries, fields, or geographic areas.

What's more, you may be worth more to one company than you would be to another.

Research what you are worth in each of your target markets. And when you are interviewing at a specific company, find out as much as you can about the way they pay.

Background Information: Compare What You Are Making (Total Compensation) with What the Market Is Paying

You need to know if you are now at market rates, below market, or above market. *This is the key* to how you will answer a hiring manager or search firm that asks you, "What are you making?" or "What are you looking for?"

How to Answer: If You Are within the Market Range

Most companies want to know what you are making. If you are within the market range, they will pay you 10 to 15 percent above what you are currently making. Therefore, if you are making $40,000 and you know the market is paying $43,000 to $45,000, then you could say, "Right now I'm at $40,000, but I'm looking to move a little away from that." The only time you can safely state your current compensation is when you are at market rates.

How to Answer: If You Are Above Market Rates

A counselor asked me to have a meeting with his client Sam, who was having problems finding a job because of his high salary. I did an interview role play with Sam. At one point I said, "So, Sam, what are you making now?" Sam replied, "Two hundred thousand dollars plus-plus-plus." I said, "I know you're a very competent person, but we simply cannot afford someone at your high level." Sam's salary was not hurting him, but his way of talking about it was. Even if your salary isn't $200,000-plus-plus-plus, you can easily put off the hiring manager who thinks your salary will be a problem. You have to give her a chance to find out about you, and you have to think about how you can create a job that is appropriate for your salary. You must tell her, "Salary will not be a problem"—*especially if you know it is a problem.* You have to think to yourself that it won't be a problem when she gets to know you better and understands what you will do for her. Otherwise, you will not get anywhere.

> **Your position has to be that "salary won't be a problem." It is your job to reassure the hiring manager that you are both on the same team and can work this out. When they get to know you better—and what you have to offer—salary *won't* be a problem.**

If you are making more than the market rate, do your best to create a job that warrants the salary you want and defer the discussion of salary until you have the offer. When you're asked, "What are you making now?" use a response from the list below to reassure the hiring manager that you are both on the same team and can work this out. These responses are listed in sequence from easiest to most difficult. Try the easy response first. If the hiring manager persists, you may have to move on to one of the other responses. You are simply trying to postpone the discussion of salary until she knows you better and you have an offer.

The manager asks, "What are you making now?" You respond:

- "I'd prefer to postpone talking about the salary until I'm clearer about the job I'll be doing. When we come to some agreement on the job, I know that salary won't be a problem."

- "Salary won't be a problem. But I'm not exactly sure what the job is, so maybe we can talk more about that. I'm very flexible, and I'm sure that when we come to some agreement on the job, we can work out the salary."

- "Salary won't be a problem. I know that you do not want to bring someone in at a salary that makes you resentful, and I'm sure you do not want me to be resentful either. I know that we'll come to a happy agreement."

- "I'm making very good money right now, and I deserve it. But I'd hate to tell you what it is because I'm afraid it will put you off. I know that salary will not be a problem. I'm a fair person and I'm sure you are, too. I know we'll come to an agreement."

- "I'm being paid very well, and I'm worth it. But I'm very interested in your company and I'm willing to make an investment in this if you are. As far as I'm concerned, salary won't be a problem."

Marie successfully postponed the discussion of salary for two years. When she came to The Five O'Clock Club, she had been unemployed for a long while. It took six months before she was on the verge of a job offer at a major fashion house, the company of her dreams. On the day she was to receive the offer, the company went *into play.* That is, another company was trying to take this one over, so all hiring was put on hold. Marie was more desperate than ever. Within a month or two, she received an offer from a major entertainment company, went to work there, and continued to keep in touch with the fashion house.

Over the next year and a half, she had meetings with the president and most of the senior executives at the fashion house. Each one asked her about her salary, and to each one she replied with one of the statements previously listed. She eventually got a tremendous offer—after having postponed the discussion of salary for two years. By the way, Marie's boss at the entertainment company told her that he hired her because she was so persistent in her follow-up. He thought she acted a little desperate, which she was after having been unemployed for so long, but he gave her the job because it seemed to mean so much to her. And, of course, she later got the job at the fashion house because she followed up with them for *two years!* If this desperate job hunter could postpone the discussion of salary, so can you. But you need to practice with someone. It does not come naturally.

How to Answer: If You are Making Below Market Rates

Again, you have a few options. For example, if a manager asks what you are making, you could answer instead with what you are looking for:

Manager: "What are you making right now?"

You: "I understand the market is paying in the $65,000 to $75,000 range."

Manager: "That's outrageous. We can't pay that."

You: "What range are you thinking of for this position?"

Note: You haven't revealed either what you are making or what you want—but you've still tested the hiring manager's expectations. The person who states a number first is at a negotiation disadvantage.

Or you could say, "My current salary is $32,000. I know the marketplace today is closer to $45,000. I have been willing to trade off the salary in order to build my skills [or whatever]. But now I am in a position where I don't need to trade off money, and I'm ready to take a position at market rates."

I was taught that the way of progress is neither swift nor easy.

Marie Curie

If You Are Pushed to Name Your Salary

Don't simply state your salary—develop a line of patter to soften it. Simply stating a number can be very confrontational, as with the $200,000-plus-plus-plus job hunter. If you have exhausted all the responses, and the hiring manager throws you up against the wall and shouts, "I want to know what you are making!" you can still soften your answer by saying, for example:

- "I'm earning very good money right now—in the $90,000 to $120,000 range, depending on bonus. And I'm certainly worth it. But I'm very interested in your company, and I know we can work something out."

- "My salary is very low—only $20,000, and I know that's dramatically below market rates. But I was willing to do that as an investment in my future. Now, however, I expect to make market rates."

You should name your salary only as a last resort. Managers want to know your last salary as a way of determining your worth to them, but it is certainly not the most reasonable way to decide what you are worth. For example, you would want to be paid more if the job requires 70 hours a week and lots of travel, versus one that requires only 35 hours a week. How do you know how much you want unless you know what the job entails? You are being sensible to talk about the job first and the salary later.

Some managers cannot deal that way, so you have to be prepared in case you are forced to discuss salary prematurely. And even if you do name your salary, there are different ways you can couch it. For example:

- "My current salary is $32,500."

- "I make in the high 60s."

- "My base is around $25,000 and my bonus [commissions] is usually around $15,000, which brings my total package to $40,000."

- "I make in the range of $100,000 to $200,000, depending on my bonus." (This, of course, tells them very little.)

Remember to soften your mention of your salary with a line of patter or your response will sound too confrontational and too much like a demand: "I make . . . but salary won't be a problem because. . . ."

More Complex Compensation Situations

Most people are in the position of negotiating salary, perhaps a bonus or commission, and perhaps a training program, association membership, or the timing of the first salary review.

Others have a more complex situation. For example, a senior executive may say (at the appropriate time), "You'd like to know how much I'm now making? Let me write it out for you." (Or perhaps he or she would go into the meeting with the information already filled out.) The following table contains the current year's compensation, the next year's compensation (if it is relevant) to account for bonuses, pay increases, and so on. The third column would contain a skeleton of what you are looking for or would be left blank and used as a worksheet. Be sure to write footnotes as commentary on those lines requiring it. For example, you may want to document that if you leave before April you will lose your year-end bonus. Therefore, you could not start work until after April, or the hiring company would have to make up for your loss:

	2005	2006	Looking For
Base salary	$89,000	$95,000	$95,000
Bonus	26,000	35,000	
Deferred Comp.	20,000	30,000	
Car Allowance	8,000	8,000	
Stock Options	40,000	40,000	
Addtl Medical	4,000	4,000	
TOTAL COMP.	187,000	212,000	250,000

You may leave the third column completely blank and fill it in as you are speaking. For example, you could say, "This is an exciting opportunity you are presenting, and I want to be part of it. To make it easier for you, I could imagine staying at my present base compensation level for next year, $95,000. To make the move worth my while, I could imagine a total package of $250,000, for example, and we could figure out the numbers in between."

In stating your *requirements* in a collaborative way, there is plenty of room for flexibility as well as for their comments and input. You do not run the risk of having the offer fall apart before you have actually gotten one. As you will see later, you want to hear their best offer, and *then* you can accept it or reject it.

Are you not ashamed of heaping up the greatest amount of money and honor and reputation, and caring so little about wisdom and truth and the greatest improvement of the soul, which you never regard or heed at all?

Socrates

CASE STUDY *Betsy*
Simplifying the Request

Betsy went to Europe on a consulting assignment and was later offered a full-time position. She had a list of 20 or so expenses that she thought the company should cover: moving expenses, household purchases, trips home, phone calls home, gym, and so on. When we added up the entire package it exceeded $200,000, but it would have been too clumsy and too unprofessional to itemize all the things on her list.

Instead, we came up with a very neat package that included having the company pay completely for her apartments in both Prague and Dusseldorf, where housing was very expensive. Those items alone more than made up for the extra expense of phone calls and other miscellany. The resulting package was well in excess of what she had originally wanted and gave her the comfort of knowing that unexpected expenses would not cause her great loss.

> **You are trying to postpone the discussion of salary until after you have an offer, but in real life that is not always possible. Therefore, postpone it if you can. And if you can't, be sure you *know* how you want to answer the questions:**
> - **"What are you making now?"**
> - **"What are you looking for?"**

No Absolute One Way

Salary negotiation is the most nerve-racking part of the job hunting process. At the beginning of your job hunt you are at loose ends—not knowing where you are going and feeling like you will never get there. But salary negotiation is the part people fear the most. It is a surprise monster at the end of your search.

> **You're in a great negotiating position if you can walk away from the deal. Therefore, make sure you have 6 to 10 things in the works. If this deal is the only thing you have going, see how quickly you can get something else going.**

Search Firms

Search firms must know the *range* of salary you are making or the amount you are looking for. They do not need an exact amount.

Ads

In answering ads, you will rarely give your salary requirements. The trend at the moment is for many ads to read, "Please state salary requirements." Most job hunters do not, and the hiring company does *not* exclude them. Stating your salary or requirements not only puts you at a negotiating disadvantage but also allows you to be eliminated from consideration because you are too high or too low.

On the other hand, some ads state, "You will absolutely not be considered unless you state your salary requirements." Then, you should state them.

Armies of worried men in suits stormed off the Lexington Avenue subway line and marched down the crooked pavements. For rich people, they didn't look very happy.

Michael Lewis, *Liars Poker*

What Is Negotiable?

Everything's negotiable. That doesn't mean you'll *get* it, but it is negotiable. First, think of what is important to you. Make a personal list of what you must have versus what you want. Decide where you can be flexible, but know the issues that are deal breakers for you.

Think of your musts versus your wants. If you get everything you *must* have, then perhaps you won't even mention items on your *want* list. Go in knowing your bottom-line requirements, what you would be willing to trade off, and what benefits/perks could compensate you if you hit a salary snag. Have your own goals in the negotiation clearly in mind.

Salary is not the only form of compensation that might be negotiated. Other items might include:

- the timing of the first review
- closing costs on a new home or a relocation package
- use of a company car

- association or club memberships
- reimbursements for education
- bonus

Which is the most meaningful or valuable to you?

The pay is good and I can walk to work.

John F. Kennedy, on becoming president,
quoted by Ralph G. Martin, *A Hero for Our Time*

Forms of Compensation

Basic Compensation

- the timing of the first review
- base salary
- deferred compensation
- incentive compensation (short and long term)
    — performance bonus
    — sales commission
    — sales incentive plans
    — stock options
- sign-on bonus
- matching investment programs
- profit sharing

Vacations

- extra vacation: vacation length is becoming tied to level or length of work experience rather than time spent with one company.

Prerequisites

- expense accounts
- company car or gas allowance
- memberships
    — country club
    — luncheon club
    — athletic club
    — professional associations
- executive dining room privileges
- extra insurance
- first-class hotels or air travel
- personal use of frequent-flyer awards
- paid travel for spouse
- executive office
- private secretary
- employee discounts
- financial-planning assistance
- C.P.A. and tax assistance
- tuition assistance
- continuing professional education
- conventions
- furlough trips for overseas assignments

Relocation Expenses

- moving expenses
- mortgage-rate differential/housing allowance
- mortgage prepayment penalty
- real estate brokerage fees
- closing costs, bridge loan
- home-buying trips
- lodging while between homes
- company purchase of your home
- mortgage funds/short-term loans
- discounted loans/mortgages
- temporary dual housing
- trips home during dual housing
- outplacement assistance for spouse

Related to Severance

- severance pay and outplacement
- consulting fees after termination
- insurance benefits after termination

Glossary

Deferred compensation: Ability to make deposits to a deferred salary plan from your pay on a before-tax basis so that amount of income is subject to taxation in the year you make the deposit.

Employment contract: A formal written agreement between yourself and the employer guaranteeing certain benefits, such as severance pay should you lose the job through no fault of your own. At high levels sometimes known as a golden parachute.

Letter of intent: A written confirmation of a job offer summarizing the items agreed upon (salary, benefits, perks, etc.). Not a formal contract but hard for a company to rescind. If you write it, it's called a reverse letter of intent.

Matching investment programs: Savings incentive plan in which company matches employee basic award or personal contribution toward investment.

Performance bonus: An amount of money to be paid to you contingent on your performance on the job. May be a specific amount or a percentage. Can be tied to individual, group, or corporate performance.

Perks or prerequisites: Extra benefits that come with the position, such as executive dining room privileges or company car. May be negotiable or standard company policy.

Profit sharing: Cash award based on corporate earnings. Unusual outside of banks.

Sales commissions: Compensation directly related to sales at a predetermined percentage.

Sales incentive plans: Additional compensation based on sales volume.

Signing bonus: A one-time amount of money paid as an inducement for you to join the company. Also known as a signing, or up-front, bonus.

Stock options: A grant to purchase stock at a fixed price.

Want a Signing Bonus?

Everyone's getting them, right? But those who do are often giving up something—usually base salary. Most companies give signing bonuses to keep payroll costs down!

Louis Uchitelle reports in *The New York Times:* "The hiring bonus is just the latest tool that companies have turned to in recent years to hold down wages. The others include profit sharing, flexible schedules, tuition subsidies, stock options, health club memberships and 'performance' bonuses in lieu of raises for those already on the payroll. While wages are now rising a bit faster than they have in a decade, hiring bonuses are ballooning and spreading across the work force—absorbing some of the pressure for still-greater income" (Louis Uchitelle, "Signing Bonus Now a Fixture Farther Down the Job Ladder," *New York Times,* June 10, 1998).

The bottom line for you? You've made a deal when you get a signing bonus to make up for a lost bonus if you leave your present job. Otherwise, try to get money in your base rather than in a signing or other bonus.

The
Five
O'Clock
Club

PART SIX

Keeping It Going

AFTER YOU'VE GOTTEN THE JOB YOU WANT

The Five O'Clock Club

Starting Out on the Right Foot in Your New Job

. . . be patient toward all that is unsolved in your heart and try to love the questions themselves like locked rooms and like books that are written in a foreign tongue.

Rainer Maria Rilke

Starting out can be tricky: You are *on board* but *the jury is still out* on you. It is a time of trial. You are often being watched to see if you will work out. Here are some things you need to do to start out on the right foot and keep moving in the right direction.

Before You Start

Say thank you. Contact all the people who helped you get the new position. Often people don't make this effort because they feel they'll be in the new job for a long time. But today, when the average American changes jobs every four years, the odds say you're going to change jobs again soon. You need to keep up those contacts.

Then think about ways to keep in touch with these contacts—if you read something that someone on your list would appreciate, clip it and send it.

It is not the critic who counts; not the man who points out how the strong man stumbled or where the doer of deeds could have done better. The credit belongs to the man who is actually in the arena, whose face is marred by dust and sweat and blood; who strives valiantly; who errs and comes short again and again; who knows the great enthusiasms, the great devotions; who spends himself in a worthy cause; who, at best, knows in the end the triumph of achievement, and who, at worst, if he fails, at least fails while daring greatly, so that his place shall never be with those timid souls who knew neither victory nor defeat.

Theodore Roosevelt

Right Away

• Don't fix things or do anything *big* for the first three months. That is one of the biggest mistakes people make. Take time to learn the system, the people, and the culture.

You cannot possibly understand, in those first months, the implications of certain decisions you may make. You may be criticizing a project that was done by someone really important. Or you could be changing something that will affect someone on the staff in ways of which you aren't aware.

• Make yourself productive immediately. This does not contradict the point I just made. Do things that are safe. For example, install a new system where there has been none. This is *safe* because you aren't getting rid of some other system. What isn't safe? Firing half your staff the first week!

• Introduce yourself to everybody. Be visible—walk around and meet people as soon as possible, including those who work for you. Meet everybody. Too many managers meet only the *important* people while ignoring those who will actually do the day-to-day work.

• Don't make friends too fast. Someone who befriends you right away could also be on the way out. That doesn't mean you shouldn't be friendly, however. Go to lunch with several people rather than becoming known as someone who associates only with so-and-so. Get to know everybody, and then decide with whom to get closer.

• Take over compensation of your subordinates immediately. Look at review and raise dates, and make sure no one is overlooked. You can't afford to wait three months to get settled while one of your people is stewing about an overdue salary review.

• Get your budget—quickly. If it isn't good, build a better one. If you spend some time at the beginning trying to understand the budget, the things you hear over the next few weeks will mean more to you.

> **Try not to do anything too daring for the first three months. Take time to learn the system.**

Destiny is not a matter of chance, it is a matter of choice; it is not a thing to be waited for, it is a thing to be achieved.

William Jennings Bryan

In the First Three Months

- Learn the corporate culture. People new to jobs lose those jobs often because of personality conflicts rather than a lack of competence.

  Keep your head low until you learn how the company operates. Some companies have certain writing styles. Some expect you to speak a certain way. In certain companies, it's the way they hold parties. Do people work with their doors open or their doors shut?

  All those things are part of the culture, and they are unwritten. To learn them, you have to pay attention.

  I had a client, for example, who lost his job because his management style rubbed everyone the wrong way. He is a *touchy-feely* manager who, when he wants his employees to do things, schmoozes with them, saying things such as, "You know, I was kind of thinking about this and. . . ." But the corporate culture was such that the employees liked and expected to be asked straight out. His style made them feel patronized and manipulated. And his own staff did him in.

  Pay your dues before doing things at a variance with the corporate culture. After you build up some credits, you have more leeway. Let your personality emerge when you understand the company and after you have made some contribution.

- Learn the organizational structure—the real structure, not the one that is drawn on the charts. Ask your secretary to tell you who relates how with whom, who knows what, who thought of this project, who is important. You could be surprised.

- As far as subordinates are concerned, find out other people's opinions and then form your own. Consider that you may have a different perception because you have different values.

- Find out what is important in your job. For example, when I counsel people for a corporation, counseling is not the only important thing in my job. The people who come to me are sent by human resources, and I must manage my relationship with these people. It doesn't matter how good a counselor I am if I don't maintain a good relationship with human resources.

- Pay attention to your peers. Your peers can prove as valuable to you as your boss and subordinates. Do not try to impress them with your brilliance. That would be the kiss of death because you'd cause envy and have a very large reputation to live up to. Instead, encourage them to talk to you. They know more than you do. They also know your boss. Look to them to teach you and, in some cases, protect you.

I know one executive who found out that her last three predecessors had been fired. She knew from talking to people that her boss was the type whose ego was bruised when someone had ideas. He had a talent for getting rid of these people.

> **Pay attention to your peers. Look to them to teach you and, in some cases, protect you.**

Know how to ask. There is nothing more difficult for some people. Nor for others, easier.

Baltasar Gracian, *The Art of Worldly Wisdom*

To protect herself, she built relationships with her peers, the heads of offices around the country. After a year and a half, her boss's brother took her to breakfast and told her that, unlike her predecessors, she could not be fired: It would have been such an unpopular decision that it would have backfired on her boss.

- Don't set up competition. Everyone brings something to the party and should be respected for his or her talent, no matter what their level. Find ways to show your respect by asking for their input on projects that require their expertise.

- Set precedents you want to keep. If you start out working 12-hour days, people come to expect it of you—even if no one else is doing it. When you stop, people wonder what's wrong.

- Set modest goals for your own personal achievement and high goals for your department. Make your people look good, and you will, too.

The character of a person is formed as well as revealed by his own concept of self-interest.

John Lukacs, *A History of the Cold War*

> **You'll be busy in your new job and may not keep up your outside contacts. In today's economy, that's a big mistake.**

Three Months and Beyond . . .

- Continue to develop contacts outside the company. If you need information for your job, sometimes the worst people to ask are your boss and the people around you. A network is also a tremendous resource to fall back on when your boss is busy—and you will seem resourceful, smart, and connected.

- Keep a hero file for yourself, a hanging file where you place written descriptions of all your successes. If you have to job hunt in a hurry, you'll be able to recall what you've done.

   You will also use it if you stay. If you want anything, whether it be a raise or a promotion or the responsibility for a particular project, you can use the file to build a case for yourself.

- Keep managing your career. Don't think, "I'll just take this job and do what they tell me," because you might get off on some tangent. Remember where you were heading and make sure your career keeps going that way.

Be proactive in moving toward your goal. Take on lots of assignments. If a project comes up that fits into your long-term plan, do it. If one doesn't fit into your plan, you can do it or you can say, "Oh, I'd love to do that, but I'm really busy." Make those kinds of choices all the time.

To act with confidence, one must be willing to look ahead and consider uncertainties: "What challenges could the world present me? How might others respond to my actions?" Rather than asking such questions, too many people react to uncertainty with denial.

Peter Schwartz, *The Art of the Long View*

Thank-You Note after Getting a Job

Someday soon you'll be able to write one of these too.

Anita Attridge
400 First Avenue
Dayton, Ohio 22090

May 8, 2005

Mr. Ellis Chase
3450 Garden Place
Des Moines, Iowa 44466

Dear Ellis:

The happy news is that I have accepted a position at Ohio State Trust as Controller for their Ohio branches. I'll be responsible for financial reporting and analysis, loans administration, budgeting, and planning. I think it's a great match that will make good use of both my management skills and banking experience, and the environment is congenial and professional.

I really appreciated your interest in my job search. I very much enjoyed speaking with people like you about your career, and I appreciated your advice and encouragement. The fact that you so willingly gave of your time meant a great deal to me, and it certainly was beneficial.

If I can reciprocate in some way, please feel free to be in touch with me. I will also probably be in contact with you in the months ahead. My new office is at 75 Rockfast Corner, Dayton 22091. You can reach me at 200-555-1212.

Sincerely,

Anita Attridge

The
Five
O'Clock
Club

PART SEVEN

What Is
The Five O'Clock Club?

AMERICA'S PREMIER CAREER-COACHING NETWORK

The
Five
O'Clock
Club

How to Join the Club

The Five O'Clock Club:
America's Premier
Career-Coaching
and
Outplacement Service

"One organization with a long record of success in helping people find jobs is The Five O'Clock Club."

Fortune

- Job-Search Strategy Groups
- Private Coaching
- Books and Audio CDs
- Membership Information
- When Your Employer Pays

THERE *IS* A FIVE O'CLOCK CLUB NEAR YOU!

For more information on becoming a member, please fill out the Membership Application Form in this book, sign up on the web at: www.fiveoclockclub.com, or call:
1-800-575-3587
(or **212-286-4500** in New York)

The Five O'Clock Club Search Process

The Five O'Clock Club process, as outlined in *The Five O'Clock Club* books, is a targeted, strategic approach to career development and job search. Five O'Clock Club members become proficient at skills that prove invaluable during their *entire working lives.*

Career Management

We train our members to *manage their careers* and always look ahead to their next job search. Research shows that an average worker spends only four years in a job—and will have 12 jobs in as many as 5 career fields—during his or her working life.

Getting Jobs . . . Faster

Five O'Clock Club members find *better jobs, faster*. The average professional, manager, or executive Five O'Clock Club member who regularly attends weekly sessions finds a job by his or her 10th session. Even the discouraged, long-term job searcher can find immediate help.

The keystone to The Five O'Clock Club process is teaching our members an understanding of the entire hiring process. A first interview is primarily a time for exchanging critical information. The real work starts *after* the interview. We teach our members *how to turn job interviews into offers* and to negotiate the best possible employment package.

Setting Targets

The Five O'Clock Club is action oriented. *We'll help you decide what you should do this very next week to move your search along.* By their third session, our members have set definite job targets by industry or company size, position, and geographic area, and are out in the field gathering information and making contacts that will lead to interviews with hiring managers.

Our approach evolves with the changing job market. We're able to synthesize information from hundreds of Five O'Clock Club members and come up with new approaches for our members. For example, we now discuss temporary placement for executives, how to use voice mail and the Internet, and how to network when doors are slamming shut all over town.

The Five O'Clock Club Strategy Program

The Five O'Clock Club meeting is a carefully planned *job-search strategy program*. We provide members with the tools and tricks necessary to get a good job fast—even in a tight market. Networking and emotional support are also included in the meeting.

Participate in 10 *consecutive* small-group strategy sessions to enable your group and career coach to get to know you and to develop momentum in your search.

Weekly Presentations via Audio CDs

Prior to each week's teleconference, listen to the assigned audio presentation covering part of The Five O'Clock Club methodology. These are scheduled on a rotating basis so you may join the Club at any time. (In selected cities, presentations are given in person rather than via audio CDs.)

Small-Group Strategy Sessions

During the first few minutes of the teleconference, your small group discusses the topic of the week and hears from people who have landed jobs. Then you have the chance to get feedback and advice on your own search strategy, listen to and learn from others, and build your network. All groups are led by trained career coaches with years of experience. The small group is generally no more than six to eight people, so everyone gets the chance to speak up.

Let us consider how we may spur one another on toward love and good deeds. Let us not give up meeting together, as some are in the habit of doing, but let us encourage one another.

Hebrews 10:24–25

Private Coaching

You may meet with your small-group coach—or another coach—for private coaching by phone or in person. A coach helps you develop a career path, solve current job problems, prepare your résumé, or guide your search.

Many members develop long-term relationships with their coaches to get advice throughout their careers. If you are paying for the coaching yourself (as opposed to having your employer pay), please pay the coach directly (charges vary from $100 to $175 per hour). **Private coaching is *not***

included in The Five O'Clock Club seminar or membership fee. For coach matching, see our website or call **1-800-575-3587** (or **212-286-4500** in New York).

From the Club History, Written in the 1890s

At The Five O'Clock Club, [people] of all shades of political belief—as might be said of all trades and creeds—have met together. . . . The variety continues almost to a monotony. . . . [The Club's] good fellowship and geniality—not to say hospitality—has reached them all.

It has been remarked of clubs that they serve to level rank. If that were possible in this country, it would probably be true, if leveling rank means the appreciation of people of equal abilities as equals; but in The Five O'Clock Club it has been a most gratifying and noteworthy fact that no lines have ever been drawn save those which are essential to the honor and good name of any association. Strangers are invited by the club or by any members, [as gentlepeople], irrespective of aristocracy, plutocracy or occupation, and are so treated always. Nor does the thought of a [person's] social position ever enter into the meetings. People of wealth and people of moderate means sit side by side, finding in each other much to praise and admire and little to justify snarlishness or adverse criticism. People meet as people—not as the representatives of a set—and having so met, dwell not in worlds of envy or distrust, but in union and collegiality, forming kindly thoughts of each other in their heart of hearts.

In its methods, The Five O'Clock Club is plain, easy-going and unconventional. It has its "isms" and some peculiarities of procedure, but simplicity characterizes them all. The sense of propriety, rather than rules of order, governs its meetings, and that informality which carries with it sincerity of motive and spontaneity of effort, prevails within it. Its very name indicates informality, and, indeed, one of the reasons said to have induced its adoption was the fact that members or guests need not don their dress suits to attend the meetings, if they so desired. This informality, however, must be distinguished from the informality of Bohemianism. For The Five O'Clock Club, informality, above convenience, means sobriety, refinement of thought and speech, good breeding and good order. To this sort of informality much of its success is due.

Fortune, The New York Times, Black Enterprise, Business Week, NPR, CNBC and ABC-TV are some of the places you've seen, heard, or read about us.

The Schedule

See our website for the specific dates for each topic. All groups use a similar schedule in each time zone.

Fee: $49 annual membership (includes Beginners Kit, subscription to *The Five O'Clock News,* and access to the

Members Only section of our website), **plus** session fees based on member's income (price for the Insider Program includes audio-CD lectures, which retails for $150).

Reservations required for first session. Unused sessions are transferable to anyone you choose or can be donated to members attending more than 16 sessions who are having financial difficulty.

The Five O'Clock Club's programs are geared to recent graduates, professionals, managers, and executives from a wide variety of industries and professions. Most earn from $30,000 to $400,000 per year. Half the members are employed; half are unemployed. *You will be in a group of your peers.*

> **To register, please fill out form on the web (at www.fiveoclockclub.com) or call 1-800-575-3587 (or 212-286-4500 in New York).**

Lecture Presentation Schedule

- History of the 5OCC
- The 5OCC Approach to Job Search
- Developing New Targets for Your Search
- Two-Minute Pitch: Keystone of Your Search

- Using Research and the Internet for Your Search
- The Keys to Effective Networking
- Getting the Most Out of Your Contacts
- Getting Interviews: Direct/Targeted Mail
- Beat the Odds When Using Search Firms and Ads
- Developing New Momentum in Your Search
- The 5OCC Approach to Interviewing
- Advanced Interviewing Techniques
- How to Handle Difficult Interview Questions
- How to Turn Job Interviews into Offers
- Successful Job Hunter's Report
- Four-Step Salary-Negotiation Method

All groups run continuously. Dates are posted on our website. The textbooks used by all members of The Five O'Clock Club may be ordered on our website or purchased at major bookstores.

> **The original Five O'Clock Club was formed in Philadelphia in 1883. It was made up of the leaders of the day who shared their experiences "in a spirit of fellowship and good humor."**

The Five O'Clock Club

Questions You May Have about the Weekly Job-Search Strategy Group

Job hunters are not always the best judges of what they need during a search. For example, most are interested in lectures on answering ads on the Internet or working with search firms. We cover those topics, but strategically they are relatively unimportant in an effective job search.

At The Five O'Clock Club, you get the information you really need in your search—*such as how to target more effectively, how to get more interviews, and how to turn job interviews into offers.*

What's more, you will work in a small group with the best coaches in the business. In these strategy sessions, your group will help you decide what to do, this week and every week, to move your search along. You will learn by being coached and by coaching others in your group.

---

*We find ourselves not independently of other people and institutions but through them. We never get to the bottom of our selves on our own. We discover
who we are face to face and side by side with others in work, love, and learning.*

Robert N. Bellah, et al., *Habits of the Heart*

Here are a few other points:

- For best results, attend on a regular basis. Your group gets to know you and will coach you to eliminate whatever you may be doing wrong—or refine what you are doing right.
- The Five O'Clock Club is a members-only organization. To get started in the small-group teleconference sessions, you must purchase a minimum of 10 sessions.
- The teleconference sessions include the set of 16 audio-CD presentations on Five O'Clock Club methodology. In-person groups do not include CDs.
- After that, you may purchase blocks of 5 or 10 sessions.
- We sell multiple sessions to make administration easier.
- If you miss a session, you may make it up any time. You may even transfer unused time to a friend.
- Although many people find jobs quickly (even people who have been unemployed a long time), others have

more difficult searches. Plan to be in it for the long haul and you'll do better.

Carefully read all of the material in this section. It will help you decide whether or not to attend.

- The first week, pay attention to the strategies used by the others in your group. Soak up all the information you can.
- Read the books before you come in the second week. They will help you move your search along.

To register:

1. Read this section and fill out the application.
2. After you become a member and get your Beginners Kit, call to reserve a space for the first time you attend.

To assign you to a career coach, we need to know:

- your current (or last) field or industry;
- the kind of job you would like next (if you know); and
- your desired salary range in general terms.

For private coaching, we suggest you attend the small group and ask to see your group leader, to give you continuity.

The Five O'Clock Club is plain, easy-going and unconventional. . . . Members or guests need not don their dress suits to attend the meetings.

(From the Club History, written in the 1890s)

What Happens at the Meetings?

Each week, job searchers from various industries and professions meet in small groups. The groups specialize in professionals, managers, executives, or recent college graduates. Usually, half are employed and half are unemployed.

The weekly program is in two parts. First, there is a lecture on some aspect of The Five O'Clock Club methodology. Then, job hunters meet in small groups headed by senior full-time professional career coaches.

The first week, get the textbooks, listen to the lecture, and get assigned to your small group. During your first session, *listen* to the others in your group. You learn a lot by listening to how your peers are strategizing *their* searches.

By the second week, you will have read the materials. Now we can start to work on *your* search strategy and help *you* decide what to do next to move your search along. For example, we'll help you figure out how to get more interviews in your target area or how to turn interviews into job offers.

In the third week, you will see major progress made by other members of your group and you may notice major progress in your own search as well.

By the third or fourth week, most members are conducting full and effective searches. Over the remaining weeks, you will tend to keep up a full search rather than go after only one or two leads. You will regularly aim to have 6 to 10 things *in the works* at all times. These will generally be in specific target areas you have identified, will keep your search on target, and will increase your chances of getting multiple job offers from which to choose.

Those who stick with the process find it works.

Some people prefer to just listen for a few weeks before they start their job search and that's okay, too.

How Much Does It Cost?

It is against the policy of The Five O'Clock Club to charge individuals heavy up-front fees. Our competitors charge $4,000 to $6,000 or more, up front. Our average fee is $360 for 10 sessions (which includes audio CDs of 16 presentations for those in the teleconference program). Those in the $100,000+ range pay an average of $540 for 10 sessions. For administrative reasons, we charge for 5 or 10 additional sessions at a time.

You must have the books so you can begin studying them before the second session. (You can purchase them on our website or at major bookstores.) If you don't do the homework, you will tend to waste the time of others in the group by asking questions covered in the texts.

Is the Small Group Right for Me?

The Five O'Clock Club process is for you if:

- You are truly interested in job hunting.
- You have *some* idea of the kind of job you want.
- You are a professional, manager, or executive—or want to be.
- You want to participate in a group process on a regular basis.
- You realize that finding or changing jobs and careers is hard work, but you are absolutely willing and able to do it.

If you have no idea about the kind of job you want next, you may attend one or two group sessions to start. *Then* see a

coach privately for one or two sessions, develop tentative job targets, and return to the group. You may work with your small-group coach or contact us through our website or by calling **1-800-575-3587** (or **212-286-4500** in New York) for referral to another coach.

How Long Will It Take Me to Get a Job?

Although our members tend to be from fields or industries where they expect to have difficult searches, *the average person who attends regularly finds a new position within 10 sessions.* Some take less time and others take more.

One thing we know for sure: **Research shows that those who get *regular* coaching during their searches get jobs faster and at higher rates of pay than those who search on their own or simply take a course.** This makes sense. If people come only when they think they have a problem, they are usually wrong. They probably had a problem a few weeks ago but didn't realize it. Or the problem may be different from the one they thought they had. Those who come regularly benefit from the observations others make about their searches. Problems are solved before they become severe or are prevented altogether.

Those who attend regularly also learn a lot by paying attention and helping others in the group. This *secondhand* learning can shorten your search by weeks. When you hear the problems of others who are ahead of you in the search, you can avoid them completely. People in your group will come to know you and will point out subtleties you may not have noticed that interviewers will never tell you.

Will I Be with Others from My Field/Industry?

Probably, but it's not that important. If you are a salesperson, for example, would you want to be with seven other salespeople? Probably not. You will learn a lot and have a much more creative search if you are in a group of people who are in your general salary range but not exactly like you. Our clients are from virtually every field and industry. The *process* is what will help you.

We've been doing this since 1978 and understand your needs. That's why the mix we provide is the best you can get.

Career Coaching Firms Charge $4,000–$6,000 Up Front. How Can You Charge Such a Small Fee?

1. We have no advertising costs, because 90 percent of those who attend have been referred by other members.

   A hefty up-front fee would bind you to us, but we have been more successful by treating people ethically and having them pretty much *pay as they go.*

   We need a certain number of people to cover expenses. When lots of people get jobs quickly and leave us, we could go into the red. But as long as members refer others, we will continue to provide this service at a fair price.

2. We focus strictly on *job-search strategy,* and encourage our clients to attend free support groups if they need emotional support. We focus on getting *jobs,* which reduces the time clients spend with us and the amount they pay.

3. We attract the best coaches, and our clients make more progress per session than they would elsewhere, which also reduces their costs.

4. We have expert administrators and a sophisticated computer system that reduces our overhead and increases our ability to track your progress.

May I Change Coaches?

Yes. Great care is taken in assigning you to your initial coach. However, if you want to change once for any reason, you may do it. We don't encourage group hopping: It is better for you to stick with a group so that everyone gets to know you. On the other hand, we want you to feel comfortable. So if you tell us you prefer a different group, you will be transferred immediately.

What If I Have a Quick Question Outside of the Group Session?

Some people prefer to see their group coach privately. Others prefer to meet with a different coach to get another point of view. Whatever you decide, remember that the group fee does *not* cover coaching time outside the group session. Therefore, if you wanted to speak with a coach between sessions—even for *quick questions*—you would

normally meet with the coach first for a private session so he or she can get to know you better. *Easy, quick questions* are usually more complicated than they appear. After your first private session, some coaches will allow you to pay in advance for one hour of coaching time, which you can then use for quick questions by phone (usually a 15-minute minimum is charged). Since each coach has an individual way of operating, find out how the coach arranges these things.

What If I Want to Start My Own Business?

The process of becoming a consultant is essentially the same as job hunting and lots of consultants attend Five O'Clock Club meetings. However, if you want to buy a franchise or existing business or start a growth business, you should see a private coach.

How Can I Be Sure That The Five O'Clock Club Small-Group Sessions Will Be Right for Me?

Before you actually participate in any of the small-group sessions, you can get an idea of the quality of our service by listening to all 16 audio CDs that you purchased. If you are dissatisfied with the CDs for any reason, return the package within 30 days for a full refund.

Whatever you decide, just remember: *It has been proven that those who receive regular help during their searches get jobs faster and at higher rates of pay than those who search on their own or simply attend a course.* If you get a job just one or two weeks faster because of this program, it will have more than paid for itself. And you may *transfer unused sessions to anyone you choose.* However, the person you choose must be or become a member.

The
Five
O'Clock
Club

When Your Employer Pays

Does your employer care about you and others whom they ask to leave the organization? If so, ask them to consider The Five O'Clock Club for your outplacement help. The Five O'Clock Club puts you and your job search first, offering a career-coaching program of the highest quality at the lowest possible price to your employer.

Over 25 Years of Research

The Five O'Clock Club was started in 1978 as a research-based organization. Job hunters tried various techniques and reported their results back to the group. We developed a variety of guidelines so job hunters could choose the techniques best for them.

The methodology was tested and refined on professionals, managers, and executives (and those aspiring to be) from all occupations. Annual salaries ranged from $30,000 to $400,000; 50 percent were employed and 50 percent were unemployed.

Since its beginning, The Five O'Clock Club has tracked trends. Over time, our advice has changed as the job market has changed. What worked in the past is insufficient for today's job market. Today's Five O'Clock Club promotes all our relevant original strategies—and so much more.

As an employee-advocacy organization, The Five O'Clock Club focuses on providing the services and information that the job hunter needs most.

Get the Help You Need Most: 100 Percent Coaching

There's a myth in outplacement circles that a terminated employee just needs a desk, a phone, and minimal career coaching. **Our experience clearly shows that downsized workers need qualified, reliable coaching more than anything else.**

Most traditional outplacement packages last only 3 months. The average executive gets office space and only 5 hours of career coaching during this time. Yet the service job hunters need most is the career coaching itself—not a desk and a phone.

Most professionals, managers, and executives are right in the thick of negotiations with prospective employers at the 3-month mark. Yet that is precisely when traditional outplacement ends, leaving job hunters stranded and sometimes ruining deals.

It is astonishing how often job hunters and employers alike are impressed by the databases of *job postings* claimed by outplacement firms. Yet only 10 percent of all jobs are filled through ads and another 10 percent are filled through search firms. Instead, direct contact and networking—done The Five O'Clock Club way—are more effective for most searches.

You Get a Safety Net

Imagine getting a package that protects you for a full year. Imagine knowing you can come back if your new job doesn't work out—even months later. Imagine trying consulting work if you like. If you later decide it's not for you, you can come back to The Five O'Clock Club.

We can offer you a safety net of one full year's career coaching because our method is so effective that few people actually need more than 10 weeks in our proven program. But you're protected for a year.

You'll Job Search with Those Who Are Employed—How Novel!

Let's face it. It can be depressing to spend your days at an outplacement firm where everyone is unemployed. At The Five O'Clock Club, half the attendees are working, and this makes the atmosphere cheerier and helps to move your search along.

What's more, you'll be in a small group of your peers, all of whom are using The Five O'Clock Club method.

Our research proves that those who attend the small group regularly and use The Five O'Clock Club methods get jobs faster and at higher rates of pay than those who only work privately with a career coach throughout their searches.

So Many Poor Attempts

Nothing is sadder than meeting someone who has already been getting job-search *help,* but the wrong kind. They've learned the traditional techniques that are no longer effective. Most have poor résumés and inappropriate targets and don't know how to turn job interviews into offers.

You'll Get Quite a Package

You'll get up to 14 hours of private coaching—well in excess of what you would get at a traditional outplacement firm. You may even want to use a few hours after you start your new job.

And you get up to one full year of small-group career coaching. In addition, you get books, audio CDs, and other helpful materials.

To Get Started

The day your human resources manager calls us authorizing Five O'Clock Club outplacement, we will immediately ship you the books, CDs, and other materials and assign you to a private coach and a small group.

Then we'll monitor your search. Frankly, we care about you more than we care about your employer. And since your employer cares about you, they're glad we feel this way—because they know we'll take care of you.

What They Say about Us

The Five O'Clock Club product is much better, far more useful than my outplacement package.

Senior executive and Five O'Clock Club member

The Club kept the juices flowing. You're told what to do, what not to do. There were fresh ideas. I went through an outplacement service that, frankly, did not help. If they had done as much as the Five O'Clock Club did, I would have landed sooner.

Another member

When Your *Employer* Pays for The Five O'Clock Club, *You* Get:

- **Up to 14 hours of guaranteed private career coaching** to determine a career direction, develop a résumé, plan salary negotiations, etc. In fact, if you need a second opinion during your search, we can arrange that too.

- Up to **ONE YEAR of small-group teleconference coaching** (average about 5 or 6 participants in a group) headed by a senior Five O'Clock Club career consultant. That way, if you lose your next job, you can come back. Or if you want to try consulting work and then decide you **don't like it, you can come back**.

- **Two-year membership** in The Five O'Clock Club: Beginners Kit and two-year subscription to *The Five O'Clock News*.

- **The complete set of our four books** for professionals, managers, and executives who are in job search.

- **A boxed set of 16 audio CDs** of Five O'Clock Club presentations.

COMPARISON OF EMPLOYER-PAID PACKAGES

Typical Package	Traditional Outplacement	The Five O'Clock Club
Who is the client?	The organization	Job hunters. We are employee advocates. We always do what is in the best interest of job hunters.
The clientele	All are unemployed	Half of our attendees are unemployed; half are employed. There is an upbeat atmosphere; networking is enhanced.
Length/type of service	3 months, primarily office space	1 year, exclusively career coaching
Service ends	After 3 months—or *before* if the client lands a job or consulting assignment	After 1 full year, no matter what. You can return if you lose your next job, if your assignment ends, or if you need advice after starting your new job.
Small-group coaching	Sporadic for 3 months Coach varies	Every week for up to 1 year; same coach
Private coaching	5 hours on average	Up to 14 hours guaranteed (depending on level of service purchased)
Support materials	Generic manual	• 4 textbooks based on over 25 years of job-search research • 16 40-minute lectures on audio CDs • Beginners Kit of search information • 2-year subscription to the Five O'Clock Club magazine, devoted to career-management articles
Facilities	Cubicle, phone, computer access	None; use home phone and computer

The
Five
O'Clock
Club

The Way We Are

The Five O'Clock Club means sobriety, refinement of thought and speech, good breeding and good order. To this, much of its success is due. The Five O'Clock Club is easy-going and unconventional. A sense of propriety, rather than rules of order, governs its meetings.

J. Hampton Moore, *History of The Five O'Clock Club*
(written in the 1890s)

Just like the members of the original Five O'Clock Club, today's members want an ongoing relationship. George Vaillant, in his seminal work on successful people, found that "what makes or breaks our luck seems to be . . . our sustained relationships with other people." (George E. Vaillant, *Adaptation to Life,* Harvard University Press, 1995)

Five O'Clock Club members know that much of the program's benefit comes from simply showing up. Showing up will encourage you to do what you need to do when you are not here. And over the course of several weeks, certain things will become evident that are not evident now.

Five O'Clock Club members learn from each other: The group leader is not the only one with answers. The leader brings factual information to the meetings and keeps the discussion in line. But the answers to some problems may lie within you or with others in the group.

Five O'Clock Club members encourage each other. They listen, see similarities with their own situations, and learn from that. And they listen to see how they may help others. You may come across information or a contact that could help someone else in the group. Passing on that information is what we're all about.

If you are a new member here, listen to others to learn the process. And read the books so you will know the basics that others already know. When everyone understands the basics, this keeps the meetings on a high level, interesting, and helpful to everyone.

Five O'Clock Club members are in this together, but they know that ultimately they are each responsible for solving their own problems with God's help. Take the time to learn the process, and you will become better at analyzing your own situation, as well as the situations of others. You will be learning a method that will serve you the rest of your life, and in areas of your life apart from your career.

Five O'Clock Club members are kind to each other. They control their frustrations—because venting helps no one. Because many may be stressed, be kind and go the extra length to keep this place calm and happy. It is your respite from the world outside and a place for you to find comfort and FUN. Relax and enjoy yourself, learn what you can, and help where you can. And have a ball doing it.

There arises from the hearts of busy [people] a love of variety, a yearning for relaxation of thought as well as of body, and a craving for a generous and spontaneous fraternity.

J. Hampton Moore
History of The Five O'Clock Club

The Five O'Clock Club

Lexicon Used at The Five O'Clock Club

Use The Five O'Clock Club lexicon as a shorthand to express where you are in your job search. It will focus you and those in your group.

I. Overview and Assessment

How many hours a week are you spending on your search?

Spend 35 hours on a full-time search, 15 hours on a part-time search.

What are your job targets?

Tell the group. A target includes industry or company size, position, and geographic area.

The group can help assess how good your targets are. Take a look at *Measuring Your Targets*.

How does your résumé position you?

The summary and body should make you look appropriate to your target.

What are your backup targets?

Decide at the beginning of the search before the first campaign. Then you won't get stuck.

Have you done the Assessment?

If your targets are wrong, everything is wrong. (Do the Assessment in *Targeting a Great Career*.) Or a counselor can help you privately to determine possible job targets.

II. Getting Interviews

How large is your target (e.g., 30 companies)? How many of them have you contacted?

Contact them all.

How can you get (more) leads?

You will not get a job through search firms, ads, networking, or direct contact. Those are techniques for getting interviews—job leads. Use the right terminology, especially after a person gets a job. Do not say, "How did you get the job?" If you really want to know, ask, "Where did you get the lead for that job?"

Do you have 6 to 10 things in the works?

You may want the group to help you land one job. After they help you with your strategy, they should ask, "How many other things do you have in the works?" If *none*, the group can brainstorm how you can get more things going: through search firms, ads, networking, or direct contact. Then you are more likely to turn the job you want into an offer because you will seem more valuable. What's more, 5 will fall away through no fault of your own. Don't go after only 1 job.

How's your Two-Minute Pitch?

Practice a *tailored* Two-Minute Pitch. Tell the group the job title and industry of the hiring manager they should pretend they are for a role-playing exercise. You will be surprised how good the group is at critiquing pitches. (Practice a few weeks in a row.) Use your pitch to separate you from your competition.

You seem to be in Stage 1 (or Stage 2 or Stage 3) of your search.

Know where you are. This is the key measure of your search.

Are you seen as an insider or an outsider?

See *How to Change Careers* for becoming an insider. If people are saying, "I wish I had an opening for someone like you," you are doing well in meetings. If the industry is strong, then it's only a matter of time before you get a job.

III. Turning Interviews into Offers

Do you want this job?

If you do not want the job, perhaps you want an offer, if only for practice. If you are not willing to go for it, the group's suggestions will not work.

Who are your likely competitors and how can you outshine and outlast them?

You will not get a job simply because "they liked me." The issues are deeper. Ask the interviewer: "Where are you in the hiring process? What kind of person would be your ideal candidate? How do I stack up?"

What are your next steps?

What are *you* planning to do if the hiring manager doesn't call by a certain date or what are you planning to do to assure that the hiring manager *does* call you?

Can you prove you can do the job?

Don't just take the *trust me* approach. Consider your competition.

Which job positions you best for the long run? Which job is the best fit?

Don't decide only on the basis of salary. You will most likely have another job after this. See which job looks best on your résumé and will make you stronger for the next time. In addition, find a fit for your personality. If you don't *fit,* it is unlikely you will do well there. The group can help you turn interviews into offers and give you feedback on which job is best for you.

> *"Believe me, with self-examination and*
> *a lot of hard work with our coaches,*
> *you can find the job . . . you can have the*
> *career . . . you can live the life*
> *you've always wanted!"*
>
> Sincerely,
> Kate Wendleton

Membership

As a member of The Five O'Clock Club, you get:

- A year's subscription to *The Five O'Clock News*—10 issues filled with information on career development and job-search techniques, focusing on the experiences of real people.

- Access to *reasonably priced* weekly seminars featuring individualized attention to your specific needs in small groups supervised by our senior coaches.

- Access to one-on-one coaching to help you answer specific questions, solve current job problems, prepare your résumé, or take an in-depth look at your career path. You choose the coach and pay the coach directly.

- An attractive Beginners Kit containing information based on over 25 years of research on who gets jobs . . . and why . . . that will enable you to improve your job-search techniques—immediately!

- The opportunity to exchange ideas and experiences with other job searchers and career changers.

All that access, all that information, all that expertise for the annual membership fee of only $49, plus seminar fees.

How to become a member—by mail or E-mail:

Send your name, address, phone number, how you heard about us, and your check for $49 (made payable to "The Five O'Clock Club") to The Five O'Clock Club, 300 East 40th Street - Suite 6L, New York, NY 10016, or sign up at www.fiveoclockclub.com.

We will immediately mail you a Five O'Clock Club Membership Card, the Beginners Kit, and information on our seminars followed by our magazine. Then, call **1-800-575-3587** (or **212-286-4500** in New York) or e-mail us (at info@fiveoclockclub.com) to:

- reserve a space for the first time you plan to attend; or

- be matched with a Five O'Clock Club coach.

The Five O'Clock Club Way

The
Five
O'Clock
Club

"One organization with a long record of success in helping people find jobs is The Five O'Clock Club."

FORTUNE

Do not skip Assessment.

Even if you are rushed or know what you want to do with your life, the Seven Stories Exercise will help you develop a great résumé and cover letter, ace your interviews and feel more confident. After you've done the **Seven Stories Exercise** and tried The **Forty-Year Vision,** your private coach can help you!!! These are a must!

CDs for Assessment:

How The Five O'Clock Club Works

The Five O'Clock Club Approach to Job Search

How to Develop New Targets for Your Search

Successful Job Hunters Report

ASSESSMENT: TARGET AND RÉSUMÉ DEVELOPMENT

Assessment helps you develop a career direction—and a good résumé. Go through *all* of the exercises in our *Targeting* book—*especially* the **Seven Stories Exercise** and the **Forty-Year Vision.** You will come up with job targets—and be better able to focus on what you want to do next.

Assessment results in Job Targets, and a Résumé that makes you look appropriate to those targets.

A job target is:

- an industry or organization size (e.g., banking),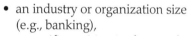
- a specific position in those industries (e.g., marketing),
- a certain geographic area (e.g., St. Louis).

Do preliminary target research (internet, networking) on your first list of targets. Refine your list. Use *Finding Jobs That Don't Exist.* Brainstorm as many alternative targets as possible in case you need more targets later on in your search.

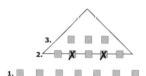

Target Development

- Segment your targets.
- Rank your targets.
- Measure your targets (Average number of positions per organization).
- Target 200 positions.

> **Target 200 *positions* —not job openings, but positions. It's okay if the positions are filled right now.**

"For profit" is not a target. "Not-for-profit" is not a target. They are too broad. For example, "not-for-profit" could include: associations, hospitals, universities, the government – and all of those sub-targets are huge!

Break down your targets into sub-targets. Healthcare, for example, could include: hospitals, home healthcare, HMO's, pharmaceutical companies, nursing homes, hospice care, health insurance companies, crisis intervention programs, congregate care facilities, medical billing, healthcare consulting firms, medical device manufacturers, distributors, anything having to do with the aging of America, vitamin companies, healthcare publishing, and more!!

MOST PEOPLE START OUT WITH TARGETS THAT ARE JUST TOO SMALL. THEIR SEARCHES ARE DOOMED!

Measuring Effectiveness of Your Search

You sent 100 résumés and talked to 75 people. But was it effective? *Measure* where you are.

- Stage 1 *Keeping in touch* with 6 to 10 people in your target area. Get feedback.
- Stage 2 is the core of your search. Keep in touch with 6 to 10 of the right people at the right level in the right organizations, AND when they say, "I wish I had an opening right now – I'd love to have someone like you on board," you have a GREAT search. Now, aim for 10 to 20 ongoing Stage 2 contacts.

If you're *not* getting positive feedback, your target is wrong or your positioning is wrong.

- Stage 3 will happen naturally: 6 to 10 *job* possibilities. *Aim for 3 concurrent offers.*
- Don't select the job that simply pays $2,000 or $20,000 more. Select the job that positions you best for the long term. You *will* have to search again.

Assessment results in a **RÉSUMÉ** that makes you look appropriate to your targets – so that you will be desirable when you go in for an interview. Remember, the average résumé is looked at for only 10 seconds. What ideas or words pop out? (It should *not* be your name!) Can the reader easily figure out your level? If you say I "install computer systems," you could be making anywhere from $15,000 to $200,000. Is your résumé accomplishment oriented or just a job description? Work with your private coach and your small group to make your *résumé* stand out.

HAVING TROUBLE FIGURING OUT WHAT YOU WANT TO DO WITH YOUR CAREER? YOUR PRIVATE COACH CAN HELP YOU.

If You Will Be Working with a Private Coach

in addition to your small group coach: Prior to the first private coaching session, send your coach your current résumé, in whatever state it is in, and the results of the Seven Stories Exercise. You and your coach can address your thoughts about the Forty-Year Vision and brainstorm potential targets. Your coach may assign you other exercises or instruments that are right for you, and will help you with your résumé.

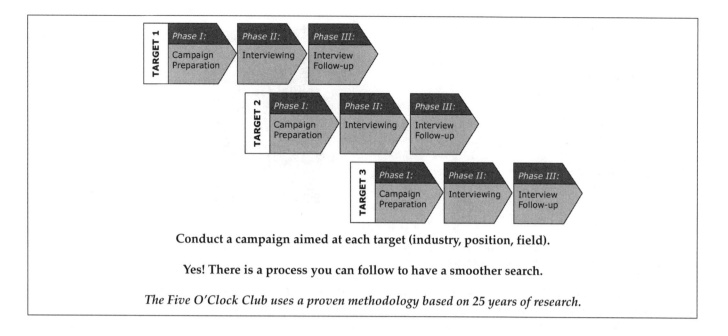

Conduct a campaign aimed at each target (industry, position, field).

Yes! There is a process you can follow to have a smoother search.

The Five O'Clock Club uses a proven methodology based on 25 years of research.

CDs for Campaign Preparation:

Your Résumé and the Two-Minute Pitch

How to Use Research and the Internet for Your Job Search

How to Get Interviews: The Keys to Effective Networking

How to Get Interviews Through Direct and Targeted Mail

Beat the Odds When Using Search Firms and Answering Ads

YOUR SMALL GROUP CAN REVIEW YOUR SEARCH PLANS AND HELP YOU PRACTICE YOUR TWO-MINUTE PITCH.

PHASE I: CAMPAIGN PREPARATION

- **Conduct research** to develop a list of all the companies in your first target. Find out the names of people you should contact in the appropriate departments in each of those companies.

- **Develop your cover letter.** (Paragraph 1 is the opening; Paragraph 2 is a summary about yourself appropriate for this target; Paragraph 3 contains your bulleted accomplishments ("You may be interested in some of the things I've done"); Paragraph 4 is the close. (Lots of sample letters are in *Getting Interviews*.)

- **Develop your plan** for getting lots of meetings in this target.

Methods for Getting Meetings in Your Target Areas:

- Networking (40% of meetings),
- Direct Contact (40%),
- Search Firms (10%), and
- Ads (print and Internet) (10%).

"Networking" means using someone else's name to get a meeting ("Sue suggested I contact you."). "Direct Contact" means pursuing people whom you may have known in the past or people you have never met: association members, or key people identified on the Internet, through newspaper or magazine articles, or from library research. (For entry-level people, it includes going from one Human Resources office to another in an office center.)

Segment Your Targets

Your A-list: organizations you would love to work for.

Your B-list: organizations that are okay.

Your C-list: organizations that don't interest you much.

Contact C-list companies first. Practice. Are they interested in *you* or not? You are researching. If C-list likes you, contact B-list. "I am already talking to a number of companies in our industry, but I didn't want to accept a job with any of them until I had a chance to talk with you." If B-list likes you, contact A-list.

Divide Up Your List

If you have a list of 60 organizations:

- Network into 5 or 6, if you can;
- Send a targeted mailing to 20 (requires follow-up phone call); and
- For the remaining 35, use a direct mail campaign (no follow-up phone call)

Condense Your Search

If Target #1 is hospitals, contact all of the hospitals. "Just yesterday, I talked to . . . " You appear interested in hospitals. Gives you credibility.

Segment your targets. The pitch that you use with one of these targets, say, hospitals, will be very different from the pitch you would use with a different target, say, healthcare manufacturers.

The "Two-Minute Pitch"

—the way you position yourself—is used throughout your search

- at the top of your résumé;
- in your networking meetings; and
- in your cover letters (2nd paragraph).

It is the answer to the question, "So, tell me about yourself." A great pitch helps people see you as appropriate for the kind of job you are going after. At the Five O'Clock Club we say, "If your pitch is wrong, everything is wrong." That is, if the way that you are positioning yourself is wrong, everything else about your search is wrong. It can't work.

The top of your résumé is your *written* positioning. Two-Minute Pitch is the *verbal* positioning of yourself. And they must correspond. So, the top of Wally's résumé could say:

Web Press Supervisor
With 20 years' experience
and an emphasis on quality
and productivity

In an interview, when an employer asks, "So tell me about yourself," Wally could start with the verbal version of that same pitch: "I'm a Web Press Supervisor with over 20 years' experience. I've always emphasized quality and productivity. For example . . ." And then he would go into examples of his accomplishments, which would correspond to some of the bulleted accomplishments at the top of his résumé. When your pitch is correct, you will use it throughout your entire search.

CDs for Interviewing:

The Five O'Clock Club Approach to Interviewing

Advanced / Strategic Interviewing Techniques

How to Handle Difficult Interview Questions

How to Develop New Momentum in Your Search

Making the Most of Your Contacts

YOUR SMALL GROUP CAN HELP YOU PREPARE AND PRACTICE FOR YOUR INTERVIEWS AND NETWORKING MEETINGS, AND NOTICE WHEN THINGS ARE GOING WRONG IN YOUR SEARCH.

PHASE II: INTERVIEWING

Most people think interviews result in job offers. But there are usually a few intervening steps before a final offer is made. **Interviews should result in getting and giving information.**

- Did you learn the issues important to each person with whom you met?
- What did they think were your strongest positives?
- How can you overcome the decision-makers' objections?

Don't think like a job hunter. Think like a consultant trying to land a $40,000, $90,000, or $150,000 consulting assignment—whatever your salary is. What consultants do:

- Research beforehand.
- Dress and look the part.
- Prepare your 3x5 card including your pitch as well as your key points.

Find out:
- What is going on? What are their needs?
- How can I satisfy those needs?
Consider your competition.
- Ask how you stack up against others.
- Have all the information you need.
- Are they ready to decide?
- Try to keep in the running.

Plan your follow-up
- Get and give information.
- Don't try to get an offer right now.
- Get the next meeting.
- Consultants write proposals. So will you!

Conduct a campaign aimed at a company
- If Miss Gold is the hiring manager, don't try to see her just yet. *Surround* the hiring manager. Meet with others, so when you finally get in to see her, you will have a lot of advocates and know a lot about the organization.

Prepare for the interview
- Say to the person who set up the meeting: "I'd like to go in prepared. With whom will I meet?" Ask:
  - names and job titles
  - issues important to each of them
  - what they are like
  - tenure with organization

Uncover their objections
- Where are you in the hiring process?
- How many others are you considering?
- How do I stack up against them?
- Is there any reason why you might be reluctant to bring someone like me on board?

Have each person see you as the ideal
- Each should advocate having you on board. If anyone objects to you, handle it now.

Always have 6 to 10 possibilities going
- Try to get an offer (even if you don't want the job), or you'll never get 6 to 10 possibilities.
- Do *not* drop other search activities when an offer seems certain.

Mistake: Trying to get an offer too soon
- Instead, get that next meeting.
- Give and get information. Move it along.
- Address issues that concern *them* rather than what's bothering you (getting the job).

Questions to Ask

Responsibilities
- What is the most important part of the job?
- What is the first problem that would need the attention of the person you hire?

Resources
- May I meet other people who work in the area?
- What are the department's employees' experience, training and tenure with the company?

Authority
- How is the department organized?
- What would be the extent of my authority in carrying out the responsibilities of this position?

Performance
- What are the short- and long-term goals of the position, and how are they established?
- How is one's performance evaluated? By whom? How often?
- What would you like to say about the person in this job one year from now?

Culture
- What do you find most satisfying about working here? Most frustrating?
- Who tends to get ahead here?
- How would you describe your management style?

Remember . . .
- You are being interviewed by everyone including receptionists and peers.
- They say they are going to call you back in 2 days. Do they ever? No, never.

> **Consultants don't expect to get the offer on the first visit. Neither should you.**

Handling Difficult Interview Questions

Your 3" x 5" card with the information you want to cover during your interview

??? Questions that divert you from your main agenda

Off on a tangent

Handle them quickly and get back to the topic

Do not allow the interview to get off track. When the interviewer brings up something that takes you in a direction in which you don't want to go, briefly give a response that satisfies the interviewer, and then *get back on track.*

Give your answer, and then say, for example, "But I really wanted to tell you about a special project I worked on." It is your responsibility to get the conversation back on track.

CDs for Follow-up and Salary Negotiation:

How to Use the Four-Step Salary Negotiation Strategy

How to Turn Job Interviews into Offers

THIS IS THE BRAINIEST PART OF THE PROCESS. YOUR SMALL GROUP WILL HELP YOU TURN INTERVIEWS INTO OFFERS AND GET THE SALARY YOU DESERVE.

PHASE III: INTERVIEW FOLLOW-UP
(including salary negotiation)

Follow-Up After a Job Interview

- The brainiest part of the process.
- Takes as much time as getting interviews and interviewing.
- Keep things alive with 6 to 10 organizations.
- Don't write a silly "thank-you" note after a job interview. Instead, *influence* them.
- Tailor the follow-up to each situation.
- Build a relationship. Company says that they're not hiring until February. That's OK.
- Whether to call, write or e-mail is not the issue. Uncover their objections to you.
- The best you can do: **If they were going to hire someone, would you be the person?**
- Your coach will want to know:
  – Who did you meet with?
  – What are *each* person's key *issues*?
  – Why would each want you there?
  – *Each* person's objections to you.
  – What can you offer vs. competition?
  – Problems *each* interviewer has.
- Decide the next steps, such as:
  – another meeting; meeting w/others
  – an in-depth review of documents
  – developing a few ideas and then meet
  – drafting a proposal

- State the "next steps" in your follow-up note. For example, "I'd like to get together with you to discuss my ideas on . . ."
- Influence the influencers.
- Be in sync with their timing, not yours.
- If unemployed, be open to consulting work.

Salary Negotiation

- Starts with your first meeting: position yourself so they see you at a certain level.
- Mantra: "Salary will not be a problem."
- Manage the process to get the right offer.
  – If original offer is too low, okay for now.
  – Don't try to close too soon and ruin deal.
- The Four-Step Salary Negotiation Process:
  1. Negotiate the job
  2. Outshine and outlast your competition
  3. Get the offer
  4. Negotiate the salary
- *Must* be done in this order. For example, don't negotiate salary if you have competitors.
- "Grow the job" to make it worth more.
- Find out what you personally are worth.
  – Network: "What would you expect to pay someone with my background?"
  – Salary.com and others. Associations.
- Make yourself in demand: 6 to 10 a must.
- Don't reject the offer—talk about the job.
- Keep process open; hear their best offer.
- Postpone salary discussion until offer.
  – Person who names a number first loses.
  – Talk more about the job.
- Discuss salary using a collaborative tone.
  – May take more than one meeting.

The amount of money you receive will always be in direct proportion to the demand for what you do, your ability to do it, and the difficulty of replacing you.

Dennis Kimbro, *Think and Grow Rich: a Black Choice*

You ain't goin' nowhere . . . son.
You ought to go back to driving a truck.

Jim Denny, Grand Ole Opry manager,
firing Elvis Presley after one performance.
From an interview on October 2, 1954.

Have 6 to 10 job possibilities in the works at all times. Five will fall away through no fault of your own.

With 6 to 10 things going, you increase your chances of having three good offers to choose from.

When you are in the Interview Phase of Target 1, it's time to start Phase I of Target 2. This will give you more momentum and insure that you do not let things dry up. Keep both targets going, and then start Target 3.

Research shows: those who regularly attend a small group, headed by a Five O'Clock Club coach, get jobs faster and at higher rates of pay than those who search alone or only work privately with a coach.

Remember . . .

- Get 3 hours of fun a week—like it or not!!
- Job search in summer and over holidays.
- "They" never call when they say they will, so follow up by being creatively persistent.

Follow-Up After Networking

- Immediate "thank-you" note.
- Then, at least every three weeks.
- Status report of search; send articles.

When You've Lost the Spirit to Job-Hunt

They're all doing terrific! You're barely hanging on. You used to be a winner. Now what can you do?

1. **Put things in perspective.**
   You've worked 10 or 20 years, and you're not done yet. You *do* have a future, you know.

2. **Get support.**
   Join the Club! Relying solely on yourself is not the answer. Job hunters can feel vulnerable and uncared for. They walk into walls and have accidents.

3. **Remember that this is part of a bigger picture.**
   Learn from this experience and make some sense of it. Decide what is now important to you.

4. **Continue to do your job.**
   Sometimes you didn't feel like doing your old job, but you did it anyway. Job hunting is now your job. Get it done. Organize. Make that call. Have fun.

It's true that when God closes a door, He opens a window. But the hallways are hell.

Sol Wachler, former New York Supreme Court Justice, after serving time in jail.

Join Your Small Group

You will have help from:

- Your Small-Group Coach
- Your Job-Search Buddies
- Your Small-Group Team
- Hundreds of Five O'Clock Club Alumni

The first week, listen to other members. Observe their search strategies. You can learn a lot from them. The second week, we start working on *your* search: help you figure out how to get more interviews in your target areas or how to turn those interviews into offers.

Study the Materials

- The books
- The audiotapes (or lectures at the in-person branches)
- **Website:** "How to Find a Job" Section and Worksheets in the Members-Only section

**SEE YOUR PRIVATE COACH
USE *ALL* OF YOUR RESOURCES!**

**THE FIVE O'CLOCK CLUB
300 EAST 40TH STREET
NEW YORK, NEW YORK 10016**

**CALL 212-286-4500
FOR INFORMATION ON BECOMING
A MEMBER AND SUBSCRIBING TO
*THE FIVE O'CLOCK NEWS.***

**OR CALL TOLL FREE: 1-800-575-3587
EMAIL: INFO@FIVEOCLOCKCLUB.COM**

**WEBSITE:
WWW.FIVEOCLOCKCLUB.COM**

Start Here:

1. Targeting a Great Career

- Figure out who you are, what you enjoy doing, and what you want to do with your life—and your career.

- Develop your job targets by industry, field or profession, and geographic area.

2. Packaging Yourself: The Targeted Résumé

- Develop a résumé that separates you from your competition and makes you look appropriate to your targets.

- Then you'll be desirable when you go in for an interview.

- Remember, the average résumé is looked at for only 10 seconds.

3. Shortcut Your Job Search: The Best Ways to Get Meetings

- Use the Internet and other techniques properly.

- Get lots of interviews.

- Refer to the extensive bibliography to uncover lists of organizations in your target market.

4. Mastering the Job Interview and Winning the Money Game

- Turn those job interviews into job offers.

- Answer those difficult interview questions The Five O'Clock Club way.

- Use our Four-Step Salary Negotiation Method to get what you deserve.

- Start out on the right foot in your new job.

5. Navigating Your Career: Develop Your Plan, Manage Your Boss, Get Another Job Inside

- Learn how to get ahead in your present organization.

- Enhance your interpersonal skills.

- Have a career-development discussion with your boss.

- Get the assignments you really want.

And be sure to listen to our audio CDs on each topic.

He that will not apply new remedies must expect new evils.

Francis Bacon, English philosopher

Membership Application

The Five O'Clock Club

❑ **Yes! I want to become a member!**

I want access to the most effective methods for finding jobs, as well as for developing and managing my career.

I enclose my check for $49 for 1 year; $75 for 2 years, payable to "The Five O'Clock Club." I will receive a Beginners Kit, a subscription to *The Five O'Clock News,* access to the Members Only area on our Website, and a network of career coaches. Reasonably priced seminars are held across the country.

Name: _____

Street Address: _____

City: _____ State: _____ Zip Code: _____

Work phone: (_____) _____

Home phone: (_____) _____

E-mail: _____

Date: _____

How I heard about the Club: _____

Job Search Workbook

The following *optional* information is for statistical purposes. Thanks for your help.

Salary range:

❑ under $30,000   ❑ $30,000–$49,999   ❑ $50,000–$74,999

❑ $75,000–$99,999   ❑ $100,000–$125,000   ❑ over $125,000

Age: ❑ 20–29   ❑ 30–39   ❑ 40–49   ❑ 50+

Gender: ❑ Male   ❑ Female

Current or most recent position/title: _____

Please send to:
Membership Director, The Five O'Clock Club,
300 East 40th St.-Suite 6L, New York, NY 10016

The original Five O'Clock Club® was formed in Philadelphia in 1893. It was made up of the leaders of the day who shared their experiences "in a setting of fellowship and good humor."

Index